HOW THE WORLD EATS

Also by Julian Baggini

How to Think Like a Philosopher

The Godless Gospel: Was Jesus a Great Moral Teacher?

How the World Thinks: A Global History of Philosophy

Freedom Regained: The Possibility of Free Will

The Virtues of the Table: How to Eat and Think

The Ego Trick

*Should You Judge This Book by Its Cover? 100 Fresh
Takes on Familiar Sayings and Quotations*

*Do They Think You're Stupid? 100 Ways of Spotting Spin
& Nonsense from the Media, Pundits & Politicians*

Welcome to Everytown: A Journey into the English Mind

The Pig That Wants to be Eaten: And 99 Other Thought Experiments

What's It All About? Philosophy and the Meaning of Life

By Julian Baggini and Jeremy Stangroom

Do You Think What You Think You Think?

HOW
THE
WORLD
EATS

A Global Food Philosophy

JULIAN BAGGINI

PEGASUS BOOKS
NEW YORK LONDON

HOW THE WORLD EATS

Pegasus Books, Ltd.
148 West 37th Street, 13th Floor
New York, NY 10018

ISBN: 978-1-63936-819-8

10 9 8 7 6 5 4 3 2 1

Printed in the United States of America
Distributed by Simon & Schuster
www.pegasusbooks.com

'It is high time for each nation to study the others and by mutual agreement and co-operative effort, the results of such studies should become available to all concerned, made so in the spirit that each should become coordinate and mutually helpful component factors in the world's progress.'

F. H. KING,
Farmers of Forty Centuries, or Permanent Agriculture in China, Korea and Japan (1911)

CONTENTS

INTRODUCTION

Which foods best represent your part of the world? If you are in Maharashtra in western India, you might think of your prized local produce, the Alphonso mango. In South Africa, it could be biltong, a speciality product. Many Persians would nominate Ghormeh sabzi, a traditional stew. Delicious as all these may be, none are truly indicative of how we typically eat today, at least not in the industrialised world. Asked to bring back the most typical Earth foods, an anthropologist from Mars would fill its shopping basket with sliced bread, frozen pizzas and ready meals, picking up a burger and fries on the way back to the spaceship.

Curious extraterrestrials might also want to know how this food is produced. But if they stopped a random person and asked them, they probably wouldn't discover very much. Despite the growth of interest in healthy eating, provenance and fair trade, most of us still have only a sketchy idea of the stories behind the foods in our fridges and cupboards. Our ignorance should embarrass us. Every well-informed citizen should know the basics about how food is grown, reared, processed, traded and controlled. We should all know how it affects our culture, economy, health and environment.

There is a lot to learn, and the first lesson is that it is all much more complicated than you could ever imagine.

Consider a bowl of cornflakes, the kind of meal that is usually given no consideration. It is bought out of habit, eaten in a hurry and quickly forgotten. But think for a moment about how it got into the bowl. You might imagine that it starts with a farmer, but there is no way to trace your breakfast back to a single farm. The maize, for example, would have been bought from an intermediary, whose bulk containers would hold grains sourced from many different farms, all mixed up together. The chances are that most of this corn was grown from patented seeds, bought from one of a handful of big companies that dominate the global market. That seed would have been bred by one of a number of modern techniques, perhaps even genetic modification.

Each farmer would have been dependent on a number of pieces of machinery, and almost certainly on synthetic fertilisers, herbicides and insecticides. Irrigation was unlikely to have been provided by rainwater alone. Computers would have helped to plan harvests, which would have required storing and then transporting.

Cornflakes are usually fortified with vitamins and minerals, all supplied by specialist manufacturers. Other more sugary cereals may include highly processed ingredients such as high-fructose corn syrup or invert sugar syrup. Once made, the flakes will be packed, shipped to vast distribution centres and delivered to shops at just the right time so they don't have too much or too little in stock. All of this depends on labourers throughout the supply chain, who are often badly paid and working in poor conditions.

Then there's the milk. Most dairy cows are kept indoors, where every aspect of their environment is carefully controlled. Their feed may have come from the other side of the world, possibly grown on land that was cleared from rainforests. Their milk has to be heat-treated, packaged and shipped, chilled the whole time, if it is fresh.

All of this results in more than just the food you eat. The packaging needs to be disposed of, ideally recycled, but all too often not. The manure and urine from the industrial dairy cows need to be treated and disposed of, and when, as is often the case, this isn't done properly, local water supplies can be polluted. If the corn growers are not careful with their fertilisers, these too can run off and contaminate neighbouring land and waters. If the farm is a liberally sprayed monoculture, with nothing but corn as far as the eye can see, local wildlife suffers. And, of course, there are the greenhouse gas emissions both from the energy required at each stage and the methane released by the animals and their waste.

Let's not even get going on the tea or coffee you're having with your breakfast.

Cornflakes are relatively simple by the standards of modern breakfast cereals. Apart from the added vitamins and minerals, the most famous brand has only four ingredients: maize, barley malt extract, sugar and salt. Yet when you think of everything that needed to be in place for you to be able to eat it, you uncover a tangled, complicated story. Imagine what is involved in your total weekly shop.

Picture a map of the world, with places and routes lighting up whenever and wherever some part of this process of making and selling cornflakes is taking place. You would see a kind of spider's web of flickering filaments and nodes. Now imagine the illuminated web for another foodstuff. If every food's earth print were superimposed on one image, all detail would be lost and almost the entire world would be glowing.

This incredibly complex network is usually called the food system, which is difficult to clearly define, let alone describe. The Food and Agriculture Organization (FAO) of the United Nations (UN) says that food systems 'encompass the entire range of actors and their interlinked value-adding activities involved in the production, aggregation, processing, distribution, consumption and disposal of food products that originate from agriculture, forestry or fisheries, and parts of the broader economic, societal and natural environments in which they are embedded.'[1] More pithily, Henry Dimbleby, who led the independent report for the UK government's National Food Strategy, defines the food system as 'the sum of all the elements that combine to produce, process, market and sell the food we eat'.[2] It has become the hidden wiring of the modern, industrialised lifestyle, an essential part of the engine that keeps us going, and that nobody even notices unless it breaks down.

Food systems change and vary across time and space, often considerably, but there is always a sphere of human existence which they govern, guide and control. This can be thought of as the sum total of all the agents, practices, flora, fauna, land and water that are involved in and affected by the process of producing, eating and digesting food. Strangely, we do not have a word for that domain. In the absence of the proper Latin- or Greek-derived name it deserves, such as the nutrosphere, I'll refer to it simply as our food world. This domain is not a discrete, separable part of the wider world but, rather, every feature of the world that would show up if you had a kind of infra-red camera that captured everything that affects and is affected by human food.

Using the concept of the food world subtly but importantly reframes our thinking. The food system is something outside ourselves that we sometimes participate in as consumers and workers. But as people who eat daily, we are always within the food world. Whereas 'food system' evokes associations of a massive global machine, controlled by pulleys and levers, the idea of the food world invites us to think of an organic ecosystem, in which every part is connected to every other. And while asking how our food system should operate sounds technocratic, thinking about how our food world should be managed foregrounds the ethical and existential import of how we feed ourselves. We have to think about values as well as processes.

The contemporary food systems debate is highly polarised and contested, but on one thing there is remarkable agreement: it is broken and we need to fix it urgently. Ask how and why it is wrong, however, and discord reigns once more. At the heart of the problem is a paradox: while humanity's perennial challenge has been to provide enough food to feed the world adequately, many of our current difficulties are the result of overproduction. The worry is that we have only been able to produce large surpluses by depleting natural resources far more quickly than we can replenish them. The price of producing too much today could be that we cannot produce enough in the decades to come. In the meantime, we face both hunger and obesity, bumper crops and unprecedented environmental damage, food that is at the same time cheap for many and unaffordable for others.

There is no shortage of people offering solutions. Unfortunately, most proposals are far too simplistic: use technology to fix everything, return to traditional practices, go organic, let the market decide. All such prescriptions defy the incredible complexity of our food world, which can only be fully understood with a mastery of agronomy, ecology, biology, geography, sociology, anthropology, psychology, politics, history, economics, meteorology, chemistry, nutrition, business, cookery and more. It is precisely because a comprehensive understanding of the food world is beyond any single expertise that I dared to think I was in as good a position as anyone to take on the task of identifying its key features, joining the dots and sketching the big picture. I am by background a philosopher, and as Wilfrid Sellars put it, the aim of philosophy is 'to understand how things in the broadest possible sense of the term hang together in the broadest possible sense of the term.'[3] Substitute 'the food world' for 'things' and there is no better description of my goal: to understand how the food world in the broadest possible sense of the term hangs together in the broadest possible sense of the term. To enable me to do this, I have interviewed more than two dozen people for this book, and have surveyed the most important reports and studies from leading academics and authoritative bodies such as the United Nations. I see my endeavour as a form of 'philosophical journalism': finding the key facts, speaking to reliable informants, and using my philosophical skills to bring a picture of our food world together into a theoretically coherent and conceptually clear whole.

My interest in food has been intellectual as well as gastronomic for many years. In 2014 I published *The Virtues of the Table*, which explored the connections between the art of eating and the art of living. Two years later, I was invited to join the Food Ethics Council. The more I learned from my council colleagues about how the food system works, the more I realised that almost all received opinion about food and farming is simplistic at best, riddled with myths at worst. I realised that I wouldn't have a good answer for the Martian asking about how we do and should feed ourselves. I wanted to inform myself and, by reporting back, inform others as well.

The need for a better understanding of the food world has become urgent because arguably it has never been in such a fragile state. To appreciate the scale of the problem, we need to dig deeper into the paradox of the simultaneous overproduction and undersupply of food, whereby a large global minority of human beings suffers from eating too much while another large minority suffers from eating too little.

Start with the deficit side of the equation. One of the UN's key Sustainable Development Goals is to end hunger by 2030. Spoiler alert: it isn't going to happen. The UN itself calls it a 'daunting challenge' and predicts that almost 600 million people will still be facing hunger in 2030. Many more will have an inadequate diet. In 2022, the UN said that 2.4 billion people did not have year-round access to 'nutritious, safe and sufficient food', with women and people living in rural areas suffering disproportionately. Worse, after decades of gradual improvement, these figures reached their lowest levels in 2014 and deteriorated badly as a result of the Covid-19 pandemic, later exacerbated by the Russian invasion of Ukraine. In 2022, 9.2 per cent of the world's population was undernourished, compared with 7.9 per cent before 2019. An even greater number face food insecurity, meaning they 'lack regular access to enough safe and nutritious food for normal growth and development and an active and healthy life'. In 2022, nearly three in every ten people on Earth – 2.4 billion people – were moderately or severely food insecure, with more than one in ten severely food insecure. Perhaps the most sobering statistic is that in 2021 more than 3.1 billion people – 42 per cent of the global population – were unable to afford a healthy diet.[4] Behind these numbers are untold human lives, people all across the planet struggling to meet their basic needs.

And yet, according to the World Health Organization (WHO), more people live in countries where being overweight is a bigger killer than undernourishment than live in countries where lack of food takes more lives. Obesity worldwide has tripled since 1975, and by 2016 13 per cent were obese, with 39 per cent overweight.[5] Although obesity is often portrayed as a problem of affluence, it is not that straightforward. Obesity rates are higher in Libya, Lebanon, Egypt and Iraq than they are in Canada, the United Kingdom, Spain or Israel.[6] Levels of inequality within industrialised nations are greater predictors of obesity than average wealth.[7]

Malnutrition is mainly a problem of distribution and consumption. But Tim Lang, a professor of food policy, also thinks that the production side of the food system is facing a crisis of sustainability. Most believe that with the global population due to keep rising to nearly ten billion by the middle of the century, so too must agricultural output.[8] The UN thinks that global food production needs to increase by 60 per cent by 2050 from a 2005 baseline.[9] Some dispute this. But even if we can get by with a lesser increase, or even none at all, the world is already suffering the consequences of so much land and so many resources being used for food production. The global food system is responsible for a third of anthropogenic greenhouse gas emissions.[10] It is also the primary driver of biodiversity loss, mainly due to the conversion of natural ecosystems to arable land or pasture.[11] In Britain, once-common birds such as the turtle dove and the corn bunting have been pushed to the brink of extinction. Between 1970 and 2018, wildlife populations around the world declined by 69 per cent, and extinction rates are 1,000 times higher than historical averages and set to rise tenfold by the middle of the century.[12] In many parts of the world, farming is also degrading soils, causing erosion and a reduction in nutrient content. By 2050, an estimated 90 per cent of the world's soils will be degraded.[13]

Agriculture is also depleting one of our most plentiful resources: water. Farming is responsible for about 70 per cent of global water usage, and it is leaving the planet parched.[14] In southern Spain, for example, subterranean aquifers are running dry as more and more water is drawn to irrigate the endless rows of crops being grown in polytunnels, most destined for export. Even in historically soggy England, fifteen out of twenty-three water-company areas were recently judged by the Environment Agency to be under water stress.[15]

We've faced food challenges before, but as Lang tells me, 'The difference now is that some of the pressures today are so enormous, they will completely reshape the capacity of humans to be able to do anything about it. That is existentially different. And because it's so huge, it troubles me hugely.'

Our health, our environment, our peace and our prosperity all depend on the food system doing its job to maintain a healthy food world. But no serious commentator says that we can continue with business as usual. 'Go and talk to anyone in the industry, experts, specialists – very few think it is fine,' says Lang. 'Most think we're in the calm before the storm. And indeed the storm is already beginning.' Lord John Krebs, the first chair of the UK's Food Standards Agency, calls it a 'perfect storm', created by the confluence of a rising population, low- and middle-income nations increasing their consumption of animal proteins, natural resources being in short supply, rising energy costs, diminishing returns from productivity gains, and climate change.[16] Add to that poor nutrition and wars disrupting food supply, and you have what many now call a 'polycrisis'.

Getting out of this mess requires technical innovations and changes in practice. But we cannot leave it to scientists and technologists to determine which farming systems are most efficient and what diets are most nutritious, and then press policy-makers to follow their prescriptions. As Lang says, 'Food policy is not and cannot be neutral. Of course not, it is framed by assumptions, informed by values.'[17]

What we need to guide us is a global food *philosophy*, and articulating one is the aim of this book. By a 'food philosophy' I mean, with a nod to Sellars, the principles and values that should guide our management of the food world, understood in the broadest possible sense. This breadth means that such a food philosophy might be compatible with a variety of different *practices*: agricultural, industrial, commercial, culinary, social. It is also broader than a food *ideology*, which specifies in some detail how the food world should be managed, demanding that we all go organic, biodynamic, vegan, or that we depend on free trade or technology to sort us out. A global food philosophy need not be so prescriptive, but it will involve prescriptions. It will rule some practices out, demand others, but often leave multiple options open for how they are put into practice.

A global food philosophy is needed because anything thinner would leave us without a compass to guide us as we seek to repair our broken food world. At the same time, anything thicker has no chance of commanding enough agreement for all the most important actors to work together. For example, even if you think that the food world should be governed by organic principles, it would be naive to imagine that there is any chance of that happening in the foreseeable future. Advocates of food ideologies need to accept that their best cannot be the enemy of the common good, and that to heal the food world they need to find common ground alongside people they sometimes disagree with profoundly.

Because the food world is so vast, my broad sketch cannot be comprehensive. The seventeen chapters that follow focus either on some of the most significant aspects of the food world or on entire historical food systems. We'll be looking at the many ways in which humans have fed off the land, from hunter-gatherers, nomadic herders and subsistence farmers, through to intensive industrial agriculture. We'll examine how humans have been both pawns and players in the global food system, as slaves, producers of commodities, regulators of the food economy and titans of the food business. We will look at how other animals fit into this picture, such as cattle grazing the expanses of the Pampas, chickens kept in tiny cages, fish bred in vast farms, and live animals spreading diseases to humans. And we'll explore how technologies such as meat grown without livestock, genetic modification, and methods of processing and packaging have changed and will continue to change what we eat.

This panoramic overview will take us across the world, to the Maasai of East Africa, the Inuit of the Arctic, the gauchos of Argentina, the Hadza of Tanzania, the smallholders of Bhutan, the Rohingya refugees in Bangladesh, the market traders of Wuhan, the industrial farmers of the Netherlands and the astronauts of the International Space Station. We will visit both the present and the past; the industrialised world, low- and middle-income nations and traditional societies – ones where the norms and practices remain largely continuous with their long past, which means by definition they are very different from one another, since they are highly self-contained.

Although the goal to formulate a global food philosophy may seem wildly ambitious, even hubristic, in practice it is anything but. When you look closely at the global and historical food world, key principles emerge naturally. They are already to be found in the food systems that work, held by the people for whom they are effective. Our food philosophy does not need to be invented or discovered, but simply recognised in the good practices found the world over. And when it is articulated, it should resonate. It needs to. As Lang says, the debate about how we feed ourselves is 'a battle for hearts, minds and mouths'. To win it, we need a global food philosophy everyone can rally behind.

PART ONE

Land

I

THE HUNTER-GATHERERS

Hyrax and honey in Tanzania

Mwapo talks with the birds. Near Lake Eyasi in northern Tanzania, all Hadzabe men do. They call their interlocutor the *Tikiriko*, otherwise known as the honeyguide bird. The bird signals to the men when it has found a killer bee nest and the men reply in a back-and-forth that leads them to its exact site. Starting a fire with sticks, they climb twenty to thirty feet up the tree that houses the hive and smoke out the bees for long enough to remove the honeycomb. If it is lucky, the bird is left with some waxy scraps in reward for its assistance.

Mwapo is one of only a thousand Hadza left in Tanzania today, of whom fewer than 300 continue to live entirely as hunter-gatherers, with no permanent agriculture or architecture. 'Hunter-gatherer' or 'forager' communities have historically obtained all of their diet from wild foods. Anthropologist Richard Wrangham points out that it would be more accurate to call them gatherer-hunters because they gather daily, but every day doesn't necessarily include a successful hunt. Whatever we call them, they move with the seasons, living in grass-covered huts that dissolve back into the landscape when they leave. They take from the natural environment what they need to survive, leaving it able to fully replenish itself, so that any extraction of resources can go on indefinitely without depleting them. This exemplifies the definition of 'sustainability' agreed by the UN in 1987: 'meeting the needs of the present without compromising the ability of future generations to meet their own needs'.[1]

A typical hunter-gatherer only 'works' for around twenty hours a week, half the load of a standard full-time worker in an industrialised society. Outsiders may feel relieved that agriculture, trade and technology have made it unnecessary for entire communities to have to dedicate themselves to finding food. But our reliance on professional farmers has not made us more food secure. The Hadza have no food supplies in reserve, storing nothing for the future, but that is because they have no need to do so. They know that the next meal is always out there, waiting to be collected. Our storehouses and warehouses may appear to give us more security, yet we are only a few days away from hunger. Our international supply chains are extremely vulnerable, and if a city were to find its supermarket shelves empty, its citizens would have no alternative sources of nutrition. The industrialised world's food security hangs by a thread, whereas that of the Hadza is almost unbreakable.

The Hadza represent one of our last living links with the first *Homo sapiens*. They provide a window into how we all used to live. They are inevitably a source of fascination, but they can also become objects of romanticisation. For many who bemoan the destruction of the environment unleashed by the Industrial Revolution, the consumerist culture of constant striving for more, and the obesity and illness created by modern diets, hunter-gatherers like the Hadza provide a model of a different way to manage the land, organise society and eat.

*

The diet of the Hadza is without doubt the aspect of their life that draws the widest interest today. The twenty-first century has seen the rise of the 'paleo diet', and many foods are labelled 'paleo', lending them a healthy halo, on the assumption that anything our Palaeolithic ancestors would have eaten must be good for us too. Public fascination with this idea grew with the publication in 2002 of the book *The Paleo Diet*, written by an American doctor of exercise physiology, Loren Cordain. Innumerable iterations followed, including 'Stone Age' or 'caveman' diets. All were based on the argument that the human body evolved to survive on the kinds of food our Palaeolithic ancestors ate. According to this theory, cancer, cardiovascular disease, diabetes and many other illnesses are modern ailments caused by a switch in diet that began when we started to farm, increasing our consumption of grains. Our health then deteriorated further as we processed our food more, increasing the amount of refined carbohydrates in our diets, especially sugar and white wheat flour. The scientifically plausible basis of the paleo diet is the so-called mismatch hypothesis: the theory that society has evolved faster than our biology, and so we are 'stone-agers living in the fast lane'.[2]

There may well be lessons to be drawn from the diets of hunter-gatherers, but adopting the so-called paleo diet should not be one of them. Take the idea that we should avoid legumes and whole grains. In fact, there is evidence from fossilised tooth plaque that these foods were eaten in the Palaeolithic era, a conclusion supported by the discovery of stone tools like mortars and pestles, used to crush seeds and grains 20,000 years before the beginning of agriculture.

Behavioural ecologist and nutritional anthropologist Alyssa Crittenden is better placed than anyone to call out the unfounded claims of the paleo diet. For two decades she has been spending several months of every year with the Hadza. What she has observed flies in the face of the rigidity advocated by modern paleo diets, which overtly try to limit the kinds of foods that we eat. 'Foragers themselves are very flexible in terms of their subsistence strategy, based on seasonality and resource availability,' Crittenden told me. For example, she was informed that the Hadza never eat fish. But she was once in their territory during an El Niño year of 'unbelievable, massive torrential rain'. 'Lake Eyasi, an alkaline lake which often doesn't have any water in it, had a lot of water. I was there when all of a sudden, I saw Hadza men stand up to their calves in the lake, take an arrow, wait really patiently and then stab a catfish. Guess what? The Hadza eat catfish. We human beings are resilient and we're generalists and so in any environment where you can get a beautiful, fat, delicious catfish at the end of your arrow, who isn't going to take it?'

This adaptability contradicts claims that there has not been enough time for us to evolve to eat foods which our Palaeolithic ancestors did not. In fact, we can eat many totally novel foods without millennia of adaptation. As Crittenden points out, 'We did not evolve to eat a raw food diet. We did not evolve to eat a meat diet. We did not evolve to eat a plant diet. We evolved to eat all of it. We were able to essentially conquer all sorts of environmental obstacles because we ate a generalist diet.'

Our ability to vary what we eat is a huge human strength. For example, the genetic mutation that allows around a quarter of the world's adults to tolerate lactose and so drink milk without any adverse effects only emerged around 10,000 years ago in Turkey, before spreading widely in Europe when farming had become the human norm. Similar mutations occurred in Africa and the Middle East. In the Bronze Age people drank goats' milk in what is now northern Italy, while in Roman Britain they were consuming the milk of sheep and cows. The idea that the human body has made no significant genetic adaptations to our agrarian diet for more than 12,000 years has no scientific basis.

The adaptability of hunter-gatherers also reminds us that

nothing was made to be food for anything else: animals have simply evolved to be able to extract nutrients from a huge variety of sources. So, for example, the primary purpose of the milk of other animals is to feed their own young, but it is no less natural for us to drink it than it is for us to eat anything else that originally evolved for other purposes, such as nuts, seeds or honey. Milk has been a core component of many diets for centuries, which would not have been the case if it were not nutritious.

Nutritionists today, such as those at Harvard Public Health, advise against the paleo diet's wholesale exclusion of entire categories of foods like whole grains and dairy, arguing that it may increase the risk of deficiencies in calcium, vitamin D, and B vitamins, among others.[3] Supplements and fortified foods may not be a good alternative because our ability to absorb vitamins and minerals depends upon the form in which they are ingested. For example, very little of the plentiful calcium in spinach is absorbed by the body because it binds to the oxalates and phytates that are also abundant in the vegetable. The exclusion of whole grains can also decrease the amount of fibre in the diet, which carries numerous health risks.

While it excludes some whole categories of food, there is one the paleo diet especially promotes: meat. Even if we set aside the current consensus that very high levels of meat consumption are bad for our health, the paleo prescription ignores the fact that the kinds of meat eaten by our ancestors were very different from the steaks and chicken breasts eaten today. Hunter-gatherers eat every part of lean, wild game, not prime cuts of farmed meat. The varieties of fruits and vegetables our ancestors ate also bear little relation to the cultivated varieties we eat today. They were much more fibrous, with more seeds and less flesh. Rather than scooping out a delicious plump avocado, for example, you'd have to peel and de-stone dozens of smaller ones in order to get anything like a meal. Even if we were able to source such wild, pre-farmed varieties, we would find them bitter and unpalatable.

There just isn't any such thing as *the* paleo diet anyway. As anthropologist Christina Warinner points out, there was a plethora of paleo diets, varying according to where and when our ancestors lived.[4] There were sub-tropical foragers, coastal foragers, Arctic foragers. There are 'immediate-return' foragers, who consume what they eat more or less straight away, and 'delayed-return foragers', who store their food for longer lengths of time. For example, in the pan-Arctic seal poke storage system, Inuit women process the skin of a whole seal into a waterproof container used to store and preserve precious rendered seal oil and other foods.

However, the fact that most fashionable paleo diets are neither truly paleo nor advisable as diets does not mean we have nothing to learn from the way hunter-gatherers ate. For instance, both Crittenden and Warinner have researched the hunter-gatherer gut microbiome. In recent years, there has been an explosion of interest in the importance of the microbes in our digestive system for human health. Like all frontier fields, some of the claims made are almost certainly hyperbolic, but there can be little doubt that a healthy, diverse population of gut microbes is an important indicator and determinant of wider health.

'Microbiome' is defined by the Nobel Prize-winning molecular biologist Joshua Lederberg as 'the ecological community of commensal, symbiotic, and pathogenic microorganisms that literally share our body space and have been all but ignored as determinants of health and disease'.[5] Crittenden and her peers have found that the gut microbiome of the Hadza contains more species and more types of bacteria than those of people in more industrialised countries. Warinner has also shown that the hunter-gatherer biome is similar to that of rural agriculturalists. In other words, it was not the move from hunter-gathering to farming that was the cause of our biome diversity loss but the move from natural, seasonal whole foods to highly processed manufactured ones. Industrialisation, not agriculture, is the culprit. One indicator of this is that the guts of people in industrialised societies have completely lost the Treponema bacteria that specialise in digesting fibres, creating important fatty acids in the process.

The healthy biome of the hunter-gatherers is adapted to a broad-spectrum carbohydrate metabolism, meaning it is tailored to the digestion of mostly plant-based foods. At the same time, Warinner has also reported that a comparison of the composition of the human biome with those of other species of herbivores, omnivores and carnivores shows that humans are definitely omnivorous.

The diet that produces this healthy biome has four main features – it comprises diverse, fresh, whole and seasonal food. Diversity is now recognised as being one of the defining features of a healthy diet. The American paleoanthropologist Peter Ungar and his colleagues have argued that the fossil, archaeological and paleoenvironmental evidence shows that increased dietary diversity and versatility was actually key to the early evolution of humans.[6]

The importance of fresh and whole foods has been appreciated for many decades now. Hunter-gatherers like the Hadza eat only fresh foods because they store nothing. Many forms of preservation, such as salting and drying, kill off the living microbes in food, which act as important 'prebiotics' that feed the gut microbiome. However, traditional forms of preservation that use fermentation encourage the growth of some microbes while killing those that cause the food to rot. Whole foods are also more effective prebiotics that those that have been refined.

That is one reason why seasonal eating is important: it tends to increase the proportion of the freshest food in the diet. Fruits and vegetables that have been transported across continents to places where they are not in season pay a nutritional price, largely because they tend to be picked before they are fully ripe, and hence not at their nutritional peak. Seasonal eating is also a sure route to more diverse eating. When we eat the same foods every day of the week we inevitably reduce the range of foods we consume. Seasonal variations in the diet also alter the composition of the biome over the annual cycle, to the extent that research has found that some microbes become undetectable at some parts of the year, only to reappear at others.[7]

In industrialised countries, diets tend to be the precise opposite of the one modelled by the Hadza. Instead of being diverse, fresh, whole and seasonal, foods are limited, preserved, processed and largely the same all year round. So, for example, in place of the natural sugars from fruits, vegetables and honey there are refined sugars, often in the form of high-fructose corn syrup, which overload the body in an intense, heavy blood glucose hit. Processed food provides less of the dietary fibre and living, organic matter that feed the gut microbiome.

The good news is that we have no reason to think that we have to eat exactly like hunter-gatherers to have a well-balanced, diverse seasonal diet which is as good as theirs. Rather than trying to mimic a largely fictional and restrictive paleo diet, you can simply eat more varied and fresh foods, from all the major food groups. Crittenden told me that if you take someone with a typical western, industrialised diet and get them to eat 'a decent amount of animal protein, a lot of fresh fruits and veggies, not a lot of domesticated grains, and so really uptick the amount of fibre they're eating', then 'even within six weeks or two months, all of a sudden you have a gut microbiome profile that looks like that of a forager'.

It is probably because the hunter-gatherer diet has these advantages over the industrialised one that anecdotally many people report health benefits of paleo diets, even though controlled studies fail to back these up. Anyone who goes on a paleo diet is almost certain to be 'cutting out processed foods and ramping up fruits and vegetables', as Deirdre Tobias, assistant professor in the Department of Nutrition at Harvard, put it.[8] This, rather than the specific paleo prescription, could provide a health dividend.

There is a sense in which the hunter-gatherer diet actually

created the problems we face today. Several studies have revealed that among foragers there is a strong link between highly calorific foods and food preferences. Among both male and female Hadzabe, for instance, their most energy dense food – honey – is also their most preferred, while tubers are least preferred and also the worst source of energy. The high importance placed on honey is reflected in the fact that men may spend up to five hours a day trying to acquire it during the rainy season, when game is harder to hunt. The Hadza language has a different name for each type of honey, varying according to the species of bee that makes it. The best is Ba'alako from the African killer bee. This alignment of energy content and preference works to our advantage when overeating is almost impossible and not getting enough food is the major risk, but it works against us when energy dense food is cheap, plentiful and engineered to be both tasty and moreish.[9]

Hadza food preferences also reveal that despite living in the same environment with the same resources, the diets of men and women differ, with women having a greater preference for berries and men for meat.[10] In macronutrient terms, this can be seen as a greater male preference for protein and a female preference for sugar. It should not be surprising that there are such differences, given the different physiologies of the sexes. For example, men have more muscle as a proportion of their body weight and women more fat. But dietary medical research has rarely distinguished between male and female subjects, so the advice we get is almost identical for men and women, with relatively few exceptions, such as greater calorific intake for men and greater importance of calcium and iron for women. Studies of the hunter-gatherer diet perhaps suggest that we should be paying more attention to the differing nutritional needs of the sexes.

To learn from hunter-gatherers, we need to be able to overcome some deep-seated assumptions. Consider the question of why individuals who kill an animal then share the meat with others. The theory widely held by behavioural ecologists and evolutionary psychologists is that sharing is a form of 'reciprocal altruism'. That is, by sharing the meat, the hunter is acting altruistically, but doing so is also in his long-term interests. The hunter cannot rely on himself for future meals because he does not know when he will next be able to kill an animal. By sharing, he creates an obligation from those he shares with to reciprocate when they are the successful hunters. This strategy is called 'risk-reduction reciprocity'.

A team of anthropologists set out to test this theory by studying Hadza meat-sharing. If the risk-reduction reciprocity theory were true, then you would expect certain patterns of behaviour to follow, the most obvious one being that 'the meat a man's household gets from the kills of others depends on the meat the others get from kills by him'. But the anthropologists found that this was not what happened. Food was shared equally. There were no rewards for more successful hunters or penalties for those who were less successful.[11]

The team of anthropologists came to believe that a major reason why the risk-reduction reciprocity thesis failed is that 'a large carcass among the Hadza is like a public good until it is distributed'. In other words, killing it does not make it yours. You only get to own a share after the group has allocated it to you. This also seems to be the case for the Aché, hunter-gatherers in what is now Paraguay. As with the Hadza, they show 'no bias in the shares to better hunters or their wives and children' and 'hunters play no role in meat distributions'.

Interestingly, anthropologist Lorna Marshall found that the !Kung of the western Kalahari Desert do attribute nominal ownership of a carcass to an individual: it belongs to 'the owner of the arrow that first penetrated the prey', who 'may or may not be the hunter who shot it'.[12]

Still, the anthropologists found themselves feeling the need to find some kind of egocentric motivation for hunters to 'give up' their kills. Their conclusion was that being a good hunter bought you status. 'Everyone knows who acquired the carcass,' they say, and 'the effects on the hunter's reputation are not the same as title to the meat'. This 'status rivalry' 'or 'show-off' hypothesis would also explain why hunters talk incessantly about their kills and remember each one.

The risk-reduction reciprocity hypothesis and its refutation tell us at least as much about the thinking of western anthropologists as they do about the Hadza. The original misunderstanding of meat-sharing behaviour only arose because western observers brought with them the assumption that a food system must contain some kind of food economy in which participants in food production are rewarded in proportion to their contribution. But in hunter-gatherer societies the importance of sharing and mutual aid is so obvious that you don't need material incentives to make your contribution. Even if status is a reward for being a good hunter, it does not follow that it is a necessary motivation. A parent who looks after their children well is usually rewarded by filial love, but the motivation for parenting is love for the child, not the desire to get it back. In the same way, a hunter might be motivated to play their part by their fidelity to the group, not by the status that playing their part well might bring.

It has become too easy to assume that every aspect of food systems must be understood in terms of trade and transaction. It is of course true that commerce is a widespread feature of our food world. Even the Hadza now trade some of their honey with Swahili and Datoga for cornmeal, a recent addition to their diet. Many also wear manufactured clothes such as T-shirts, which are obviously not home-made. But at the very basis of the Hadza food system is a cooperative effort in which trade and exchange play no role at all. For them, interdependence is part and parcel of daily life.

*

Much as there is to admire in Hadza society, it involves several practices that few outsiders would wish to adopt. Although there is a refreshing lack of political hierarchy, with no one in the role of chief, there are very strong and rigid sex-determined roles: men hunt, women gather; men make weapons, women make almost everything else, including dolls from termite nest mud. Crittenden has to rely on juvenile informants and her adult male colleagues for information about Hadza hunting practices because it is taboo for her, as a female, to accompany the male hunters.

Hunting itself is of course something that tests the squeamishness of societies in which veganism is increasingly seen as the most morally pure position. Hunting wild animals may seem to be more humane than factory farming, but animal welfare is hardly a Hadza priority. Animals are killed with darts tipped with a poison derived from a neurotoxin extracted from the desert rose by three hours of boiling. It is powerful enough to bring down anything other than an elephant, which the Hadza don't hunt anyway. (Snakes are also off the menu, although deadly black mambas are killed on sight.) Little wonder the Hadza are very careful not to eat the bit of meat around the poisoned arrow tip.

People are commonly appalled by slaughterhouses, but the instantaneous unconsciousness induced by the stun guns used in abattoirs leads to a much cleaner and less painful death than being taken down by a toxin. 'People don't often think about what this means for the animal when it is not only shot with a poison-tipped arrow but, after you hit one, it takes some time to track the animal to find them,' says Crittenden. 'These large animals take a long time to die.' *National Geographic* photographer Matthieu Paley reported following a Hadza hunt in which a giraffe was hit and wandered off, slowly getting more wobbly as the poison took effect. In this case, the giraffe overcame the poison, meaning it suffered hours of torment for no creature's benefit.[13] Paley had to feast instead on some roasted game: a hyrax, a small, furry herbivorous mammal which often ends up as a Hadzabe dinner.

Perhaps even more unsettling for those in most developed countries, where the eating of our fellow primates is taboo, is that the Hadza will hunt and eat baboons. Human beings descended from primates in the Rift Valley and are therefore very closely related to them. The Hadza have no theory of evolution, but they do believe another story of what happened in the same geographical location that makes the connection between them and baboons even more intimate.

Haine is a mythical giant, comparable to a god, who one day gathered some baboons and sent some to get food and others to bring water. The foraging primates returned with the food, tired and thirsty, but hours later, the ones sent for water had still not returned. When Haine and the foraging baboons went down to the river to see what had happened, they found the other baboons splashing around in the water. Haine told the food foragers that from now on they would be Hadzabe, while the others would remain baboons. The Hadzabe would live in the bush and eat berries, tubers, the fruit of the baobab tree, but first and foremost, meat.[14]

It is always discomforting for people who have grown up in industrialised food environments to realise that people who are evidently infinitely more in touch with the natural world than they are see the killing and eating of other animals as good and natural. Of course, that does not mean they are right. But it should at least give pause for thought: is disgust at meat eating really a sign of a more civilised society or simply a mark of one that has become detached from the realities of life and death?

Modern attitudes to animal welfare and sexual equality are not the only reasons you'd be hard-pressed to find a single example of someone from an industrialised nation choosing to irreversibly live among hunter-gatherers. Another reason might be the high infant mortality rate of 21.8 per cent, with only 55 per cent making it to their fifteenth birthday. Those who make it that far typically live into their sixties or beyond, but those brutal early years mean that life expectancy at birth is a mere 32.7 years.[15] Even those convinced that Hadza are happier than the typical urban dweller may find that they value more than just contentment in life. Few would trade the opportunities, diversity and richness of the modern world for the simpler but heavily restricted and monotonous life of the hunter-gatherer. We want to grow, to learn, even if that makes life harder.

It is difficult enough for the few remaining hunter-gatherers who were born into this way of life to maintain it. Their lifestyle depends on being able to move around a large territory following seasonal food supplies, with a population density low enough to avoid depleting the resources they utilise. This is getting increasingly difficult for the Hadza as they face competition for land from others moving in to cultivate crops or raise cattle. Around the world the few remaining hunter-gatherer communities find themselves penned in by towns and land dedicated to agriculture or nature reserves.

Our planet certainly does not have enough space for seven billion people to hunt and gather. Biologists Lynn Margulis and Dorion Sagan have calculated that it requires 1,000 hectares to feed a single palaeolithic hunter-gatherer.[16] So with a land mass of 24,853,200 hectares, the United Kingdom could sustain a population of fewer than 25,000. It is currently home to 68 million. In other words, a Britain of hunter-gatherers would have to get rid of more than 96 per cent of its people. The global population would have to be more than decimated to make hunter-gathering viable.

In any case, Crittenden believes there are no hunter-gatherer communities that are still collecting and eating only wild foods: 'All foraging communities around the world are mixed subsistence, meaning they rely on other forms of nutrition and other types of food economies for at least part of the year. The community I work with in Tanzania have not yet started growing crops or tending domesticated ungulates like cattle or goats, but they do rely very heavily on donations from tourists, tour companies, missionaries and aid organisations. Many of them also participate in wage labour and are part of a market economy. So they're also spending money to buy farmed and processed foods to supplement their diet.'

Not everyone wants to continue living strictly according to the old ways anyway. Crittenden says that 'at the turn of the last century, when there were arguably far greater amounts of Acacia-Commiphora woodland available for people to live in and to access resources on, many individuals were choosing to turn away from the foraging lifestyle in order to engage in wage labour and a different type of economy'.

Times are hard for the last remaining hunter-gatherers. Crittenden sees their current situation as 'fundamentally a human rights issue. The area of land in which foraging communities can exist varies around the world and it is tethered to national policies. In northern Tanzania there are parts of the community who still want to forage for as much of their food as possible. They have been deeded a section of land from the Tanzanian government on the eastern shores of Lake Eyasi, covering two of the four historic territories that the community resided in. But this customary right of occupancy also happens to be the same plot of land that Datoga pastoralists often share. The Datoga have lost 100 per cent of their homeland, they have actually been kicked out. They had to move south because they were displaced further to the north by other pastoral groups. So you have both communities displaced by national parks, which has turned both communities into what a lot of applied human geographers, human rights activists and Indigenous scholars refer to as "conservation refugees". We have these wildlife conservation areas that are pushing populations into smaller and smaller plots of land.' On top of this, climate change is reducing the carrying capacity of the land that is left, especially as a result of water stress.

Once hunter-gatherer communities contract, they don't rebound. Hardly anyone who has grown up with indoor toilets, smartphones and international food is going to give it all up to live on honey, wild meat and tubers. We probably couldn't do it even if we wanted to. Hadza boys start learning to hunt from the time they are given their first toy: a tiny bow and arrow. They start by killing and eating small birds, and by the age of ten they are bringing home small-game meat. To learn these skills from scratch as an adult would be incredibly difficult. If we are to learn from the Hadza it cannot be by trying to copy them. Rather, we should see whether the way they have always lived provides any pointers towards how we should live tomorrow.

Such pointers are there, if we look carefully enough. For the Hadza, how they live and how they eat are inseparable. That's not how it seems to the typical denizen of the industrialised world, for whom food is something to be bought as and when it is needed, and very often does not even require preparation. The Hadza spend around six hours a day gathering food and yet more time preparing it. In the UK and the USA, people spend less than 8 per cent of their income on food and less than six hours a week cooking. In more gastronomic cultures like Spain and Italy, the latter figure is only around an hour greater.[17]

However, these differences do not show that the link between how we eat and how we live has been broken. The connection remains fundamental, just not as obvious. Everything about how we live is related to how we eat. It is precisely our ability to outsource food production and preparation that allows us to structure our lives around other things, primarily paid employment and leisure. Furthermore, it is only because this outsourcing demands such a small percentage of our income that we can live consumerist lifestyles, creating brochure-perfect homes filled with high-tech gadgets.

Everything about how we live has always depended on a

functioning food world. But whereas every Hadzabe knows exactly how their food system works and how to feed themselves, few in developed economies have any idea where most of their food even comes from, and most are entirely dependent on others to get it for them.

Perhaps the most uncontroversial lesson the Hadza provide is that living sustainably requires a profound appreciation of the interdependence of all things. Within their communities, sharing is a daily fact of life and competition is absent. Within their environment, they live in such a way as to sustain rather than deplete. The history of industrialised societies, however, is one in which the attitude has been one of resource extraction and capture, trade and competition. Anything non-human is seen as something to be exploited rather than something that we depend on and that depends on us. We need to appreciate, as the Hadza do, that food supply is not just another area of consumer choice, a discrete part of the economy that can be left to business to run, but is fundamental to human life and society.

2

THE OUTLIERS

Fat and flesh in the Great Rift Valley and the Arctic

The food pyramid is perhaps the most recognisable and common health-information graphic ever created. The first was produced in Sweden in 1974, but perhaps the most famous is the one introduced by the United States Department of Agriculture (USDA) in 1992. At the bottom of the pyramid are the foods that should provide the basis of the diet: breads, grains and cereals. On the next level up are fruits and vegetables, the pyramid narrowing to indicate that they need to be eaten less. An even smaller third level contains meat and dairy, while sweets and oils are at the apex, to be consumed in moderation.

These days the pyramid has largely been superseded by the food plate, divided to indicate the recommended proportions of the food groups on it. In content, it differs only slightly from the old pyramid. In the British version, fruits and vegetables occupy the same amount of space as bread, pasta and other starchy carbohydrates, with an encouragement to eat whole grains. Vegetable proteins such as beans and pulses are grouped together with meat and eggs, while dairy has been given its own, squeezed segment. Sweets and snacks are left out completely, to be eaten only as occasional indulgences. In the USDA version, fruit and vegetables take up half the plate.

The shifts in dietary advice over the past century are less remarkable than the continuities. Exact proportions may have varied, but grains, fruits and vegetables have always made up the bulk of the recommended healthy diet. As far back as 1943, the USDA was recommending eating from seven different food groups, four of which (green and yellow vegetables ... ; oranges, tomatoes, grapefruit ... ; bread, flour and cereals; potatoes and other vegetables and fruits) comprised plants. The enduring and wide degree of consensus is striking.

Yet in certain parts of the world, people have for centuries, even millennia, been living on diets that bear no resemblance to these orthodoxies. In the Rift Valley in Kenya, the basis of the traditional Maasai diet is milk, meat and blood. In and around the Arctic Circle, Eskimos – the collective term for the indigenous Inuit and Yupik – used to eat barely any plants at all, living almost entirely on the harvest of the sea. For both peoples, consumption of fat and protein far exceeds the levels recommended by most health experts, and consumption of plants is far below. Yet not only have these societies survived for centuries, their health outcomes have actually become worse the more they have left behind their traditional food ways. How is this possible?

The Maasai live on the plains and uplands of East Africa's Great Rift Valley in Kenya and Tanzania. They are spread across sixteen politically autonomous and geographically defined *iloshon*, each of which has its own dress, dialect and customs. However, there is a distinct and unified identity and culture shared by all and reflected in their name: 'Maa-sai' means 'my people'. There are estimated to be around a million Maasai people, although the Maasai Association says this number is inaccurate because many distrust the national census and either deliberately provide inaccurate information or refuse to take part.

The Maasai are pastoralists who consider plant food dirty – literally soiled. Although they have traditionally consumed some plants, the basis of their diet comprises the milk, blood and meat that come from their livestock. Milk is the main component of this triad, with studies in the early 1970s suggesting that they typically drank four to five litres a day. Overall, their diet provided two thirds of their calories from fat. Yet their levels of blood cholesterol and of the beta-lipoproteins that transport 'bad' LDL cholesterol through the arteries were low, as were incidences of atherosclerosis – hardening of the arteries.[1]

Similarly, sea animals form the basis of the traditional diet of the peoples of the north polar regions, which means around half of all their calories are derived from fat (a quarter of which is saturated), around a third from protein and 20 per cent or less from carbohydrates.[2] But again, not only have these people thrived for millennia, it has long been thought that their incidence of coronary (or ischemic) heart disease is lower than in industrialised societies.

The main reason for this is that evolution ensures that all species adapt to their environments, and human beings are no exception. The Maasai, for example, have been found to have several distinctive adaptations that allow the tribe to live on a diet that most other human beings would struggle with, including an ability to cope with high dietary cholesterol.[3]

But some aspects of the Maasai and Inuit diets are healthy simply because they are good for any human, not just those adapted to them. For instance, one common factor that traditional foods seem to have over their modern, processed alternatives is that they are whole foods in the truest sense of the term. Most people today pay lip service to the idea of whole foods, but only seem to apply it to grains. Fat is skimmed off milk and trimmed off meat. People happily eat the muscle tissue from animals but turn their noses up at all the other parts. Even the fruits and vegetables that we cultivate have been bred to rid them of as many seeds as possible, so we are left only with the flesh, and many people don't even eat the skins.

Consider also the high fat consumption of the Inuit. Until very recently, fats had long been demonised by western nutritionalists, leading to a trend for lean meat. But if the Inuit were to throw away anything from a carcass, it would be flesh, not fat. The archaeologist John Speth has found evidence that, even at times when food was scarce, they would leave fat-depleted animals with plenty of meat left on them. There is even a form of malnutrition known as rabbit starvation, *mal de caribou* or plain protein poisoning, which is the result of surviving on the too-lean meat of rabbits or caribou. The Icelandic American explorer and ethnologist Vilhjalmur Stefansson experienced this first hand on his journeys in the Arctic and later tried a fat-free meat diet at Bellevue Hospital in New York as an experiment. He found that the symptoms brought on 'were exactly the same as in the Arctic . . . diarrhoea and a feeling of general baffling discomfort'.[4]

However, it is not just the quantity of fat that matters but the type. The meat of wild animals tends to contain more monounsaturated fats, the kind found in olive oil, and fewer saturated ones. In addition, cold-water fish and sea mammals are rich in omega-3 fatty acids, a kind of polyunsaturated fat. In contrast, the meat of shedded farm animals, fattened up on grains, contains more saturated fat, while the polyunsaturated fats in the most popular commercial vegetable oils are high in omega-6 fatty acids. There is some good evidence that the imbalance between omega-3 and omega-6 fatty acids in the western diet is a key factor in its unhealthiness.[5] Worse, much of this fat is highly processed, meaning it is ingested in an altered form.

Anthropologist Kristen Borré has also found that the traditional Inuit diet ranks better on conventional nutrition scales than one might have thought. It is 'low in sugar and saturated fat, high in quality protein and polyunsaturated fats, and rich in iron and vitamins'. 'Country foods' – traditional hunted and foraged foods – score better than 'store foods' – packaged and processed ones – for all nutrients except calcium, vitamin C and carbohydrate. What's more, the more Inuit eat store foods, the more they suffer from tooth decay, acne, obesity, anaemia and deficiencies in vitamins A, C, D and folic acid.

Karen Fediuk, a nutritionist with expertise in traditional food systems, made some similarly surprising discoveries. As a graduate student, she investigated the vitamin C intake of Inuit on Baffin Island. Given the lack of plants in the polar regions, you might have thought vitamin C would be hard to come by. Scurvy was for a long time the scourge of western travellers without sources of fresh fruit and vegetables. But many traditional animal-based Inuit foods turn out to be rich in vitamin C, including raw cisco eggs (cisco is a whitefish of the Salmonid family), raw beluga whale meat, narwhal maktak (made from the frozen skin and blubber of narwhal whales) and mountain sorrel. Other good sources include aged and boiled maktak, ringed seal and caribou liver, blueberries and kelp.

Similar stories can be told for other nutrients. Most people around the world make most of their vitamin D by exposing their skins to the sun. That's not an option where it is virtually constant nighttime for half the year and it's too cold to undress for most of the rest. But the vitamin can also be found in the oils and livers of cold-water fish and sea mammals.

Notice two things about many of these foods. First, the best animal sources of nutrients are raw. Vitamin C, for example, is destroyed by cooking. Second, many of the most nutrient-rich parts of animals are the innards, not the muscle tissue. Unfortunately, from a nutritional point of view, these are two of the food ways that are being abandoned as Inuit adopt more western diets. 'My grandmother used all parts of the caribou, even to the bones,' one woman told Fediuk. 'We no longer boil the bones, we waste lots of the caribou as not all parts are eaten.' Another reported that now, 'very small parts of the meat or intestines are taken, and the parts that were eaten as a delicacy are hardly touched'.

Fediuk found that at the turn of the twenty-first century, the primary sources of vitamin C for the Inuit were fortified processed foods such as fruit-flavoured beverages (often made from dried crystals), evaporated milk, apple juice and potato chips. Taste, availability and affordability were all factors driving these changes, as well as a cultural norm that country foods should not be purchased but obtained through hunting and sharing with family.[6]

Studies of traditional diets such as those by Borré and Fediuk are becoming increasingly difficult to conduct since vanishingly fewer people now live on them. In East Africa, Alaska and Northern Canada, indigenous peoples are undergoing what is called a 'nutrition transition'. Traditional lifestyles are being abandoned or significantly modified, which, along with increased access to shops and markets, leads to more consumption of purchased foods, many of which are processed, high in carbohydrates, fatty and low in fibre.

These studies provide evidence that people undergoing the transition tend to have worse health outcomes as a result. The nutrition transition in Inuit communities is leading to an increase in cardiovascular disease and type 2 diabetes, both of which used to be uncommon there.[7] Across all low- and middle-income countries, it has been found that 'changes are occurring very rapidly and the costs, in terms of health, are great'. One surprising consequence is that there are many lower-income households which have both underweight and overweight members. Similarly, some are overweight and undernourished, because people increasingly eat calorie-rich but nutrient-poor processed foods.[8]

There can be little doubt that the traditional diets of peoples such as the Inuit and the Maasai are under threat, along with their ways of life. Just as the Hadza of Tanzania are facing increasing competition for the land they depend on, so too the Maasai are being squeezed in to make way for grazing land, a trend accelerated by increased drought due to global warming. Herds are getting smaller and more cattle are being sold, often at 'throwaway' prices. There is increasing dependence on purchased foods, but in the frequent absence of secure incomes, this decreases food security and self-sufficiency. Undernutrition is widespread and half of all Maasai children have stunted growth. In one community studied, milk, blood and meat made up only 7 per cent of the calorific intake, with maize and beans now the primary staples. The study concluded that indigenous food knowledge is being lost and that 'if some measures are not put in place, complete loss of traditional food practices appears inevitable'.[9] As the Maasai Association laments, what 'once was a proud and self-sufficient society' is now seeing a level of poverty 'beyond conceivable height' and has become 'a beggar for relief food' because of 'imposed foreign concepts of development'.

Not all the negative changes in health can be attributed to the nutrition transition. As one study concluded, 'the life style of the Inuit is rapidly changing towards an increased cardiovascular risk factor profile. Physical activity declines, obesity is widespread, the reliance on imported food increases, and the smoking rates are alarmingly high.'[10] One intriguing study tried to disentangle lifestyle and diet factors by looking at two Inuit groups in the northwestern part of Greenland that both had physically demanding jobs. One group had a traditional life involving fishing and hunting and the other were doing manual labour at an airbase for up to sixty hours a week. The first group ate a traditional diet while the second consumed a westernised one. Although the study was small, no one was found to have glucose intolerance or type

2 diabetes, both common problems in Inuit communities transitioning to a western lifestyle, despite the fact that many had high body mass indexes, a common predictor of metabolic disease. It was still true that 'the metabolic profile of traditionally living Inuit were more favourable than in those who had changed to a westernised diet'. But these differences were not extreme, suggesting that lifestyle mattered more than diet.[11] The experience of East African pastoralists also suggests that the transition journey itself seems to be more harmful that the destination. Those undergoing the nutrition transition have been found to have worse health outcomes than both those still eating traditional diets and those who have become settled urban dwellers.[12]

Nor should claims about the healthiness of these traditional diets be exaggerated. Several studies have questioned received opinion about the good cardiovascular health of the Inuit, for example. Bjerregaard, Young and Hegele point to a claim made in 1975 that 'coronary atherosclerosis is almost unknown among these people [the Greenland Eskimos] when living in their own cultural environment'. They argue that although this has 'attained axiomatic status in the atherosclerosis literature', it lacks a solid evidential basis. The general claim that Eskimos have a low incidence of coronary artery disease 'is fragile and rests on unreliable mortality statistics'. Indeed, some evidence points the other way. In Greenland and among Alaska natives, there was a decrease in mortality from coronary heart disease from 1955 to 1965, a period of rapid westernisation. Whereas in 1952, 54 per cent of the daily energy intake in the villages of Northwest Greenland came from traditional food, by 1991 it had fallen to 25 per cent.[13]

Perhaps one reason why the general healthiness of traditional diets has sometimes been overlooked is that the ways it is conceptualised by indigenous people themselves seem unscientific. For instance, illness is often treated by eating 'country foods', especially the 'strong medicine' of seal meat. Borré explains that the Inuit say that the nutritional value of seal meat is due to the fact that 'the cycling of animal blood and human blood creates a healthy human body and soul'. Inuit blood must be enriched by seal blood, or else it will be thin and weak. As one elder of the Clyde River community on the shore of Baffin Island told Borré, 'Seal blood gives us our blood. Seal is life-giving.'

These are not forms of explanation that would pass muster in a journal of nutritional science. However, as Borré argues, although Inuit food ways are not based in science, science ends up vindicating them.[14] This raises the question of what we accept as sources of knowledge about the food world. The global gold standard today is science. The ability to measure, quantify and test is the only reliable method we have for arbitrating between competing truth claims. However, many argue that science is not the only valid way of knowing and that there is great value in forms of indigenous or traditional knowledge, often referred to by the initials IK and TK. In particular, it is claimed that traditional ecological knowledge (TEK) leads to the best management of ecosystems. One striking example is the resurgence of interest in the Aboriginal Australian practice of starting controlled fires to create breaks in the bush. These buffers are protective against the spread of the kinds of devastating wildfires that have become more common in Australia in recent decades. They also help promote biodiversity.[15]

Admiration for traditional ecological knowledge is not new. At the beginning of the twentieth century, American agricultural scientist F. H. King studied the farming practices in China, Korea and Japan. He had wondered 'how it is possible, after twenty and perhaps thirty or even forty centuries, for their soils to be made to produce sufficiently for the maintenance of such dense populations as are living now in these three countries'. When he went to find out, he reported that 'almost every day we were instructed, surprised and amazed at the conditions and practices which confronted us whichever way we turned; instructed in the ways and extent to which these nations for centuries have been and are conserving and utilizing their natural resources, surprised at the magnitude of the returns they are getting from their fields'.[16]

Sceptics argue that although there are cultural and political reasons to respect traditional knowledge, it is absurd to give it equal status with science. But these two ways of knowing may not be as different as they seem. Both can be seen as complementary routes to the same destination: empirical knowledge.

Start with the empirical part. Empiricism – the belief that all knowledge is rooted in experience – is the central tenet of most modern western philosophy and the keystone of natural science. The early empiricists were happy to reach their conclusions on the basis of their ordinary observations. But over time science developed an experimental method that strove to control for nature's variables and isolate precisely what was responsible for what. Empiricism thereby became systematised.

But conducting experiments and making measurements is not the only way to learn from experience. Trial and error is more venerable and often just as potent. It is, after all, the blind mechanism behind evolution by natural selection, creating organisms more complex than any human artefact. Traditional knowledge is based on the trial and error of generations possessing an intimate knowledge of their land and all that lives on it. When it is used to feed a people, and so its success or failure is measured by life and death, we have every reason to consider it as having a firm empirical basis.

We also have to think more about what kind of knowledge this empiricism yields. 'Knowledge' comes in different forms. One key distinction is between 'knowledge-that' (facts) and 'know-how' (skills and abilities). A scientist may know everything there is to know about growing tomatoes yet be totally incompetent at farming. On the other hand, someone may be able to grow tomatoes brilliantly yet not be able to give an account of their methods or why they work.

A lot of traditional knowledge is in effect a form of know-how. Eskimos and the Maasai know how to hunt, gather and eat. However, they may lack a scientific understanding of why what they do works. Traditionally, they had no idea about vitamins, minerals, proteins or carbohydrates. So the way they conceptualise their know-how may well be literally false. It isn't true that the spirit of the seal or the cow mingles with their own, but that doesn't matter. These accounts do not need to be scientific. They are just ways of making sense of their practical knowledge, and that is both robust and of deep scientific interest. If traditional knowledge suggests that ways of living off the land and eating are good and sustainable, scientists have a good reason to try to find out if and how those ways of being work. As we have seen, more often than not, there turns out to be a wisdom in the old ways which is ahead of, not against, the science.

The beliefs and practices of traditional societies raise questions for our ethical values as well as for our scientific understanding. In particular, they challenge the way we think about other animals. Like the Hadza, both the Inuit and the Maasai have an intimate sense of kinship with the same animals that they kill and eat. The Maasai's identification with cattle is, if anything, deeper than that of the Inuit with seals. Like many East African pastoralists, they share names with their favoured oxen and refer to each other by these cattle names.[17] The Maasai also refer to themselves as a people by using their word for cattle, *inkishu*. Anthropologist Kaj Århem says the overlapping words for cattle and people are 'symbolic ways of saying that cattle and men are interdependent, that the life of the one depends on that of the other'. The importance of cattle is reflected in the Maasai prayer *'Meishoo iyiook enkai inkishu o-nkera'*: May the creator give us cattle and children.[18]

For the Maasai, cattle are symbols of the important distinction between the spheres of humanity and the wild. 'Human beings are defined in opposition to wild beasts,' says Århem, 'society in opposition to nature and the wild.' Cattle 'embody the virtues of humanity' since they are 'gregarious and docile herbivores' and 'prototypical non-predators', they 'live in community' and they 'are peaceful, and do not hunt for food'. By drinking milk, the Maasai indirectly feed on grass and so share the life of the cow.

The identification of the Maasai with cattle is also a way of distinguishing themselves from a variety of 'others'. Most obviously, it separates the Maasai and their cattle from the wild, predatory and scavenging beasts whose base behaviour has only one useful function: that of eating the corpses of dead humans, which are left out for them. In contrast to the savagery of wild beasts, the Maasai value restraint, formalised in a code of proper conduct which sets clear rules and restrictions, particularly on sex and eating. This restraint is also manifest in a belief that causing bloodshed pollutes and that the optimal behaviour is non-violent whenever possible.

This othering of the wild means that the Maasai are prepared to treat certain animals in ways that conservation-minded outsiders might find objectionable. In particular, there is a strong tradition of lion hunting. Sometimes this is simply to protect livestock, in the same way that many European farmers kill wolves to defend their sheep, even though wolves are a protected species. But sometimes the killing is purely ritual, known as *Ala-mayo*, a rite of passage for young *morani* warriors.

Such was the case in April 2014 when a Daniel Rosengren, a field observer for the Serengeti Lion Project, detected a no-movement signal from the collar of a female lion known as MH35. His worst fears were confirmed when he found her dead as a result of spear wounds. There were no Maasai livestock in the area, and Rosengren eventually concluded it must have been a ritual killing. Six days later a second female called VUM was also found killed by the same means. Rosengreen believed two other lions from the same pride had also been recently killed.[19]

What seems especially objectionable is that Maasai do not even use the lions' meat, as they see all game meat as inferior to that of domesticated animals. They only take trophies, such as the mane, the tail or, in the case of VUM, her claws. As the Maasai Association explains, 'The mane is beautifully beaded by village women and given back to the hunter. The mane is worn over the head, only during special ceremonies. The mane helped warriors from far areas to identify the toughest warrior.' For the Maasai, the lion is not a noble beast but a savage one, inferior both to human pastoralists and to their pacific cattle. There is a Maasai saying: 'Until the lion learns to roast his meat he cannot challenge the warriors.'[20]

The Maasai no longer advocate lion hunting. But the carefully chosen words of the Maasai Association show that they justifiably resent being demonised for their occasional kills when non-indigenous people can do it for fun. 'The practice of lion hunting and other wildlife has been banned in East Africa,' they say. 'Unless, of course, you are wealthy enough to join the Western Hunters Club who pay an enormous amount of money to hunt lions for trophy.' They add with understated irritation, 'A share of revenue generated from game reserves in Maasai land could only improve the situation.'

The differing attitudes towards lion hunting provide a vivid example of how moral norms vary cross-culturally. Some worry that this means moral values have no validity and are nothing more than conventions. But there are good reasons why ethics is and should be shaped by environment and situation. For example, the philosopher Patricia Churchland argues that differing ecological conditions for the Inuit and Polynesians have led to different moral norms. This explains why lying is considered by the Inuit to be much more serious. As she explains, 'deception really jeopardises the group as a whole, because they're always on the knife-edge of survival. Starvation is always just a seal away. So when someone deceives them about something, and the whole group undertakes an activity as a result, they waste precious resources, energy.'

In Churchland's view, all ethics is essentially an attempt to deal with 'constraint satisfaction problems'. That is to say, there are certain things we want and need to do – eat, find shelter, stay safe, and so on – but there are numerous constraints that limit what we can do in pursuit of these aims. If we only try to stay warm we can never go out to get food; we can't both stay completely safe from predators and hunt; we can't distribute food completely equally and make sure everyone has what they specifically need. Ethics concerns the social rules we put in place to ensure that collectively we can solve such problems.[21]

In this view, ethics is a practical means of negotiating competing needs and demands. Food waste is only a moral issue because it causes practical problems, potentially of life and death. Environmental degradation is a moral issue because it harms all living things. Poor diet is also a moral issue, because it hinders people's ability to flourish. Because ethics is in this deep sense pragmatic, ethical norms rightly change depending on the actual situation we find ourselves in.

Accustomed to an idea of ethics as universal and absolute, perhaps even divine, some find this thought troubling. They fear it opens the door to a kind of relativism in which nothing is really right or wrong, it all depends on your, or your culture's, point of view. But it does not follow from 'ethics is always situated' that 'anything goes'. Ethics is anchored in objective facts about what causes harm and what does good. These can't be altered on a whim.

However, if the facts change and ethical values don't, that might lead to some moral rules becoming obsolete. Indeed, various studies have argued that the moral values shaped by ecology may endure after those conditions have changed. For example, there is evidence that societies where there has historically been greater 'parasite stress'– in other words, more infectious disease – are more authoritarian and traditional, since having strict rules on such things as how food is handled helps combat disease transmission.[22] Another study sought to explain the Chinese culture of collectivism by the fact that rice farming is an extremely collaborative endeavour. It concluded that 'a history of farming rice makes cultures more interdependent, whereas farming wheat makes cultures more independent, and these agricultural legacies continue to affect people in the modern world'.[23]

The concern about such ethical inertia is that we end up working with values that are ill-suited to our current problems. Ritual hunting may have been acceptable when lions were much more numerous, but not now that they are endangered. And as our food world changes, the rules that govern its use may need to change too.

Despite the complexities involved in assessing the healthiness of traditional diets, several conclusions can be safely drawn. First, the idea that all societies at all times have to conform to the same ideal diet doesn't add up. There are no essential foods, only essential nutrients – a principle widely attributed to the late biochemist Harold Draper. What's more, there are many sources of these nutrients, and if we eat a diverse range of whole foods, we are more likely to get them.

Human beings have evolved to make the most of the resources available to them in ways that are subtle and complicated. When we change our diets, especially when we do so quickly, we are effectively conducting huge experiments in nutrition. We ought to have more humility. Nutritional science is still young and there is so much we do not know. If we have eaten certain foods in certain ways for millennia, we should assume until it is proven otherwise that there is probably a good reason why. Traditional foods that don't fit neatly on the contemporary dietary food plate should generally be chosen over highly processed ones that do. We should assume that traditionally made fatty blood sausages are prefer-able to lean, factory-made salamis; that lard full of saturated fat is better than industrial margarine boasting of its polyunsaturated fat content; that spoonfuls of honey are superior to sprinkles of sweet-eners. Witnessing how poorly traditional societies are faring as they undergo a nutrition transition should make those who have already completed it question whether their diets have moved too far.

3

HUMANITY'S
GREATEST MISTAKE?

Rice and kharang in Bhutan

How can the happiest country in the world still be making what an-thropologist Jared Diamond called 'the worst mistake in the history of the human race'? Diamond popularised the idea that the 'Neolithic Revolution' from hunter-gathering to agriculture around 11,000 years ago was a disaster for humankind. It was at that time that people began what we now call subsistence farming: families and small communities growing crops and keeping animals to feed themselves, not to sell.

Huge swathes of humanity still live in basically the same way today, although as Ken Giller, emeritus professor of Plant Production Systems at Wageningen University in the Netherlands, told me, very few are pure subsistence farmers. 'Many of the poorer people have extremely small plots and are largely earning their food by working for other farmers,' he says. Moreover, 'they don't want to just grow food to eat. They want to be able to send their kids to school and to have a better life.'

Giller argues that 'the idea of a subsistence farmer is an outdated concept that we need to escape'. A more accurate term is a smallholder, running a farm of less than two hectares (around two and a half soccer pitches), almost always with one family. According to the most recent data from the FAO, around two billion people – a quarter of the world's population – live on such farms, predominantly in Asia and Africa.[1]

Bhutan is one of many countries where smallholding is still a widespread way of life. As recently as 1980, 90 per cent of its population lived in rural areas. Despite rapid urbanisation, that proportion is still around 56 per cent, most of whom rely on arable crops, livestock and forestry to make a living.[2] If the turn to an agricultural society was a terrible mistake, the Bhutanese are still making it. Yet Bhutan has become internationally famous as the country that puts happiness first. In 1972, King Jigme Singye Wangchuck declared that 'Gross National Happiness is more important than Gross Domestic Product'. This was embedded in the country's first constitution, enacted in 2008.[3] Bhutan is also a global happiness champion, sponsoring a 2011 UN resolution that urged governments to 'give more importance to happiness and well-being in determining how to achieve and measure social and economic development'. Its passing led to the creation of the annual UN World Happiness Report.[4]

But aspiring to be the happiest country in the world is not the same as actually being it. Bhutan does sometimes punch – or perhaps hug – above its weight, as it did during the Covid-19 pandemic when, by July 2021, it had vaccinated a higher proportion of its people than any other country in the world.[5] But the last time Bhutan was included in the UN's World Happiness Report it ranked 95th out of 156 countries, lower than the likes of Mongolia, Nigeria, Azerbaijan, Lebanon, China and Vietnam.[6] Its blushes have been saved in recent years by the country not being included in the report at all, officially due to the difficulties of collecting data during the pandemic.

The government's plans to enhance its citizens' well-being require balancing change with preservation of the country's most valuable traditions. Nowhere is this challenge greater than in rural life. To understand what is good and bad in Bhutan's farming system is to understand some of the most fundamental problems and opportunities that humanity's switch to agriculture brought.

Before looking at Bhutan, the argument that the adoption of agriculture was a horrendous mistake merits closer attention. Jared Diamond's famous 1999 article summed up the case against farming with persuasive succinctness.[7] Much of the evidence he drew on had been set out in greater length a decade earlier by anthropologist Mark Nathan Cohen in his landmark book *Health and the Rise of Civilization*.[8] Using archaeological evidence and studies of contemporary hunter-gatherer societies, both Cohen and Diamond found that cultivation came out worse than hunting and gathering by pretty much every health and well-being metric they looked at.

Take labour. Hunter-gatherers were observed to spend less than twenty hours a week getting food, while farmers work almost all their waking hours. Then there is diet. Farmers eat a narrower range of foods, mostly high-carbohydrate crops such as maize, rice and wheat. Hunter-gatherers, in contrast, eat a wide variety of foods and get a good balance of fat, protein and carbohydrates, plentiful calories, and all the essential micronutrients. Farmers' dependence on a limited number of crops also raises the risk of famine and starvation if even one of them fails, as inevitably happens from time to time. In contrast, as Diamond said, 'It's almost inconceivable that Bushmen, who eat 75 or so wild plants, could die of starvation.'

This impacts on life expectancy at birth, which anthropologist George Armelagos told Diamond was about twenty-six years in pre-agricultural communities but fell to nineteen once humans started settling and farming. One reason for this is that once humans were living in larger, more crowded, enclosed settlements, parasites and infectious diseases could spread more easily. There was no tuberculosis or diarrhoeal disease before farming, no measles or bubonic plague before the appearance of large cities.

Agriculture was not only the reason for declining health, it was also responsible for increased incquality and hierarchy. As we have seen, hunter-gatherers have very egalitarian societies, albeit ones where roles are clearly divided according to sex and age. Because nothing is stored, there are no riches to amass. With farming, however, those who had the best land could have more than those that didn't, and in time many of those who owned land didn't even need to farm it themselves. As Diamond concludes, 'Only in a farming population could a healthy, non-producing elite set itself above the disease-ridden masses.'

The link between farming and inequitable ownership is found in the very word 'farming'. It comes from the Old French *ferme*, derived from the medieval Latin *firma*, meaning 'fixed payment'. This referred to the annual rent or tax paid to the landowner. Only in the early nineteenth century did the verb 'to farm' come to mean 'to grow crops or keep livestock'.

Many find Cohen and Diamond's argument intuitively implausible, disingenuous even. If they really thought hunter-gatherers' lives were superior, why didn't they give up their professorships and go and live among them? But Diamond argues that this objection misses the point. A comfortable life in a developed economy is fuelled by natural resources imported from poorer countries where life is often miserable. The West is the largely 'non-producing elite' benefiting from a system that is still worse for the vast majority of people. The question we should ask is not whether it is better to live in LA than in the Kalahari, but 'if one could choose between being a peasant farmer in Ethiopia or a bushman gatherer in the Kalahari, which do you think would be the better choice?'

The final defence of agriculture is that it made art and

civilisations possible. There is no Franz Kafka of the Hadza, no Mozart of the Maasai, no Sistine Chapel of the San, no Picasso of the Pirahã. Arguably, there is not even any cuisine as we understand it before the existence of settled human communities. Hunter-gatherers ate what they foraged raw or cooked simply over an open fire. Diamond's best reply is that 'great paintings and sculptures were already being produced by hunter-gatherers 15,000 years ago, and were still being produced as recently as the last century by such hunter-gatherers as some Eskimos and the Indians of the Pacific Northwest'.

If the case against agriculture looks damning, that is in part because the before-and-after comparisons don't extend as far as they might. Even Diamond agrees that, over time, the losses in life expectancy brought on by agriculture were reversed. Examination of skeletons from different parts of the world suggests that while the average height of an early farmer was ten to thirteen centimetres less than that of a hunter-gatherer, by classical times people were as tall as the foragers. Another study suggested that 13,000 years ago, 40 per cent of a hunter-gatherer population in what is now Egypt showed a defect called linear enamel hypoplasia in their layers of tooth enamel, which indicates prolonged illness or malnutrition. A millennium later, when farming had become established, the proportion of the population affected rose to a startling 70 per cent. But by 4,000 years ago, this figure had fallen to just 20 per cent, half the hunter-gatherer level.[9]

Furthermore, as Alyssa Crittenden, whom we met earlier, said, 'it wasn't just a clean story where everything was healthy and great and then we moved to farming and everything fell apart'. She pointed me to fascinating work by the archaeologist Jim Watson. 'Jim found something that surprised a lot of people. When foragers were consuming sugary fruits, those fruits have glucose in them that led to a very cariogenic environment. So it resulted in a lot of cavities in the mouths of foragers long before the transition to agriculture. This makes the story messy. You see the same thing with the Hadza, because those who are consuming a much larger amount of wild honey have a much higher rate of caries in their mouths.'[10]

Overall, the evidence suggests that the switch to agriculture did initially impact *Homo sapiens* badly, but very slowly we recovered and after 8,000 years of toil on the land, we were at least as well off as we had been hunter-gathering. But crucially, this new form of society allowed for the development of technologies and learning. As the evolutionary anthropologist Jay Stock puts it, without agriculture we wouldn't be able to stack innovation upon innovation. 'Without the surplus of food you get through farming, we couldn't have the runaway technological innovation we see today. For instance, I can spend a lifetime in school, years doing a PhD, and then teach my students everything I know in a few months. They can then go on to become more expert than I am, pushing the boundaries of knowledge.'[11]

Although much of the case against the agricultural turn rests on facts and statistics, gauging the relative merits of smallholding and its alternatives is not a scientific process of measuring which is more efficient. The question of how we feed ourselves is a normative one, meaning that it involves value judgements. Very often those debating how to manage the food world talk as though it is simply a factual matter about what works best. But 'best' is the superlative of 'good', which is clearly a normative term. Is it better to have lower yields but less environmental impact? Is it better that we have plentiful meat for everyone or that we don't eat meat at all? Is it better to farm more efficiently but lose traditional practices? A food system needs to be underpinned with principles, and if we are not clear what they are, they will often default to values we may not hold to be the highest, such as economic efficiency, convenience and productivity.

The main normative question raised by the switch to farming

concerns the nature of the good life. Is it better to live within a stable but restricted community, hunting, foraging, eating, dancing, talking; or in a more expansive world, where we are able to write down our literature, develop science, build monuments and buildings, meet with and learn from people from very different cultures? By some metrics the latter kind of life could be less happy and more stressful. But many of us prefer a richer, more challenging life over an easier but less varied one.

There is no simple way to determine which life is better. The nineteenth-century British philosopher John Stuart Mill concluded that the 'higher pleasures' enabled by literacy, the arts and culture are superior to simpler ones, even if those 'lower pleasures', such as those derived from sex and food, are more intense and more frequent. He argued that people who have experienced both kinds of pleasures are the only competent judges of their relative merits, and their consensus verdict is that higher pleasures are more valuable.

It might be objected that Mill self-selected his judges, since there are plenty of hedonists who have tried art and learning and still prefer beer and dancing. And if we wanted to consult judges who were competent to assess foraging and farming, we might find it difficult to find suitable appointees. For someone who has grown up with the opportunities that modern, industrialised economies offer, becoming a hunter-gather is inconceivable. But for those who have always lived as foragers, it might be equally impossible to countenance giving up family and community to farm the land, or to live in a dirty, bustling city. Still, there is one form of implicit judgement that informed people make: voting with their feet. The sparse movement we see between these forms of life goes only one way, from traditional to industrialised societies.

Agriculture may not have been such a mistake, but the experience of Bhutan suggests that many people still seek an escape from the smallholder life. They are attracted by the prospects of education and a well-paid job in a city or overseas. Those who freely choose to stick with farming, or to go back to it, usually do so because they see its entrepreneurial opportunities, not because they want no more from life than self-sufficiency. Outsiders, however, often have a rosier view of smallholding, focusing only on its merits. For example, a report released as part of the UN Decade of Family Farming said that 'family farmers are custodians of biodiversity and better preserve rural landscapes as well as cultural heritage'.[12] So we have the paradox that some affluent people in industrialised economies look wistfully to a form of farming that poor people in less developed ones are keen to abandon. Bhutan can help us to understand this contradiction and what we can learn from it.

Landlocked Bhutan contains a remarkable diversity of ecosystems within its 14,824 square miles (38,394 km²). Its six agro-ecological zones – wet subtropical, humid subtropical, dry subtropical, warm temperate, cool temperate and alpine – range from as low as 150 metres above sea level to 4,600 metres, close to the elevation of western Europe's highest mountain, Mont Blanc. The majority of its nearly 800,000 people work the land, almost all on their own families' farms, with few large enough to hire workers. About 71 per cent of Bhutanese households own land, on average just 2.16 acres, not much bigger than three soccer pitches.[13] Land inheritance laws have caused farm sizes to get smaller over time as farms are divided up between heirs.

Yet farming contributes less than 20 per cent to the national gross domestic product (GDP).[14] This is partly due to the dense forest cover and the steepness of much of the terrain: nearly a third of agricultural land is on slopes with a gradient of 50 per cent or more. Only 8 per cent of the land is cultivable and less than 3 per cent is actually under cultivation.[15] Farmers also have to spend on average nearly fifty nights a year guarding their farms against wild animals that destroy crops or prey on livestock. Add to that the other historical challenges of inadequate irrigation and small farm sizes, more recent problems of labour shortages as an increasing number of younger people move to the cities, and a loss of agricultural land to urbanisation, and you get an exceptionally tough farming environment.

A vivid picture of rural Bhutanese life is painted by Sonam Kinga in an academic paper that is both rich in information and deeply evocative.[16] Kinga comes from the place that he took as his subject: Gortshom village, lying 1,800 metres above sea level in eastern Bhutan. It can only be reached on foot, a day's walk from an eight-shop settlement called Gorgan. From there, a steep descent takes you into a river valley of the Kuri Chhu, following a mule track that Kinga says 'alternates between steep and gentle climbs through an expansive forest of pine, gooseberry trees, lemon grasses and onto more sub-alpine growths like oak, rhododendron, walnut and others'.

In this region, maize is the main crop, and when mixed with rice, which is considered superior, it forms the staple food, served alongside the vegetables that grow plentifully. Pure rice dishes are for special occasions only. Cattle and other livestock are also kept, but their numbers are declining, partly because the young children who would have traditionally acted as cowherds are increasingly going away to school. The arrival of shops in Gorgan in the 1980s also opened up the opportunity for farmers to barter for animal products rather than produce them.

Complex social systems have evolved over centuries to make smallholder farming in these conditions possible. There are always times of the year when extra labour is needed, which means everyone relies on everyone else. These labour exchanges are regulated through five conventions. One is to pay wages in kind (*pheu* or *chieu*), a form of bartering of goods for labour. More common is *lakpho*, under which a person who has borrowed the labour of someone else must reciprocate with the same number of days in return. No one keeps a ledger and the work exchanged need not be identical or even as difficult. A day's ploughing, weeding, harvesting or fetching wood all count for the same.

If farmers are unable to promise reciprocation or to pay, they might organise a day of feasting and working called *danpa*. Kinga says it is generally a form of support for a household in difficulty, but the hosts are expected to provide plentiful good food – rice, meat or fish, eggs, cheese or butter – as well as tea and alcohol. Kharang, the plain traditional staple of ground maize, should never be offered. Although *danpa* is not a reciprocal arrangement, it is understood that the hosts will usually take part in any future one hosted by a helper if needed. A short form of *danpa* is *drola*, morning work, that starts very early and ends at sunrise, so the worker can do their own full day's work as well.

A fifth form of labour exchange is *ruba* (help), which is more common for construction tasks. But if someone is ill and another kind of help is needed, it will be requested, on the understanding that it will be paid back if needed in future.

This merely scratches the surface of the complex networks of exchange and cooperation. For example, there is also transhumant agro-pastoralism, the practice of migrating cattle to lower elevations during the winter to access snow-free pastures. However, this isn't just about relocating livestock. As farmers move they establish relationships with people in different villages. Yak herders at higher elevations, for instance, host people from lower down in their own homes. They barter meat, wool and cheese for products like rice produced lower in the valley.

All this makes it clear that when we talk about smallholding, we are not just describing a form of agriculture. It is part of a whole way of life and set of social structures. As Kinga puts it, 'The foundations of a stable and cohesive society in traditional Bhutan were small and sustainable rural communities. As subsistence agricultural communities, they are more inter-dependent, more interactive and their lives more integrated. [...] An interactive environment fomented by the necessities of inter-dependence at all levels fostered the sense of community vitality and strong sense of belonging.'

Such interdependence and mutuality are probably found in any flourishing food world. The food system is so complex that it is impossible to keep it compartmentalised. Everything affects everything else. There are two possible consequences of this – conflict or cooperation – and it is obvious which is preferable. In the industrialised food system, there is conflict over land, natural resources, market share, intellectual property. But there is also cooperation, in the form of trade, subsidy, consumers supporting independent shops. Sometimes there can be both conflict and cooperation. Big supermarkets and other buyers can use their might to enhance the well-being of their suppliers or to drive hard bargains. Nations can open their doors to fair trade or dump their surpluses abroad and put up protectionist barriers.

The interdependence that characterises traditional farming is strikingly different from the vision of complete self-sufficiency that drives many in developed countries to start smallholdings. The 'traditional' form of life they seek is given a modern, individualistic twist. 'Self-sufficiency' is one of those values that sounds positive but needs to be questioned. This is not the only way in which smallholding is both romanticised and misrepresented. It is often claimed that these traditional farms, far from being obsolete, are still the bread baskets of the world, since they produce 80 per cent of the world's food. But although this figure has been attributed to the FAO, it's a zombie statistic: a false number that just won't die. Although 80 per cent of the world's food is produced by *family-owned* farms, many of these are very large indeed. Smallholder farmers actually produce under a third of the world's food, which is a lot, but far from the majority.[17]

*

The old Bhutanese way of life is now under threat. Even the kind of food being eaten is changing. The Food Corporation of Bhutan is a state-owned company created in 1974, mandated 'to maintain food reserves and provide food security to the nation at all times'. Its four retail stores and twenty-four warehouses increasingly stock 'fast moving consumer goods' (FMCG) such as cheese slices, instant noodles and dairy whitener. In 2022, for the first time, the value of its FMCG sales exceeded that of core grains and essential commodities, such as cooking oil.[18]

Rural populations are also declining. When Kinga reported that the official population of Gortshom was 118, only half of these actually lived in the village. Forty attended school, most in the village, but many a day or more's walk away. Ten women had married outside of the village and no longer lived there. Add a few soldiers, monks and civil servants working elsewhere and that leaves only forty-six people to work in the fields. As the population becomes more mobile, ties of kinship and community are becoming more diffuse, weakening the system of informal labour exchange. Barnaby Peacocke, who has had a long career in international development and knows Bhutan well, told me that many village populations now comprise children of primary school age and those aged thirty-five-plus, with very few in between. People increasingly depend on the remittance culture, in which family members working in cities or overseas send money home.

Given the hard work and poor financial returns of smallholder life, it is not surprising that many younger people aspire to find easier, better-paid work in towns and cities. Ulrike Čokl has seen this for herself. She did the fieldwork for her PhD in social and cultural anthropology in Bhutan and co-founded the Bhutan Network in Austria, which set up skills exchange programmes with Bhutanese and European farmers. 'Life in the villages is not really interesting for many young people,' she tells me. 'You can go to bed at seven because there's nothing happening in terms of entertainment.' Indeed, many parents and grandparents encourage the youth to seek a seemingly better life. 'They sometimes tease the grandchildren or children if they have a degree from some college and come back and want to be farmers. They tell them, "Why are you here? You should be now going to the town and get a job and earn money."'

One sign of this is that Gortshom village has four households with only one working person, all four of them women. Traditionally men were needed for heavy labour. But with the arrival of machines and power tools, women have taken on jobs such as tilling. 'The men go out for a month and work in the forests, the hydroelectric dams or in construction sites,' says Peacocke. The smallholders are interdependent not only with each other but with the wider economy.

Ai Tshomo, one of these women left to farm alone, says, 'Because there are no men in my family, people do not readily agree to work for me. [. . .] I am the only one working in the fields. People are afraid they won't get back their *lakpho*.' Since much farm work requires men, women like Ai Tshomo are effectively left outside the labour exchange system. Her fellow lone women farmers Dekimo and Dorjimo can only get labour by *pheu*, wages paid in kind, made possible by the butter and cheese from their dairy cows. Machinery can't fully compensate for a lack of able hands, especially since most of it has been built with male operatives in mind, which means it is too heavy for many of the women to use. Much of the land is too steep for machines anyway.

Despite these challenges for the traditional farming life, or perhaps partly driven by them, according to a recent UN report, 'Bhutan has made remarkable achievements in agriculture and livestock production over the years.' There has been a shift from subsistence to commercialised or entrepreneurial farming, assisted by investments in irrigation, roads, fencing and the development and promotion of high-yielding crop varieties. By 2023 the Bhutanese government was talking of its ambition to 'boost high-value agriculture and livestock commodities to make our farmers rich and contribute to economic development', saying that 'tech-enabled agricultural farming will be adopted as the way forward in enhancing performance as well as to encourage the young population into farming professions for long term food system sustainability.'[19]

The transformation began in the 1960s after Bhutan emerged from the self-imposed isolation it had maintained for most of its history. The continued 'modernisation' of Bhutanese agriculture and society presents several challenges, threats and opportunities. The push for greater productivity has resulted in some clear gains. There is more double-cropping, when vegetables are planted in a paddy field after the rice has been harvested. Low-yielding local breeds of dairy cattle have been replaced by high-yielding foreign ones such as the Jersey and the Brown Swiss. Although most farmers still plough the land with oxen, power tillers are becoming increasingly common, which can help increase output and compensate for some of the problems created by the loss of labour.

The intensification which comes with the push for greater productivity also has costs. While nomadic herding continues in the higher mountains, elsewhere domesticated farm animals are increasingly being stall-fed, which is generally worse for animal welfare. The Bhutanese are also abandoning the old 'shifting cultivation' model in which farmers cleared and burned patches of forest to plant cereal crops for a few years before moving on to another area, leaving the trees to regrow, and so on, in unending cycles. This practice is better known disparagingly as 'slash and burn agriculture' and many international environmental agencies oppose it, claiming it results in deforestation, habitat loss and soil erosion. But as the American anthropologist Harold C. Conklin argued back in 1957, there is a world of difference between traditional shifting cultivation that is well adapted to local conditions and the destructive, unsustainable forest-clearing of pioneers expanding agricultural land. Simplistically labelling it all as 'slash and burn' demonises practices that are more sustainable than some of the ones proposed to replace them. Call it 'shifting cultivation', which is more accurate, and it suddenly sounds much more benign.

This is not the only change of dubious merit being made in the name of conservation. The Bhutanese government also has a policy of not killing any wildlife, even though farmers around the world have always had to control animals that destroy crops or prey on livestock. Take wild pigs. They live in an ecosystem where 'there's no apex predator,' says Čokl. 'Or rather, they're called humans. I wake up at five in the morning and there is this happy wild pig family running around and ruining the potato field because nobody can do much about it. They used to have traps and sometimes shot them.'

The rules against killing wild boar are puzzling because historically dried pork is a traditional dish and pork rind is an indicator of status. But today many are importing their pork from India. This may surprise people who know Bhutan as a Buddhist and therefore supposedly vegetarian country. The Bhutanese government helps buttress the myth of a vegetarian, Buddhist nation. For example, there is no legal animal slaughter in Bhutan, although it is perfectly legal to eat meat butchered in India, which many do. Čokl believes animal slaughter goes on, but says 'you won't hear about it'.

Valuable traditional ways are also threatened by the largely welcome introduction of the latest science and technology. As we have seen elsewhere, much indigenous knowledge is based on experience and observation of repeated events by multiple people, both touchstones of the scientific method. Yet our paradigm of science is the white-coated laboratory investigator, away from the front line, with knowledge that is different from and superior to that of practitioners on the ground. Peacocke rejects this, saying, 'My experience from doing my doctorate is that you don't have to have the scientific method or the analytical, statistical tools to incorporate the complexities of a multi-variant system. One of the reasons why I left research is that reductionism cannot be the be all and end all for agriculture. It's a system. You're part of an economy. You're part of a society. You're part of an environment. There are so many dimensions in here. Real science is much more complicated than repeating an experiment for three years in a row so that it will be statistically valid.'

An example of a potentially happy marriage of technology and tradition can be seen in the evolution of the customs of informal sharing and cooperation that have always been a part of the Bhutanese farming system. Alongside new, more formal community institutions such as cooperatives and farmers' groups, networks are also forming on social media platforms such as WhatsApp. For example, Čokl says, 'Death is a very important event in Bhutan and if somebody dies, it incurs a lot of costs for the cremation, the rituals. They have ways of networking on social media groups to help each other out. It's an extension of traditional relationship fostering, only now it's easier.'

Čokl hopes that new technologies will help preserve the best characteristics of Bhutanese culture. 'I would be very unhappy if they totally abandoned a traditional way of relating to each other through the framework of hospitality, hosting each other, eating traditional food. If everything became a transaction I would be very sad.'

Traditional smallholder farming faces an uncertain future. Subsistence farming in its traditional form has more or less vanished already. In a world of opportunity, the returns from tilling the land alone cannot meet people's reasonable aspirations for a varied, comfortable life. Čokl says that 'there has been a tendency to look down on manual labour because there was so much focus on getting a higher education and an office job, bureaucracy and earning a regular income'. This prejudice is strongest when the gap between the toil and low pay of farm work and the comfort of white-collar work is at its widest, which it currently is in Bhutan. As Adrian von Bernstorff of Bhutan's Jigme Singye Wangchuck School of Law put it, 'Subsistence farming, which is an ultimately sustainable and independent way of life, does not offer conditions and opportunities that young people seek. Farming has to become economically viable as well as socially attractive so youth start to see a future in it.'[20] And to be attractive, it has to be seen as 'potentially lucrative and creative'.[21]

There are signs that this is beginning to happen and, paradoxically, urbanisation and globalisation are two of the major reasons. The growing number of more affluent urban dwellers creates a market for higher-value produce, and with that, opportunities for farmers. A promised move to 100 per cent organic farming also creates export opportunities. Bhutan's usage of agrochemical inputs is among the lowest in the world, with none used at all on more than 80 per cent of farmland.[22] Although traditional farming has always more or less conformed to organic standards, certification allows farmers to attract premium prices on international markets.

Peacocke sees the future of smallholder farming as involving a mixture of high-value animal products such as dairy and eggs, vegetables and plants for local markets and domestic consumption, and 'niche products which can go into the international market, ideally light so you can fly them out, or non-perishable so that you can take them down to India', with a greater focus on food processing that adds value. If smallholder farms in Bhutan are to thrive, as the government wants them to, they have to do what they do best, which is producing high-value specialist crops, like green tea and black cardamom.

There are some indications that these trends towards a more dynamic, entrepreneurial and future-orientated agricultural sector are making farming more attractive to younger people. One benefit of Čokl's exchange programme is that the young Bhutanese 'meet farmers in Austria from a diverse range of backgrounds who have university degrees and went back into the farming profession. It gives them a different perception of what farming or a manual profession can be and how it can be a meaningful career. It's about enhancing their identity as a farmer.'

Perhaps the greatest challenge facing Bhutan is whether its agriculture can advance without repeating the mistakes of countries that industrialised earlier. Steven Newman of BioDiversity International thinks it can. He rejects the idea that there is a universal linear progression from subsistence to commercial to industrialised farming. 'Things don't have to be like that for Bhutan,' he says, in large part because 'we're now in the world of the internet.' A World Food Programme Evaluation report found that 'Bhutan has achieved a high level of digital access' and that 'mobile broadband subscriptions in 2018 had reached over 87 per cent coverage compared to 62 per cent globally'.[23] Newman's idea is that younger people can stay in their villages and enjoy the friendships, meaning and respect offered by that kind of life. But the internet also allows them to be 'connected to the world and make use of the commercial potential'. Newman cites as a model the black mulberries he orders online that probably come from a remote area of Afghanistan.

For smallholder farmers to compete in the wider market, however, there has to be a level playing field with big business. Industrial agriculture usually benefits from subsidies and gets away with not having to pay for the pollution and environmental degradation it creates. 'I hope that the external costs of industrial agriculture are factored in one day,' says Peacocke. 'And when they are, the smallholder will be at a comparative advantage. We can feed the world based on smallholder producers.' But 'until policies and resources are better targeted towards smallholder farmers, there will continue to be bigger incentives for young people to go elsewhere as they become educated'.

Čokl believes that some of the country's limitations will turn out to be sources of strength. 'I'm hopeful because they don't have the capacity for as huge monocultures as places like India or other countries that have huge amounts of land. They will have to focus on multi-resource farming, which is the best option, including home-stay tourism. It works well because it's not like in Austria where you have masses of tourists. You have the occasional guest and it fits well into the traditional hospitality system, so they can get some niche income but at the same time they still grow their cash crops.'

In the right place, with the right natural, social and economic conditions, smallholder farming can be a viable, fulfilling and productive way of life. But most of the time it is extremely tough, and increasingly those who can escape it choose to do so. A country like Bhutan that depends heavily on smallholder farming is not only poor in cash terms but struggles with its health. 'Diets in Bhutan are characterised by low dietary diversity and high consumption of staple and processed foods,' says Peacocke. 'It costs more than four times as much to meet nutrient needs as energy needs.' The World Food Programme found that despite making significant progress in addressing child undernutrition, Bhutan is 'facing a triple burden with over a fifth of children under five stunted, a high prevalence of micronutrient deficiencies reflected in high rates of anemia and outbreaks of vitamin B deficiency, and a rapid increase in overweight [people] and obesity'. It reported that 'progress in addressing malnutrition has been uneven, with worse nutrition outcomes among households in rural areas and in lower wealth quintiles,' and that 'nearly 3 in 10 households (27 per cent) cannot afford to meet their nutrient needs.'[24]

If smallholding is to have a future, it has to be very different from its past. It will need supportive governments that are able at the very least to provide the education, infrastructure and health care that farmers themselves could never afford. There are good reasons for governments to do this. Good farmers are custodians of the land and tradition, and the value of the smallholding life cannot be measured in agricultural outputs alone.

As more and more farming becomes larger scale, we should not lose sight of the things that smallholding gets right. First and foremost, it is a way of farming that recognises the interdependence of everyone in the food world and of the natural environment it depends on. Industrial farming, in comparison, has too often become separated from the rest of society and neglectful of the long-term health of the land it cultivates.

When human beings first settled down to farm, they created an entirely new food world and transformed their relationship with the land. The price we paid was initially high, but eventually we got our reward. In the Anthropocene we have transformed agriculture so profoundly that we risk paying a second, even higher price. The transition from subsistence to commercial agriculture is, however, still under way. We have time to learn from our early mistakes and make sure that when countries like Bhutan modernise, they do not lose all that is good for their food culture and replace it with all that is worst in the alternative. How we reshape the food world for the second time is still in our hands.

4

THE INTENSIVE TURN

Tomatoes and potatoes in the Netherlands

If you didn't know which country has been the world's second largest exporter of agricultural goods in recent decades, you'd be unlikely to guess it was the Netherlands. With a total land mass of 13,019 square miles (33,720 km²), it is smaller than Switzerland, the Indian state of Punjab, or West Virginia in the USA. Yet, measured by value, it still exports more food than Brazil, which is 205 times bigger; China, 231 times its size; and even Russia, which could accommodate 412 Netherlands-sized parcels of land. Its population is a mere seventeen million people, just 0.22 per cent of the global total. Over nine in ten of them live in urban areas and only 2 per cent work in agriculture. It is one of the top 15 per cent most densely populated countries in the world, and more than a quarter of it is below sea level. On paper, it looks like one of the worst places in Europe for farming, yet it exports more agricultural products than any country in the world except the USA. It is also responsible for a third of all global trade in vegetable seeds.

Despite its cool northern climate, the Netherlands is the world's leading exporter not only of potatoes and onions, but also of sun-loving tomatoes. The country squeezes out over 505,000 kg of tomatoes per hectare, 30,000 more than the second-best performer, neighbouring Belgium. In contrast, traditional tomato-growing nations such as Spain and Italy have much lower yields of only 88,000 and 57,000 kg per hectare respectively.[1]

The seeds of this apparent success story were germinated in one of the darkest periods of Dutch history. In the last year of the Second World War, with the Allied liberators closing in, the Dutch began a railway strike that hindered the German occupiers. In retaliation, the Germans erected a blockade. What followed became known as the Dutch Hunger Winter.

At the start of the blockade in 1944, in the big cities, the average adult was consuming only 1,000 calories of food a day, around half the needs of an average female and 40 per cent of an adult male's. By winter's end in February 1945, that figure had dropped to 580. Around 20,000 people died due to the famine, exacerbated by the exceptionally cold winter.

Despite its short duration, the famine had lasting health effects, even on future generations. The children and grandchildren of women who had been malnourished in the famine were more likely to suffer from certain negative health outcomes, such as obesity and mental health problems. This knock-on effect helped change our understanding of genetics. Evolutionary theory holds that our life experiences do not alter our genes. But we now know that how these genes are *expressed* can be affected by what happens to us in life. The legacy of the Dutch Hunger Winter is a stark example of the power of these epigenetic effects.

The famine also had a lasting social legacy. Across Europe, governments vowed that they would never endure hunger again. Given their bitter experience, the Dutch understandably took up this challenge more urgently than most. They were helped by their history and collective mythology. In countries like France, agriculture was associated with ancient traditions and bucolic landscapes. The role of technology and innovation was downplayed, while romantic ideas like *terroir* – the unique qualities of every local ecosystem – focused on the almost mystical link between people and soil. In the Netherlands, by contrast, the public imagination is shaped by the *polder* – land reclaimed from the sea by dykes on which cattle graze and crops are grown. The national psyche was steeped in the values of human ingenuity and innovation. It was accustomed to having to make the most of little. So it was ripe to embrace new farming methods. This would be the continuation of a noble tradition, not the destruction of one.

The food agenda was taken up enthusiastically by the post-war Minister of Agriculture, Sicco Mansholt. A former farmer and a resistance fighter in the war, his first responsibilities were born of desperation. In a radio address to the nation, he called upon everyone able to work 'to roll up his sleeves, so that we may succeed in saving the harvest which, now more than ever, we so sorely need'. Knowing that this wouldn't be enough, Mansholt also had to secure the importation of food to keep his people alive.

To improve efficiency, he encouraged land consolidation, where larger, more productive farms gobbled up smaller, less profitable ones. The country went from having over 400,000 farms in 1950 to fewer than 55,000 today.[2] Guaranteed rates for produce were introduced, not to prop up small unprofitable farms but to support the development of larger ones. At the same time, there was a strong desire to protect the landscape. Every plan for changes in land use had to be approved by the *Staatsbosbeheer*, the government organisation responsible for forestry and the management of nature reserves.

Between 1950 and 2015 the value of agricultural production in the Netherlands increased more than tenfold.[3] Albert Hoekerswever, who works on improving collaboration in the supply chain, told me, 'We created a system that grew very fast. We produced too much for ourselves. It's like a train, it's very difficult to stop.' The solution to this novel problem of oversupply was ready to hand. The country was also a great trading nation, with Europe's busiest container port in Rotterdam. So it was natural that the Dutch would also begin to excel at exporting their abundant harvests. This combination of trade and modernised food production led the Netherlands to become a food superpower.

Indeed, the major role the Netherlands plays in global trade makes its status as the world's second largest exporter of food misleading. Although this is true, a lot of that food was previously imported rather than produced in the Netherlands. Still, the country massively outperforms in terms of food production for land area, and ranks a lofty seventh in the world as a producer of food for export, ahead of much larger countries like Canada, Russia and Australia.[4]

The Netherlands achieved these efficiencies by becoming the most zealous and thorough implementer of the global 'green revolution', the collective name given to a series of innovations that revolutionised agriculture in the twentieth century, vastly improving yields. The first transformational development was the industrial manufacture of synthetic fertilisers. In the nineteenth century, it was already known that nitrates were important for soil fertility, but although nitrogen is an abundant element, it cannot be applied in its pure form. Before synthetic fertilisers, the main source of agricultural nitrates mined was potassium nitrate, or nitre (KNO_3), and guano, bird excrement that was also rich in two other soil nutrients, phosphate and potassium. Guano was such an important and valuable product that it generated something of a gold rush, with traders seeking out the richest sources. These were mainly found in the tropical areas of Latin America, especially Peru. As an incentive to its exploitation, the US government passed the Guano Islands Act in 1856, which made it lawful to claim any unoccupied island, rock or key laden with guano for the

USA. However, by the late nineteenth century, the trade in guano had been so intense that many sources had been all but depleted.

The search for new fertilisers became urgent. In the first decade of the twentieth century, the German chemists Fritz Haber and Carl Bosch made a breakthrough. They developed a process in which ammonia (NH_3) could be created from atmospheric nitrogen and hydrogen using a metal catalyst under high pressure and temperatures. The Haber–Bosch process, as it became known, was energy-intensive and not initially very efficient. But as the century progressed, so did humanity's capacity to harness the process. The impact of this on food production can hardly be overstated. By the turn of the twenty-first century, it is estimated that food grown with the help of fertilisers made by the Haber–Bosch process fed between 40 and 50 per cent of the world's population.[5]

However, it wasn't until the middle of the twentieth century that the global agricultural output began to rise steeply. For fertilisers to become widely used, they needed to be affordable for farmers, and that took a combination of lowering production costs and introducing government subsidies. But there was also another major contributor to improved yields: plant breeding. This was transformed by the agricultural scientist Norman Borlaug, who came from an Iowan farming family. The pivotal moment in his career, and arguably in the history of humankind, came when he went to work in Mexico for the Cooperative Wheat Research and Production Program, a collaboration between the Mexican government and the Rockefeller Foundation. The program sought to use technology to improve Mexican farming.

Over the next two decades Borlaug helped to develop wheat varieties that were higher yielding and more disease resistant. The techniques used were far simpler than the genetic technologies of today. The basic method was F1 hybrid breeding, which is simply cross-pollinating two different strains of a seed to produce a third. (F1 stands for Filial 1, or first children.)

One key feature of these varieties was that they had shorter stems. Traditional wheat stands very tall, but that makes it more vulnerable to weather damage and requires it to put more energy into vertical growth, with less to spare for the grains. The shift to shorter stems has continued ever since. The reason wheat fields are not as tall as many of us remember from our childhoods is not just that we have grown taller: they really have shrunk. Up to half the productivity gains of the twentieth century have been attributed to shorter stems.[6]

The impact in Mexico was immediate. Borlaug's new Mexican wheat variety was released in 1962, and a year later 95 per cent of Mexico's wheat production came from one of his seeds. The country went from importing over 200,000 tons of wheat a year in the 1940s to exporting 63,000 tons in 1963. Along with synthetic fertilisers and hybrid crop breeds, the green revolution also saw an increase in the use of pesticides. This triad of innovations spread out across the world, increasing global crop yields on average by a factor of more than two and a half. Production increased without a commensurate increase in land use. In Asia, cereal production doubled between 1970 and 1995 while requiring only 4 per cent more land. Globally, grain output in the second half of the twentieth century only took up 10 per cent more land.[7]

The Dutch embraced these methods with gusto. But like the rest of the world, they pushed them too hard, and their advances in production are now taking their toll on the environment. In later life, Mansholt himself saw some of the problems his boom had unleashed. In a letter to the president of the European Commission, Franco Malfatti, in 1972, he lamented the 'disruption of the ecological balance as a result in particular of the use of pesticides and insecticides which are required for mass production'. Some of his remarks seem very prescient today. He advocated 'a nonpolluting production system and the creation of a recycling economy' in order to 'prevent the destruction of precious natural materials'.

He also said that 'hitherto, research has in practice been centred on growth' and suggested that we should 'replace the GNP [gross national product] by gross national utility' or even 'gross national happiness'.[8]

The Dutch farming system may already have exceeded the limits of sustainability. 'More and more we realise that we've become too intensive and too much focused on cost minimisation without accounting for the environmental costs,' says Martin van Ittersum, a professor at the Plant Production Systems group at Wageningen University. Hoekerswever made a similar point more colourfully: 'About 80 per cent of our production is for export and the shit stays here.'

Take the problem of nitrogen leaching. Nitrogen is the most important component of chemical fertilisers, ahead of phosphorus and potassium. However, it is extremely volatile and easily drained away by water, especially after heavy rain. If too much gets into the groundwater and runs into the water supply, it can be toxic to young children and many animals. So there is a limit to how intensively you can farm outdoors because it is impossible to keep leaching under close control.

It is widely accepted that there is too much agricultural pollution in the Netherlands. At the start of the 2020s, its emissions of ammonia, nitrogen and phosphorus as well as its use of pesticides per hectare were among the highest in the European Union.[9] A major part of the problem is livestock production, which is staggeringly high and increasingly intensive. It is the world's second largest importer of soybean animal feeds after China, and one third of its cows never graze on open pasture, with the proportion set to rise to half.[10]

Just as the Netherlands once symbolised the gains of the green revolution, now it represents its costs. Around the world, the limits of intensive farming have been breached. But healing the wounds is not easy. In 2019 a proposal was made in the Dutch parliament to halve the nation's livestock to tackle agricultural pollution. Farmers took to the streets in protest, leading to the formation of a political party, the Farmer–Citizen Movement (BBB, *BoerBurgerBeweging*), to act as a voice for these grievances. Undeterred, in 2022 the Dutch government committed to halving nitrous oxide and ammonia emissions by 2030. Farmers and their supporters took to the streets again, complaining that jobs and businesses would be lost, especially in the livestock sector, which would have to see a 30 to 50 per cent reduction to meet the targets. In the 2023 senate elections, the BBB won more than 20 per cent of the vote and became the largest party in the Dutch parliament's upper house. The Dutch experience shows how hard it will be for governments to curb the excesses of intensive agriculture, because it requires stopping a lot of people from doing what earns them a living.

However, we have to be careful not to throw the baby out with the bathwater. Today, we have a romantic idea that 'sustainable' means minimal human intervention. As Ernst van den Ende, then managing director of Wageningen University & Research's Plant Sciences Group, told *National Geographic*, this is a misconception. He points to Bali, where for thousands of years farmers have farmed ducks and fish in the flooded rice paddies, all irrigated by canals running along human-made mountain terraces. 'There's your model of sustainability,' said van den Ende.[11]

Not everything about industrial agriculture is irredeemably bad. Although synthetic fertilisers have been massively overused, there is no good reason to get rid of them altogether. One often-repeated prophecy of doom is that we cannot depend on synthetic farming inputs because Earth's resources are finite and they will run out. The finitude of resources is, however, sometimes merely theoretical. We only have finite carbon dioxide in the atmosphere, but in practice that supply is endless for the needs of photosynthesis. We similarly have plentiful supplies of nitrogen in the atmosphere. Apart from excessive use, which can be curbed, the main problem with synthetic nitrogen fertilisers is that they are energy intensive to produce. But by using solar or wind power, the supply could be unlimited.

This is just as well, since as Ken Giller, the professor of Plant Production Systems we heard from earlier, says, 'Most calculations are that we could only produce about 40 per cent of the food we need without using nitrogen fertilisers.' Crops that fix nitrogen, like legumes and clover, are useful contributors to soil fertility, but not all the nutrients the world's crops require can be produced by rotations that use them. Nor can we afford to do away with insecticides and herbicides. In many parts of the world, the problem is their underuse, not their overuse. The FAO estimates that every year up to 40 per cent of global crop production is lost to pests, by which it means 'any species, strain or biotype of plant, animal or pathogenic agent injurious to plants or plant products'. These losses add up to nearly $300 billion. Global warming is set to increase these losses even further.[12] At the start of the twentieth century, a farm labourer would spend up to a third of their time removing weeds, and even today in many countries farmers spend 25–120 days a year hand-weeding, only to still lose a quarter of the potential harvest due to competition from weeds.[13]

Just as synthetic inputs have become demonised, so too the term 'intensification' is associated with all that is wrong with farming today: thousands of cattle rammed into indoor feedlots, barely seeing the light of day; acres of commodity crops with no other vegetation to support wildlife; overuse of pesticides and chemical fertilisers. Yet in recent years, the Netherlands has been a hub of innovation for a model of agriculture known as 'sustainable intensification'. Superficially, this might seem to be an oxymoron. But all that 'intensification' means is getting more food from fewer resources, mainly inputs and land. Human beings have been trying to do this ever since they started farming. They selected the crops that produced the highest yield and bred livestock that grew fatter more quickly. They irrigated, fertilised, pruned and thinned to increase production.

Intensification only becomes unsustainable when it goes beyond the limits of what the land can tolerate. The Dust Bowl of the American and Canadian prairies during the 1930s testifies to how badly things can go wrong when you try to extract too much too quickly and too harshly. Heavy ploughing, resulting in the removal of native deep-rooted grasses, meant that when drought hit, the newly friable topsoil dried up and literally blew away. Around 3.5 million people left the affected areas after their livelihoods were destroyed. Today, intensification is also unsustainable when it relies too much on external inputs such as feed, fertilisers, herbicides and insecticides, which are depleting resources elsewhere.

Sustainable intensification, in contrast, seeks genuine efficiency, improving the input-output ratio year after year. It aims to decrease the use of pesticides, insecticides, fertilisers, energy and water, as well as the levels of unwanted outputs such as greenhouse gases, waste, nitrogen and ammonia. One major area of technology that helps with this is precision agriculture, in which, instead of blanket spraying fields of crops, each plant receives the optimal amount of nutrients or pesticide, no more and no less, resulting in fewer inputs overall. Irrigation can also be made precise, so instead of watering whole fields, you only give water where it is needed. This not only reduces inputs, it makes sure that crops do not suffer from being over- or under-watered.

Put simply, sustainable intensification is about getting more out of less. The Royal Society, the world's oldest scientific academy, defines it as 'global agriculture in which yields are increased without adverse environmental impact and without the cultivation of more land'.[14] That is why the EAT–Lancet Commission, which set thirty-seven world-leading scientists the question 'Can we feed a future population of 10 billion people a healthy diet within planetary boundaries?', concluded that one of the five strategies for a much-needed Great Food Transformation was to 'sustainably intensify food production, generating high-quality output'.

An example of sustainable intensification in action is found at Lodge Farm in North Suffolk, England, run by cousins Patrick and Brian Barker. The 500-hectacre farm featured on the BBC's landmark documentary series *Wild Isles*.[15] In an episode focusing on the environment, Patrick proudly described Lodge Farm as 'a proper intensive arable farm'. At the same time, he said, 'the natural environment is at the forefront of everything we think about' and 'our environmental impact is assessed on every operation we do'. So they know that thanks to actions like nurturing and planting hedgerows, sowing wild flower meadows and digging ponds, 400 species of wild animals from insects to mammals live on the farm, including, for the first time in decades, barn owls. They minimise ploughing and insecticides and have seen their soil structure improve.

The farm practises Integrated Farm Management (IFM), described as 'a site-specific farm business approach that uses the best of modern technology and traditional methods'.[16] It has nine areas of focus, including soil management and fertility, crop health and protection, animal husbandry, energy efficiency, water management, and landscape and nature conservation. That's really just a list of what all good farmers should be thinking about, not a radical blueprint for farming. But that's the point. As long as you're running a farm properly and getting results like those of the Barker cousins, you can use whatever tools you have in your kit.

IFM is promoted in the UK by the charity LEAF (Linking Environment And Farming), and Lodge Farm has become one of its demonstration sites, where others can come to learn good practice. 'I believe that we can have a farm that is productive, that grows food or grows crops for industry, and at the same time we can have a farm that's full of wildlife,' Patrick said. 'So I don't accept anyone saying to me it's one or the other.'

One form of intensification that promises increased productivity with none of the harmful side effects is indoor farming. This allows a degree of control that is impossible in the open air. Pests can be kept out, which reduces the need for insecticides. Temperatures can be controlled, which prevents crops being ruined by frosts or excess heat. Water can be tightly controlled, recaptured and reused, avoiding waste and ending reliance on the vagaries of the weather. Nothing leaches into the soil because there is no soil, or at least none that is directly in contact with the ground. Phosphorus can be recaptured and reused.

Indoor farming also allows for specialisation without the usual drawbacks of monocultures in which the same crop, and only that crop, is grown on the same fields every year. This creates all sorts of problems, from nutrient depletion to the build-up of pests and diseases. That is why crop rotation has been basic good agricultural practice for centuries. Indoors, however, fresh growth mediums can be brought in every year and the facility can be sanitised, so you can grow only tomatoes, or only lettuce, or only any other crop, again and again.

Sustainable intensification can not only avoid or get around many of the problems and limitations of industrial agriculture, it can also seek to replicate many of the virtues of the old ways. Take the circularity of traditional mixed farms. Livestock would eat waste and parts of the crops not suitable for human consumption, like straw, and then provide not only meat, but also manure to fertilise the land. Specialisation in industrial agriculture makes this kind of farm-level circularity impossible. But why not reintroduce it at a higher level? The manure from a large dairy farm can be trucked to a nearby arable farm, from which it could collect the straw and other feeds in return. The same principles that made single mixed farms efficient can be applied to make a number of specialised farms more efficient. Circularity does not require that the circumference runs along single-farm boundaries.

'You cannot get circular on your own,' says Hoekerswever. 'You have to collaborate with your chain partners.' The weak link in this chain is in another sense also the strongest – namely, the big retailers. As in most industrialised countries, a handful of big retailers dominate the food supply in the Netherlands and, according to Hoekerswever, 'they are not circular in any way. They are selling their products in a linear system.' He is optimistic this can change but thinks it will take at least ten years.

However, it is not obvious how this change will come about. Hopes of a consumer-led transformation of the food world are naive. Even when shoppers say that they are prepared to pay more for suitable produce, in practice they are usually unwilling to do so. Noud Janssen, an animal scientist and former poultry farmer, told me of a Dutch colleague who talked about the people who would come to his city farm. 'They come at weekends, when they have time to think about food, to make it themselves and to enjoy it. But for five days a week they go to the supermarket and buy the cheapest option. They just want to eat.'

Sustainable intensification does not look pretty. Acres of polytunnels, greenhouses and livestock sheds lack rustic charm. It also comes at a cultural loss. There was a human scale to the family farm, with a farmhouse, home to several generations of the same family. Even Sicco Mansholt, who enthusiastically ushered in the modernising revolution, regretted at the end of his life that small farms had all but disappeared from the Netherlands.[17] But most gains involve trade-offs. No one denies that there are losses with sustainable intensification. The question is whether, on balance, the gains are worth it.

Ken Giller makes a persuasive case that they are, saying, 'Turn it around and ask, what is the alternative? Extensification?' That doesn't sound very appealing either. He continues, 'Deep at heart I love nature. I'm a botanist. I spend all my free time looking at wildflowers and walking in nature. I want to see how we can preserve the best of that while meeting the need to feed people throughout the world with nutritious food. I think to do that we need intensive agriculture desperately in order to spare land for nature.'

Giller is referring to a big debate which pits the merits of 'land sparing' against those of 'land sharing'. Land sparing is about farming as little land as possible as intensively as possible, in order to preserve wilderness for biodiversity. Critics reject the premise of this trade-off, arguing that we should instead pursue land sharing: making agricultural land more biodiverse and hospitable to wildlife. Land sharing has become the favoured strategy of proponents of most forms of so-called nature-friendly farming. They point to many farms which are able to be both productive and biodiverse.

However, the very framing of the debate needs to be questioned. It suggests a neat binary, when in reality there is more of a spectrum than an either/or. No farm need be a biodiversity desert, and not all farmed land can be as biodiverse as wilderness. Which approach is best depends on the specifics of crop, location, weather and land. Giller worries that if we tried to follow the land-sharing model everywhere, we would end up 'trying to combine everything in one place where we end up often getting the worst of both worlds: poor yields and poor nature'.

Giller's thinking is more in line with that of Henry Dimbleby, who led an independent review for the UK government's National Food Strategy. His final report rejected the idea that land sharing and land sparing should been seen as 'conflicting schools of thought', arguing that 'the greatest benefits come from using both together'. The evidence suggested that 'creating a mosaic of different landscapes – wild land, low intensity farmland and higher intensity farming – had the broadest beneficial effect for the most species.'

This is not the only way in which the future of our food world requires taking a variety of approaches. There are many alternatives to industrialised agriculture which can and should be part of this diversity, but claims that they provide templates that all farms can follow don't stack up. Take organic agriculture, which represents the largest and best-known alternative both to the dominant modes of intensive industrial farming and sustainable intensification.

In its Green New Deal, the European Union (EU) has set a target of at least 25 per cent of agricultural land to come under organic farming by 2030. 'That's never going to happen in our country,' says Janssen. 'We don't have the land.' Although most organic farms are highly sustainable, they are less productive. Van Ittersum sums up the current scientific consensus when he says that multiple studies have found that on average, organic systems produce 75–80 per cent of the food of non-organic ones. You can find exceptions, but they don't disprove the rule. That's why Giller says that the EU target would be 'a disaster for the world because we'll reduce production in Europe. That means if we don't reduce our consumption as well, then our own environmental footprint globally will be extended elsewhere to meet our demands.'

The organic movement also often objects that yield comparisons are not fair. Organic farms are more circular, using manure fertilisers, green manures and so on. Non-organic systems rely on external inputs, and those hidden costs are not counted. As van Ittersum explains, 'you need to include in the equation the energy that is needed for the conventional system to produce mineral fertilisers, and if that's fossil energy, it leads to emissions etc. That is part of the energy and emission footprint of the conventional system, which may be lower in the organic system.'

However, van Ittersum believes the studies looking at overall efficiency are robust and that, if anything, the 75–80 per cent figure is an overestimate, because organic farming also relies on land use that is missed out of the calculations. For example, 'an organic wheat crop is fertilised with livestock manure, clover or whatever other legume crop, and that requires land. So if you look at the systems level, beyond that single field, the yield of the organic system will probably be closer to 50 or 60 per cent, than 80 per cent of that of the conventional.'

It seems beyond reasonable doubt that to feed the world entirely organically would require more land to be given over to agriculture. The evidence on yields has become so overwhelming that many organic organisations no longer challenge the data, arguing instead that yields aren't everything. 'It's no secret that yields are often lower in organic systems compared to conventional,' admitted the Soil Association's Sarah Compson on an official blog. However, focusing on yields 'fails to take into account the hidden costs that are often inherent in conventional farming systems', including 'the biodiversity losses and pollution from pesticides'.[18]

Organic farms are also not always as self-sustaining as might be imagined. There is a big trade in concentrated organic animal feed, which means that organic cows in the Netherlands could be fed with food produced in South America, a supply chain that is hardly a model of sustainability. Indeed, one artisan British cheese producer gave up its organic certification because the only source of supplementary organic feed it could find was from far overseas. They decided to use local, non-organic feed instead. Other external inputs may not even be organic. A 2012 USDA guide for organic crop producers, for example, stated: 'Manures from non-organic systems are allowed in organic production, including manure from livestock grown in confinement and from those that have been fed genetically engineered feeds.'

The only major attempt to convert a whole country's food system to organic was a complete disaster. In 2019, Gotabaya Rajapaksa made an election campaign pledge to make all farming in Sri Lanka organic in ten years. When he won the presidency, he swiftly imposed a nationwide ban on the import and use of synthetic fertilisers and pesticides. Domestic production of rice, a staple crop, fell by 30 per cent. Having been self-sufficient in the crop, Sri Lanka now had to import $450 million worth, with retail prices skyrocketing by 50 per cent. At the same time, the drop in the production of tea, a major export, cost the economy $425 million.[19] Within seven months, the government was forced to reverse most of its changes. While it is possible that the problems were caused by the speed and manner of the transition rather than by deficiencies with organic farming itself, the episode should at the very least make those demanding a wholesale switch to organics think again.

For the moment, organic food is the preserve of two very different demographics: the wealthy of the industrialised world, able to pay the premium prices organics command, and the very poorest, who farm without chemical inputs only because they can't afford them. But there is still an important place for organics. What makes for the best farming system is very context specific. Van Ittersum's view is that 'there can be many locations, maybe close to nature or in fragile areas, where you have to be careful with emissions and so on, where organic is a very good solution. So it's not either/or.'

There are other alternative models to mainstream industrial farming that are less prescriptive than organics. One of the biggest noises in farming at the moment is regenerative agriculture, often referred to simply as 'regen'.[20] Its basic idea is to farm in ways that restore the land rather than deplete it, putting as many nutrients back as are taken out, without the use of external inputs, or at least using as few as possible.

One problem with regen is that there is no agreed definition of what it is. Like sustainable intensification, it places great emphasis on soil health and preserving biodiversity. The main difference Giller sees is that sustainable intensification talks of 'producing the food we need while doing no harm' whereas regen talks of 'producing the food we need but doing good at the same time'.

Giller sees this as 'the same idea with more of a positive spin' since although good farming can restore soil health on land that has been depleted, nothing is going to keep improving soil indefinitely.

Although sustainable intensification and regen have similar ends, advocates of each tend to promote different means. Broadly speaking, sustainable intensification is pursued by all means available, whereas proponents of regen tend to promote traditional methods, such as integrating livestock and arable farming, minimising soil disturbance and avoiding synthetic inputs. However, there are also many who argue that the test of whether a method of farming is regenerative or not is entirely in the results. If a farm can show that it has improved soil quality without external inputs, it is regenerative, whatever specific methods it uses.

Regenerative agriculture in its wider sense is just good farming practice, and there is no reason to think that all farms should follow its most purist version. Some never could, no matter how sustainable they are, because 'regenerative' is defined in terms of soil health. So any agricultural practice that bypasses soil altogether – like hydroponics, which grows plants using water-based nutrient solutions – is by definition not regenerative.

Yet another model is conservation agriculture, which the FAO defines as having three principles: minimum soil disturbance, maintenance of a permanent soil cover, and diversification of plant species.[21] The first of these is often described as 'no-till', an idea that grew in popularity after the disaster of the Dust Bowl. No-till farming is a relation of the no-dig method favoured by a lot of gardeners. The idea is that rather than disturbing the soil, which accelerates the loss of nutrients, you just add manures and composts to it each year.

No-till may sound like it avoids the excesses of industrial agriculture, but on farms it often works by depending very heavily on technology. Huge mechanical planters add fertiliser and seeds at precisely the required points and depths. 'With one individual machine you can plant up to five hundred hectares a day,' says Giller. 'It's quite phenomenal.' Even more surprising is that the crops being sown are often pesticide resistant, allowing the fields to be blanket sprayed. So with the machine making one pass for sowing, one for applying pesticide and one for harvesting, the farmer makes efficient use of both time and diesel.

The method is very popular all over the Americas and has some surprising supporters. Giller remembers being at a conference and hearing a farmer from Argentina confessing that when he was young he did terrible things – meaning ploughing – before converting to conservation agriculture. 'He showed a picture of himself receiving a prize from Prince Charles, an ardent organic farmer who would completely abhor the idea of this huge commercial type of agriculture. But because the word "conservation" is used it appeals to everybody from all corners.'

In agriculture, as in the rest of the food world, there are too many partisan camps offering one-size-fits-all solutions. But the debate over which method of farming is best is a red herring. There are some things that are almost always wrong in agriculture, like polluting, treating animals badly, degrading soils. But when it comes to more specific practices, what is best depends on the situation. No-till may be a great method in most cases, but sometimes you need to plough. Avoiding all pesticides can work on some farms, but there are times when it is perverse to lose a crop when you could save it with a judicious spray. There are some farms that can get by without animal manures or synthetic fertilisers, but others will need one or both.

Different conditions may push us towards different solutions. For example, in some areas farming ninety acres more intensively and having ten acres reserved for wildlife could create a more biodiverse hundred acres than if the entire area were farmed regeneratively. Similarly, growing tomatoes in greenhouses may make no sense in Scotland, but in Iceland, where there is abundant geothermal energy, it can be very efficient. Indeed, in the Netherlands, a farm entirely housed in greenhouses was named the world's most innovative tomato producer by an international jury of horticultural experts. The Duijvestijns' family farm is powered by renewable energy, with only rainwater for irrigation, and the entire operation is carbon neutral. It uses only biological controls for pests and produces most of its own fertiliser. It is close to its ambition of being fully circular. It meets all the key desiderata of organic and regenerative agriculture, but it does not match either description.[22]

Henry Dimbleby is a rare example of someone who fully embraces pluralism in the food system. He told me, 'What you're seeing is regenerative agriculture at one end, which at the extreme is agroecological or organic, and then at the other end there's sustainable intensification, with lots of stuff in the middle. We're solving it from both ends and that's the right way to do it.'

Perhaps the most important feature of the Dutch model is its spirit of collaboration and innovation. Hoekerswever believes that one reason the Netherlands is ahead of other countries is that 'in Holland we have a very small tiny country so all the people live and work close together. So it's very easy to connect people and innovations.' Hoekerswever's vision of 'glocal' agriculture is one in which the kind of sharing and collaboration that is traditionally found in local food systems extends globally. This encourages not uniformity of approach but diversity, as people respond to varying local needs and conditions. 'Let's learn from each other,' says Hoekerswever. 'I think the main challenge is that we are open for new ways of thinking and sharing knowledge about several systems.'

TAKING STOCK

Towards a Global Food Philosophy

Throughout history and across the globe, we have seen that people have found incredibly diverse ways to feed themselves from the land. Not only has there been a gradual change from foraging to subsistence farming to industrial agriculture, each of these general approaches has also contained multitudes. The methods and diets of hunter-gatherers are very different in the polar regions from how they are on the Serengeti. The crops and techniques of smallholding in Central America are not the same as those in Bhutan.

This diversity might appear to undermine the very possibility of a single global food philosophy. In fact, it tells us that plurality must itself be a universal principle. This is no paradox. Think of how diversity is a general dietary rule. Variety of foodstuffs is one strength of the foraging life and also the Achilles heal of agriculturalists. Despite depending heavily on animal protein, the Inuit get diversity in their diet not only by eating small quantities of various plants but also by consuming every part of the animal. Seasonal eating also increases dietary diversity wherever it is practised. The fact that there are many ways to eat a diverse diet fits the general principle that diversity in diet is good. Similarly, the fact that there are many ways to farm, hunt, prepare and eat food fits with the general principle that diversity in the food world is good.

However, to embrace variety does not mean embracing everything, believing that anything goes, or that there is nothing more to say other than that we need plurality. A varied diet that includes too few plants and too much processed food is not a good one simply because it is diverse. Humans have subsisted on an incredible range of diets, but their differences mask some key commonalities. Most notably, healthy diets are based on whole foods. The ability of human beings to stay healthy as long as they eat whole grains, seeds, plants, milk and all the different parts of animals is extraordinary. One key reason why the nutritional transition of traditional societies towards industrialised diets invariably leads to worse health seems to be that they start to eat more refined and processed foods.

Similarly, a food world that includes too many polluting, environmentally destructive and resource-depleting farms is not a good one simply because people are messing up in many different ways. Plurality is an important value, but it is not the only one, and it is not difficult to discern several other key characteristics that all successful food systems share.

One is sustainability. This is a concept that has become debased by overuse and misuse. Everyone is in favour of it and everyone claims their methods of production support it. It is not a meaningless concept, but it refers to an outcome rather than an underlying principle: a system is sustainable if it satisfies our present needs without compromising the needs of the future. We have seen how sustainability has always been achieved through some form of circularity. Food production and consumption have to be in a closed loop in which inputs are renewable and as much waste as possible goes back into the system, usually as feed, fuel or fertiliser.

Foragers take only as much as the land can spare and give nature time to renew itself. Good farmers work with crop rotations to allow soil to recover from heavy use and also use animal or green manures to enrich the earth. Industrial farming has too often ignored this need for circularity, but at its best it too can achieve it.

Circularity has been a perennial demand of food systems, but today we have the unprecedented option of not having to close the loop completely, since some inputs, such as synthetic nitrogen fertilisers, could be produced indefinitely using renewable energy. However, we should be wary of being led into complacency by such exceptions that prove the rule. Circularity must be the default, and any deviations from it must be taken with care.

The principle of circularity sits alongside a more general need to consider each aspect of the food system as it relates to everything else, not just in isolation. Because food systems are so complicated and involve an extended food world, we have to think about them holistically, taking into account the many networks of cause and effect. One manifestation of this we have seen is the mutual dependence of actors in the food world. Foragers own nothing and depend on each other to find and share food. In traditional Maasai and Inuit societies, individualists just couldn't survive. Smallholder farmers own or rent their own land but need to help each other out in order to cope with busy times and to compensate for the fact that not everyone has all the skills and equipment they need.

In a consumer society, the plethora of choice gives us a sense of almost unbounded autonomy. But in reality our interdependence has never been greater. We depend upon global producers and manufacturers, refrigerated supply chains, distributors and retailers. Wars, political upheaval and natural disasters can play havoc with all of these. This new scale of interdependence means that if the food system needs fixing, it cannot be done by individuals choosing to shop differently, or even by businesses opting for better practice. In a globalised food world, only national and transnational actions have the power to make a big enough difference.

Overall, we have found much to admire and emulate in traditional societies. But there can be no going back. Foraging is neither a practical nor a desirable choice for the vast majority of us living today. Smallholder farming is toil and cannot provide most of us with the yields or the standards of living that we reasonably expect. While some in the remaining traditional societies around the world have a right to have their ways of life protected, more will continue to abandon them than go back to them. And with the global population set to exceed nine billion sometime this century, we have no choice but to pursue much greater efficiencies than we have had for the vast majority of our history. Technology cannot save us by itself, but we will have to use it as well as we can, just as our forebears have always innovated. Science is our friend, but we should also draw on traditional knowledge, which embodies know-how gleaned from long experience. When humanity appears to be hurtling towards a cliff edge, it is natural to want to stop or even turn back the clock. But human resourcefulness – demonstrated by our adaptability and ingenuity – has been manifest in how the world eats throughout our entire history and should continue to play a part as we adapt to our changing ecological conditions.

Our survey so far suggests that resourcefulness should be a key principle of a global food philosophy, along with plurality, circularity and holism. This philosophy needs to be able to guide us to new solutions as well as to help us preserve the best of the old ones. Our food history shows that we have never stopped learning and that even the oldest traditions evolve and change. We learn best from experience when we use our knowledge to take us forward into the future, not back into the past.

PART TWO

People

5

FROM FOOD TO COMMODITY

Chocolate and more chocolate in Belgium

The anticipated and actual pleasures of food and drink do not always match. A delicious-looking cake emitting a freshly baked smell can be a bland, sweet, dry disappointment in the mouth. An unfamiliar plate of cuttlefish in black ink may arouse wariness and suspicion, yet may induce a culinary epiphany on eating.

With coffee, anticipation commonly exceeds pleasure. Most people find its smell pleasing yet many do not actually like its bitter taste, which is why they smother its flavour with milk and sugar. With cheese, it's the opposite. Its smell typically reminds people of sweaty feet, yet it is wildly popular both on its own and in or on numerous foods.

There is, however, one food that people firmly expect to enjoy and that rarely disappoints: chocolate. A box of chocolates remains one of the safest, most popular gifts, especially for people we don't know, because nothing is more likely to please most people most of the time.

Yet behind the chocolates we buy lies one of the most complex, opaque and arguably unjust supply chains in the contemporary food world. At the heart of this are a small number of large companies most people have never heard of, such as Callebaut, Cargill, Mondelez, Olam and Blommer. These corporations turn over more than $15 billion a year, yet they are neither cacao growers nor chocolate makers.[1] They are processors.

Processing cacao is a major part of chocolate production, which, from tree to bar, is incredibly complicated. It begins with harvesting the fruit of the cacao (Theobroma) tree, from which the beans are extracted. These are then fermented, a process that starts spontaneously in the humid, hot countries where cacao is grown. Fermentation is critical for releasing many different aromatic compounds in the beans. After fermentation, the beans are dried, reducing the moisture content from as high as 60 per cent or more to less than 8 per cent. Until this point, the beans are generally referred to by their plant name, cacao. From the next stage on, they are more likely to be referred to as cocoa. The dried beans are roasted, which is another important step in creating the full flavour profile of the end product. Next, the roasted beans are winnowed, and the separated shells discarded. This leaves cacao nibs, which are ground into cocoa mass, which contains both cocoa butter and fine cocoa particles. Now the cocoa is ready to be used as an ingredient. In a pure dark chocolate, only sugar is added to the cocoa powder and butter. The mix is gently heated and stirred to form a liquor, a process called 'conching' that was invented by Swiss chocolatier Rodolphe Lindt, the founder of the famous company that still bears his name. Finally, the mixture is tempered – gradually cooled so that it sets with the desired shape and texture.

Compare this process with that of coffee, which essentially involves harvesting the green cherries, removing the pulp by one of several different processes, drying, hulling and eventually roasting. Or with that of wine, which only requires harvesting, crushing and fermenting grapes. Not only is chocolate more complicated to make than wine or coffee, it can have a comparably complex flavour profile. What we call flavour is a combination of taste, detected by the tongue, and smell, detected in the nose, often retronasally – from aromas rising through the nasal passage from the mouth as we chew. These flavours are produced by volatile and non-volatile compounds, the former smelled, the latter tasted. It is the volatile compounds that give foods their complex flavours, since the mouth only detects sweet, salty, sour, bitter and umami. The number of volatile compounds varies enormously depending on how each wine, chocolate or coffee is made, and a good-quality chocolate has a comparable number of compounds to most coffee and many wines.

The initial stages of harvesting, fermenting and drying are typically done at or close to the cacao farms. But from there on, processing almost always continues off-site, usually in another country. In fact, in the industry, fermentation and drying aren't typically considered part of 'processing' at all. It is as though the language of the cocoa business refuses to acknowledge that farmers do more than just pick the fruits.

Most processing is done in countries which are not cacao producers. The biggest cacao-growing country in the world by a long shot is Côte d'Ivoire, which produces in excess of two million metric tonnes a year, more than a third of the global production. The next largest producer, Ghana, produces less than half this, while Africa as a whole accounts for two thirds to three quarters of global production. But while Côte d'Ivoire is also the largest cocoa processor, collectively, the Netherlands, Germany, Malaysia and the USA process around two and a half times more, despite not being producers. Indonesia also processes much more than the small amount it grows.[2]

In the industrial production chain, for which most cacao is destined, processing does not result in a finished product, but in liquid liquor or solid couverture, made from partially tempered liquor.

Sometimes other ingredients such as vegetable oils are added to make cheaper compound chocolate. Manufacturers add other in-gredients to the liquor, couverture or compound chocolate to create their signature textures and flavours, set in the moulds of their trade-marked shapes. Even in the days when chocolate bars were 'made in Britain' by companies such as Mars of Slough or Terry's of York, the chocolate itself was usually processed overseas. Today, even high-class chocolatiers buy in couverture. The only people who do the bulk of the processing themselves are the so-called bean-to-bar makers, and even they rarely take care of fermenting and drying.

Where is this chocolate sold? The biggest markets by far are Europe (nearly $6 billion per year) and North America (nearly $3 billion), followed by Asia Pacific (around $2 billion), with the rest of the world accounting for only around $1.5 billion of trade. The big six chocolate companies are based in the USA (Mars Wrigley, Mondelez and Hershey), Luxembourg and Italy (Ferrero), Switzerland (Nestlé) and Japan (Meiji). No African or South or Central American company features in the global top ten, despite these regions dominating in cocoa production.

The fingerprints of colonialism are all over these chocolate statistics. The growers see little of the profit, since most of the value is added at the stages of processing and manufacture. By the time chocolate is a retail product, it is mostly being sold in rich countries, where the bulk of both pleasure and profit is taken. Farmers receive less than 7 per cent of the sale price of chocolate, with retailers taking around 44 per cent and manufacturers 35 per cent. And while the average cocoa farmer in Ghana earns $1 a day and those in Côte d'Ivoire around 78 cents, America's most pop-ular bar, Hershey's Milk Chocolate, costs $1.24.[3] In other words, a European or American consumer pays more for a single bar of chocolate than the cacao farmer earns in a whole day. This is a pattern found in many agricultural goods produced in low- and middle-income countries. Food is bought as a raw or minimally processed ingredient at a rock-bottom price and shipped out to wealthier countries where it is used to make consumer products, which are sold at high prices.

The inequity becomes most evident when these products make it back to the markets of their countries of origin. For example, Uganda sells 96 per cent of its coffee for export, the vast majority of which is taxed by the importing countries. It is then used to make instant coffee, which Ugandans import, since they drink very little ground coffee. So Uganda sells its coffee for very little and buys it back for quite a bit more. The value is added abroad and charged back home. As the country's president, Yoweri Museveni, said, 'For each kilo of green beans, the farmer gets two dollars or less. When somebody roasts the same kilo, he has 50 dollars. We are losing money and losing jobs.'[4]

Colonialism is also a big part of the reason Belgium has become so associated with quality chocolate. 'Belgian chocolate', like 'Italian coffee', is almost an oxymoron because no cacao or coffee is grown in either country. Chocolate was introduced to Belgium during the period of Spanish rule in the seventeenth century, when cocoa beans were imported (or rather expropriated) from Spain's South American colonies. In the late nineteenth century, under King Leopold II, Belgium became a colonial power of its own. After it colonised Congo with its abundant cocoa production, Belgium became the world's leading trader in the beans.

Three Belgian innovations led the way in developing the production of luxury chocolate. In 1912, Jean Neuhaus invented the praline, and three years later his wife, Louise Agostini, invented the ballotin, the elegant gift box that housed the chocolates. This innovation is arguably as significant as the development of the chocolate itself. The Belgian chocolate brand was built on an idea of affordable indulgence, with chocolates laid out in shops modelled more on jewellery stores than on traditional sweet shops. When the Belgian chocolate maker Godiva started selling its chocolates in this way in US department stores in the 1960s, the international image of Belgium as a centre of chocolate excellence took root. In the 1920s, Octaaf Callebaut shifted the focus of his large family chocolate business to couverture, which opened the divide between cacao processors and manufacturers of chocolate, as well as making it easier for the latter to create a number of different products from the same base ingredient.

Chocolate provides the clearest example of how the modern international industrial food system allows primary agricultural products to be bought cheaply from farmers in order for profit to be added by intermediaries and manufacturers. Colonialism is a major part of the history of how this happened, and its legacies loom large. But colonialism does not explain how the system now works or why it is sustained. To understand that, you need to understand how agriculture ceased to primarily be a producer of foods and instead became a producer of commodities.

To see what commodification is, take two highly simplified scenarios. In the first, farmers sell food to customers. They harvest potatoes, tomatoes, cassavas or whatever and take them to market, where someone buys the food to eat. Sometimes the sale may not be quite as direct. A wheat harvest may be taken to the miller and then sold to bakers, who sell their bread to customers. But in this simple kind of supply chain there is a direct, easily traceable route from field to fork.

However, most of what farmers produce today is not eaten as food or sold as an ingredient to a small, local artisan, such as a miller, cheesemaker or *charcutier*. Today, most food products are produced industrially, at scale, like pasta, sliced bread, ready meals, biscuits, breakfast cereals, sauces, instant noodles. These large manufacturers do not generally go out and find their suppliers themselves. Rather, they buy through intermediaries who work in the global commodities market. These intermediaries buy up grains, fruits, vegetables, coffee beans and so on from innumerable farms, large and small. Furthermore, there are often several layers of intermediaries, all taking their cut. A miller may buy wheat from growers in a relatively limited area of a country and sell it on to a national company, which then sells it on to an international one. So the wheat and rye for an industrial bread maker may come from hundreds, even thousands, of farms, passing through many hands before it gets turned into bread. Similarly, a chain like Starbucks gets its coffee beans from thousands of growers, since most coffee farms are relatively small.

Almost all the cacao grown in the world is sold as a commodity. As craft chocolate seller Spencer Hyman explained to me, this means that 'it is bought primarily on price not on quality, and you use it as an ingredient which is relatively easy to substitute: one bean is the same as another. It meets a minimum standard and the most important criterion for purchasing is generally price. You wouldn't know how or where it's been sourced from except in very broad terms.'

The key feature of a food commodity is that it is replaceable. Its individual characteristics are not only irrelevant, they should be minimal. As an ingredient it needs to meet a minimum standard and have as standard a flavour as possible. The one thing it should not be is different or interesting because buyers in the commodity market are looking for consistency. With chocolate, for example, every major consumer product has a distinctive taste: a Galaxy bar doesn't taste the same as a Cadbury's Dairy Milk or a Hershey's. This is not because of the cocoa content, which is typically very low. The minimum cocoa content for milk chocolate in the EU is 25 per cent, while in the UK it is 20 per cent and in the USA only 10.[5] Still, the manufacturers will be careful to ensure that the cocoa they buy from numerous sources is mixed together to create a blend with a consistent flavour. With coffee, this blending is even more important. Every jar of Nescafé or bag of Lavazza beans has to taste the same, which requires blending together beans from different sources and adjusting the roast times. This means that farmers are incentivised to grow for yield and consistency, not for maximum quality, and certainly not for maximum taste.

Hyman argues that one reason quality doesn't count for much in high street chocolate is that most of the flavour comes from what is added to the couverture. The cocoa is simply a 'vector for other tastes and flavours', not something you want to bring out the flavours of itself. All sorts of shortcuts can be taken that sacrifice flavour. For example, as we have seen, cacao beans are usually roasted before they are shelled, but Hyman says that much commodity cocoa is shelled before it is roasted. Why? 'Because it's three to five per cent more efficient. It dramatically changes the flavour profile but that doesn't matter because when you're dealing with commodity, you're assuming that you can add tastes and flavours back in later.' It doesn't even matter if the cacao hasn't been properly fermented.

The push for quantity can also create environmental problems. According to Hyman, 'One of the tragedies is that because cacao has become a commodity crop, the easiest way to make more money if you're a farmer is to cut down trees to free up land to grow more cacao. Before the 1950s, over 50 per cent of Côte d'Ivoire and Ghana were virgin rainforest. By the 1990s it was down below 30 per cent and today it's two or three.' Between 2001 and 2014 alone, one quarter of Côte d'Ivoire's forests and 10 per cent of Ghana's were cleared for cocoa production, with an estimated 40 per cent of Ivorian plantations sited illegally inside supposedly protected areas.[6]

Another environmental impact is that because commodity crops have to be high yielding and substitutable, and deliver consistency, there is a trend to less diversity. Just three crops – maize, rice and wheat – account for nearly 90 per cent of all global grain production worldwide and nearly half of all calories consumed.[7] There is also less variety of cultivars for each crop. The most extreme case is the banana. Until the 1950s, the most grown variety was the

Gros Michel, but it was killed off by a strain of fungus that caused Panama disease. It was replaced by the Cavendish, which was smaller and less tasty but was immune to the fungus and travelled well. Once again, the commodity markets prioritised reliability, and yield trumped quality. (The fact that a tropical fruit is named after the English employer of a British head gardener, Joseph Paxton, who first bred the variety in 1835, tells you a lot about the historical power dynamics in the global food system.)

Almost all bananas sold for export are Cavendishes, and the variety accounts for nearly half of all production worldwide. But in recent years, new strains of Panama disease have started killing them too. Even if this is overcome, the reliance on a single variety makes the banana industry very vulnerable to disease or infection, especially because Cavendish bananas are sterile and so every propagated tree is a genetically identical clone.[8] That they are grown in huge monocultures adds to the vulnerability. When one crop dominates a large area, any pest or pathogen is presented with a feast to feed on, free from competitors or predators that would be found in a more diverse ecosystem.

Farmers who grow for commodity markets have little to no control over the price they charge. That is set by the global markets. When supply is low relative to demand, prices rise and when supply is high, prices can plummet. There are many years when farmers may have to sell their commodity crops at less than what it cost to produce them. 'It's just a roller coaster,' cocoa processor and trader Jeff Steinberg tells me. 'What ends up happening is that when it goes down to a certain level people decide to cut down cacao trees because it's not worth the money compared to another thing they can be doing. Then when the market climbs back up everybody goes and plants.'

This is a far cry from the image of the commodity farmer portrayed in the famous series of advertisements for Del Monte fruit juices that ran in the late 1980s. A white-suited white man would arrive by private seaplane, be treated like a VIP and go to taste fruit while the darker-skinned farmer would watch apprehensively. When the farmer finally got the nod, he would rush out and announce to all the peasants, 'The man from Del Monte, he say yes!' Everyone would whoop, cheer and throw their hats in the air. The advert suggested that the best thing that could happen to a farmer in a low- or middle-income country, and the highest praise for their fruit or vegetables, was that the man (and it would have been a man) from the large international company wanted to buy their produce. In reality, such a deal would bring low or even negative margins and would be indicative of minimum, not top, quality, as any one farmer's oranges or peaches would be blended in with those from numerous other farms to produce the consistent Del Monte taste.

The commodification of the food trade could even be contributing to ill health. In 2002, a joint World Health Organization and FAO report linked the rise of the commodity market and poor nutrition. 'Food and food products have become commodities produced and traded in a market that has expanded from an essentially local base to an increasingly global one,' it says. These commodities are used to make processed foods, which are drivers of changes in dietary patterns, with an 'increased consumption of energy dense diets high in fat' and 'low in unrefined carbohydrates'.[9] To put it more simply, junk food is the result of foods ceasing to be sold to be eaten as they are and becoming industrial ingredients instead.

If commodity crops are such a bad deal, why do farmers grow them? Because the alternatives either don't exist or are even worse. Imagine a wheat farmer who wants to sell flour directly to local people and shops. First, they either have to mill the wheat or pay someone else to do it, which adds expense and time. Then they would have to find customers, who are generally quite poor and so can't pay high prices. Demand and supply are also both likely to be somewhat unpredictable, which means that in a good year the farmer will have a useless surplus and in a bad one won't have enough and so may lose customers when they switch to a new supplier. Selling wheat as a commodity may be a bad deal, but you know that someone will regularly turn up to take what you have produced and hand over some cash for it. It's simple, predictable and reliable – although no guarantee of a living income.

Still, most farmers would take an alternative if there were a good one. And for some crops, such alternatives do exist, albeit not extensively enough to be viable for most farmers. Coffee and cacao are two such crops. The best-known alternative to the mainstream commodity market is to sell under a fair trade label, such as Fairtrade or Rainforest Alliance. These schemes typically pay farmers a premium over the market price. While this is an improvement, they are limited in what they can achieve. As Hyman explains, 'Let's say a farmer is earning eighty cents a day and they need $2.50 to live. The fair trade premium is about 20 per cent maximum. So even if you could pay people the maximum premium you're moving them from eighty cents to ninety-six cents and that just isn't even halfway to getting what they need to live on.'

For consumers, fair trade isn't always what it seems either. For example, back in 2009, Cadbury committed to buying 10,000 tonnes of cocoa under the Fairtrade scheme from Ghana, enough to have its flagship Dairy Milk bar certified as Fairtrade. But that did not mean that Dairy Milk bars were made with only Fairtrade-certified cocoa. Cadbury was permitted to label a proportion of its output as Fairtrade, in line with the proportion of Fairtrade cocoa that it bought as a company. But any given product could have a mixture of Fairtrade and regular commodity cocoa.

Another complication is that many schemes, such as Fairtrade International, require suppliers to be cooperatives, which means that ethically aspirational small companies can't get certified. That's one reason why Simran Bindra, co-founder of the privately owned cocoa trader Kokoa Kamili, is not enthusiastic about fair trade, even though he supports its aims. 'If you show me one well-functioning cooperative here I can show you fifty where the management tends to be the politically connected, rich people in the area,' he told me. This leads to situations where, for example, 'the fair trade premium gets spent on a truck for the cooperative and that truck just happens to be parked at the co-op manager's house and just happens to be used for his hardware supply business or his piggery instead of being used only for their cooperatives.' Bindra believes it is better to 'take it a step further and give that money directly to the farmer who did the work on growing that cocoa'. Steinberg broadly concurs.

The biggest criticism is that certification schemes lack the capacity to ensure that environmental and labour standards are being met. Take the issue of child labour. In 2001 the major chocolate manufacturers signed the Harkin–Engel Protocol, an international agreement aimed at ending the worst forms of child labour in cocoa production. That same year, the big chocolate companies – Cadbury, Ferrero, Hershey, Kraft, Mars, Nestlé, ADM Cocoa, Barry Callebaut and Cargill – formed the Global Issues Group (GIG) 'specifically to address the labor challenges in the cocoa sectors of West Africa as articulated in the Harkin–Engel Protocol'.

Yet in 2019 the *Washington Post* ran a series of reports on the continued use of child labour in the cocoa supply chain. One key problem was that the inspection regime just wasn't rigorous enough. The *Post* found that 'inspections for the labels typically are announced in advance and are required of fewer than one in ten farms annually'. A 2017 Nestlé report concluded, 'Put simply, when the auditors came, the children were ushered from the fields and when interviewed, the farmers denied they were ever there.' In 2010, the Fairtrade Labeling Organization (FLO, now Fairtrade International) acknowledged that 'the industry in fact does not know of any system that currently, or in the near term, can guarantee the absence of child labor, including trafficked labor, in the production of cocoa in West Africa'.[10] Research reports co-sponsored by UTZ, which started certifying coffee in 2002 and merged with the Rainforest Alliance in 2018, found that certified farms in Côte d'Ivoire were actually more likely to have child labour than non-certified farms. The *Post* also found that trees in the rainforest were still being cut down for cocoa production despite environmental pledges.[11] Steinberg sums it up pithily: 'Just thinking that it's the solution to all the problems and that if I buy fair trade or organic cocoa, my conscience is clean – it's not as clear cut and black and white as that.'

Another alternative for farmers comes in the form of the recent rise of craft coffee and chocolate makers, championing top-quality growers. This offers three opportunities for farmers and their communities. First, they can concentrate on growing higher-quality beans that can command a higher price. Second, because they trade more directly with the roasters and makers, less is taken as a cut by intermediaries. Third, some bean-to-bar makers and roasters shift more of the production closer to the source, adding more value locally. This means that the places where these crops are grown can share more of the profits generated by the products that are eventually sold.

Bindra's Kokoa Kamili is one such company, based in the Kilombero Valley in Tanzania. The valley sits at the edge of the Udzungwa Mountains, which lie partially in a protected national park. It looks beautiful, but Bindra warns, 'People tend to romanticise village life in Africa but when the closest hospital is sixty kilometres away I think it's a hard life. You don't have a government providing a social safety net. Most people who are farming in the village are completely non-mechanised.'

When Bindra left university, he was looking for a job not in business but in international development. But while doing a consulting job in Tanzania for a non-governmental organization (NGO) working on a project to improve the quality of local farmers' cacao, disillusion set in. 'I remember reading a report where the organization was patting itself on its back for farmer incomes going up something like 15 per cent in that year and I was like, "Hang on: global cocoa prices went up 20 per cent, so how is this a success story?"' He also found himself disliking the short timelines: 'I was working on a four-year project and one of the goals was to boost the yields of cocoa farmers. But a cocoa tree takes four years from planting to first production, and seven to eight years to reach maturity.'

Bindra moved on, joining an agribusiness investment fund that was looking at opportunities in Tanzania. There, the idea formed of starting a cocoa business, buoyed by the burgeoning bean-to-bar sector and the more mature specialist coffee market, both of which proved there was an appetite for quality, well-sourced cocoa and coffee beans with a story to tell. And so, with his business partner Brian, who had experience in the coffee trade, he founded Kokoa Kamili. The move from international development consultant to entrepreneur might seem a strange one, but for decades a development mantra has been 'trade not aid'. It is widely agreed that the best way to raise living standards in low- and middle-income countries is to increase their capacity to produce and do business. And many people who go into craft chocolate and specialty coffee are motivated to give farmers a better deal.

Take Jeff Steinberg, founder and managing director of Latitude. When describing his company to me he foregrounded not what he sells but who he buys from: 'We basically work with small farmers, support them with training and resources to help them grow cacao.' Like Bindra, he didn't start out as a businessman but worked first in academia and consulting. 'After a number of years doing that I decided I was done telling people what they should be doing and I wanted to actually do it myself.'

Both Steinberg and Bindra know that they are not radically transforming the lives of local farmers. 'A smallholder farm is not a path to prosperity anywhere in the world,' says Bindra. 'I'm under no illusions that anyone is being lifted out of poverty farming a couple of acres by receiving a higher income from us.' But, like Steinberg, he is confident their way of doing things is much better for producers. 'Before we started, the farmers in Kilombero received the lowest prices in Tanzania for their cocoa. I'm pretty sure that they could now be receiving the highest prices in Africa, definitely in Tanzania, for their cocoa, which is pretty rewarding. If you're making $500 a year because you work with us instead of $300 a year working with a commodity market, it's a big percentage. It's not going to mean that you're suddenly going to buy a car. But it will mean that you might be able to send your kid to a better school in the next town or that you can upgrade to a tin roof. It might mean that you have extra meat in the pot or an extra beer on Sunday.'

Many of the beneficiaries are women. Although only around 30 per cent of the farmers registered are women, that is because as 'heads of the household' men are more likely to control the method of transportation, whether it's a bicycle or a motorbike, and sign formal documents. Bindra believes the actual gender ratio of who's doing the work would flip the balance in favour of women.

The craft chocolate and coffee model isn't completely different to the mainstream commodity market. Many bean-to-bar makers talk of their 'direct trade' with growers, but this is misleading. It is relatively *more* direct, but they are still using intermediaries, like Kokoa Kamili and Latitude. No foreign maker could buy direct from farmers because each farm is so small. In Uganda, up to a million farmers keep at least some coffee trees.[12] 'There are always going to be middlemen in the chain,' says Steinberg. 'People make this direct trade / commodity distinction. That's too simplistic. We are still a middleman, selling to a third party. It's just a better version of the mainstream system. We, as a vertically integrated chocolate company, occupy the space in a traditional supply chain of anywhere from eight to twelve different companies, but this is very difficult to do and there are many good and economically efficient reasons why those companies in between normally exist and have a role to play. Shortening the supply chain is just one way to increase transparency and (potentially) increase margins within the supply chain, both of which ultimately can benefit everyone if done well and at scale.'

Specialty processors also do more than just buy and sell. 'When you're talking about middlemen, the common thought is that somebody is just taking product and basically taking advantage of an arbitrage opportunity,' says Steinberg. 'They're buying it in one place and bringing it to another and not changing or doing anything to it. We, along with many of the more traditional exporters and traders, take on significant risk in the value chain and, in some cases, do a significant amount of value addition. At Latitude, we're buying at farm-gate directly from farmers, carrying out all primary processing, manufacturing chocolate bars and delivering those chocolate bars to retailers.'

As with commodity coffee, specialty beans are almost always a mix from different farms. Whereas much fine wine is 'single estate', the concept doesn't translate well to coffee or chocolate, where farms are too small to supply enough beans for even a niche producer. (Occasional limited edition bars and coffee 'microlots' are the exception to this rule.) If a coffee or chocolate is single estate, that almost certainly means the farm is a large one owned by a very wealthy individual or, more likely, a company.

Overall, although there are alternatives to the mainstream commodity market, none are straightforward and none result in profoundly transformational changes for primary producers. And it would be naive to believe that every commodity crop grown could be sold using alternative models. 'People can be anti-middlemen but they do play a role,' says Bindra. 'If someone said tomorrow you can buy all the cocoa in Tanzania direct from farmers, we wouldn't know what to do with it. The specialty market isn't big enough. If the commodity market were to disappear tomorrow, the farmers would definitely be worse off because who's going to buy their cacao?'

Steinberg agrees. 'The commodities marketplace is pretty efficient, with the exception of traders who are just speculating, but even speculators play a role in terms of buying and selling risk and uncertainty in the market. These are very big supply chains with a lot of actors and a lot of dynamics. It's like moving mountains in order to get that quantity of any product from so many different suppliers in such rural, volatile areas to a manufacturer in another market.'

The other problem is that chocolate made by the specialty bean-to-bar makers is comparatively expensive. The chocolate makers who use Kokoa Kamili cocoa typically sell bars for upwards of £5 ($6), four times the price of a mainstream brand. But the premium paid for specialty chocolate is not all accounted for by higher cocoa costs. The chocolate is marketed as a premium, gourmet product and the packaging reflects this. One maker was able to reduce its prices by around a dollar a bar when it switched to less fancy packaging. There is also a handful of bean-to-bar makers whose price point is closer to premium mainstream brands like Lindt or Godiva.

Most of the time, says Bindra, 'Cocoa is not a big driver of the retail price. You could double the amount of spend on the cocoa to a farmer and I guarantee you it would have an insignificantly small impact on the finished price.' So why don't all companies just pay more? 'I don't know of any situation where a huge multinational would be willing to pay a higher price than they're able for any commodity in any industry,' says Bindra. Every company tries to keep all its costs as low as possible. Why double what you pay for cocoa but not what you pay for sugar, energy, packaging, labour, shipping and so on? The ethical answer is that some low costs mean people are paid too little whereas others do not. Paying double for electricity would enrich already hugely profitable energy companies; paying double to a farmer gives them a better liveli-hood. But, as Steinberg says, 'Many of those manufacturers have shareholders and boards that they're responsible to, and people who have invested in their companies that expect certain returns and outcomes. It's hard to deny that a decent chunk of the problem has to do with our kind of capitalism.'

Latitude and Kokoa Kamili are for-profit businesses working in a capitalist economy, so it is not inevitable that companies see max-imising shareholder or owner profit as the overriding goal. Nor is it inevitable that consumers in affluent countries only buy on price and flavour. However, based on their impact so far, the ability of enlightened entrepreneurs and ethical consumers to drive radical change in the food system is very limited. Fairtrade-certified or otherwise fairly traded craft chocolate has been around for decades, but relatively few consumers choose to buy it. Several years ago, Cadbury and Nestlé moved to certify some of their core range as Fairtrade, in response to perceived consumer demand. But in recent years both have withdrawn from the Fairtrade scheme, fail-ing to see clear benefits. In its place, Cadbury's owner, Mondelez, set up its own Cocoa Life programme and Nestlé opted for the less onerous Rainforest Alliance certification. If we leave it to consumers to drive change in the commodity markets, we could be waiting a very long time.

A more equitable food world should be everyone's goal, but real-istic reform requires a fairer commodity market, not its abolition. That is easier said than done, and neither Steinberg nor Bindra knows how to fix it. But there is a possibility of real change, because 'capitalism' is not a pre-given system that comes in only one form. Capitalism is any form of economy where capital is allowed to be privately owned, and such economies can be more or less regulated, in myriad ways, as we'll soon see. But first, we need to understand how the raw deal for commodity crop growers is far from the worst way in which the people who provide our food are treated.

6

HARD LABOUR

Spices and slaves in Zanzibar

In the late nineteenth century, travellers arriving off the coast of Zanzibar reported that from their ships they could smell the fragrant spices, especially cloves, growing on the East African island. In the eponymous main town, however, the air was less agreeable. The Victorian explorer Henry Stanley called it 'extremely malodorous', complaining of the 'compound smell of hides, tar, filth and vegetable refuse'. Cholera outbreaks, a sure sign of poor sanitation, were regular occurrences.[1] As a metaphor for the historical inequities in the food system, this is almost too perfect. Trade brings food to relatively affluent consumers for whom it is a sensory delight. For those who sell it, along with those who own the land, food is a source of wealth. But for the vast majority of people working on the ground, growing and harvesting, food production is usually pure toil, for little or even no pay.

The Atlantic slave trade played a central role in food production. From the start of the sixteenth century to the end of the seventeenth, around 12–15 million people were taken to be used as slaves in the Americas. Almost as many people died while being marched to the coast of Africa from the interior as made it across the ocean, while nearly 15 per cent who were put on ships in Africa never made it to port in America.[2] It was the largest forced migration in history, and the vast majority of slaves were put to work on farms, with around three quarters working on sugar plantations.[3] Because the legacy of this trade still affects the lives of people today, it has naturally become the paradigm of slavery: Europeans and their white North American descendants exploiting black Africans.

However, in his comprehensive and concise overview of slavery and the slave trade in eastern Africa, Professor Abdulaziz Y. Lodhi makes it clear that slavery was not a creation of the imperialist western powers. A specialist in East African Area Studies, Lodhi reminds us that slaves have been kept by Mayans and Aztecs and in other American societies; by Sumerians and Babylonians in the Near East; by Chinese and Japanese in the Far East; by Ottomans and Egyptians in the Middle East; and by Romans, Egyptians and Greeks in antiquity. Religion has been actively supportive of slavery. 'All the three Semitic religions of Judaism, Christianity and Islam recognise slaves as a separate class of people in society,' says Lodhi. The caste system of what we now call Hinduism also meant that people from lower castes 'provided ample free or cheap labor to the upper castes'.[4]

The ubiquity of slavery in human history becomes even more undeniable if we count serfdoms as slave-owning societies. Serfs were labourers, usually agricultural, who were required to work the land of their feudal lord. Serfs had no freedom to work for anyone else, let alone themselves. They were, in effect, the property of their lords. In England, the Peasants' Revolt in 1381 heralded the beginning of the end of serfdom, although it wasn't until 1574 that Elizabeth I freed the last serfs. In Russia, the system persisted until 1861.

Slaves have been kept to fulfil many roles, including in trades, construction and crafts, and as soldiers and administrators. Women have often been kept as sex slaves, sometimes under the euphemistic label of 'concubines'. But the majority of slaves have been put to work to produce and prepare food.

Zanzibar is a good case study. In East Africa, there was domestic slavery and a thriving slave trade before Vasco da Gama reached Mozambique in 1498, opening up the region for the Portuguese. Human beings were being exported to the Middle East, especially the Persian Gulf. Black African slaves made up a large part of the armies that fought for Muslim Arabs in the eighth century. Under the Abbasid Caliphate in the ninth century, slaves of mostly African origin worked in terrible conditions to convert land into arable plantations in what is now Baghdad. In 869, a number of them rose up against their oppressors, their rebellion finally suppressed after two years. Over the coming centuries, Persia, Oman and Mesopotamia continued to be major importers of human cargo.[5]

The arrival of the Portuguese in East Africa created new markets, enabling this (in)human trade to expand. But perhaps its biggest effect was to change how trade was conducted. Until then, the region was a kind of free-trade area, in which no one country sought to dominate by military power. Da Gama's men counted 'around fifteen hundred Moorish vessels arriving in search of spices' but were amazed that they were all unarmed. This struck them as bizarre since in the Mediterranean, from time immemorial, naval power had been used to control sea lanes and trade. So, like hawks finding themselves surrounded by doves, they saw an opportunity to assert their military might to become the dominant regional power.[6]

This might-is-right strategy was successful for a couple of centuries but, unsurprisingly, foreign occupation was unpopular with the major regional powers. Eventually, in 1650, the Omanis expelled the Portuguese from Muscat, their main naval base in the region. However, this did nothing to reduce slavery. For example, around the beginning of the eighteenth century, Imam Said bin Sultan, owner of a third of Oman's date palms, had 1,700 slaves. Throughout the century to follow, slaves were used on Omani-owned date and sugar cane plantations on the Mascarene islands colonised by the French in the Indian Ocean, and in the Americas. As the European powers began to abandon the slave trade, increasingly slaves were kept to work within the region, both in the Middle East and in the interior of Africa, rather than exported far overseas. As the historian Abdul Sheriff put it, merchants 'realised that if slaves could not be exported, the product of their labour could', which became the basic principle of human exploitation for agriculture since the abolition of the Atlantic slave trade.[7]

One of the most prolific regional slave traders was the Zanzibari Arab Ḥamad ibn Muḥammad al Murjabī, better known as Tippu Tip. His trading and looting trips were supported by the Sultan of Oman and he was appointed governor of eastern Congo by the Belgian king, Leopold II. The British explorer Henry Stanley reported that when he first saw Tippu Tip, 'a buzz of admiration of his style was perceptible from the onlookers'.[8] Like many tyrants, Tippu Tip had an aura about him and he became quite a celebrity in his time. But this charismatic man was a violent and ruthless trader. In his authorised biography, as told to a German contemporary, Heinrich Brode, we are told Tippu Tip could 'barter a few pieces of coloured cloth for a whole herd of slaves', but if 'the natives were weak and victory seemed certain, a shorter procedure was adopted. Peaceful hamlets were surprised and plundered, and such of the natives as could be captured were carried off as slaves.'[9] Tippu Tip told Stanley, 'Slaves cost nothing, they only require to be gathered.'[10]

Slaves were useful for carrying his plunder and supplies, but back in Zanzibar, they were important for the cultivation of cloves, which had been introduced from Mauritius and quickly came to be the island's major commodity crop in the second half of the nineteenth century. As Zanzibar became a thriving trading hub, slaves passed through it as well as being brought to it, traded to North Africa, Arabia and the countries on the Persian Gulf.[11]

At the peak of this trade, 70,000 slaves a year were brought to Zanzibar. In the wider region, 1.6 million slaves were shipped out of the east coast of Africa in the nineteenth century, four times the number taken from Africa to the United States of America.[12] Despite a treaty theoretically banning the slave trade in 1873 and a declaration permitting slaves to buy their freedom in 1890, when Zanzibar was declared a British protectorate, slavery was not entirely abolished on the island until 1897.

The end of slavery changed surprisingly little for the people who worked the farms. Most remained landless 'squatters' working for their landlords in a relationship that was almost as unequal as that of slaves and masters. It wasn't until the revolution in 1964 that squatters were given their own minimum of three acres of plantation land, while larger farms were nationalised.[13]

The story of slaves and spices in Zanzibar exemplifies the ways in which, ever since food has been traded, an extreme power and wealth imbalance has existed between those working on the ground to produce it and the landowners and traders who profit from it. The same pattern has been repeated over different centuries and continents. These power and wealth imbalances are a large part of what allows food to be plentiful and cheap for those in major trading and importing nations.

Examples of how this dynamic is still at work are legion, sometimes right under our noses. A Briton does not have to look overseas to see such abuses. One of the most notorious examples was in February 2004, when at least twenty-one people were drowned by an incoming tide while gathering cockles in Morecambe Bay in the north-west of England. The bodies of at least two others believed to have been killed were never found. They were all illegal Chinese immigrants, working for a Chinese gangmaster who was sentenced to twelve years in prison for manslaughter.

A decade later, one of the authors of a major report into forced labour in the United Kingdom, Durham University's Gary Craig, said, 'People tend to think that slavery is something to do with faraway countries with poor human rights records. Well, actually, slavery is here and now in the UK and the research which I've done with colleagues suggests there may be upwards of 10,000 people at any one time in the UK in conditions which we would class as modern slavery.'[14]

Illegal immigrants are often exploited for agricultural work. The often casual, temporary and arduous nature of the labour makes it hard to find willing workers who are available for legal employment. Illegal migrants are in no position to demand minimum wages or basic rights. And away from towns and cities, it is relatively easy to employ people illicitly.

In the USA, where people spend a lower proportion of their incomes on food than in any other country, such workers are essential to the production of cheap food. Roughly half of all agricultural workers in America are foreign-born, around half of whom are undocumented and working illegally. In crop production, around a third of workers are illegal immigrants.[15]

Europe is no stranger to these issues. Tins of Italian tomatoes are sold across the continent, prized for their quality. But many are grown and harvested in southern Italy, where modern slavery is rife. Reporting on the business, Tobias Jones and Ayo Awokoya wrote that workers 'live in isolated rural ruins or shanty towns' often without residency permits or contracts. 'Desperate for work, these labourers will accept any job in the fields even if the wages are far below, and the hours far above, union standards.'[16] Where they come from varies with current geopolitical conditions.

When Jones and Awokoya were writing, there were some eastern Europeans, but most were from African nations such as Gambia, Ghana, Nigeria, Sudan and Somalia. According to the NGO Global Slavery Index, in 2018 there were 50,000 enslaved agricultural workers in Italy, more than a third of all the slaves in the country, many others of whom work in prostitution or domestic services.

There are similarly dire conditions for workers in southern Spain and Morocco, which together provide much of Europe's fruit and vegetables. In 2021, for the first time the UK imported more fresh produce from Morocco than from the Netherlands.[17] Around 15,000 workers in southern Spain are hired through a state-run process called 'contract in origin', designed to limit illegal migration. Under this system, foreign workers sign contracts before their arrival in Spain that specify the conditions and length of employment, as well as where they will live, after which the worker must return to their country of origin. Arguably, this is closer to the condition of being a serf than it is to being an employee. The worker is entirely dependent on their employer, tied to a specific farm, only free to live in the country while employed. It also has similarities with bonded labour, considered a form of slavery, where a person is forced to work for someone to pay off a debt. With little or no practical option to return home, 'contract in origin' workers are almost as tied to their employers as debt slaves.

NGOs working in Spain have uncovered all manner of abuses of these workers. Some are fitted with GPS trackers to ensure they are working hard enough. Many live in shanty towns called *chabolas*, without a fresh water supply or proper sanitation, in shelters usually made from old polytunnels. Undocumented workers are in an even worse position, paid low wages when needed and left without work when they are not, sometimes for days or weeks.[18]

Overall, around the world 2.1 million people are being exploited through forced labour in farming, comprising 13 per cent of the global adult forced labour workforce, excluding those in forced commercial sexual exploitation. Of these, 31 per cent are in debt bondage. Five per cent of the children trafficked for forced labour work in agriculture, and seasonal migrant workers are also at particular risk. In recent years, these numbers have been rising.[19]

'There are 50 million people in modern slavery today,' says Louise Nicholls, who spent years trying to improve labour conditions in UK food retailer M&S's supply chain, leading its Corporate Human Rights programme. She tells me it persists because, 'unlike a product, which you sell once, you can sell a person over and over again. It's a very profitable crime and exploiters are very clever. No sooner have you put in some rules and regulations than they find a way around them. Exploitation will always be an issue in supply chains.'

Consumers would like to think that the tomatoes they buy in reputable supermarkets are not tainted by this exploitation. After all, producers and retailers have numerous policies and codes of conduct that are supposed to stop such abuses. But those who monitor modern slavery do not believe these policies are effective enough. Much of the exploitation is driven by organised crime, which is very adept at avoiding detection. Inspection regimes are not rigorous enough, and it is too easy to cover up malpractice when audits are scheduled. Worse, no matter how good the intentions of big companies might be, their demand for cheap ingredients and produce fuels the problem. Rachel Wilshaw, ethical trade manager at Oxfam, said that 'in squeezing their suppliers so hard commercially that they can only make a profit by exploiting workers, supermarkets themselves are driving the conditions that can result in modern slavery in their supply chain'.[20]

Exploitation in agriculture does not end with forced labour. Many people are growing food in countries that are poor, lack basic human rights, or both. In the two largest cacao-producing countries, Côte d'Ivoire and Ghana, around 1.5 million children work on plantations, 10,000 of whom are trafficked, often from Mali and

Burkina Faso. Children work so much because without their help, the adults can't earn enough to live. In Côte d'Ivoire the typical cacao farmer's family earns one third of a living wage.[21]

Ironically, the reason Côte d'Ivoire and Ghana became the main producers of cacao is that production was shifted from where conditions were even worse. In 1905, a journalist called Henry Nevinson went to the West African island country of São Tomé and Príncipe and found that although the Portuguese colonial rulers had banned slavery, almost all the workers were indentured. He published articles and photographs in *Harper's Magazine* which were turned into a book, *A Modern Slavery*, published in 1906. It was four years before Cadbury, one of the biggest buyers of cacao from São Tomé and Príncipe, moved its production to Côte d'Ivoire and Ghana.

'The history of chocolate has always had a very bad taste of slavery,' says craft chocolate entrepreneur Spencer Hyman. 'It's not just Africa. In South America, when the Spanish wanted more chocolate they couldn't get it from Mexico or Honduras because their invasion introduced smallpox and a host of other diseases which destroyed the population, so there weren't enough people to grow it.' Production was moved south to countries like Venezuela and Ecuador, where the Spanish introduced the *encomienda* system. Under this system, colonial settlers were 'entrusted' with natives to 'civilise' and convert to Christianity. This was basically enslavement, and in return the settlers would provide labour, taxes or goods to the Spanish Crown.

Similar stories can be told of pretty much every foodstuff that is consumed in developed countries and grown in less developed ones. These injustices have been well publicised for decades, but most actors in the food system ignore them. Governments in countries that benefit from the cheap food the system provides feel unwilling and/or unable to try to affect the labour conditions in supplying countries, in large part because they don't want to make food imports more expensive. As for abuses in their own countries, farm work has become so unattractive that agriculture has become dependent on badly paid migrants. To put it cynically, there are two labour problems – the conditions of migrant workers, and the shortage of agricultural workers – and governments ignore the first to help them deal with the second. Supermarkets and food multinationals are similarly incentivised to do very little. Although scandals in supply chains present reputational risks, to address the issues properly would require increasing prices, putting them at a competitive disadvantage. That is why ethically minded CEOs want more government intervention, to ensure that there is a level playing field. As for consumers, most of us shop on price and preference, rarely choosing to pay more for the reassurance of ethical sourcing. For those on low incomes, buying the cheapest food possible is a necessity. For people on middle to high incomes, it is optional. Across Europe, people spend around 13 per cent of their household income on food and non-alcoholic drinks.[22] Most people could easily pay more, but prefer not to.

The fact that people have been enslaved and exploited to feed us across millennia and continents suggests an uncomfortable explanation for why change is so difficult: labour abuses in the food-supply chain are a feature, not a bug. They are not flaws that crop up despite people's best efforts to avoid them, but are structural features of the system itself that have still not been designed out. No one designed our complex food system, but as it evolved, exploited labour brought with it adaptive advantages. Any person, company or nation that could get away with mistreating food producers got more and cheaper food, satisfying themselves, their customers or their citizens. Any individual or entity that wants to break this dependence on exploited labour increases the costs of life's most basic necessity.

The global market economy as a whole shares this built-in inequity. In their more reflective moments, consumers in industrialised countries realise that the era of cheap goods can only last as long as the era of cheap labour. Most obviously, it is difficult to even find an electronic device that is not made in China, and those that are not are almost all made in other middle- or low-income Asian countries. If such goods were made in Europe or the USA, they would be much more expensive, due mainly to higher labour costs. And if countries like China become richer, workers will expect to be paid more and the goods they produce will become more expensive too.

Up until now, most of what we have learned from global food systems past and present has been positive. We've been looking for the principles of a global food philosophy in practices and food ways worth emulating or reproducing. Now we can see that a core feature of how we have been feeding ourselves is deeply problematic. But can and should we try to reduce or even eradicate these ingrained inequities? There are many who argue that although there are some egregious abuses that ought to be eradicated, it is naive and utopian to believe that we have some kind of moral duty to make working conditions as good as possible for everyone. To put it bluntly, they say that the system may be ugly and objectively unjust, but that's life.

Crude though this argument is, it has to be taken seriously, and meeting it is not easy. One major problem is that there is no general agreement on moral principles. The closest thing we have to a global moral code is the Universal Declaration of Human Rights, adopted by the United Nations General Assembly in 1948. However, it would be very difficult to use the rights framework as a moral basis for much greater global economic equality. Most philosophers agree that rights are not natural, meaning that they do not exist until human beings create them. The things upon which we base rights – such as sentience and the capacity for autonomy – may be natural, but rights themselves are artefacts of common or state law. This argument was put most forcibly and clearly by the philosopher and social reformer Jeremy Bentham (1748–1832), who wrote that 'there are no such things as natural rights – no such things as rights anterior to the establishment of government – no such things as natural rights opposed to, in contradistinction to, legal.' We may talk of 'natural rights', but that is just a figure of speech and 'in the moment you attempt to give it a literal meaning it leads to error, and to that sort of error that leads to mischief – to the extremity of mischief.'[23]

Today, rights are enshrined in both international and national law, although too often they are not respected. In any case, while it is necessary for national law to respect the rights enshrined in the Universal Declaration, additional rights granted by nation states have no authority outside them. So while we may not like it that many people in low- and middle-income countries work all hours and receive little in return, as long as farmers and agricultural workers in global supply chains are working in accordance with national and international law, their legal rights are not being violated.

Of course, when people are being mistreated we often believe that this indicates that we ought to grant them more rights. That's how slaves were freed and women got the vote. Similarly, if we think that we have moral duties to treat those we trade with fairly, there is a case for granting them more rights. But it is difficult to agree on what our duties to people in the food system are. Everyone would agree that companies should not hold workers as slaves, that they should pay them on time, honour contracts and so on. But beyond that, many would say that they have no additional positive duties of care. If a farmer is willing to sell a crop at a certain price, no one has a duty to offer them more.

A global food philosophy cannot put at its heart any principle that is highly contested. So if it is to appeal to morality, it has to do so at the most general, least controversial level possible. Perhaps the most universally accepted principle of morality is that we should consider the well-being of others as well as ourselves. This seems to be an innate human predisposition rather than a principle we need to be persuaded into endorsing. As Adam Smith wrote in *The Theory of Moral Sentiments* (1759), 'How selfish soever man may be supposed, there are evidently some principles in his nature, which interest him in the fortune of others, and render their happiness necessary to him, though he derives nothing from it except the pleasure of seeing it.' This is the same Adam Smith who wrote of the efficacy of markets. There is no contradiction in asserting the value of both human sympathy and free trade.

The same basic idea was endorsed by Smith's contemporary, the philosopher David Hume. Hume emphasised that only fellow feeling could motivate us to behave morally. We could be persuaded of the cogency of rational arguments and abstract principles, but without an altruistic impulse, we would not act on them.

Smith and Hume provide a naturalistic basis for moral sympathy. Others may see it as a demand of a God-given moral code, or as a kind of natural law. It doesn't matter that we disagree over its foundations, as long as we agree on its importance. In short, to be a moral agent is to care about the well-being of everyone. So if we step back and see that we are all deeply implicated in a food system that is characterised by injustice and gross inequality, we all have reason to do something about it. If we ignore the welfare of people down the supply chain, we are taking them off our moral radar, choosing not to notice suffering and hardship that would make us uncomfortable.

That leaves very big questions about how much can and should be done, and how. We have to think not only of general moral principles, but of the practicalities of trying to engineer a fairer food system. Many argue that there can be unintended consequences of well-intentioned efforts to counter market forces. For example, in the 1990s, the Vietnamese government encouraged coffee cultivation and production boomed, almost all of which was the lower-quality robusta bean, not the more valuable arabica. Vietnam became the second largest producer of coffee in the world after Brazil, and with prices in the mid-1990s fluctuating between $1.50 and $2 per pound for green beans, everyone was happy. But the growth that was initially so welcomed contributed to a global oversupply which sent prices crashing below $1 per pound in 1999 and bottoming at 50 cents in 2001, far below the cost of production.[24] It was a disaster for Vietnamese coffee farmers. Think also of how Sri Lanka's dash for organics caused more harm than good.

So we need to use our heads to work out what to do about inequity, to avoid causing inadvertent harm. Such practical plans require expert knowledge and cannot be prescribed by anything so general as a food philosophy. But there are three broad reasons to believe that it is not only possible to address injustice, it might be easier to do so than it might seem.

First, fair pay does not mean starting to pay everyone industrialised-world wages overnight. It costs less to have a decent quality of life in a low-income country than it does in a high-income one. So the increased costs of fair food need not be enormous. Consider how in the UK, Fairtrade-certified bananas, which pay a premium to growers, sell for almost the same consumer price as non-fair trade equivalents. This is one reason why around one in four bananas sold in the UK are Fairtrade certified.[25] In one major British supermarket today, all its cheapest ground coffees are fair trade. Because the cost of raw ingredients is typically a small fraction of the cost of finished products, the extra costs of fair pay can easily be absorbed. With whole, unprocessed foods, such as berries and tomatoes, the additional costs will be larger, but still manageable.

Second, automation means that we may need less manual labour to produce food anyway. Already machines do a lot of the work that has previously required strenuous human toil. Many of the tasks that remain require more care and attention to detail than machines have been capable of reproducing. But the next generation of robot harvesters and planters may be able to overcome these limitations. For example, picking soft fruit is extremely difficult because it is easily damaged and it is not easy to judge whether it is ripe, but now robots are being developed that are able to do even this.

Some may worry that this will leave people who currently have bad jobs with no jobs at all. It could, however, free them up to do more profitable work. Most of the profit from food is added by processing, far away from the primary producers. For instance, coffee roasters and chocolate makers in developed countries make a greater profit than coffee and cacao growers in low- and middle-income ones. So there is an opportunity for more of the profits from food to stay closer to the producers. The principle of adding value closer to source has already been tried by farmers in many industrialised nations. Dairies that used to sell milk with a tiny profit margin to wholesalers found that if they made cheese, yogurt or butter themselves, they made much more money. The growth of farm shops also reflects this desire to cut out intermediaries. In the future we could see producers in low- and middle-income countries also adding more value themselves, rather than exporting raw materials. We could have more coffee growers roasting beans, more cacao growers actually making chocolate, and so on. Instead of an extractive model, where raw materials are taken from farms and turned into profitable foodstuffs elsewhere, we could have more of a genuinely productive model, in which farmers and farmworkers have to spend less time getting food out of the ground and can devote more energy to turning it into valuable products.

Third, we have encouraging precedents for fair pay raising consumer prices without any disasters. If you are used to the cheap dining-out culture of the USA, it is sobering to find yourself in Scandinavia, realising that you can't afford to go to restaurants as often as you are used to. But this different status quo is, in the round, preferable. Restaurant staff in the USA are typically very low paid and rely on generous tips to eke out a living. The staff in

Scandinavian restaurants, in contrast, are paid a higher minimum wage and receive greater state benefits, such as health care. Tips are not expected because customers know staff don't rely on them and it would be demeaning to suggest that they do, as though they were beggars on the street who needed to be tossed a few coins. Better to dine out less, knowing that your pleasure isn't dependent on others being paid a pittance, than to eat out a lot, dependent on badly paid service staff, like a medieval aristocrat. The same is true of a fairer food system in general. It is better to have a little less choice than to have more options only because producers have hardly any at all.

At a time when food banks have become normalised in many rich nations, to talk of food needing to be more expensive might seem horribly elitist. In the UK, for example, it was calculated that in order to eat in line with health recommendations, the poorest fifth would have to spend 42 per cent of their disposable income on food.[26] That was in 2018, before the recent rise in food prices and 'the cost-of-living crisis'. Food politics expert Marion Nestle thinks that 'the country would go into a major depression if we had to pay the true cost of food'. Tim Lang, professor of food policy, is similarly sceptical: 'No democratically elected government is going to say we're going to raise the price of food, particularly not in a time of a cost-of-living crisis.'

But the solution is to give poorer people enough to eat well, not perpetuate their dependence on cheap (and often nasty) meals. It has become standard to disaggregate poverty, so that we talk of food poverty, energy poverty, period poverty. But these are all manifestations of poverty, full stop. The right goal is for people to have enough money to eat, not for food to be made so cheap that even the destitute can afford to eat it and only the desperate are willing to produce it. As Nestle says, 'solve the poverty problem and you've solved your food problem'.

With all the will in the world, ending exploitation in the food chain is not easy. 'The challenge with global supply chains is the complexity,' says Louise Nicholls. By way of illustration, she tells me about the first time she went to a cocoa farm, finding that it was deep in the jungle, a two-and-a-half-hour drive beyond the end of the last metalled road. 'Then I realised that the nearest school was a walk back to that tarmac road. It wasn't any wonder children didn't go to school. So when I read of big brands saying "we have zero tolerance for child labour and we're insistent every child goes to school" I think that they haven't been to look at cocoa. If they had, they'd know that it wasn't that easy.'

A food world in which everyone involved in production and distribution was paid a fair wage, with good working conditions, would be unprecedented. It would require us to fundamentally change the value we place on food and price it accordingly. It can be done, but it would be a revolution in social and economic practices. Relying on voluntary action alone to achieve this is not enough. Bananas are an exceptional fair-trade success story, but even so, 75 per cent of those sold in the UK are at the lower market prices, which short-changes growers. Even with coffee, which has a healthy and mature fair-trade market, less than 10 per cent of that sold in the UK is Fairtrade certified.[27] Low pay and exploitation both took root in the food trade from the time it first began. It will take some digging to remove them.

7

THE BIG BUSINESS OF FOOD

Soda and cereal in the USA

In August 2023, the *Financial Times* reported on how Modelo Especial had become America's best-selling beer, ending Bud Light's 22-year run as market leader. Less than a decade before, Modelo Especial was a little-known Mexican beer drunk mainly by Latinos in California. So how had sales tripled in such a short time, expanding the customer base to include 50 per cent non-Hispanics?

The *FT* identified several factors, including: the growing appeal of America's Hispanic culture; effective advertising and marketing centred on the beer's 'fighting spirit' slogan; sponsorship of major sporting competitions; a general rise in both the production of Mexican beer and its consumption by Latinos; the improved conditions for export facilitated by the North American Free Trade Agreement (NAFTA); a consumer backlash against competitor Bud Light caused by the brand's controversial collaboration with a transgender TikTok influencer; and a wider trend of 'trading up' to more premium alcoholic drinks. Not once in the article's 1,200 words was there any mention of the beer's flavour.[1]

Ask someone why they buy a certain food or drink and they'll almost certainly say it's because they prefer its taste, texture and so on to other options in the same price range. That is not, however, how the people charged with making money out of mass-produced food think. Of course, they require their products to be tasty, but what makes the difference between a hit and a flop, a market leader and an also-ran, is not primarily flavour. It's the ability of the manufacturer to sell the *idea* of the product.

That idea doesn't even have to have much substance. Much food and drink is sold on the basis of its national or cultural identity: German lager, Italian pasta sauce, Indian curry. But a lot of 'authentic' ethnic and national food has only a passing relationship with its supposed motherland. 'German' beers are brewed in other countries, 'authentic Italian' pasta sauces are made the world over, while many 'Indian' curries are actually dishes created for consumers outside the subcontinent and not eaten there at all.

Modelo Especial's cultural identity is also somewhat impure. It is still exclusively brewed in Mexico, but since 2012 its global owners have been Belgium's Anheuser-Busch InBev, who quickly had to sell the American division to Constellation, a US company, to satisfy antitrust regulators. Even its marketing plays fast and loose with Mexican identity. Two of its advertisements featured Ennio Morricone's music from the film *The Good, the Bad and the Ugly*, directed by an Italian, filmed in Italy and Spain, and with its leading Mexican character played by an American, the son of Polish Jewish immigrants.

The beer market is typical of the food and drink industry. The best-selling products are made by a handful of large, often multinational corporations, competing in a game where quality isn't what makes you a winner. Food lovers lament this, appalled that so many people drink bland, mass-produced lager; rubbery block cheddars; long-life, springy sliced bread; watery bacon from intensively reared pigs. If this were just a matter of taste, it would not be serious. But the concentration and use of corporate power in the food world has more than just gastronomic consequences.

The question of where power lies in any system is always important. In the case of food, many believe that business holds the most cards. In theory, sovereign nations could have the upper hand and call the shots, but in a relatively deregulated global market, governments have a loose grip and allow business to take the lead role in shaping and guiding the food system.

One influential concept used to capture this is the 'corporate food regime'. The sociologists Harriet Friedmann and Philip McMichael first coined the term 'food regime' in 1989.[2] They argued that in the modern era we have seen three successive food regimes – distinct historical periods in which the dominant power in the food world resided in different places. The first was the British imperial regime, from around 1840 to 1914, in which the British Empire established the first 'global provisioning system', importing, exporting and trading to suit its own needs. The second was the period of American dominance after the Second World War, which McMichael and Friedmann saw as another kind of imperialism. By the use of subsidies, tariffs and food aid, the USA used its might as a huge commodity producer to bolster its international power.

In the 1980s, however, we saw the emergence of the first non-state-centred food regime that, as Friedmann and McMichael argued, established an international trade and investment system, with the interests of global business at its centre. This corporate food regime was sealed by the establishment in 1995 of the World Trade Organization (WTO), which sought to reduce trade barriers and facilitate global free trade. (We'll look more closely at the WTO in chapter 8.) McMichael has said that one key feature of the regime is 'the way in which agri-business has established all kinds of privileges and incredible subsidies, to the tune of almost $500 billion a year from governments across the world, to maintain and extend its power'.[3]

Supporters of food regime theory tend to be broadly Marxist in their analysis, seeing it as a manifestation of the grip of capital on the political economy. However, acceptance of its key message does not require buying into a communist world view. The central idea is simply that there is always a dominant power in the food world, that it has changed over the years, and that today business occupies that role. You could accept that and think that the consequences are not all or necessarily bad. However, many argue that corporate power has become too strong and that, as a result, the food system is not meeting our health, environmental or social needs.

No one has done more to raise awareness of these problems than Marion Nestle, professor emerita of Nutrition, Food Studies, and Public Health at New York University. In 2002, her landmark book *Food Politics* opened a nation's eyes to the often unscrupulous means that large food companies have used to sell their products. Especially disturbing are the relentless efforts to sell high-fat, -sugar and -salt (HFSS) food to children. For instance, the very young have been targeted with branded counting books, which invite the kids to count by placing candies, cookies or pieces of sweetened cereal on designated areas of the page. Nestle highlights one book licensed by Oreo cookies which 'requires children to count (and, presumably, eat) their way through ten cookies before reaching 'and now there are none'.[4]

Another initiative Nestle describes was Channel One News, which freely installed TVs in schools on condition that 80 per cent of their classrooms watch its twelve-minute news programme on 90 per cent of school days. Two of these twelve minutes were taken up by commercials, many of which promoted products like Pepsi and

Snickers bars. A thirty-second slot cost around $200,000, showing how much companies valued reaching this impressionable, captive audience. It is puzzling that freedom-loving Americans who were horrified when they heard about children in non-democratic countries being forced to listen to state broadcasts somehow thought it was OK that their kids were forced to watch corporate propaganda. Thanks to Nestle and many outraged parents, many schools turned against Channel One News, and it folded in 2018.

Yet another way in which big companies tried to turn schoolchildren into loyal and regular customers was to buy 'pouring rights', which gave companies exclusive licences to sell their products in school districts. Sometimes this exclusivity meant that children could not bring other brands of drinks into school or even display any competing logos. Many of these contracts incentivised the schools to encourage their students to buy more drinks, as payments were linked to sales. Vending machines also started stocking fewer 12oz cans and bottles and pushing larger 20oz bottles instead. Given that the high levels of consumption of carbonated sugary drinks is a major cause of increased childhood obesity, this kind of promotion was irresponsible, to say the least.

Nestle tells me that she does not think that businesses are 'sitting around a conference table saying how are we going to make Americans and everybody else in the world fat?' They're just trying to sell more product in order to make more money. 'That's what business is about,' she says, and 'making profits is fine'. The problem is that on Wall Street today, 'it's not enough just to make a profit. Their profits have to increase and if they don't, then business looks on them unfavourably and their stockholders are unhappy.' She thinks this growth imperative is relatively new. 'Prior to the 1980s, companies could make a profit and everybody was perfectly happy with them. IBM is the classic example. This was a company that gave long-term, extremely slow returns on investment.'

Nestle says the change can be traced 'practically to the minute' to a speech given in 1981 by Jack Welch, CEO of General Electric. The *Financial Times* concurs that the 'birth of the shareholder value movement' is 'commonly traced' to that speech, titled 'Growing Fast in a Slow-Growth Economy'.[5] The idea of shareholder value is that the primary purpose of business is to increase returns to investors. The focus is on quarterly profits and share price gains, and everything else is subordinate to this goal.

On closer inspection, however, the truth about shareholder value is a little more complicated. The idea that publicly listed companies have a legal obligation to serve their shareholders is not a recent one. It goes back more than a century, to the case of Dodge v. Ford Motor Co., heard in Michigan in 1919. Henry Ford's Model T car was transforming America and the world. But Ford wasn't just a businessman. He wanted his car to be a force for social good, creating jobs and prosperity, and giving ordinary people more freedom and independence. In 1916 he said, 'My ambition is to employ still more men, to spread the benefits of this industrial system to the greatest possible number, to help them build up their lives and their homes. To do this we are putting the greatest share of our profits back in the business.'[6] That, of course, meant less going to shareholders, much to the chagrin of brothers John Francis Dodge and Horace Elgin Dodge, who owned 10 per cent of the company. They took Ford to court, which ruled in their favour, declaring: 'A business corporation is organized and carried on primarily for the profit of the stockholders. The powers of the directors are to be employed for that end. The discretion of directors is to be exercised in the choice of means to attain that end, and does not extend to a change in the end itself, to the reduction of profits, or to the non-distribution of profits among stockholders in order to devote them to other purposes.' This is referred to as the doctrine of 'shareholder primacy'.

Ever since, this idea has dominated thinking in business and economics. One of its most famous reiterations was made by the Nobel Prize-winning economist Milton Friedman, who wrote in 1976 that 'there is one and only one social responsibility of business – to use its resources and engage in activities designed to increase its profits'.[7] Friedman was a major influence on Ronald Reagan and Margaret Thatcher's Wall Street and City of London–friendly policies.

However, the 1919 affirmation of shareholder primacy did not mean that American businesses could think of nothing but paying the largest dividends possible. First of all, nothing in the ruling said that *short-term* profit maximisation must be the aim. Indeed, the best interests of shareholders are more sensibly interpreted as requiring long-term stability and sustainability. Second, the ruling left the means of achieving this goal to the discretion of directors. As long as they plausibly believe that things like not being a polluter and treating staff well serve the business in the long term, no court can make them do otherwise.

Ever since Dodge v. Ford, people have continued to dispute what is or is not compatible with the principle of shareholder primacy, but it has never been a crude short-term injunction to return as much money to shareholders as possible or always pursue growth. Even after the idea of shareholder value took hold in the 1980s, far from everyone thought it entailed an obsessive focus on share price and dividends. In 2009, Welch himself called this 'the dumbest idea in the world'. He said that 'shareholder value is a result, not a strategy ... your main constituencies are your employees, your customers and your products. Managers and investors should not set share price increases as their overarching goal ... Short-term profits should be allied with an increase in the long-term value of a company.'[8] If some large food businesses have put ever-increasing profits above all else, that is not because shareholder capitalism forces them to.

Nestlé thinks there is another reason, aside from profit, behind the food business's relentless push to get us to eat more: there's a lot of food to sell. In 2018, the US food system provided 3,782 calories per person per day. In the UK, that figure was 3,344.[9] This level of food supply is remarkable given that, historically, major famines have been regular occurrences. The Roman Empire suffered twenty-five, Britain had been through ninety-five before 1500, and in the first eight centuries of the second millennium, France averaged one every six years.[10] As Tim Lang says, our global food system 'has delivered unprecedented quantity and choice of food to millions of people'.[11] However, Nestle believes that this oversupply means that to grow sales, companies have to get people to buy more food than they should be eating. As she writes, 'many of the nutritional problems of Americans – not least of them obesity – can be traced to the food industry's imperative to encourage people to eat more in order to generate sales and increase income in a highly competitive marketplace'.[12]

This unholy combination of excess supply and the profit motive isn't quite as deterministic of bad corporate behaviour as this brief summary suggests. Companies are motivated to grow profit, not waistlines. Indeed, some of their most profitable lines are low-calorie products, such as ready meals, snacks and drinks. Others are premium ranges that often provide many fewer calories per dollar than cheaper ones. 'Selling more' in business terms means increasing the quantity of income earned, not the quantity of food produced. So even though there is a pressure on shareholder-owned companies to grow profits, their main tool for doing that is to increase market share and profit margins rather than the total quantity customers buy. Oversupply can help manufacturers achieve these goals. It is basic economics that when supply of an input exceeds demand, prices go down. Oversupply allows food businesses to reduce their costs and so increase their profits.

The combination of the profit motive and an oversupply of food does not seem to be sufficient to explain why bad practice in the food industry is so widespread. It is certainly true that a food business with access to endless cheap raw ingredients, determined to grow sales at all costs, is going to try to get people to eat as much of its food as possible, and damn the health consequences. But not all businesses are the same, and although they all have to make money, many care about other things too. Take Unilever, the British consumer goods company that has historically owned many famous food brands, including Ben & Jerry's, Hellmann's, Knorr, Magnum, Marmite and Wall's (Heartbrand). The company traces its roots to Lever Brothers, founded in 1884 as a soap manufacturer. Like several other Victorian companies, it had a strong interest in employee welfare, building the model village of Port Sunlight in Merseyside in north-west England to house its staff. (Also, like many of its contemporaries, it was not so benevolent in its operations in the colonies. Its subsidiary Huileries du Congo Belge used forced labour in the Belgian Congo from 1911 to 1945.)

The importance of social responsibility has ebbed and flowed throughout Unilever's history but has always been part of its identity. So it was in keeping with tradition that soon after becoming CEO in 2009, Paul Polman launched a 'Sustainable Living Plan' for the company. Under Polman, *The Economist* said, 'Unilever has again become the exemplar of the "good company", the poster child of sustainability . . . generally reckoned to have the most comprehensive strategy of enlightened capitalism of any global firm.'[13]

There are also an increasing number of businesses that use independently accredited schemes to validate their green and ethical credentials. One of the most important such certifications is the B Corporation, or B Corp for short. B Lab is a privately owned business that grants B-Corp status to any company that meets its standards for impact on its workers, the community, the environment and its customers, as well as for governance structure and accountability.

However, the fact that many food companies care about more

than profit arguably misses the more important point that people like Nestle are making. Irrespective of motives, the structure of our economies and the ways in which businesses are regulated create conditions in which it is almost impossible for the food industry to put ethics first. A comparison could be made with the idea of institutional racism, defined in the Macpherson report into the investigation of the murder of the black teenager Stephen Lawrence in 1993 as 'The collective failure of an organisation to provide an appropriate and professional service to people because of their colour, culture, or ethnic origin.'[14] The critical feature of institutional racism is that it does not presuppose racist individuals, goals or motives. An organisation could operate in ways that are institutionally racist without any of its employees themselves being racist.

In a similar way, large food corporations could be said to suffer from institutional rapacity. That is to say, even though the motivations and characters of the owners and employees may be morally blameless, as a corporate entity, the companies behave in ways that are morally objectionable. The need to make a profit, even if it is not the only goal, can end up pushing companies to compromise on their values.

Take, for example, Unilever's Sustainable Living Plan, which, according to *The Economist*, aimed 'not only to reduce Unilever's environmental footprint and increase its "positive social impact", but also to double sales and increase long-term profitability.' But by 2019, many shareholders had become impatient with the company's focus on social purpose, and the architect of the plan, Paul Polman, was replaced as CEO by Alan Jope, described as 'less preachy than his predecessor, more pragmatic and, possibly, more profit-oriented'.[15] Jope toned down the social mission and prioritised health and hygiene brands over the sluggishly performing food ones.[16] Still, when he said of one of Unilever's brands, 'Fighting against food waste – that is the purpose of Hellmann's,' many investors rolled their eyes. One major shareholder, fund manager Terry Smith, famously said that a firm 'which feels it has to define the purpose of Hellmann's mayonnaise has ... clearly lost the plot'. In a letter to investors he wrote, 'Unilever seems to be labouring under the weight of a management which is obsessed with publicly displaying sustainability credentials at the expense of focusing on the fundamentals of the business.'[17] *The Economist* lamented that Unilever 'has cast itself as a sustainability icon, but its shareholder returns have lagged far behind those of its rival, Nestlé'.[18]

It is not just Unilever's social mission that has creaked under pressure to deliver profits. In 2021, the CEO of French food giant Danone, Emmanuel Faber, was forced to step down by activist shareholders who complained that under his leadership the company 'did not manage to strike the right balance between shareholder value creation and sustainability'. As Arturo Bris, professor of finance at the International Institute for Management Development, put it, 'Danone is perceived to have cared more about people, the planet and social responsibility than its shareholders, and Faber is paying the price.'[19]

Even companies with a social purpose at their heart find it difficult to uphold their values completely. Henry Dimbleby's experience as co-founder of the Leon fast-food chain bears this out. Leon aspired to be as tasty and affordable as the mainstream alternatives while serving food that was both healthy and responsibly sourced. 'It made me realise that there was a junk food cycle,' Dimbleby told me. 'We were trying to do food that tasted good and did you good. But in some areas we ended up doing slightly better versions of junk food. So we did baked fries, not a nutritious foodstuff, but slightly better than fried fries. Our vegan burgers were not ultra-processed but they were in a soft white bun. We found it impossible to make money doing just the stuff that did you good. That was what gave me the insight that these aren't wicked people.

These are people who are bonused to make a buck and they go where it's easier to make a buck.'

Nestle has seen how commercial pressures erode values. 'Everybody that I've known who has gone to work for a food company thinking that they can have high motivations and strong ethics has run into trouble, because if the company is not making a profit, it can't stay in business.' She accepts that 'every company wants to have social responsibility as part of its portfolio', but based on people she knows, she thinks that 'the social responsibility officers are the unhappiest people. They know that if they want to do anything they're fighting their entire corporation because it's going to cost money.'

Intelligent, thoughtful people are always reluctant to divide the world into villains and heroes, but sometimes fingers need to be pointed and bad practice needs calling out. It is telling that Tara Garnett, an academic expert in food-systems analysis who makes a constant effort to see food-system issues and arguments from different angles, agreed when I asked her if big food businesses deserved a kicking, albeit with the caveat that retailers belong in a slightly different category and the firmest boot should be reserved for the big manufacturers and agritech companies. She pointed to the example of Nestlé, which has the corporate strapline 'Good food, good life' and whose self-stated purpose is 'to unlock the power of food to enhance quality of life for everyone, today and for generations to come'.[20] Yet in 2023 it was still launching egregiously unhealthy products, such as a KitKat breakfast cereal, which may be 31.4 per cent whole-grain wheat and 'a source of five vitamins, calcium and iron', but is also nearly 25 per cent sugar. 'How can you claim to be doing anything and then put this out?' asked Garnett.

Plenty of people within the big companies know that their actions do not match their professed values. An internal presentation at Nestlé in 2021 admitted that 60 per cent of its lines did not meet 'a recognised definition of health' and that 'some of our categories and products will never be "healthy" no matter how much we renovate'.[21] Still, many reject the charge that it is simply impossible to pursue socially responsible goals in a corporate setting. One is Louise Nicholls, who went on to become managing director of Human Rights and Sustainability at the consultancy Suseco.org after leading the corporate human rights programme at M&S for many years. Her general assessment of the challenges facing the food industry sounds indistinguishable from any number of statements made by NGOs critical of business: 'We're living beyond the planet's boundaries. We need to really think about how we use natural resources in a way that we replenish them. We need to really think about how we decarbonise food systems so that we are not contributing to climate change, and we need to do so in a way that has a positive impact on nature, people and society.' She also accepts that although there is much more happening around sustainability labelling, 'there is masses of greenwash going on that makes it very hard for the consumer to make informed choices'.

Not surprisingly, Nicholls believes that 'retailers, farmers and food producers have to be part of the solution' even though historically 'we've also been part of the problem'. Business has to take a lead because 'if we're waiting for the consumer to want something different, we will always be waiting'. Retailers in particular can be change-makers. 'What I think is exciting for brands and retailers is that they've been good at introducing consumers to new things.'

There is a certain irony that Nicholls is saying that one of the very things big business is criticised for – shaping consumer demand – is what could help them to drive positive change. Similarly, retailers and manufacturers have been accused of exerting too much pressure on farmers. But they could choose to use this power for good, getting their suppliers to adopt more regenerative and higher animal welfare practices. M&S already does a lot of this. Its power to demand whatever standards it likes means that it is the only UK retailer to have 100 per cent of its fresh chicken meet Compassion in World Farming's Better Chicken Commitment standards.[22] All its UK growers have the LEAF (Linking Environment And Farming) Marque, an environmental assurance system recognising more sustainably farmed products. And all its milk is produced to RSPCA standards for animal welfare, which the company claims are the highest in the dairy industry. (Compassion in World Farming disagrees, ranking Pasture for Life, Organic, and Pasture Promise higher.)

Tim Lang agrees that, overall, 'retailers mostly have the power because they mediate between many, many primary producers, distributors, processors and hundreds of millions of mouths'. But he is less optimistic about their capacity to drive positive change. 'They're a baronial class, but they are on treadmills, looking over their shoulders neurotically all the time. They are ruthless but twitching!'

One obstacle to big business grasping the ethical mantle is the comforting idea that 'good ethics is good business', and so doing the right thing morally leads to higher profits. This slogan has become the rallying cry of people promoting corporate social responsibility, and many have been persuaded. Environmental, social and governance (ESG) investing has enjoyed a purple patch, with many putting their money into companies with ethical credentials in the belief they offer better returns. But although it may indeed be possible to be highly profitable and ethical – especially if being ethical is part of your brand appeal – the idea that there is never a choice between ethics and profit is wishful thinking, as Unilever and Danone have shown all too clearly. Doing the right thing in business, as in life, sometimes comes at a material cost. In our personal lives, this can be compensated for by a warm glow and a clear conscience. In business, such intangibles don't count so easily.

Some good businesses are prepared to make that trade-off.

Take Boston Tea Party, a small chain of cafés in the southwest of England. In 2018 they decided they would not sell takeaway coffee in single-use cups because of their environmental impact. Customers had to bring their own, or hire or buy a reusable cup. In five years, they saved almost one million cups going to waste. But the change led to sales going down by 25 per cent, and in less than a year, the company estimated it had lost £250,000 in revenue.[23] 'The step-change in behaviour we dreamt of inspiring just hasn't happened,' lamented CEO Sam Roberts in 2023. As a privately owned company, it could take the view that good ethics is good business, because it accepted that a good business is not simply one that makes a profit.[24]

Not surprisingly, given its patent falseness, the 'good ethics is good business' mantra seems to be losing its shine with investors. At the time of writing, the business media is full of scepticism about the merits of ESG investment.[25] In a leader, *The Economist* declared: 'The fundamental contradiction of ESG is being laid bare.'[26] Because 'it is the mission of companies to generate long-term value for their investors . . . it will often be more profitable for a business to dump costs, such as pollution, on to society than to bear them directly.' Similarly, when junk food contributes to poor health, the bill is passed on to health-care providers, not paid by the manufacturers. When food production contributes to global warming, future generations pick up the tab.

The Economist is not arguing against the idea that companies should operate in socially responsible ways. Its argument is that it cannot and should not be left to them to do so voluntarily. 'It falls to governments to reconcile the goals of profit maximisation and a safer climate.' In short, good business requires good regulation, not just the good will of businesspeople. The simplest way to do this is to make business pay for the costs it imposes on society. If you produce something that harms the health of people, animals or the planet, the cost of that damage must be covered by the producer.

Only that provides a robust business incentive for companies to make the right choices.

If this argument is right, then voluntary third-party certification is no long-term solution to the problems of bad business practice. The limits of certification are already all too evident. They are supposed to place onerous responsibilities on companies, but few if any will take on, or retain, the burdens of certification if their profits suffer. Indeed, the decision to certify or not is often itself a commercial one. Many products that carry the logos of Fairtrade, the Rainforest Alliance, the Marine Stewardship Council and so on are premium ones which consumers are willing to pay a little extra for. This can actually allow companies to make more profit. Back in 2005 economist Tim Harford dug into Costa Coffee's option for customers to have Fairtrade beans for an extra 10p. The additional cost of the beans to the company was just a penny or two. In other words, the ethical upgrade made them more money, not less.[27]

Companies happily sign up for certification when they calculate it will not cost them profits, but rarely when it will. McDonalds long ago switched to organic milk and free-range eggs in its British operations, but it didn't move over to free-range poultry because it calculated that doing so would make the costs of its chicken products higher than its customers would tolerate.[28] For several years, both Nestlé and Cadbury certified some of their leading lines – KitKat and Dairy Milk, respectively – as Fairtrade. But as we have seen, Mondelez found that third-party certification no longer suited them and they made Dairy Milk under their own in-house fair trade scheme, Cocoa Life, instead. KitKat's owners also switched to their own Nestlé Cocoa Plan, with only the cocoa content of the bar (less than 20 per cent), not the sugar, certified by the Rainforest Alliance.

Even when companies commit to third-party certifications that raise ethical standards, many argue that they do not go nearly far enough. Take B-Corp status. Companies that can boast of it include Nestlé Health Sciences US, Nespresso Global, Brewdog, Maker's Mark distillery, Hello Fresh, Graze, Volvic, Innocent Drinks and many international divisions of Danone. For critics, a club this inclusive just can't be demanding enough of its members. An eighteen-month study into its processes concluded that the 'assessment only weakly captures human rights impact', and 'does not contain meaningful measures of human rights harms that Business and Human Rights (BHR) advocates would expect to see, such as information on land grabbing or violence by police or private security companies in connection with the company's operations'. The report argued that 'a company can reach the required minimum score without, for example, ensuring a core labor right like freedom of association and collective bargaining, or without conducting a human rights impact assessment'.[29]

Reaction to Nespresso's certification caused an especially loud howl of outrage. Critics pointed to decades of accusations of human and labour rights violations by the parent company, Nestlé, as well as to issues with Nespresso's coffee supply chains. They also pointed out that the Nespresso system, which makes coffee from single-use individual pods, by definition falls short of environmental best practice.[30]

Nicholls thinks that certification is 'a tool in the toolbox', but that schemes are mis-sold as showing everything will be perfect when that isn't the case. 'If you buy something that's certified you need to read the small print. In many cases, it is certifying that the product comes from X source and that it has had an audit that met a certain standard. Let's say the audit happens on the first of February. What it is not saying is that there'll be no issues that happen in that farm after the first of February. What it says is that on the first of February there were management systems in place which should have prevented X or Y happening.'

These critiques of ESG and certification offer qualified support for Marion Nestle's analysis of the food industry. They demonstrate that not all businesses are the same, that many people in business want to do the right thing, and that some of them manage to work to higher social and environmental standards. But commercial pressures are such that business can only go so far before, as Nestle says, push comes to shove.

Debates about food have always featured demons. Sometimes these are nutrients, like saturated fat, sugar or other refined carbohydrates. Sometimes they are foods: red meat, junk food, sodas. Sometimes they are actors in the food system: big agritech companies, supermarkets, large international manufacturers. It is tempting to put all the blame on big, bad business, with greed built into its DNA. But Marion Nestle is not fundamentally anti-business. She even acknowledges that in the USA 'the industry has created a plentiful, varied, readily available, relatively safe, and relatively inexpensive food supply that is the envy of people throughout the world'.[31] She is not against industry making profits, and nor does she go along with more radical critics who think the only solution is the dismantling of the whole capitalist system, telling me, 'We aren't there yet. I wish I knew what a meaningful alternative might look like.' She thinks that 'the food industry has to be part of the solution for now, but only if it's regulated appropriately. Let's put some regulatory controls on it. Let's not let them have unfettered access to children, to pick just one example. They're not going to lose money. They're just not going to be gaining in the inappropriate way that they have been.'

Nestle argues there is 'nothing particularly radical' in her calls for more regulation. Many in the food industry tell her that 'if there were regulations that applied across the board to all food companies, they would be able to work within those guidelines in a much more ethical way and they would be able to sleep at night'. Better regulation would ensure that those who care less about their social and environmental impact cannot gain an unfair competitive advantage.

Henry Dimbleby agrees. 'Behind the scenes,' he wrote, 'several company bosses have told me they would like government legislation designed to reduce junk food sales. They know the food they are selling is terrible for their customers, and they want to do the right thing. But they need a level playing field. They can't act alone. They can't even be honest – at least in public – about what they know.'[32] They want to sell fewer unhealthy products, but, he tells me, 'when they try to act they realise that they put themselves at competitive disadvantage'. So, 'fundamentally this is a transition that is going to be led by regulation'.

Louise Nicholls also advocates many regulatory interventions, saying that 'through a mixture of regulation, taxation and better labelling, we can drive the kind of changes that we're looking for'. She too thinks businesses want this and has seen many engaged in 'advocacy work to improve national legislation and international legislation, to get a consistency of standards'. Companies can't enforce high standards on their own, even when they want to. She points to headlines about slavery in the Thai fishing industry. 'That's seven tiers down a big retailer's supply chain.' The solution is 'not just effective regulation but effective enforcement'.

There is a certain irony that some of the very people who praise private enterprise for its efficiency and ability to innovate talk as though it would not be able to adapt to even the slightest regulatory change. And if cynics are right that business cares only for profit, the only practical solution is to put in place regulation to ensure that trading ethically is the surest way to be profitable. As Roberta Sonnino, a professor of sustainable food systems, puts it, 'The private sector goes where the market goes. They could rebrand themselves overnight if that was going to make them more successful.' Sonnino gives me a striking example of how business is more than capable of dancing to a more ethical tune. 'The most sustainable school food system I've ever seen was the one of the city of Rome up until 2008. It took them twelve years of work to get to where they arrived. I was informally advising them during the time for the last call for tenders. I remember we introduced criteria such as guaranteed freshness for the food. You know who got the contract? Sodexo.' Sodexo is Europe's second largest food services and facilities management company, the kind of large-scale operator that generally uses the cheapest ingredients with minimal concern for provenance. Yet, given the conditions for the tender, they just adapted their offering. 'This gives me hope,' says Sonnino.

But regulating well isn't always easy, with the laws of unintended consequences difficult to read. For example, sugar taxes that raise the cost of sodas have been credited with reducing consumption and encouraging reformulation to give drinks a lower sugar content. However, this has also led to an increase in the use of artificial sweeteners, about which there are increasing concerns. In 2023, the WHO issued new guidelines 'against the use of NSS [non-sugar sweeteners] to control body weight or reduce the risk of noncommunicable diseases (NCDs)'. This followed a systematic review of the evidence suggesting that sweeteners had no long-term effects on body fat loss in adults or children and that 'there may be potential undesirable effects from long-term use of NSS, such as an increased risk of type 2 diabetes, cardiovascular diseases, and mortality in adults'.[33]

Another set of regulatory interventions with questionable results concerned France's attempt to protect small local shops against the power of large supermarkets. As early as 1973 it put in restrictive planning regulations through the *Loi Royer*, measures strengthened in 1996 by the *Loi Raffarin*. In the same year, the *Loi Galland* was passed to prevent supermarkets attracting business through 'loss leaders' – foods sold at below cost price. However, the impact of these laws has been minimal at best, harmful at worst. There is evidence that they have raised prices and decreased employment, and there is no good evidence that they slowed the rate of closure of small independent stores, which was the primary intention. Many small shops have stayed open but have been bought by the chains or have become franchises of them.[34] Although these laws were intended to shield the country from the growth of big retailers, in 2021 France's Carrefour was the leading supermarket by sales in Europe.[35]

These examples show that framing legislation to be effective is more difficult than it might seem. Banning this or limiting that often looks like a quick fix, but the food world is highly complex and unintended consequences are always a danger. Regulation is needed, but it must be smart.

Many dislike the idea of more regulation, complaining of the 'nanny state' and the deprivation of liberty. However, we already have innumerable regulations governing the food industry and a lot of state interventions in the form of subsidies. Established rules tend to become invisible over time and taken for granted, whereas any new proposed rule stands out. It is conceivable that a more rational system of laws and regulations could be put in place that did not increase the total number of regulations at all. 'We're not changing the system,' says Nestle. 'We're tweaking it. The entire agricultural subsidy system and everything else dealing with agriculture in the United States needs to be reconfigured so it promotes public health rather than corporate health. That doesn't throw out regulations, it tweaks and redefines their purpose.' The question is not whether to regulate, but how, and for what purpose.

8

WHO GOVERNS?

School dinners in Finland

In 1773, tea ignited a revolution. A total of 342 chests of it, worth $18,000, were dumped into Boston harbour. It was a protest against taxes on teas imposed on the American colonies from London, violating the widely held principle of 'no taxation without representation'. The furious British parliament responded by passing the Coercive Acts, which established British military rule in Massachusetts, compelled the colonised locals to house British troops, and made British officials in America immune from criminal prosecution. This further fuelled the colonists' grievances and in 1775 a full-blown revolutionary war of independence broke out.

On 12 March 1930, Mahatma Gandhi and his supporters began a twenty-four-day march in protest against the British colonial ruler's salt monopoly. Gandhi and many others saw the control of such an essential ingredient as an act of oppression, blaming the increasing incidence of leprosy in India on reduced intake. On reaching the coast at Dandi, Gandhi said his morning prayers, took some muddy salty water from the sea and said, 'With this, I am shaking the foundations of the British Empire.' He boiled the water to produce salt, illegally breaking the monopoly and encouraging his supporters to do likewise. Many view this as the start of the liberation movement that would see India finally achieve independence in 1947.

In 1987, Russia, which, before the First World War, had been the world's biggest grain exporter, became its biggest importer. 'We cannot survive without it,' the General Secretary of the Communist Party of the Soviet Union, Mikhail Gorbachev, told the party's Central Committee Plenum. The grain had to be bought with hard currency, but the country had very little. Its industry, like its agriculture, was in a dreadful state, the result of decades of poor central state planning. By the end of 1991, the Soviet Union had collapsed, its economy a wreck. Yegor Gaidar, acting prime minister of Russia for six months in 1992, later said, 'The story of the collapse of the Soviet Union could be told as a story about grain and oil.'[1]

History turns on wars, revolutions, and the rise and fall of regimes. The fundamental causes of these seismic events are often the slowly moving tectonic plates of food supply. Although natural events like drought play their part, more often than not the fundamental source of the breakdown is policy. This is even true when the catalyst is famine, as the Nobel prize-winning economist and philosopher Amartya Sen has demonstrated. Most famously, his landmark study of the 1943 Bengal famine, which he experienced as a nine-year-old boy, showed that there was no significant drop in food production. Rather, the British rulers had co-opted the food system to help their preparations for a feared Japanese invasion. They stockpiled food for troops and exported more to their armies in the Middle East. They also confiscated the boats, carts and elephants of fishermen and traders in Chittagong, depriving them of their livelihoods. Three million died, not because of food shortages, but due to an 'entitlement failure' born of policy.

Similarly, the blight that ruined the potato crop was not the whole reason for Ireland's great famine of 1845–1852, which killed nearly one fifth of the population. During this time, grain continued to be *exported* from Ireland. Although there were severe shortages, at times there would have been enough to feed everyone, had the grain been distributed more equally. The effects of the famine were also made worse in its later years, as landlords were allowed to evict tenant farmers who had become too poor to pay their rent.

Today, failures of policy to provide sufficient, affordable and nutritious food continue to be vital and often under-appreciated drivers of social and political unrest. A study by *The Economist* concluded that 'rises in food and fuel prices were a strong portent of political instability, even when controlling for demography and changes in GDP'.[2] With the cost of living becoming a chronic problem, food costs risk becoming tinderboxes that could set societies ablaze. 'I don't see riots breaking out in the street tomorrow,' Tim Lang tells me. 'But there are many, many of my colleagues who think it's not impossible, if and when food troubles worsen.[3] And I agree.'

Food systems have been shaped by laws, regulations and policies ever since the first nations emerged to rule over their subjects. Leaders have demanded a proportion of their subjects' harvest, herd or flock and have imposed taxes on food leaving or entering their territories. In medieval times many countries had feudal systems in which peasants worked on land they did not own and had to pay taxes to their lords, usually in the form of a share of the produce. Nations have also demanded a cut of the food production in conquered territories as tribute. Such practices were common in ancient Egypt, Rome and Greece, as well as in the Ottoman and colonial empires.

Ruling powers used food to generate income to support their armies and often their own lavish lifestyles, and to guarantee food security to prevent revolt. The biblical story of Joseph shows the pharaoh gathering grain during seven good years in order to have reserves to distribute in the seven years of famine. This is not history, but it reflects common practices of state collection and distribution. The Roman Empire became very dependent on its conquered North African territories to feed the citizens of Rome and its dispersed armies.

Food policy may sound dry, but at the international, the national and the regional levels it has changed the course of history, and how the food world is governed will determine its future.

At the transnational level, for millennia there was no food governance. Who took what from whom was determined primarily by who wielded the most power. A significant change to the global order was heralded in 1648 with the signing of the Treaty of Westphalia, ending the Thirty Years' War in central Europe. Many historians believe that this was the first treaty to implicitly endorse the principle that states have sovereignty over their own lands and territories that other states are required to respect. A direct line can be traced from 1648 to the 1945 signing of the United Nations Charter, which states that the organisation is 'based on the principle of the sovereign equality of all its Members' and that the relationship between those members 'shall be based on respect for the principle of sovereign equality'.[4] The modern system of nation states is known as the Westphalian order, as the treaty marks the first stages of the formation of sovereign nation states as we know them today.

The Treaty of Westphalia was significant for food governance in that it marked the beginning of the end of the hitherto universal law that might is right in international relations. Trade, which had for time immemorial mainly been about the stronger taking from the weaker, was moving to an era where treaties and agreements, not force, were supposed to have the last say. Of course, in practice, might continued to be right in many, if not most, cases. In particular, European powers considered the Americas, Africa and most of Asia to be *terra nullius*, no man's land, to be claimed by the first monarch to have their flag planted there. In the post-colonial era, richer nations still tended to dictate the terms of trade to suit themselves, even when they were patently unfair.

In the twentieth century, after two disastrous world wars, a renewed effort was made to build a rules-based global order with the United Nations at its centre. The UN has several branches which, to a greater or lesser extent, concern food, notably the Food and Agriculture Organization (FAO), the International Fund for Agricultural Development (IFAD) and the World Health Organization (WHO). Although each commands a certain amount of moral authority, none has strong powers. Members may sign up to principles and aspirations, but these do not bind. Like all UN bodies, their resources do not compete with those of its largest member nations. The size of the annual budget of the FAO in 2022 was almost exactly half the $6.5 billion spent by the US government's Food and Drug Administration (FDA). The UN has a history of fine words and little action, for which it cannot be blamed, given that it is shackled by its member states and the Security Council. Given the UN's toothlessness, it is not surprising that Article 25 of its Universal Declaration of Human Rights – 'Everyone has the right to a standard of living adequate for the health and well-being of himself and of his family, including food, clothing, housing and medical care and necessary social services' – remains little more than an aspiration.

A far more important body for world food governance is the World Trade Organization (WTO), which in 1995 took over the responsibilities of the General Agreement on Tariffs and Trade (GATT). The first GATT was signed on 30 October 1947 in Geneva by twenty-three nations, comprising several members of the British Empire, the USA, and a seemingly random assortment of other nations, including Belgium, Czechoslovakia, Norway, Syria and Cuba. The basic premise of GATT was that trade was to the benefit of all and 'should be conducted with a view to raising standards of living, [...] developing the full use of the resources of the world and expanding the production and exchange of goods'. The primary means of achieving this would be 'the substantial reduction of tariffs and other barriers to trade and to the elimination of discriminatory treatment in international commerce'.[5]

However, in the GATT era, food was largely exempted from liberalisation through a number of vague clauses in the treaty so open to interpretation that governments could effectively decide what they would or would not allow in and out of their countries.[6] One key exception to this power of discretion was the prohibition on subsidies for 'non-primary agricultural exports', meaning any foodstuff that had been more than minimally treated or processed. This ban was designed mainly to help low- and middle-income nations by stopping 'export dumping', whereby rich nations offloaded their excess production at fire-sale rates or as aid, often undercutting local producers and threatening the viability of their farms.[7] However, because primary products were excluded from this ban, much export dumping persisted.[8]

With the forming of the WTO in 1995, food was given explicit recognition with a specific Agreement on Agriculture which restricted 'trade-distorting' domestic subsidies. It also required decreases in import tariffs – greater in developed countries, less in low- and middle-income ones, with least-developed nations exempt. Developed countries also had to reduce export subsidies on primary agricultural products. Countries were explicitly allowed to restrict trade in food for 'a range of public policy objectives, such as protecting human health and safety or protecting the environment, providing consumer information and ensuring product quality'.[9] At the time of writing, the WTO has 164 members, with most non-members being war-torn or failed states.

Critics of the WTO charge that its rules trump state sovereignty and trample over member nations' legitimate concerns and interests. Consider a case initially brought by the USA, and supported by Canada and Argentina, against the EU's de facto moratorium on genetically modified (GM) products in 1998. The USA claimed that this was an unfair restriction on trade as it breached articles of four key agreements. It took the WTO three years to rule that the EU had broken the rules, by which time the moratorium had ended.

Anti-GM groups saw the verdict as a defeat for Europe and national sovereignty. Sue Mayer of the NGO GeneWatch UK said the ruling 'will be used by the US government to pressure countries around the world to further liberalise trade rules'. Clare Oxborrow of Friends of the Earth called it 'a desperate attempt to force these products on an unwilling market'.[10] Eric Gall of Greenpeace said, 'All this verdict proves is that the WTO is unqualified to deal with complex scientific and environmental issues, as it puts trade interests above all others.'

However, the verdict did not amount to saying the EU was not entitled to place its moratorium. It merely judged that it had not followed the correct procedures. As Adrian Bebb of Friends of the Earth Europe said, 'Countries still have the right to ban or suspend genetically modified foods and crops. Europe's only failure was the way they did it and not why they did it.'[11]

The case illustrates how, when it comes to international food governance, the WTO is very important but not all-powerful. It is committed to free trade but it is no wrecking ball capable of smashing trade barriers down at will. The international status quo today is one in which there is an ongoing tension between, on one side, pressure to liberalise and have open borders, and on the other, nation states' desire to protect their own interests and uphold their own standards. In this tussle, no party is all-powerful.

A second criticism of the WTO is that abolishing barriers to trade favours richer nations by forcing low- and middle-income countries to accept cheap imports, regardless of the effect on their own producers, public health or the environment. For example, most rich, developed countries still make large support payments to their farmers. These are not technically export subsidies, but they do keep prices low and so help generate surpluses for export, creating unfair competition for smaller farmers in less-developed nations.

However, WTO rules also include provisions for 'Special and Differential Treatment' that grant additional rights to low- and middle-income countries, and we have already seen how some of its rules treat their needs differently. It has also come out against wealthier nations. For example, in 2002 it ruled against the EU, which had insisted that only fish of the species *Sardina pilchardus*, found in the north-eastern Atlantic, could be marketed as preserved sardines. This was naked protectionism, since Portugal dominated the European canned-sardine market and it did not want competition from Peru, from whose eastern Pacific waters *Sardinops sagax* was caught. From a zoological point of view, there is no question that *Sardina pilchardus Walbaum* and *Sardinops sagax* are both genera of the species sardine. Following the WTO ruling, the EU had to back down.

A 2008 study also concluded that 'the rate of success in WTO Dispute Settlement cases – if measured by the share of claims "won" – is broadly similar across industrialised and developing [low- and middle-income] countries'.[12] The members of dispute panels are usually agreed by both sides, and in the less than 10 per cent of cases where they cannot agree, the WTO director-general selects the panelists. Since the turn of the millennium, that director-general has come from New Zealand, Thailand, France, Brazil and Nigeria.

Perhaps the strongest evidence that the WTO is not a servant of the world's rich is that Donald Trump loathes it. When he was the 45th president of the USA he repeatedly threatened to leave the organisation, saying, 'We know they have been screwing us for years.'[13] The fact that virtually every country is, or wants to be, a member of the WTO also suggests that it is too simplistic to portray low- and middle-income nations as the victims of the trade system it upholds. Communist China joined in 2001, Saudi Arabia in 2005, Russia in 2012 and Afghanistan in 2016. It is simply too powerful for countries not to want to join, and if the WTO ever was a western, industrialised, capitalist club, it has for some time been an inclusive global one.

Cynics may counter that countries judge it better to be bullied within the WTO than beaten up outside it. However, there is plenty of evidence that WTO membership confers benefits, especially to poorer countries. A report commissioned by the UK government's Department for International Trade concluded that 'almost all countries experienced a steady increase in trade following membership' and that 'many of the largest positive impacts were observed in low and middle income countries'. The 21 per cent that did not see a decrease in trade costs were mainly former communist or very small countries. Agriculture was the sector which showed the highest positive export changes due to a WTO membership. The overall conclusion was that 'the WTO has been effective in promoting international trade among its members, leading to significant (but heterogeneous) gains in terms of trade and welfare'.[14]

Even if it is accepted that the WTO is good for the food economies of member nations, it may also be true that it could be a lot better if the interests of wealthier nations and large corporations were not so well protected. To say that the WTO is not the imperialist hegemon it is often portrayed as being is not to say it is the best friend of the world's poor. As the most important body in the global governance of food, the WTO is neither hero nor villain.

*

In an increasingly globalised world, it might seem that food governance is now mainly a transnational matter, with national governments having less power to control their own food systems. In fact, globalisation is a double-edged sword for state sovereignty. When nation states were more autonomous, they had more power to regulate within their borders but less influence over what happened outside them. But having more domestic control does not mean having more control over the food system as a whole, since exports and imports are such an important part of it.

Despite globalisation, nations still matter. As Tim Lang argues, among the state's key purposes are protecting public health and ensuring a minimum, adequate food supply. Furthermore, 'only the state can impose power on unfettered runaway food barons and facilitate a notion of the common purpose and public interest for the food system'. National government policies can make a great difference to how food systems operate. Consider the various indices that show how well countries perform in terms of food security and sustainability. Such rankings show large differences between countries in very similar economic, political and geographic conditions. Two of the most respected such indices are the Global Food Security Index (GFSI) and the Food Sustainability Index (FSI), both complied by Economist Impact, part of the Economist Group, publishers of the eponymous weekly newspaper.[15] The general pattern of the results correlates with economic development. The highest-ranking countries are all wealthy and industrialised, while the worst include many sub-Saharan countries and worn-torn and failed states. The best-performing countries on the FSI also tend to score well on social and economic indicators such as the UN's Human Development Index, progress in achieving the UN's Sustainable Development Goals, income levels, gender equality, health expenditure and participation in higher education.

However, the correlations are far from perfect, indicating that the policies and/or circumstances of nations make a difference. Ireland and Portugal, for example, perform better on the GFSI than their GDP would suggest, while Canada does better than its richer, larger neighbour. The FSI also has several major outliers. Tanzania scores much better for food security than would be predicted by its social and economic indicators, while the USA and the United Arab Emirates perform considerably worse.

Top of the GFSI rankings in 2022 was Finland, one of three Nordic nations in the top ten. Finland also came fourth in the 2021 FSI. By the standards of the most recent of both measures combined, Finland is the number one country in the world for food security and sustainability. How did it achieve this, and what can be learned from its success?

Before answering, we need to distinguish between food security and food self-sufficiency. Food security, as defined by the UN Committee on World Food Security, means that 'all people, at all times, have physical, social, and economic access to sufficient, safe, and nutritious food that meets their food preferences and dietary needs for an active and healthy life'.[16] Self-sufficiency is more simply the ability of a nation to feed its population from food produced within its own borders. The most obvious way in which the two may come apart is that a country may be entirely self-sufficient but be ill-prepared to import foods in the case of a poor harvest, disease or some other shock to its agricultural system. A tiny country like Liechtenstein, in contrast, may be more or less entirely dependent on imports but so well connected by trade that its food supply is highly secure. So, for example, while the Netherlands ranked eighth from bottom for self-sufficiency the last time the FAO reported, it came fifth on the Global Food Security Index.[17] Argentina ranks very highly for self-sufficiency, but middling for security.

In Finland's case, despite its top ranking for food security, it was actually ranked last for self-sufficiency by the FAO. Its food policy acknowledges that 'our agricultural production is currently based largely on imported production inputs, such as machinery, energy, plant protection products and feeds, and this makes our food system highly dependent on international trade in many ways'. In this situation, the strategy is to build internal production capacity while also building strong trading relationships. Realism about what is best produced domestically and what is better imported is key to Finland's strength.

The decoupling of self-sufficiency and food security has become a central feature of the global food system. The Netherlands, for example, is a huge producer, importer and exporter, but because it does not produce a lot of the foodstuffs its citizens need, it is not very self-sufficient even though it is very food secure. However, Martin van Ittersum, the Plant Production Systems professor we met earlier, thinks that at the moment we are too dependent on food grown elsewhere. Foods travel huge distances from farms to homes, which creates both environmental and geopolitical problems. A war like the one in Ukraine or a bad harvest can severely disrupt global food supply. 'Just look at really big climate change disruptions,' says Tim Lang. He points to parts of the world where recently 'production was smashed by fires and droughts'.

Consider also how much food passes through a small number of 'choke points', such as the Panama Canal, the Suez Canal, the Black Sea, the Strait of Gibraltar and Rotterdam. Over a quarter of global soybean exports pass through the Strait of Malacca between Malaysia and Indonesia, a fifth of global wheat exports transit the Turkish Straits, while in Brazil nearly a quarter of global soybean exports are handled by just four ports. 'It doesn't take much to disrupt those choke points,' says Lang, pointing out that once already 'the Panama Canal had to close because there wasn't enough water'. A report by the London-based International Affairs Think Tank Chatham House warned that 'a serious interruption at one or more of these chokepoints could conceivably lead to supply shortfalls and price spikes, with systemic consequences that could reach beyond food markets'.[18]

However, van Ittersum says, 'I don't believe in entirely local systems, in which all the food has to be produced locally. If a certain location is not very suitable to grow rice, wheat, potatoes, tomatoes, whatever, and you still want to do that locally, that is not efficient and also not in the end sustainable.' Although every region could adopt intensive methods to improve its domestic output, in practice growing foods wherever they grow best is often more efficient, in terms of both yields and total production costs, even allowing for transport. A banana grown in the Caribbean and bought in the UK can cost around 25p even when fairly traded and organic. One grown in Surrey in heated greenhouses would cost many times more.

Van Ittersum believes we should think of increasing self-sufficiency at the continental or sub-continental, not the national, level. For instance, as long as Finland is part of a very self-sufficient European Union it doesn't matter that it is not very self-sufficient as a country. Many regions, such the European Union, West Africa and East Africa, are to a large extent already self-sufficient in main food commodities. Van Ittersum would like a target of 80 per cent self-sufficiency for such regions, to make them geopolitically more independent and stable.

Finland seems to have found the sweet spot that a resilient modern food system needs, between complete self-sufficiency and total dependence on imports. But it did not attain its status as the most food-secure country in the world by accident. It has had a clear food policy for the medium to long term, something that most countries lack. The UK, for example, set up an independent review panel to advise on a national food strategy, but even its head described the result as 'not a strategy at all ... merely a handful of disparate policy ideas'.[19] In 2017, Finland, in contrast, set out its goals for its food system in 2030, looking more than a decade ahead. It did so in fewer than one hundred words:

THE BEST FOOD IN THE WORLD

In 2030, Finnish consumers eat tasty, healthy and safe Finnish food that has been produced sustainably and ethically. Consumers have the ability and possibility to make informed choices.

A transparent, highly skilled, flexible, internationally competitive and profitable food system that responds to demand. The growth and advancement of the sector are supported by well-coordinated, high-level research, development, innovation and teaching. There is a high level of marketing and communication skills in the sector. Finland is a significant exporter of high quality and safe foodstuffs and food sector skills.[20]

Such broad statements tend to be full of aspirational words and phrases that ring hollow. Would any government not claim to want 'the best food in the world' for its people? But Finland walked the talk. For all its rhetorical flourishes, the summary captured an important feature of any successful food policy in an industrialised nation: it has to address every aspect of the food system. There are nods in this statement to consumers, farmers, food technologists, marketing, education, food manufacturers and retailers. From its first words, the Finnish food policy is not afraid to say that it is in favour of business, innovation and technology at the same time as it wishes to promote sustainability, health and ethics.

Drill down into the specifics and a clear set of commitments emerges. Start with primary production: what is grown and raised on Finnish land. The policy states that 'sustainable, ethical and competitive primary production of a high quality is the foundation of the Finnish food system'. Note again how the unapologetically economic word 'competitive' sits alongside 'sustainable' and 'ethical'. The political food discourse in many countries too often implies a choice between commerce and conservation, economics and ethics, private business and public benefit. The success of the

Finnish food system suggests that this is profoundly wrong.

Indeed, the Nordic economic model as a whole challenges these simplistic binaries. Nordic nations tax heavily and score very highly for equality, health care and education. Yet they also do very well in the major rankings of the best countries in which to do business. The most recent such list published by *Forbes* put Sweden second,[21] while the last World Bank ranking placed Denmark third.[22] The 2022 Global Entrepreneurship Monitor report ranked Finland the third best country for entrepreneurs, behind the United Arab Emirates and the Netherlands.[23] The Nordic countries are nowhere near as socialist as many admirers and detractors alike believe. The Nordic model combines high taxation and social protections with a dynamic market economy. Its governments are unapologetically interventionist when they need to be but allow their citizens and their businesses as much freedom as is compatible with the pursuit of the general good. All this applies to their food systems.

The Finns may also challenge another set of binaries: natural versus industrial, whole versus processed food. For example, its food policy acknowledges a central tenet of organics – that 'good soil management on arable land and nutrient recycling are key mechanisms for improving the sustainability of the food system'. But the country does not have an especially large organic sector. In 2022, nearly 15 per cent of its arable land was organic, but organic meat accounted for only 1 per cent of production and organic milk for less than 4 per cent. The market share of organics in the grocery trade was 2.2 per cent.[24] This compares with around 6 per cent in Austria, Switzerland and Germany.[25] Finland shares many of organics' aims but is not tied to a narrow set of methods for achieving them. It accepts that soil health can be helped by new as well as old methods, saying that 'biological and technical solutions exist and are being developed'.

While the national food policy talks very much of the

environment and health, it also unapologetically calls for more investment in 'productising and commercialising innovation, especially in processing companies so that we would produce more refined products with higher value added for the domestic market and for export'. This acknowledges the fact that profit is mostly made when raw ingredients are turned into prepared foods or ingredients. But to accept this is not necessarily to promote the excesses of ultra-processing, as we will see in more detail later. Minimally processed and well-processed foods are an essential part of any secure food system.

One interesting feature of Finland's food policy is that it includes education. Free meals are universally available in pre-primary, basic and upper-secondary schools. These include a hot main course with a side of vegetables, bread, and milk or buttermilk. Children who take part in pre- or after-school activities get an additional snack. School lunches are not just seen as fuel to get students through the day.[26] Government recommendations for vocational institutions and general upper-secondary schools 'promote regular meals as an integral part of study and work, with social eating in a welcoming environment as a key factor maintaining productivity in studies and at work and the overall wellbeing of the entire school community'.[27]

In basic and pre-primary education, school meals are part of the national core curricula, teaching the children about health, nutrition and manners. National guidelines stipulate that 'pupils will be provided with the opportunity to participate in planning and implementing school meals, which fosters involvement and community spirit'. Helsinki's curriculum for early childhood education and care, in conformity with national guidelines, values 'nutrition education', saying, 'The children are taught to eat independently and to favour diverse and nutritious food choices without any pressure. The daily mealtimes take place without a rush, and the children learn about the custom of eating together, creating a sense of community through a dialogue and good table manners. By using different senses and experimenting, the children learn about foods and their origins, appearances, ingredients and flavours.'[28] Food education also takes place in the classroom, to develop 'transversal competencies' – skills, knowledge and understanding essential to life and work – such as self-care, everyday skills and cultural awareness.[29]

Just as important as what pupils are fed is what they are not given access to. The Finnish National Board of Education recommends that sweets and sugary drinks should not be made regularly available in educational institutions. Parents and guardians are consulted when vending machines or school kiosks are introduced. These should only offer 'healthy and nutritious products' and not promote foods high in fat, sugar and salt as daily choices. Parents and guardians are also entitled to decide what marketing their children are exposed to. These rules appear designed to avoid what has happened across the USA, where branded vending machines sell junk food to kids in direct competition with school meals. Roberta Sonnino, the sustainable food systems professor we met earlier, asks, 'If you let fast-food outlets surround the school buildings, as has happened in the UK and even worse in the United States, how do you expect the children who are allowed to leave the school at lunchtime to prefer broccoli at school rather than a cheap burger from a fast-food outlet right outside? In Italy, children cannot leave the school at lunchtime. That's a systemic type of intervention that needs to be in place.'

Another lesson from Finland is that no successful food system simply copies another. Each needs to be tailored to its ecology, geography, culture and economy. Take New Zealand, which in 1984 eliminated its farm subsidies. Initially agriculture reeled, but over time farming in the country thrived. In the days of subsidies, farmers were happy to sell their milk for others to turn into higher-value products. Now they produce more than 2,000 milk products when they used to make only thirty-five. The wine industry has also grown from almost nothing to being a major international player. Yet to draw the moral that all other countries should also abandon farm support would be too quick. New Zealand is a fertile, uncrowded country with a population of only 4.6 million people, but able to produce enough food for forty million. Hence it exports about 90 per cent of its production.[30] In short, it doesn't need any subsidies to be competitive. The same is not true of many other countries with less productive land and a larger population to feed and house. It should also be said that New Zealand's de-regulated farming boom has created new environmental pressures, with the sector's greenhouse gas emissions rising more than 5 per cent in a decade.[31]

Finland has the advantages of space, more clean water than it would ever use, excellent and extensive pasture for livestock, and little need for pesticides due to its cool northern location. On the other hand, its latitude and climate mean that crop yields are low. The country has to make the best of this unique set of conditions, going with the grain of nature to take advantage of its benefits and using technological interventions to mitigate its downsides. Increasing crop yields, for example, requires 'the application of research, teaching, advice and technology', including domestic plant breeding.

Mitigation, however, costs. This is where the Nordic willingness to provide social support is critical. The national food policy recog-nises that 'the production costs of agricultural products in Finland are significantly above the EU average'. For example, Finnish milk costs twice as much to produce as its farm-gate price. That means 'a policy of strong support for basic farming is thus required in order to maintain agricultural production in the country'.

The purpose of the subsidy policy is not to make Finnish food as cheap as possible. Some of Finland's regulations actually contribute to its higher cost. The policy notes: 'Stringent requirements related to food safety, the environment or the health care and welfare of production animals push up companies' costs.' This is seen as an opportunity, not a problem: rather than competing on price, Finnish food competes on quality and sustainability.

The government is also willing to pay subsidies to achieve other desired social goals that cannot be guaranteed by the functioning of the economic market alone. It offers animal-welfare payments to improve the well-being of livestock. It also places importance on public sector food provision, such as in hospitals, schools, prisons and government canteens, which collectively serve almost as much food (measured by value) as private sector kitchens. For example, its food policy states: 'School catering services should be based on providing tasty, nutritious and healthy meals while upholding the goals of sustainable development and climate change prevention.'[32]

There may be some cultural reasons why Finland has worked so hard to create a robust and sustainable food system. The country has a strong tradition of foraging and hunting, which means that the national identity involves a sense of connection to a land that is open and natural, as expressed in the idea of *Jokamiehen oikeudet*, or 'everyman's rights', enshrined in national law. Under these rights, everyone can hike or camp in the countryside, forage, and fish with a line and rod. Hunting is also permitted, although this requires permission from the landowner and a hunting card gained through an examination. These rights are actively taken up by Finns. For example, while five million kilos of freshwater fish are caught commercially every year, thirty million are caught by leisure fishermen and women. The importance of gathering, hunting and fishing is explicitly stated in the national food policy. This culture may at the very least create a populace that is supportive of sustainable food systems.

It is important not to idealise the Finnish food system. Still, Lang is probably right to say that Finland's actions on public food and health are among 'the best interventions at state level we've got on record'. Even so, many of the fine ideals of its policy, and even its laws, are not always put into practice. One shocking study found that one in four Finnish cattle and pig farms did not comply with the legally mandated animal-welfare standards. Typically, these were not egregiously cruel breaches, but failures to maintain standards nonetheless.[33] It is also the case that, like other Nordic nations, the old social democratic model has been under strong challenge from right-wing and populist political parties, and although overall government spending as a proportion of GDP has stayed quite steady, the proportion spent on education has fallen in recent years along with public support for social spending. Finland's current high rankings for sustainability and security in food could be more the fruits of past policy than a reflection of how things are going now.

Although international and national law does most to shape the food system, recent decades have seen increasing attempts to effect change at the local level. Many cities and regions around the world have developed urban food strategies (UFS) and/or food policy councils (FPCs), including London, Milan, Toronto, Ghent and Knoxville. Food Strategies tend to be created by local government authorities, whereas food policy councils are generally collaborations of like-minded civil society organisations, which may or may not have strong local government participation. They often have ambitious and wide-reaching goals such as increasing demand for and supply of healthy foods, and promoting resilience, equity and environmental sustainability in the food system.

Roberta Sonnino tells me that a major driving force for FPCs is that 'it's at the urban level that the ills and malfunctioning of the food system become visible. It's in the city that you see people queuing up at the food bank, for example. In the countryside or at the national level, it's easier to hide the problems.' Diets in cities also tend to be worse than elsewhere. As lower- and middle-income countries have urbanised, the consumption of processed food with low nutrient value has increased by around 5 per cent per year. An FAO report found that urban areas 'often manifest significant levels of child undernutrition or micronutrient deficiencies as well as overweight/obesity and diet-related non-communicable diseases'. This trend is driven by a number of factors, including sedentary lifestyles, lack of access to green public spaces, poor cooking facilities and easy access to fast and junk food.[34] Given that over half of the global population currently lives in urban areas, and by 2050 that is set to rise to two thirds, it would not be an exaggeration to talk of a global urban food crisis.

One of the most significant local initiatives is the Milan Urban Food Policy Pact, led by the mayor of Milan, signed by 100 mayors around the world at its launch in 2015 and by more than 250 cities today. Intended to be more than a high-minded declaration of intent, it includes a Framework for Action listing thirty-seven practical recommendations in six areas, along with indicators to monitor progress in implementing them. These recommendations spotlight the areas where local action can make a real difference. *Governance* includes getting official organisations, agencies, citizens and community groups to work together. Actions on *sustainable diets and nutrition* include both education and ensuring that healthy food is available for all. *Social and economic equity* may be improved by food and cash transfers, providing or improving school meals and supporting grassroots groups. There is also a focus on *food production*, promoting sustainable urban and peri-urban farming as well as improving supply chains with sustainable producers in the wider local area. Attention should be paid to *food supply and distribution*, to ensure that a secure flow of healthy, sustainable, affordable food is available everywhere. Finally, *food waste* should be minimised and reused in some form whenever possible.[35] Although some of these actions require local government cooperation, not all do.[36]

Local food governance could be seen as a return to the long-term historical norm, in which ordinary people had more control over their food supply. It feels more democratic, and Sonnino for one argues that one good feature of local food strategies and councils is that they tend to involve civil society more than national and transnational bodies. But how much power can realistically be returned to localities?

The answer to that depends a great deal on whether enabling structures are in place. Much more can be achieved when public institutions are on board. Local governments can affect the food environment by making it easier to start community projects such as orchards, allotments and canteens, and by making it harder to open junk-food outlets. Public institutions have the potential to change food procurement and delivery in schools, hospitals, universities and local government. Collectively, these institutions represent a large share of the local food market. In 2020, the average proportion of GDP spent on public procurement in the twenty-two countries that are members of both the OECD and the EU was nearly 15 per cent.[37] In Africa, that average is 17 per cent.[38] 'It's an enormous market that needs to be steered,' says Sonnino. 'You can't continue to think of school meals as a commercial service like they do in the UK and the United States. That's a health and well-being service as far as I'm concerned.'

In Italy, says Sonnino, national legislation enables municipal governments to procure locally produced, high-quality food. In contrast, before it left the EU, the UK government 'instilled the fear in procurement managers' that such a policy would 'breach the European legislation on transparency and the common market'. It's just one example of how the ability to act locally is often constrained by uncooperative national governments. Marion Nestle agrees that no matter how strong local food movements are, 'we really need changes on the national level and for that you need real political power with money behind it'.

Sometimes, however, national governments are too willing for voluntary groups to relieve them of their responsibilities. Think of how food banks have taken the pressure off governments to deal with the root causes of people not having enough money to eat. This is especially a risk in a country like the UK, which Sonnino says is 'a master of dumping social problems on the third sector'. She says that we have to question 'whether we are witnessing a transferral (or downscaling) of state responsibility to (under-funded and under-resourced) multi-sector food partnerships . . . under the guise of "food democracy"'.[39] One potential effect of this is to de-politicise food as an issue by making it the job of food partnerships that have responsibility without power.

There are also question marks about how truly democratic voluntary organisations are. They are led by self-selecting activists and so, as one overview of urban FPCs worldwide put it, many 'are predominantly composed of white, middle-class professionals from similar socioeconomic and educational backgrounds' and 'FPCs often struggle to create a diverse membership'.[40] One study looking at the food strategy of the Dutch city of Almere found that 'not all food system actors seem to be represented in many of these emerging governance networks' and that 'the time- and money-rich were privileged in the process' because the strategy was based on 'a lot of talking and a lack of financial compensation'. The study includes a stark warning: 'As urban food governance responsibility is increasingly shared with multiple actors who are not democratically elected, the locus of governance may become further removed from citizens, highlighting the democratic tension of governance through networks.'[41]

Another worry about local food activism is that it could be parochial and inward-looking. However, Sonnino's studies suggest that this isn't the case. Far from retreating to atomised cities or regions, the local food movement is recognising what Sonnino calls 'the relational nature of place', meaning that every place is in part made by the relations it has with other places. 'I haven't encountered a single example of a city wanting to reform their foodscape at the expense of either surrounding rural areas or other cities. One of the many things they share in common is a concern for rural areas,' she said. The initiatives tend to promote translocal collaborations and knowledge exchange. The point is to enable local communities all around the world to take back power from national government and multinational businesses.

Even if UFS and FPCs lack the power to be significant players in the governance of the food world, at the very least they are what Sonnino calls valuable 'food system innovators', trying out new ways to deal with food as a policy issue. For example, they tend to be ahead of national and transnational institutions in approaching food holistically and systemically. 'Rather than just trying to look for solutions either at the demand or the supply side, they have tried to embrace the food system as a whole,' Sonnino says. 'As many are beginning to recognise now, the greatest problems we have in the food system tend to be in the missing middle between production and consumption. In many cases, they have experimented with what we call food policy integration: trying to create a dialogue, to make sure that food becomes a policy subject and recognising the multiple connections that the food system has with transport, with the environment, with the economy, with housing.'

Many people who are strongly motivated to create a better food world are excited and energised by local activism. The results may be small, but they are tangible, relevant and achievable. In contrast, ordinary citizens have little to no power to change national and international food governance. But that is, alas, where most of the power lies. Perhaps one of the most important functions of local food initiatives is that collectively they make a statement about the issue's importance, exerting bottom-up pressure on national governments to take food policy more seriously. Sonnino for one hopes that 'this food movement is going to grow so much, and it's going to start placing real pressure'.

9

CULTURE AND IDENTITY

Milpa and mosolla in Mexico and Myanmar

At the start of the nineteenth century, northern Italy's agriculture was in ruins, devastated by the Napoleonic Wars. Many farmers saw no choice but to emigrate, and large numbers left for the British Isles. By the middle of the century, 4,000 had arrived, half of them settling in London. An expat community formed in the district of Clerkenwell, one of many urban areas around the world to become known as Little Italy. Three pillars of the community were soon established. In 1841, a school for poor Italian children was opened. In 1863, the church of St Peter, built in the style of an Italian basilica, was inaugurated. And in 1878, L. Terroni & Sons opened its doors – not only the first Italian delicatessen but, its present owners claim, the first deli in the whole of England.[1]

The Italians are famous for their cuisine, but they are not the only ones who take their food wherever they go. Around the world, small food stores advertise the most significant immigrant populations in the area. For example, Indian, East Asian, Polish and other

East European stores can be found in many parts of the UK, not just the big cities. In southern Spain, it is British stores that can be found among the local *tiendas*, fulfilling the expats' desire for a taste of home.

Like religion, food culture is a source of identity and belonging, rooted in rituals and traditions. Also like religion, it changes and evolves more than its practitioners like to acknowledge. Tradition is not 'how things have always been done'. Tradition is a hybrid of continuity and change, in which current practices can trace an unbroken line back many generations without necessarily remaining identical. For instance, the 'mincemeat' of dried fruit used in British Christmas baking is very different from the literal meat that used to fill festive pies, but they are on the same branch of the food family tree.

It is easy sport to point out that the bloodlines of many cherished food traditions are far from pure. For instance, Alberto Grandi has spent a lifetime debunking comforting myths Italians have about their food. In his 2018 book, *Denominazione di origine inventata* [*Invented Designation of Origin*], he showed many cherished beliefs to be no more than shibboleths. Pizza may have originated in Naples, but it spread around the USA before it conquered its home nation. If you want to eat Parmesan cheese as it used to be made, you need to try the stuff they make in Wisconsin, USA, not Parma, Italy. Italians will insist that a carbonara must be made with *guanciale* (pork cheeks), but the earliest recipe called for Italian bacon – and it was published in Chicago in 1952. Such demythologising made Grandi unpopular with the nationalist government as it prepared its application for Italian cuisine to be added to UNESCO's Intangible Cultural Heritage lists in 2023. Deputy Prime Minister Matteo Salvini accused Grandi of 'crushing the local culinary tradition', calling his work 'yet another shot at Made in Italy'.[2]

A similar story could be told of almost all contemporary food cultures. British fish and chips is owed to Jewish immigrants. Hungarian food is unimaginable without paprika, but the spice only became popular in the late nineteenth century. And as Bee Wilson elegantly chronicled, the much-admired Japanese food culture emerged only after the Second World War, under the influence of the occupying Americans. Before then, food had been about sustenance, with little variety or protein.[3]

Grandi does not want to disparage Italian food or even deny that there is such a thing. It is just that he thinks we 'confuse identity with the roots' and 'speak wrongly of identity' because 'the cuisine is constantly changing'. Food cultures are real, but like biological cultures they grow and mutate over time. They involve what Grandi calls 'crossings' and 'contamination'.[4] If we forget or deny this, food culture becomes little more than a collection of ingredients and recipes, frozen at an arbitrary moment in time.

What people grow, rear and cook is constantly changing, and varies from region to region, village to village, house to house. Food culture is better understood not as a static, perennial given, but as a dynamic, organic feature of the wider culture. To understand why it matters so much, we need to consider how human beings are always situated in time and place. This sounds obvious, but since the Enlightenment, western culture has emphasised universal rights and characteristics, downplaying ethnic, religious and cultural differences. In English, the word 'parochial', which once referred neutrally to the church parish, has come to mean narrow-minded and insular. 'Provincial' is similarly used to express disdain. In contrast, descriptors like 'cosmopolitan', 'multicultural' and 'well-travelled' carry only positive connotations.

However, in most parts of the world, throughout most of history, connections to specific times and places have been seen more positively. For example, a key part of the southern African concept of *ubuntu* is that we are who we are through others. Nowadays, the idea is often used to promote the idea of an international family of humanity. But the concept emerged at a much smaller scale, in the idea that we can only be our true, full selves by belonging to a community. In East Asia, Confucian thought is a form of 'role ethics' in which doing the right thing requires each person to fulfil their specific social role. There are no abstract, universal rights in such a way of thinking since a baby, an adult child, a parent and a grandparent all have different rights and responsibilities.

In all such societies, the individual is not a self-contained, independent ego whose essence depends only on itself. Rather, each person is who they are because of their relations with other people, as well as with the natural environment. You cannot even imagine what it would mean to be you if you took away the adults who brought you up, the communities you have lived in, the landscapes and cityscapes that forged your way of being. To be a person is to be an individual whose life story has played out in time and space. It is a tale set against the background of land and tradition in which food plays a leading role.

Culture and tradition are central to many aspects of the food systems we have already examined. Take the Maasai. Cultural anthropologist Kaj Århem argues that their food ways cannot be understood as simply the most pragmatic means of making best use of their ecological situation since their land 'so clearly offers alternative sources of subsistence'. A full explanation of why they eat as they do requires accounting for 'the dimension of meaning, the ideas and values associated with food'. Such an understanding shows that 'their diet is a part of their social identity; it communicates the values and norms on which it rests. It is a means by which they maintain their cultural distinctiveness, and an integral – and central – part of that system of ideas and practices which gives order, coherence, and meaning to their existence – their culture.'[5]

Although culture binds internally, it creates divisions with what is external. The stronger the sense of 'us', the clearer the idea of 'them'. The pacific, restrained pastoralist identity of the Maasai is held to be superior to the two other forms of human community they would traditionally have encountered. Hunters (*ildorobo*) lack domesticated livestock, which, from the Maasai point of view, makes their lives desperate and miserable. Their constant need to kill animals and eat their flesh makes the *ildorobo* seem both gluttonous and base. The Maasai never slaughter cattle for food alone, but always as part of a ritual. *Oldoroboni* (a derivative of *ildorobo*) is an insult the Maasai use against anyone perceived to be excessively fond of meat, selfish or unable to provide for his family.

Cultivators (*ilmeek*) are also considered inferior because they eat 'soiled' food that comes straight from the ground. Whereas pastoralists respect and even revere grass as the ultimate source of life itself, cultivators destroy pastures to grow their crops. The Maasai Association says that 'utilizing the land for crop farming is a crime against nature. Once you cultivate the land, it is no longer suitable for grazing.'

The Inuit also have a strong culture and identity that their food ways underpin. 'Maintaining the relationship between humans and animals through hunting . . . maintains Inuit identity,' says anthropologist Kristen Borré. Because hunted food is shared, it is also important for strengthening social relations.[6] A major UN report into indigenous food systems reached the same conclusion as Borré: 'Traditional food (called country food among Inuit) features prominently at the centre of Inuit identity and well-being. The hunting, harvesting and sharing of country food ensured survival and provided social cohesion, as they continue to do.'[7] The same UN report argued that these shared practices also represented 'another avenue in which traditional food systems can indirectly promote health and well-being among Indigenous Peoples'.

Such is the importance of food ways that when they disappear, entire cultures go with them. Sky Carrithers fears this is happening on the Pampas of Argentina. On the farm her father bought, only two old gauchos remain. Some of the ways their minds work leave her in awe. One was unable to count but was still able to make sure all of the 200 steers he was asked to look after were accounted for. 'He knew if any were missing because he knew their tracks,' Carrithers tells me. 'These people remember so much better than us that read and write and copy everything down. I just love how well they recall everything, the memories of the years, the snowfall and the river heights.'

But this way of being is going extinct. According to Carrithers, the gaucho of old no longer exists. 'Generally our age is like, "No, this is a lot of work. It's cold, every morning you wake up early, you go to bed late. I want to have a normal comfortable life and a heated house when I get home after my eight hours." We even have a lot of friends that are of our age group, if not a little bit older, that used to be workers on properties and have their own animals, who have just sold out and gone to town. It's easier, more comfortable, they get weekends off, go places.'

As Carrithers and the UN report suggest, food cultures can also be fonts of a lot of accumulated knowledge about health and diet. We've already seen that when traditional societies undergo the nutrition transition to an industrialised diet, their health suffers. Gyorgy Scrinis, who we'll hear much more from later, tells me: 'It's important to put food and dietary patterns back into their social and historical context. There are many ways of knowing and defining what good food or a good dietary pattern is. In every country around the world there is embedded wisdom in those dietary patterns and we can draw on all of them and find ways of bringing them together. For example, there would be few communities that ate the enormous quantities of meat that are now eaten in Australia, the UK or the USA on a regular basis, and they would be consuming it in a different form. What the health effects of that level of consumption are, I don't know. But it's out of balance compared to what we've eaten historically and in most other parts of the world.

You don't have to just appeal to the biological sciences for a guide on what an appropriate dietary balance might be. There are other frameworks that we can use for making sense of food.'

It would be naive and romantic to believe that all traditional diets are optimally healthy. Life expectancies have grown enormously in developed industrial nations, so it cannot be a simple tale of old ways good, new ways bad. Still, it makes sense to assume that many dietary patterns and combinations that have been followed for centuries would have persisted in part because they worked nutritionally and agriculturally. In Mesoamerica, for example, it is thought that the *milpa* system, as the Mexicans call it, has been used for over 7,000 years. This involves growing maize (corn) together with other crops such as beans, squashes or potatoes. The maize grows tall and strong and is able to support climbing beans. These legumes fix nitrogen, helping the soil to retain fertility. The crops together also shade the ground, stopping it from drying out and suppressing weeds. It's an ingenious method that is now recognised to be highly efficient and sustainable. One typical study showed that the system is more productive than monocropped maize. Furthermore, the combination of crops provides foods which, when eaten together, form the basis of a highly balanced diet.[8]

The ways in which foods are traditionally processed also tend to have benefits. When maize started to become the basis of many diets around the world in the form of a processed commodity, the niacin deficiency disease pellagra started to become a serious public health problem. Yet in countries like Mexico, which had been eating maize as a staple for millennia, pellagra was rare. That is because they did not grind maize into flour. Instead, it was soaked and cooked in limewater before being washed and hulled. This process of 'nixtamalisation' liberated the niacin from the cellulose in the maize, allowing it to be digested.[9] As with the *milpa*, this is a form of ingenuity that transcends the knowledge and understanding of any individual. Cultures evolve ways of doing things that work without anyone knowing why or how. So when we look at them with a scientific eye and can't see why or how they work either, that is not a good reason to dismiss them.

The case for the importance of culture in the food world is made most vocally and strongly by the global food sovereignty movement, which has its roots in the international organisation La Via Campesina, founded in 1993 by peasant farmers from different continents at a meeting in Mons, Belgium. In modern English, 'peasant' has pejorative connotations that the Spanish *campesino* does not. La Via Campesina counts as peasants all 'people who till the land to produce food, the fishers, the pastoralists, the farmworkers, the landless, the migrant workers, the indigenous people, rural workers – of diverse identities, gender and age groups'.

La Via Campesina was formed largely in response to the ways in which small farmers worldwide had been pushed off their land by governments and big businesses who had put the pursuit of industrialising agriculture, clearing forests and building new developments above the interests of the people whose homes and livelihoods stood in their way. It is non-hierarchical and internationalist, as well as a vocal proponent of women's rights.

La Via Campesina first articulated the concept of 'food sovereignty' at the FAO's World Food Summit in Rome in 1996. The term rose in visibility after the International Food Sovereignty Forum in February 2007 in the village of Sélingué in Mali, at which the movement issued the Declaration of Nyéléni. The Declaration has become a keystone of the movement, defining food sovereignty as 'the right of peoples to healthy and culturally appropriate food produced through ecologically sound and sustainable methods, and their right to define their own food and agriculture systems.'

Food sovereignty has undoubtedly been very influential. It is striking that although it emerged from rural farmers, the language used in the FAO Framework for the Urban Food Agenda seems to come straight from the food sovereignty lexicon: 'this framework adopts a rights-based approach that articulates the importance of ensuring that everybody, regardless of territorial location, should have access to affordable, nutritious, diversified and culturally appropriate food and is able to determine and shape, through collective decision-making processes, local food systems rooted in sustainable livelihoods'. Much of what La Via Campesina stands for would be supported by any decent person: almost everyone can get behind 'genuine and integral agrarian reform that guarantees peasants full rights to land, defends and recovers the territories of indigenous peoples, ensures fishing communities' access and control over their fishing areas and eco-systems, honours access and control over pastoral lands and migratory routes'.

But the food sovereignty movement also has a more radical, political agenda. According to the Declaration of Nyéléni, it is fighting against 'Imperialism, neo-liberalism, neo-colonialism and patriarchy, and all systems that impoverish life, resources and eco-systems'. Against this, the movement 'offers a strategy to resist and dismantle the current corporate trade and food regime'. For those in the movement, peasant rights cannot be defended within the existing economic and political order, because the entire system is in the service of big business and neo-colonial powers. That's an analysis that believers in liberal democracies and global markets will find hard to accept. Critics also point to a tendency for the movement to overlook complexity and 'present a simplified and idealised understanding of peasants and family farmers'.[10]

Whether you fully endorse its political agenda or merely support the defence of peasant rights, food sovereignty highlights the fact that the ways in which we produce food are of deep cultural as well as economic and practical importance. One of the core phrases, 'culturally appropriate food', makes it explicit that the right to one's cultural identity is a fundamental human right that cannot be upheld if our food does not fit with that identity, even if it is otherwise sufficient and nutritious. A major reason for resisting big agriculture is not just to defend the economic power and autonomy of peasants, but to preserve traditional knowledge and practices. A great deal of value is placed on the ways in which these are passed down through the generations. A statement issued to mark the twenty-fifth anniversary of La Via Campesina made it clear that preserving the diversity of these food cultures is a big reason to resist 'a cruel and all-devouring capitalist system' which prefers 'a world of monoculture and homogenous tastes'.[11] We know that people are prepared to go to war to defend their way of life. Once we understand that food is central to that way of life, its importance cannot be denied.

If there is anywhere in the world where you might think food was simply about fuel for survival, it would be a refugee camp. Consider the rations distributed by the United Nations' World Food Programme (WFP) when people are fully dependent on food assistance. These are extremely basic, designed to provide 2,100 calories per person (10–12 per cent from protein, 17 per cent from fat), as well as micronutrients such as vitamin A, iron, iodine and zinc. They will comprise a staple such as wheat flour or rice; lentils, chickpeas or other pulses; fortified vegetable oil; sugar; and iodised salt. There is no scope to cater for individual preferences, with the rations 'designed to meet the nutritional requirements of a population rather than individuals'.[12]

Still, even in this most extreme of cases, there is some deference to culture, tradition and identity. The exact composition of the rations does not only depend upon 'demographic profile, activity levels, climatic conditions, local coping capacity and existing levels of malnutrition and disease', but 'local preferences'. Even when food has to be considered overwhelmingly as fuel, it is not *only* fuel.

Moreover, as soon as they can, refugees will seize any opportunity

to turn eating back into a socially and culturally significant practice. Nowhere is this more evident than in the Kutupalong refugee
settlement, in the Cox's Bazar region of Bangladesh. Since 2017 it
has been the largest refugee camp – or rather, collection of camps –
in the world. It houses 800,000 of the 6.6 million people living in
planned and managed or self-styled refugee camps around the
globe. Almost everyone there is a Rohingya fleeing persecution in
Myanmar's Rakhine State, and more than half of them are children.[13]

It hardly needs saying that life in Kutupalong isn't easy, especially with the annual monsoons, which cause flooding and can
sweep away the often flimsy structures of the camp. On top of this,
in March 2021 a huge fire destroyed 9,500 shelters and 1,600 infrastructure facilities, including hospitals, learning centres and aid
distribution points, leaving 45,000 refugees temporarily homeless.

Despite all these pressures, or perhaps because of them, the
inhabitants do all they can to make their food pleasurable, familiar
and comforting. 'After the bustling days, we sit down together as
families to have dinner in our shelters,' wrote Jeyabol Hoque, who
had lived in the camp for four years. 'On more joyous occasions,
we arrange mini picnics and share meals and joy. . . . Most people
in the camps enjoy dinners, meals, and picnics together.'[14]

Many refugees plant tiny gardens outside their shelters, growing
crops like beans that can climb across the bamboo roofs to supplement their rations.[15] In one part of the camp, a pond has been
built so that the refugees can farm fish, thanks to money raised by
a fourteen-year-old Bangladeshi schoolboy, Sadaqat Omar.[16]

The WFP recognises the psychological as well as the metabolic
value of food. So in 2019 it introduced an e-voucher scheme to give
the residents greater freedom to design their own menus. A set
list of eighteen items to choose from was reduced to twelve, and
the retailers contracted to run the outlets stocked another eight,
which varied according to availability. The WFP's Bangladesh
Country Director Christa Räder said that this not only increased

choice and helped bolster nutrition, it actually cost less, because vendors could stock whatever was available and were not forced to seek out mandated items. That meant it was also a boon for the local economy. Local fishermen started to supply the factories that make the kinds of dried fish prized by the Rohingya, increasing their earnings. Some of this money helped to pay for the education of local children, so that they might have a better life than the fishermen and workers who dry the fish.[17] It is a reminder that most of the burden of the world's refugees falls on poor countries, not developed ones. In 2022, 73 per cent of refugees were hosted in low- and middle-income countries.[18]

The vouchers are always given to the women. Räder says that 'this enhances the likelihood of families getting their meals regularly, as women stay in or around the camps, where food can be purchased, while men might move elsewhere looking for work'. It is also good for the women. 'Having the cards in their own names enhances women's control over resources and boosts their self-confidence and decision-making power,' says Räder. 'They feel respected, uplifted, recognised. . . . When they meet other women at the WFP shops, they discuss prices and talk about their lives – their world is no longer limited to their shelters.'[19]

The importance of soul food is demonstrated by the *mosolla* spice mix made by a refugee called Hafsa for her family. The fact that they use some of the precious little money they have to buy the seven or more spices to dry and use in the mix shows that food has to satisfy more than their energy needs. The twenty-three-year-old learned how to make the *mosolla* from her parents and grandparents, and in the camp she is helped by her mother. The scene of the two of them pounding the herbs speaks volumes for the bonding power of food.[20]

However, as we have seen several times already, respecting culture and tradition is not the same as romanticising them or seeing them as above criticism. In the camps, some norms and beliefs have to be challenged. Giving women control of the de facto currency of the camp goes against patriarchal custom. 'In this society, not only do women face great challenges going out and earning an income, they are also exposed to all sorts of harassment,' says Räder. Men are also being challenged to take on roles usually left for women, such as taking children to the nutrition centres to check if they are malnourished. And everyone is taught the importance of handwashing and hygiene, which often requires new habits and routines.[21] Once again, we see that no culture, however prized, should be preserved in aspic.

Tara Garnett is clear about the need to respect history and tradition without any illusions. 'I don't think that there was a time when we were somehow all eating better,' she tells me. But 'a sense of time, of a kind of agreed way of eating and a shared heritage is important. You can have a sense of rootedness which is not based on a mythic past. It's a question of not assuming that there is no past and today is year zero.' She also points out that because traditional food ways are based on group norms they may exclude people who diverge from them, for instance by becoming vegetarian or rejecting the obligation to eat halal or kosher food. 'You have to walk a fine line between the collective and the individual.'

Despite these complexities, it seems that in general the social and cultural functions of food and agriculture are not appreciated enough. Of course, we all know about how certain dishes and foodstuffs are deeply imbued with national and ethnic identities. When people of Caribbean descent cook ackee and saltfish, those of Gujarati origin make *kadhi*, or Italian emigrants sit down to *pastasciutta*, they are not just eating delicious food, they are reaffirming their identities. 'Tell me what you eat and I will tell you what you are,' as the great French food writer Jean Anthelme Brillat-Savarin said.[22]

However, the sense of social identity given by the food ways of peoples such as the Maasai and the Inuit runs much deeper and wider than this. It is not just about what is eaten, but also how it is eaten, where it has come from, who it is eaten with, and when. This is true of everyone, not just exotic others. An anthropologist studying an industrialised nation would be able to reveal these patterns of meanings for the food systems there too. Even without having undertaken such a thorough field study, we can easily enough imagine what sorts of things we would find. First, there are the ways in which food choices mark out the in-group as superior to out-groups. The British have long celebrated their consumption of pasteurised milk as indicating superiority over the French, who drink the foul UHT version. Italians see the essential simplicity and purity of their food as superior to the over-elaborate dishes of the French, who use strong sauces to disguise the inferiority of their raw ingredients. The French, meanwhile, look down on Italian food as too simple and rustic, and view the British as just barbaric, seeing their own tradition as on a higher gastronomic plain, and so obviously requiring more time and attention.

These meanings are so deeply ingrained that they become almost invisible to the people themselves. We tend to assume that we eat the way we do because of a simple combination of price, preference and convenience. But our preferences are deeply rooted in our social identities, and the related cultural significances of food have an awkward habit of shifting over time. Back in 1965, Harry Palmer (played by Michael Caine) in the *The Ipcress File* showed his sophistication by buying more expensive tinned *champignons*. 'You're paying ten pence more for a fancy French label,' said his colleague, mocking his pretensions and showing his own lack of them. Palmer brushed off the accusation of snobbery and responded by asserting his gourmandism instead: 'It's not just the label, these do have a better flavour.' Today, Palmer would surely be buying fresh local mushrooms and looking down on anyone who would buy a can of *champignons*.

Where we buy our food also carries positive and negative associations. Some are proud to eschew supermarkets (at least the more popular ones), while others take the fact that they shop there to be a sign of their down-to-earth ordinariness. Brands have become important signifiers, and convenience has also been valued for several decades. Both these trends have the effect of encouraging more consumption of processed foods.

There is a complex interplay between the values of health and hedonism. In traditional societies, little thought has to go into this. People can safely assume that what they eat is healthy and the most delicious foods ration themselves. In an industrialised consumer society, however, choice becomes much more powerful, which introduces tensions in preferences. People want to live a good life, full of quotidian pleasures and regular treats, but they are also aware of the need to look after their health.

It can be tempting to view the identity-forming nature of food negatively, as reflecting irrational and unconscious desires for status and acceptance. But anthropology suggests that this dimension of the food world cannot be wished away. Food is an integral part of identity formation – the only question is whether that drives positive or negative behaviours. Knowing this, we should actively try to harness the importance of identity in creating a better food system.

Of course, there is one sector already trying to do this: the food industry. Market research companies have produced numerous reports identifying consumer values, in the hope of being able to align their brand perception with them. This has become increasingly important for the largest multinational companies. As a recent report by the auditing and consulting firm Deloitte explained, until recently they could rely on customers making their purchasing choices on the basis of three 'traditional drivers': taste, price and convenience.[23] But now it seems that things are changing. Deloitte and other market research companies have identified several other factors driving consumers, such as health and wellness; safety;

social impact; experience; transparency; product origin; trust and reputation.[24] A report by Euromonitor International concluded that across 100 countries around the world, 'consumers demand that companies care beyond revenue' and that 'protecting the health and interest of society and the planet is the new expectation'.[25]

These may appear to be positive developments. The cultural values of western consumers are moving away from mere price and convenience to encompass the environment, justice and health. Two considerations, however, should make us greet these developments with caution. First, the ubiquity of such reports shows that the people most informed and ready to respond to any changes in consumer sentiment are the big companies. While that is in many ways a good thing, since they are responsible for the majority of our food supplies, there is always a risk that progressive change is harnessed for narrow commercial gain, rather than for genuine good.

A second worry is that despite what consumers say, the evidence suggests that only a minority act on these professed values. The Euromonitor report found that just 28.4 per cent of consumers make purchasing decisions based on brands' social and political beliefs, 26.4 per cent boycott brands that don't align with their social/political values, and fewer than one in four buy from purpose-driven brands.

It is evident that social identity is a powerful motivator of food choices, but one that usually operates at an unconscious level, or via the mechanism of established social practices that people do not actively have to choose to follow. Nevertheless, the power of culture opens up the realistic hope that citizens of industrialised nations will increasingly want their identities to express discernment without snobbery, culinary curiosity with environmental and social responsibility, hedonism with health. Harnessing these desires for good will be a major challenge in the years to come, both for makers and shapers of food policy and for the food industry.

TAKING STOCK

Towards a Global Food Philosophy

Food is ultimately provided by the land and the sea, rivers and lakes, plants and animals. But the food system is shaped by people, politics and business. Unfortunately, all three actors have historically tended to work primarily in their own, often short-term, interests. As a result, our food system is not so much guided by the wrong principles as plain unprincipled. Most of us today would agree that our food world should be a fair one. But were the principle of equitability to be applied, it would require wide-scale transformation of a food system that has been built on injustice.

There have been people calling for a fair food system for centuries. In Britain in the eighteenth century, the Quakers were at the forefront of campaigns to abolish slavery, culminating in a largely women-led boycott of food produced by slaves. Yet nearly 250 years later, not only is injustice still embedded in the food system, we cannot even say that slavery has been consigned to history.

Exploitation persists because the food system depends on it. The manufacture of food still follows an extractive model whereby ingredients are bought cheaply from producers and turned into valuable products by processors and manufacturers. That cannot be changed by tinkering or by well-intentioned individuals and companies paying small fair trade premiums. It requires systemic transformation, enforced by regulation.

Although it is easy to agree on the goal, there is a great deal of disagreement about what equitability means. Most obviously, for some it requires full equality while for others fair shares are not necessarily equal shares. But as the economist and philosopher Amartya Sen has argued, we don't need to agree on an ideal of perfect justice in order to recognise patent injustice when we see it and take steps to reduce it.[1] As long as we move in the direction of a fairer food system, we can save the debate about what a perfectly fair one would look like for later.

The need to approach injustice systemically reinforces a principle we have already seen when we examined how we have fed ourselves from the land: holism. The food system needs to be thought of as an organic whole in which a change to any one part has consequences for many others. For example, paying more to farmers in developing countries will have implications for the price of food everywhere. If more processing is shifted to source, that will also affect production and supply chains. So many of the harms that have been created by bad governance and rapacious business have been the result of a failure to fully consider how rules and practices that suit some in the food system harm others. A more joined-up approach is needed to ensure fairness across the whole food world.

When we think about the practical measures necessary to address inequity in a holistic way, we need to adopt a pluralistic approach. As with agriculture, it is clear that what works best depends very much on specific circumstances. For instance, there is no universal prescription for what should be left to markets and what should come under tight regulation. Where water is scarce, rules on usage need to be tighter than where it is plentiful. Subsidies that are needed where farming conditions are tough may be unnecessary where they are easier. Principles are always more general than practices, and this is especially important when it comes to designing regulation and governance.

There is also a need to ensure that well-intentioned intervention does not stifle human resourcefulness and ingenuity. Regulatory frameworks need to enable positive innovation, not erect barriers to it. This requires a delicate balancing act. Rules can be too lax or too tight. For example, while countries generally benefit from open trade, it does not always follow that the freer trade is, the better. In competitions with no rules at all, the strongest always win. At the same time, when the rules are too strict, people cannot bring their best game, and some are unable to play at all.

In Part One, it seemed that whole foods ought to be at the core of our diets. We can now begin to see how this is part of a broader principle of 'foodcentrism': whole foods, not separated parts, processed ingredients or discrete nutrients, ought to be central to how we feed ourselves. We have now seen two more ways in which food systems go wrong when this foodcentric approach is abandoned. Commodification turns whole foods into industrial ingredients. These commodity markets squeeze the poorest producers for the convenience of the richest consumers and manufacturers. This links to the second problem, which is the excessive power of big business, which is used to promote the sale of profitable processed foods, made with commodity ingredients. The power that richer wholesale buyers and retailers have over producers would not be wiped away if whole foods were more central to our diets. But it would be weaker and probably easier to control. Even if this were not the case, the benefits to our health would be significant.

A more foodcentric approach also sees what we eat as more than mere fuel. One example of this is that food is part of our culture and identity. This is not just the case in exotic foreign countries where more people are directly involved in food production. It is also true in countries like Finland, where children are taught about food not just as nutrients but as an important part of the social fabric in which we express solidarity and hospitality.

Culture permeates every part of the food world. It is evident in ways of knowing, by which good diets and farming practices are learned and passed on collectively. Culture cannot be separated from nutrition, because people who cultivate, cook and share food together are healthier as a result. It is also vital to the economics of food, since citizens become disempowered when food production and distribution are taken out of their hands, to the benefit of big business. Culture is therefore another example of how our food world needs to be understood holistically but also pluralistically, since cultures vary. We need to be able to join the dots without forcing them into a monolithic pattern.

It should not be left to the radical food sovereignty movement to make the case that people need to be put at the heart of food systems. Our food world needs to be one which is fair and which allows culture and tradition to flourish and evolve. In a globalised, industrialised world, all this is an immense challenge. But we increase our chances of meeting it if we are clear about the values that should be guiding us. Our survey thus far suggests that these should include circularity, holism, pluralism, resourcefulness, equitability and foodcentrism. But this food philosophy is not complete. It has yet to account for a key feature of our food world: the other animals in it.

PART THREE

Other animals

10

FROM EXTENSIVE GRAZING
TO EXPLODED CHICKENS

Steaks and soya on the Pampas

Sky Carrithers estimates that it would take five days to walk the length of her ranch with only six hours of sleep each night. A thousand cattle used to graze these 45,000 hectares (174 square miles or 450 square kilometres) in the Andean foothills of northern Patagonia, an area larger than Barbados. For four months of the year, her brother runs a tourism business here, offering horseback rides, treks and fly fishing. But year round, Estancia Ranquilco is a working farm producing Argentina's most famous food: beef.

To say Argentinians like beef is an understatement. The average Argentinian eats thirty-six kilograms of cow meat per year, over 25 per cent more than the second biggest eaters, the Americans, who manage just twenty-six kilograms each, which is still one fifth of all the world's beef.[1] Americans also eat the most meat per person in total, without being world leaders in the consumption of any one animal.[2] Per person, the world's biggest eaters of lamb are in

Kazakhstan, those of poultry are in Israel, and those of pork are in Vietnam and Korea.

Because beef eating is part of the culture and identity of Argentinians, the increasing consensus that cattle farming is environmentally unsustainable is a challenge to their way of life. Arguably, however, traditional Argentinian food ways have been dying for decades, and the old ones never posed a climate threat.

The Pampas of Argentina demonstrate that not all ruminant farming is equal, and that some forms of it can have a place in a world fighting climate change. These huge grasslands provide the ideal terrain for grazing cows. Cattle were introduced by European settlers in the early nineteenth century, and they flourished on the lush pastures of the humid southeastern Pampas. For centuries, beef has been produced without the need for any external inputs. With so much grass, the cows at Estancia Ranquilco don't need to be given any other food. Seasonal variation is dealt with by the traditional practice of transhumance, used by cattle herders all over the world. The animals graze at higher altitudes in the summer and come down to lower ground for the winter, always moving to where the grass is at its best.

However, such pastoral scenes are rapidly disappearing. Increasingly the old ways are giving way to the new. Land is being given over to production of crops like soybeans, grown to feed livestock that is often kept in vast feedlots. Many of these are entirely indoors, with slatted floors for the manure to fall through and little room for the cows to move. Outdoor feedlots tend to be somewhat less intensively packed, but with little or no shade from the sun and manure piling up on the ground, conditions are not necessarily any better. To give some sense of this intensification, Meat & Livestock Australia recommends feedlots allow fifteen square metres per steer, meaning you could cram 667 cattle on to one hectare.[3] In contrast, just one typical free-range cow requires between four and five hectares per year. So feedlot cows are granted around 3 per cent of the space every animal used to have to itself. Today, around two thirds of Argentinian cows live their lives in feedlots, roughly three times as many as in 2001.[4]

Feedlots are proliferating around the world, driven by an increased demand for meat. Not only is the global population expanding, but as people earn more, they tend to eat more animal protein. An FAO report concluded that meat consumption world-wide was set to rise by 14 per cent in the 2020s, faster than the population increase of 11 per cent.[5] In the industrialised world, meat eating is actually in slight decline. But if demand for meat continues to grow at the current rate in the BRICS countries (Brazil, Russia, India, China and South Africa), where 40 per cent of the world's population lives, to satisfy it, the world's farmers and agribusinesses will need to step up meat production from the current rate of 300 million tonnes every year to 470 million tonnes by 2050. Given that there just isn't 57 per cent more grazing land to meet this 57 per cent increase, the only alternative is to intensify production.

The largest, most intensive feedlots are known as 'concentrated animal feeding operations' (CAFOs), or, more colloquially, as 'mega farms' or 'factory farms'. In the USA, the definition of a CAFO is a farm containing 700 dairy cows, 1,000 beef cows, 2,500 large pigs, 82,000 laying hens or 125,000 broiler chickens. One of the largest, Green Hills Farm in Missouri, housed nearly 80,000 large pigs in 2016.[6] In the UK, the biggest poultry farm keeps up to 1.4 million birds, and three farms hold more than 20,000 pigs.[7] In China, in 2023 a twenty-six-storey farm was opened that would slaughter up to 1.2 million pigs a year.[8]

Every nation has its laws determining minimum welfare stand-ards for the animals in such farms, but it is hard to believe that life inside is anything other than miserable, at least for most of the animals. The most obvious issue is space. Intensively reared ani-mals do not have the ability to express normal behaviours, one of the basic 'five freedoms' defined by Britain's Farm Animal Welfare Council in 1979 in response to a 1965 government report on the welfare of intensively farmed animals.[9] Huge amounts of excrement and urine are created in feedlots, and in too many it is not cleared away effectively. Apart from being deeply unpleasant, untreated faeces can lead to infection and breathing problems, as the noxious gases affect the lungs of animals. Such close confinement naturally leads to behavioural issues, including fighting, so teeth are clipped, beaks trimmed, even tails docked to avoid them being chewed. These procedures are often performed on the animals without any anaesthetic. Infection is such a risk that in the US antibiotics have routinely been used as prophylactics, a practice banned in the EU.

For some calves, it is hard to say whether life is mercifully or brutally short. Baby cows are kept in veal crates so small that they can't turn around in them, for all of their lives until slaughter. These crates have been banned in the UK and the EU, but not in the USA and many other countries.[10] Other animals fare no better. Mother pigs are just as immobilised in gestation crates, while chickens don't have enough space to extend their wings. Many caged egg-laying chickens spend their whole lives in a space smaller than a sheet of A4 paper (similar to standard letter size in the USA).

One of the most grotesque problems is that to keep the price of the end products as cheap as possible, fast growth is imperative. For dairy cows, this means producing more milk per day than traditional breeds. Carrying this weight for all their adult lives, in conditions where they can barely move, makes lameness a common problem. Estimates suggest that in the United Kingdom the prevalence of dairy cow lameness is around one in four.[11] Broiler chickens have also been bred to grow so quickly that 25 per cent suffer from lameness. Compassion in World Farming also reports that 'broken bones, infections and organ failure are common health problems for factory farmed animals'.[12] Little wonder that animal rights campaigners call factory farms concentration camps for animals.

These are not rare aberrations but mainstream farming practices. In the USA, 70 per cent of cows, 98 per cent of pigs and
99 per cent of chickens and turkeys are produced in CAFOs.[13]
Globally, an estimated 72 per cent of the world's poultry and 55
per cent of the world's pork is produced in these vast industrial
units.[14] All of this is done in the name of efficiency, and as a result,
in many parts of the world, traditional pasture-reared meat is more
expensive for a simple reason: land. In more densely populated
parts of the world, competition for the land needed for extensive
grazing means that the meat produced on it costs a lot more. So it
can be cheaper to keep cattle locked up and feed them imported
soy-based feed.

But in Argentina, Carrithers tells me, 'When we sell grass-fed,
it's cheaper than the feedlot fed stuff.' The vastness of the Pampas
means that land is cheap and the feed it produces is more or less
free. However, bizarrely, the fact that Carrithers' premium traditional meat is cheaper doesn't make it more popular. She sells as
many of her mature steers locally as she can, but many have to
be sold to people who will 'finish' them in feedlots, even though
they're fully ready for slaughter. This is because, as Carrithers explains, a steer on the Pampas 'sure walks a lot, so the muscle is not
quite as tender'. Its fat is also a little yellow. It grows slowly and it's
slaughtered at around one and a half to two years. But consumers
today want the kind of meat that comes from an eight-month-old
calf which is put into a feedlot for ninety days to produce a 'very
fat, succulent small-ribbed young animal that's tender because it
never walks'. So the people who buy her steers 'keep them ninety
to one hundred and ten days, no matter what, even though they're
already fat off grass. They want to change the colour of the fat,
they want to produce this more tender muscle.' Argentina's reputation for great beef was built on pasture-reared cattle, but now
'Argentinian' has become a brand, slapped on labels of packs of
steaks coming from the feedlots.

Campaigners for the ending of all animal farming understandably focus on images of livestock in tiny cages. It seems hard to deny that much, perhaps even the vast majority, of animal farming is cruel. But out on the Pampas, it is evident that not all animal husbandry is, or needs to be, like this. 'Our animals live a wonderful happy, almost feral life up until the moment we slit their throat,' says Carrithers, with refreshing directness. 'Their lives are completely unfettered and quite natural, with very little fencing and corrals. We do herding gently on horseback. The day comes that we need to slaughter a goat – that's our main food because it's a small animal so we don't need refrigeration – it's a very simple, quick and humane process.'

Some scoff at the use of the word 'humane' to describe slaughter, but Carrithers says, 'You know, that's a good word. It's a humane instead of an animal way of dying. You have a very quick knife inserted and you bleed out very quickly, whereas when a puma gets a goat every once in a while – oh boy. They run around and get all bitten up. It's a whole different story.' The ways in which animals die in the wild are often overlooked when people recoil from slaughterhouses. Animals living free look bucolic, but the absence of vets and the presence of predators mean that pain and suffering are ubiquitous, and often long.

There are few who would prefer the cold, mechanised efficiency of an intensive animal farm over the Arcadian, wide-open freedom of a traditional *estancia*. From both aesthetic and animal-welfare perspectives, there is no competition. But today the most vocal objections to animal farming concern climate change. Livestock accounts for nearly 15 per cent of global greenhouse gas (GHG) emissions, and cattle are responsible for around two thirds of that. Beef also has the highest emission intensity of any meat, at nearly 300 kg CO_2 equivalent per kilogram of protein, more than three times that produced by pork or chicken.[15] Statistics like these lead many to conclude that production of meat, especially beef, has to be reduced or even eliminated.

However, truths about the impact of the sector as a whole disguise the fact that there is a lot of variety within it. Although cattle on average have the heaviest carbon footprint of any livestock, except goats, it can range from 19 kg to 135 kg CO_2 equivalent per 100 g protein depending on the system used. The average carbon footprint of beef produced in the UK is nearly half that produced in Brazil. To assess the climate impact of meat fairly, we cannot look only at its aggregate effects. We need to compare different modes of production.

There can be little doubt that, taken in the round, the environmental impact of feedlots is enormous. Take waste. Where once manure was an effective fertiliser, now it has also become a pollution problem. The feedlots produce more waste than the soil can absorb, usually because there isn't even any soil for it to fertilise. Instead of being a good source of nitrogen, cow urine converts into nitrates, filters down to the groundwater and contaminates it. These problems are evident in 'the capital of the feedlots', Saladillo in Buenos Aires province. As Gabriel Arisnabarreta, an agronomist, small family farmer and founder of the civil society environmental organisation Ecos de Saladillo, says, 'The huge amount of rotting dung in a small space expels gases like methane or nitrous oxide which stink, are poisonous, and make life nearly impossible here.'[16]

Manure is just the most evident problem of extreme intensification. To feed animals indoors requires crops grown on land that has been cleared, converted from pasture, or which was previously used to grow plants for human consumption. Much of this land given over to grow feed for animals is in South America, especially Argentina's larger neighbour, Brazil. The growth in Brazil's soybean production has been especially steep. Between 1990 and 2010 it rose from around fifteen million tonnes a year to over sixty million, and by 2020 it had overtaken the USA to become the largest exporter by a 20 per cent margin. It now accounts for an incredible half of all the world's soybean trade, all produced on 17 per cent of the country's arable land.[17] Nor does this growth look like stopping. It's a similar story in Argentina, where only 5 per cent of the soy grown across twenty million hectares of land stays in the country.[18] Globally, WWF has reported that soybean production has increased fifteen-fold since the 1950s, and soybeans are now cultivated on more than 100 million hectares of land, an area larger than France, Germany, Belgium and the Netherlands combined.[19]

All of this leaves a large greenhouse gas footprint. Feed crops require synthetic fertilisers and heavy machinery to harvest and process them, both of which use up fossil fuels. Where once pastures locked in huge quantities of CO_2, carbon concentrations in soils decrease when land is turned over to intensive arable farming for animal feed. Worst of all is when forests are cleared to create land for feed crops. Although Brazil has been a worse offender, in Argentina three million hectares of forest were destroyed for grain production and grazing in the decade to 2015 alone.[20] The FAO has calculated that, globally, every year '13 billion hectares of forest area are lost due to land conversion for agricultural uses as pastures or cropland, for both food and livestock feed crop production.' As well as the climate impact, the FAO says that '20 per cent of the world's grasslands are degraded', which is 'mainly due to intensified animal density per area'.[21]

The world has looked on with dismay at the clearing of the Amazon rainforest, one of the world's most biodiverse habitats and a vital carbon sink. But less noticed has been the development of the Cerrado in the east of the country, nearly two million km² (ca. 740,000 square miles) of tropical savanna that makes up more than a fifth of Brazil's land mass. The Cerrado is to the Amazon what the tooth-billed pigeon is to the polar bear: just as endangered but far less glamorous. WWF describes it as 'the world's most biodiverse savanna, home to five per cent of the planet's animals and plants. ... Of its more than 11,000 plant species, nearly half are found nowhere else on Earth.'[22] It's also an effective carbon store, because its deceptively small trees have deep root systems, and so around 70 per cent of the Cerrado's biomass is underground. It is estimated that this 'upside-down forest' sequesters about 118 tons of carbon per acre, whereas croplands are typically net carbon emitters.[23]

Some of the growth of agriculture in the Cerrado is welcome. In many areas, the savanna had already been cleared, but what had been planted in its place was unproductive. The transformation of this area into profitable, productive farmland, providing homes and incomes, has given tangible benefits to locals and the Brazilian state, with very little subsidy.[24] However, there is a lot of environmentally valuable land being cleared for agriculture. Half of the Cerrado has already been converted from savanna, most of it for arable and livestock production, with more than half turned over to soy production, most of it illegally.[25] In 2021, a study showed that in the previous year, 94 per cent of ecosystems in the Amazon and the Cerrado converted for agricultural use were repurposed illegally.[26]

Between 2000 and 2015, the Cerrado was being destroyed at a faster rate than the Amazon.[27] Yet from a narrowly economic point of view, the transformation could look like a success story. In 2010 *The Economist* hailed developments as 'The miracle of the Cerrado'.[28] But it failed to appreciate how environmentally important the Cerrado is. It celebrated the fact that converting the Cerrado meant not having to further deforest the Amazon, as though the Cerrado had no environmental value. That also reflected received opinion in Brazil, where the government only protected 1.5 per cent of the Cerrado in federal reserves.[29]

The increase in the amount of land used for animal feed has other impacts too. For millennia, good arable land was used almost exclusively to grow food for humans. Most grazing land is unsuitable for arable crops, so cattle and sheep in effect turn something humans cannot eat – grass – into something they can. Livestock would also be fed the parts of crops such as wheat, oats and barley that humans couldn't eat, again making maximal use of resources. Pigs and poultry would be fed on scraps and what humans counted as waste. Even today, the FAO says that 86 per cent of global livestock feed is inedible to humans.[30] Hence, the statistic that 80 per cent of global agricultural land is used to feed livestock even though it only provides less than 20 per cent of our energy needs, although frequently cited, is misleading.[31] Most of that land could not be used to feed people.

Still, today an enormous amount of land that could be used to grow crops for humans is instead used to grow animal feed. Many wildly different figures circulate, but all are incredibly high. The FAO says that '33 per cent of croplands are used for livestock feed production'. More than 40 per cent of the world's annual production of wheat, rye, oats and maize – nearly 800 million tonnes – goes into animal feed. An additional 250 million tonnes of oilseeds, mainly soybeans, also goes straight to livestock.[32] All of these figures would have increased since they were collated at various points in the last decade.

Using so much land to fatten animals is incredibly inefficient. The land required to produce one calorie's worth of beef could provide 100 calories' worth of plants.[33] Turning over all this land to animal-feed production increases greenhouse gas emissions and reduces biodiversity.

The case against intensive livestock farming is damning. Not only is it generally polluting and bad for animal welfare, it requires converting more and more vibrant ecosystems to arable farms to provide feed. But is traditional grazing any better?

Many extensive farmers, like Carrithers, argue that their systems help rather than harm the environment, and they have science on their side. As one research paper put it, 'regions with sparsely grazed grasslands provided an important climate cooling service'.[34] Grassland is an effective carbon sink, locking in CO_2. Soils in general contain more carbon than the world's atmosphere and vegetation combined.[35]

However, cows and other ruminant animals, like sheep, produce prodigious amounts of methane, a greenhouse gas twenty-five times more potent than carbon dioxide. But whereas CO_2 remains in the atmosphere for millennia, within twelve years most methane (CH_4) has reacted with oxygen in the atmosphere and converted it into carbon dioxide (CO_2) and water (H_2O). CO_2 is, of course, still a greenhouse gas, but through photosynthesis, if the pasture is extensive enough, every molecule produced as a result of grazing livestock is taken back by the grass and put into the land again. And so the cycle continues. As long as the number of head of cattle remains constant and there is enough grass so that they don't over-graze, this 'biogenic' carbon cycle does not increase the concentrations of greenhouse gases in the atmosphere.[36] This is not true of the methane released by fossil fuel production. This adds to the total amount of CO_2 in the atmosphere because it draws on carbon that was locked underground, not on that which is already in the atmosphere.

The science behind the biogenic cycle is robust. However, it is not an unconditional green light for extensive ruminant farming. First, although it is true that cow and sheep farming can be greenhouse gas neutral, were we to reduce the number of ruminants in the system we would go one better and get a short-term net *reduction* in greenhouse gases. For example, if you were to remove half of the world's ruminants, then you'd reduce by half the amount of methane put into the atmosphere by animals over the course of the biogenic cycle. This would have a cooling effect until the new level of lower methane stabilised, when we'd be back to greenhouse gas neutrality. However, once we made this change, we'd never be able to increase the stock again, because just as decreasing ruminant numbers temporarily decreases net greenhouse gas emissions, increasing them temporarily raises the emissions.

So the biogenic cycle cuts two ways: it justifies extensive grazing with a constant level of livestock, but it also gives a reason to reduce it as one tool to help us slow global warming. Whether this is a tool worth employing requires a much wider analysis of the costs and benefits. It could be argued that the short-term gains do not justify permanently decimating a sustainable, traditional and efficient means of food production.

For all its virtues, traditional extensive livestock production faces many challenges, and one of the greatest is climate change. The Pampas have been plagued by droughts for at least a decade. 'We go for periods of four to five months without a drop of rain,' says Carrithers. 'There's not enough snowfall in the Andes feeding our rivers, our streams, our springs. We've had a lot more dry, hot, sunny days with lots of wind. It's gotten to the point that lots of bare areas are blowing away and we are losing all of our ground cover.' With every passing year, Carrithers is having to reduce the number of cattle, which is down to 300 from a peak of over 1,000. The problem is not lack of grass but lack of watering holes. 'The situation with the drought is quite serious and if it continues even just five years from now we're not going to have enough animals to have the income necessary to maintain these huge properties.'

In reality, the distinction between feedlots and extensive grazing is more of a spectrum than a binary, and there is a great deal of variety within as well as between each system. Feedlots differ in both the intensity of the housing and the duration of time that cattle spend in them. On some farms, including many dairy ones, the cows will never see the light of day. In pig and poultry farming, 100 per cent indoor systems are common. But feedlots are often used for 'finishing'. In other words, the cows spend the first year or so of their lives grazing and are then kept indoors for the last months to fatten them up with a diet that gives the meat the kind of flavour and texture profile consumers want. At the same time, even in pasture-based systems, most cattle spend at least part of their lives indoors. In countries like the UK with damp, cold winters, even most organic and pasture-reared cows will spend the winter months in sheds, eating a mostly natural diet of hay and silage (fodder made from green forage crops preserved by fermentation). Farmers insist this is better for the cows, who dislike wind, rain and standing in mud, and who would struggle to find enough food to graze on in the winter months anyway. Few farms operate as purely as Estancia Ranquilco, where the land is not overgrazed and the animals feed solely on forage (grasses, herbal lays, silage and hay). Supplementary feed is routinely given even by farmers using pasture-based and organic systems.

Much of the sustainable animal agriculture of the future will have to be more like that of the past, on extensive, circular, regenerative farms. But we cannot afford to look only backwards. Some animal farming will look very different as human beings continue to innovate and learn. In the Netherlands, where livestock intensification has pushed at the limits of sustainability and animal welfare, we can see some of these changes coming through, in part driven by public demand.

Take broiler chickens – the birds bred specifically for meat production. In 2012 the animal welfare NGO Wakker Dier ('awake animal') started a campaign, *Stop de plofkip*. *Plofkip* means 'exploded chicken', a reference to the fast and oversized growth of the animals. Supermarkets signed up to the *Kip van Morgen* ('Chicken of Tomorrow') agreement, raising basic welfare standards and aiming to phase out production and sales of broiler chicken meat by 2020. However, in 2015 the Netherlands Authority for Consumers and Markets (ACM) ruled that the agreement was anti-competitive, while also pointing out that these chickens bred in conditions with supposedly higher standards of welfare only had 'slightly more space and slightly more litter on the floors' and that the birds only lived 'a couple of days longer'.[37]

Still, the push for higher standards had gained momentum. By the end of 2015, Unilever, Lidl, Jumbo and Albert Heijn had agreed to stop selling *plofkip*. Between 2014 and 2019 the number of slow-growing chickens increased more than fivefold. Meanwhile, between 2014 and 2017 the number of fast-growing chickens raised in the Netherlands dropped by a third, although since then the decline has been more gradual.[38] Fast-growing breeds are increasingly only for export, as Dutch shoppers lose their tolerance for 'exploded chicken'. In other countries retailers are also moving to meet this demand. In 2022 Marks & Spencer announced it was to become the first British retailer to sell '100 per cent slower-reared chicken'.[39]

Elsewhere in Europe, other measures have been taken to improve poultry welfare. In 2021 both France and Germany outlawed the routine mass killing of unwanted male chicks from hen-laying broods, effective from 2022.[40] These chicks are often sent to their death on conveyor belts that drop them into a shredder, or they are gassed. Both are brutal processes, but because they are quick and painless they are not as cruel as they look. Still, there is something offensive in the way in which the process shows a complete disregard for the value of life, treating chicks as trash to be disposed of as quickly and efficiently as possible. In 2022 it was reported that in the USA, around 260 million male chicks are killed each year and in France 50 million.[41] Italy has followed Germany and France in banning the practice, effective from 2026.

The ban has become practical because the technology is now available to identify male eggs and destroy them before they grow into chicks, just one example of how technology and innovation can help agriculture to become more humane and sustainable, not less. Another is the development of robotic milking stalls which the cows enter when they are ready, without any coercion. In such systems, cows often choose to be milked more frequently than they otherwise would be.[42]

Other organisations in the Netherlands are working to improve chicken welfare. One such hub of innovators and practitioners makes the case that better welfare could also be better business. A typical laying hen lays an average of 350 eggs during its brief 12–18 months of life. In the natural environment, a hen can live to around the age of five and lay up to 1,000 eggs. So better welfare means longer, healthier lives for the chickens and more eggs per bird for the producer.[43]

However, movement is slow. In 2022, Switzerland held a referendum on whether to give animals the right 'not to be intensively farmed', which would arguably have been no more than an overdue enforcement of the protection of the 'welfare and dignity of animals' already supposedly guaranteed in the country's constitution. However, only one of the twenty-six cantons, the city of Basel, voted in favour, and the proposal was rejected by 63 per cent of voters.[44] Still, the fact that the initiative even got to a national vote and was backed by more than a third of the electorate shows the direction of change.

We can expect more political and legal attempts to end the worst farming conditions. In 2023, in the UK, the animal law firm Advocates for Animals sought a judicial review on behalf of the Humane League UK against the Environment Secretary. It argued that 'the use of conventional meat chicken breeds which grow unnaturally large, unnaturally fast' breaches a law that stipulates: 'Animals may only be kept for farming purposes if it can reasonably be expected, on the basis of their genotype or phenotype, that they can be kept without any detrimental effect on their health or welfare.'[45] It is becoming increasingly implausible that these conditions are always being met. That the complaint was one of only 5 per cent of judicial review cases to be granted a full hearing shows how such arguments are increasingly being taken seriously. The case failed, but on the grounds that the Secretary of State had not acted contrary to her legal duties, because it is *possible* to keep what the plaintiffs colourfully called 'Frankenchickens' without detriment to their welfare.[46] But it was not a ruling that they *are always* well treated. The defeat was more technical than moral.

Few would dispute that decreasing the intensity of poultry farming is good for welfare, all other things being equal. But some argue, counterintuitively, that some indoor systems can be good for animals. Human beings prefer to live indoors even though that is not 'natural', and we should not assume animals prefer the harsh outdoors. For example, Claudia, a Dutch dairy farmer, used to allow her and her husband's 180 dairy cows to go outside. Now they are in stalls all year round. But Claudia is unapologetic. 'In the Netherlands we are very good at offering a very high amount of cow comfort,' she told a documentary crew. 'The cow does not like the sun, not the rain and not the wind. A cow cannot sweat easily. So if the sun is shining they are not having a good time in the pasture. There is not enough shade. If you were to let the cow choose, she would choose what is the most comfortable for her.'[47]

Another reason for her switch is more hard-nosed. 'Consumers want to have constant quality. ... They just want the same taste. If you let the cow graze in the meadow you will have fluctuations in the make-up of the milk and therefore also in the cheese. That gives a variation in taste.' As with feedlot beef, customer tastes have been shaped by the industrialisation of food. We may not like the reality of factory farming, but many have developed a preference for its products. Any change to the system is going to require a change in tastes as well as values.

Livestock farming is too diverse to be treated and judged as though it were one single thing. From an environmental and welfare point of view, the contrast between the traditional pasture-raising of the Pampas and the horrors of the feedlot shows that. But what of the health impact? Red meat has become demonised, and there are plenty of advocates for entirely plant-based diets. So much attention has been paid to both sets of claims that it is easy to forget that there is a lot of agreement that meat and dairy products make a valuable contribution to human health, and that although it may be possible to replace them with plant-based alternatives, there is no health advantage in doing so and there could be some loss. This comes with a major caveat: the quantities of meat and dairy eaten in developed countries are far too high. The problem is not that we eat animal fats and proteins at all, it's that we eat far too much.

The biggest study into the composition of a both healthy and environmentally sustainable diet was published in 2019 by the EAT–Lancet Commission, made up of nineteen expert commissioners and eighteen co-authors from sixteen countries, from the fields of human health, agriculture, political sciences and environmental sustainability.[48] It set itself the question 'Can we feed a future population of ten billion people a healthy diet within planetary boundaries?' It concluded that meat, eggs and dairy had an important role to play, but that in industrialised countries their consumption would have to be significantly reduced. This grabbed the headlines, but the amounts recommended by the EAT–Lancet Planetary Health Diet seem small only in comparison with the historically unprecedented amounts many eat today.

One of the novelties of the EAT–Lancet report was that it explicitly rejected a single, universal prescription. It appreciated that different cultures and ecosystems support significantly different kinds of diet. So for each element of the diet it recommended a range for healthy, sustainable consumption, not a single number. If you live in a country like New Zealand or the United Kingdom, where conditions are excellent for grazing, you might eat more beef, lamb and dairy than if you lived in the Arabian Gulf or North Africa. In Japan, you might eat much more fish than a person in Bolivia or Austria.

The daily dairy intake of 0–500g is quite liberal, unless you drink a lot of milk. It allows for decent portions of yogurt and cheese, with splashes in tea and coffee. The weekly meat and egg allocations are 0–98g of beef or lamb, the same of pork, 0–406g of chicken, 0–700g of fish and 0–175g of eggs. In many countries, the reduction in beef required by this is drastic. In the USA, a typical steak weighs a huge 340g (12oz), nearly a month's maximum allocation. To eat steak every week under the EAT–Lancet guidelines would require having just one 85g (3oz) serving, a decent portion in most cuisines. The limits on pork are also tight but achievable, while up to four eggs a week is not a lot by modern standards. Together, the amount of meat, poultry and eggs EAT–Lancet allows is significantly less than the current USDA recommendations of up to 878g (31oz) per week for an adult consuming 2,400 calories a day.[49]

However, with the addition of the chicken, fish and dairy allowances, there could be plenty of animal protein in the diet. In most places at most times meat has been consumed in moderation, with large chunks only eaten on special occasions. The famed healthy Mediterranean diet, for example, as described by Harvard Health, includes 'cheese and yogurt, consumed daily in low to moderate amounts', 'fish and poultry, consumed in low to moderate amounts a few times a week' and 'red meat, consumed infrequently and in small amounts'.[50] This diet dovetails neatly with the EAT–Lancet guidelines. It should also be noted than in many parts of the world, including sub-Saharan Africa, the EAT–Lancet diet would imply an *increase* in the amount of animal protein eaten. The world eats too much meat as a whole, but that excess is concentrated in certain parts of it.

The EAT–Lancet report faced many criticisms, including that its recommendations would result in micronutrient shortfalls, that the health case for reducing red meat consumption was weak, and that 1.6 billion people in the world couldn't afford such a diet. Such an ambitious undertaking was always going to be imperfect. But few could argue with the general thrust of the report. Without saying there is no place for livestock farming and meat in our diets, it showed how the ways we raise and eat animals now are bad for our health and that of the planet, and that our current trajectory is unsustainable. To that we can add that the present and probable future of livestock farming is bad for far too many animals. But we can have a smaller, sustainable livestock sector that treats animals humanely, and we can eat meat, eggs and dairy in quantities that for most of history would have been considered ample. There may be no going back to a bucolic past, such as we used to see on the Pampas. But that does not mean the future for meat and dairy has only two possible scenarios – either their elimination or the increased use of concentrated animal feeding operations.

We have arrived at a peculiar point in the meat debate. Tara Garnett is the director of Table, a global platform for inclusive, informed dialogue about the future of food. She thinks back to 2003, when she had a meeting with the Meat and Livestock Commission, an independent UK government-funded body that represents the industry. When Garnett suggested that the nation needed to reduce its overall consumption of meat and dairy, the idea was so heretical that the representative of the commission walked out on her. But in the years that followed, a general consensus started to emerge that consumption patterns need to change, for environmental and health reasons. But, she tells me, this *entente cordiale* has not held. Within the environmental movement a split has opened up between, at one extreme, those who are vociferously anti meat and dairy and, at the other, those who think that it is possible to rear animals regeneratively. Those with better practices are pushed into a tacit alliance with the bigger producers, because they don't like to speak out against any kind of animal farming for fear of encouraging wider criticism of their industry. As Garnett says of the pasture-fed livestock sector, 'If you caught them in a quiet one-to-one moment, they would agree that ultimately one outcome of what they're arguing for would be less meat consumption. But they won't go on record to say that in public because they feel under attack.' In this polarised atmosphere, big industry has come out fighting, refusing to countenance any suggestion that it needs to be scaled back.'

This factionalism is, ironically, fuelled by an abuse of nuance. As we have seen, because different farming systems have different environmental impacts, advocates of livestock farming are correct to say that you can't make sweeping generalisations about animal agriculture. But the meat and dairy industry uses this fact to avoid accepting that, overall, severe reductions in livestock farming are needed. Legitimate arguments for the sustainability of some live-stock systems are being used to bat off all suggestions that, in the round, we still have to reduce meat and dairy consumption.

'I'm with the need for recognising complexity and not making one-size-fits-all general statements,' says Garnett. 'And there are particular interest groups that rightly feel threatened. But we get caught up in the detail. There is complexity but there is also a general direction of travel. I think you can hold those two thoughts in your mind at the same time.'

11

Out of the blue

Carp and cobia in China and Panama

While the land has long been dominated by domesticated animals, the earth's waters have remained much wilder. We think of hunter-gathering as an ancient, long-left-behind practice, but until recently, most of the food we took from our waters was hunted or gathered, not raised or cultivated. The ornamental goldfish is one of only two fish species generally considered to have been completely domesticated. The other is a close relative, although you wouldn't know it to look at it: the common carp. Westerners, who rarely eat the fish, may be surprised to know that more than four million tonnes of it is farmed around the world every year, compared with less than three million tonnes of Atlantic salmon. Four of the six most harvested farmed fish are species of carp.[1]

The Chinese started to domesticate carp as long as 4,000 years ago, meaning that aquaculture began 8,000 years later than agriculture. Around 475 BCE, Fan Lai wrote *The Classic of Fish Culture*, the first text to include details of how to maintain and harvest ponds.

The next major development in Chinese aquaculture was down to an extraordinary combination of coincidence and serendipity. In the Tang Dynasty (618–906 CE), the emperor's family name was Li, which is also the popular name of the common carp. Homophones and synonyms have always been considered significant in Chinese culture, and so cultivation of the *li* was banned. Reluctant to give up their fish, the Chinese people turned to other species, such as the silver carp and grass carp, which remain the most cultivated species in the world today.[2]

One reason why aquaculture took off in East Asia is that carp farming helped with rice cultivation. When the fish are kept in the flooded paddy fields, they eat weeds and pests, while their excrement provides natural fertiliser. In turn, the rice shades the water, stopping it from getting too warm. And because the rice plants absorb the fish waste, the ammonia concentrations in the water remain low. This integrated rice–fish system leads to more stable yields and reduces the need for fertilisers and pesticides. The rice–fish culture is recognised by the UN as a Globally Important Agricultural Heritage System.[3] Such systems are defined as 'agro-ecosystems inhabited by communities that live in an intricate relationship with their territory'. Programmes are now in place to introduce the rice–fish model to areas outside Asia where it has not been traditional.

Some form of aquaculture has been practised in most of the world for centuries, with Latin America, Australasia, the Pacific Islands and the Middle East among the few regions with no widely established tradition of fish farming. As with so much agricultural practice, its nature and scale have changed dramatically in the relatively recent past. In 1960 less than 2 per cent of the world's fish and seafood was farmed. Now, more than half of it is. While the wild seafood catch rose by 169 per cent in that period, aquacultural production rose an astonishing 5,124 per cent. Since 1990 all of the increase in harvested fish has been the result of aquaculture, which has increased sixfold, while the numbers of wild 'capture fish' have plateaued.[4] Over the same three decades, the production of farmed finfish (as opposed to shellfish) rose from 9 to 56 million tonnes.[5] The FAO expects aquatic food production to increase by a further 15 per cent by 2030.

One driver of aquaculture is the fact that fish stocks in many parts of the world are under intolerable pressure. The FAO reported that 'the fraction of fishery stocks within biologically sustainable levels decreased from 90 per cent in 1974 to 64.6 per cent in 2019'.[6] In the UK, another report found that over a third of stocks are overfished, only 45 per cent are sustainably fished, and a quarter are in a critical condition.[7] Globally, nearly one in ten stocks have been driven to collapse.[8] All these data are estimates and fish stocks can fluctuate and bounce back quickly. But for decades the pattern has been indisputable: the seas are being harvested at an unsustainable rate. The only good news is that with capture fishing plateauing, a greater proportion – 82.5 per cent in 2019 – is coming from biologically sustainable stocks.[9]

Given the global taste for fish, it is perhaps surprising that aquaculture has taken so long to proliferate. 'It's like going to a restaurant and saying, "I'd like to have a steak of a wild cow" or "I would like to have a wild chicken." There is no such thing and we're going in that direction with fish,' says Professor Daniel Benetti, Director of Aquaculture at Miami University. His colleague, fish hatchery manager Ronald Hoenig, argues, 'If we're going to actually protect our oceans, we have to make that transition from hunting-gathering to farming. It's what we've done with all of our other food production.'[10]

The global demand for 'blue foods' – those from marine or fresh waters – is predicted to nearly double by 2050, from a 2015 baseline.[11] Seafood consumption has already increased massively. The average human eats more than twenty kilograms of fish and seafood every year, more than twice as much as fifty years ago. With the increase in the global population, this has required a fourfold increase in production. Consumption patterns vary enormously around the world. On average, our waters provide about 17 per cent of the animal protein humans eat, but in many countries in Asia and Africa they provide more than half. The world's biggest fish- and seafood-eating nations are the Maldives (87kg/head) and Iceland (84kg/head), with the Central Asian republics consuming less than three kilograms per head. Afghans eat less of it than anyone else, at around a third of a kilo per year.[12]

Often aquaculture is presented as necessary to meet this growth in demand. For instance, the FAO says, 'In the next ten years, aquaculture must expand sustainably to satisfy the gap in global demand for aquatic foods.'[13] However, whether the world needs more seafood is questionable. A report by the International Panel of Experts on Sustainable Food Systems (IPES-Food) examined the often-repeated assertion that 'we need more protein to meet the needs of a growing population'. Although this claim is promoted by the vested interests of the meat, dairy, fish and dietary supplement industries, it has historically also been made by the UN. In the 1950s, when there was a widespread belief that there was a 'protein gap' between the amount of protein needed to sustain a healthy global population and its supply, the UN created a special Protein Advisory Group to fight to close that gap. The UN continued to worry about protein well into the 1970s, issuing reports such as *Feeding the Expanding World Population: International Action to Avert the Impending Protein Crisis* and 'The Protein Problem' (both in 1968).[14] However, the IPES-Food report concluded that 'there is no "protein gap" in terms of global supply versus nutritional needs, and that poverty and poor access to food are the main drivers of various dietary deficiencies'.

Whether we need more protein from the sea or not, demand for it is rising, and the FAO believes it will be met only by 'intensifying and expanding sustainable aquaculture production'. To many, this sounds like a threatening oxymoron. There has been a steady stream of reports exposing bad practice in aquaculture, almost all of which is caused by its intensive nature.

The welfare of the fish is the most obvious issue, although historically it has barely been considered. Global figures don't even count the fish caught as individual animals but as biomass, measured by total weight. Researchers have estimated that for farmed finfish alone, these numbers translated to around 124 billion fish 'harvested' – the seafood industry's euphemism for 'caught and slaughtered' – in 2019. This number far outstrips the 80 billion farmed land animals of all species slaughtered annually, and it does not include the many fish that died in their cages before they could be killed.

The same authors concluded that 'inhumane slaughter practices cause suffering for most farmed finfishes', with 70 per cent having no legal welfare protection.[15] Compassion in World Farming (CIWF) paints a similar picture, saying, 'In fish farms, large numbers of fish are confined in a small area which can cause serious welfare problems. Salmon, while around 75cm long, can be given the space equivalent of just a bathtub of water each.' It is also concerned that 'some fish may be starved for two weeks or more' so that their guts are empty before procedures such as transport, grading and slaughter, many of which are stressful. CIWF also claims that slaughter often causes 'immense suffering', with such methods being used as gassing, cutting the gills without stunning or leaving the fish to suffocate in air or on ice.[16]

Another report pointed to very high mortality rates, which have not only 'increased dramatically in recent years' but 'far outstrip those found in other forms of intensive farming'.[17] Mortality-rate comparisons with land animals can be misleading because fish naturally produce thousands of small fry, the vast majority of which don't survive. However, the mortality rates measured in the study had nothing to do with natural causes. The main factors were all attributed to 'poor farming practices', including pollution, escapes, and parasites and disease, as well as the treatments for both. The health problems are made worse by high stocking densities.

Aquaculture raises environmental as well as welfare concerns. Many fish farms are polluting, taking advantage of clean waters but leaving them dirtier than they were. Uneaten feed and faeces are created in large concentrations, which can lead to eutrophication: an excess of nutrients in the water such as phosphorus and nitrogen. Algal blooms and dead sea life are the visible signs of this. Wild fish stocks have been harmed by pollution from farms. Wild salmon numbers have been decreasing in many areas, largely due to the disease and sea lice transmitted to them via (usually escaped) farmed salmon. One review of research into Atlantic salmon and sea trout concluded that '12–29 per cent fewer returning adult spawners can be expected for Atlantic salmon populations because of salmon lice induced mortality in farm-intensive areas.'[18] Fish farms can also pollute contiguous waters in other ways.

Another environmental impact of aquaculture is that carnivorous fish need to be fed on small wild pelagic fish – those that live in the open seas, away from shores and the seabed – such as anchovies and sardines. Catching these in vast numbers to make the fishmeal and fish oil (FMFO) used as feed for the farmed animals puts pressure on wild ecosystems and decreases the number of fish that occupy an important part of the food web. The industry also uses some plant crops for feed, which brings with it all the biodiversity loss and greenhouse gas emissions associated with converting more land to arable farming.

All of these environmental costs have a financial price. 'Dead Loss', a sober independent report on salmon farming conducted for the Changing Markets Foundation, focused on the hidden economic costs of salmon farming in four major producing countries: Canada, Norway, Chile and Scotland.[19] Mortality alone cost the salmon industry in these countries $15,539 billion over the period 2013–2019. The report also quantified the 'pollution abatement cost' (PAC), meaning 'the amount that would be required to preserve or restore a unit of an environmental good', and found it amounted to $4 billion over the six years. Together with other costs, including the industry's contribution to climate change, the report concluded that salmon aquaculture had generated costs of $47 billion. Of these, only 60 per cent fell to producers, while 40 per cent ($19 billion) fell to wider society. Economists call these negative externalities: costs that are created by economic activity but not paid for by those profiting from it or buying its products. Society picks up the bill instead.

While accepting that salmon farming has many positive benefits, the Changing Markets Foundation report concludes that 'there are substantial costs that are not included on the balance sheet' and that 'the scope for improved environmental and social performance is considerable'. The consensus is that this is true across the whole sector. But can aquaculture really do better, or are its flaws inherent in its fundamental nature?

Daniel Benetti has been working in aquaculture for over forty years, and as an academic he believes he can take an impartial view. 'I've seen the good, the bad and the ugly,' he tells me. 'We've been through many stages, from the dark ages of how aquaculture was developed decades ago to how it has been progressed to this day.' For Benetti, a case study in good aquaculture is Open Blue, one of the more advanced and sustainable operations.

Open Blue farms cobia off the coast of Panama. Cobia (*Rachycentron canadum*) is the only genus of the Rachycentridae family of fish. It has a light, firm flesh, cooks similarly to tuna and is classified as a species of least concern to conservationists. To farm it, Open Blue does a lot more than put huge concentrations of the fish into large netted pens until they are big enough to eat. Every stage in the process is carefully managed and aims to model best practice in marine farming.[20]

Start with the eggs. The broodstock is kept in tanks in Miami. Because spawning is triggered by water temperature, three different breeding groups can be cycled to provide a year-round supply of eggs. They don't need a lot of mother fish because each one produces a million to three million eggs in a single spawn. In the wild, almost all of these would either be eaten by other fish or die. In the controlled conditions of the tanks, many more will grow into adult fish.

The fertilised eggs float to the surface of the tank, where they are skimmed off and sent immediately to the inshore hatchery in Panama, supplementing the local egg supply. Within a day, they begin hatching in the incubator. For three to four days the newly hatched larvae feed off their own yolk sacs. From that point on, the animals need to be fed.

From day three, the tiny fish feed on rotifers, small plankton cultivated in the facility. The rotifer has no nutritional value of its own but is enriched by whatever the company feeds it. From day nine, the fish start also to feed on artemias, brine shrimp. These are again enriched with the vitamins, minerals and essential oils that the fish need not only to grow but to have the right kind of omega oils that make cobia attractive as a healthy product.

From day eighteen the fish are weaned on to the food that they will consume for the rest of their lives: dry pellets made from fish-meal and fish oil. After thirty days in the hatchery the fish will have reached a gram in weight and are moved to the nursery, still inland but outdoors. Around fifty to sixty days later they will weigh 150 grams and be ready to be moved out to sea, where they will spend around eight months before they are harvested. Crucially, the cages are eight miles from land, lined up 330 feet apart, perpendicular to the deep, strong current so that any potential pollutants are dispersed as much as possible. This seems to work: the Monterey

Bay Aquarium's Seafood Watch programme scored the farm green for effluent, indicating that there were no concerns about it.

Moving fish farms so far out to sea could be a game-changer in terms of countering pollution. But until recently, it just wasn't possible. 'The technology was such that if you were in exposed areas your cages would be destroyed and you would lose the fish,' says Benetti. He believes that fish farms in open seas could actually bring a net environmental benefit. 'Those farms would accumulate waste, no doubt about it, but then they would become what is known as an FAD – a fish aggregating device.' FADs attract ocean-going pelagic fish. 'In a good location it could be a source of fertilisation rather than a source of pollution, as long as it doesn't cross a threshold that means you produce too much for the capacity of the environment to take it.'

However, the fish still require feed, and Seafood Watch reported that 'to supply the fish oil to grow one ton of farmed cobia, 3.84 tons of wild fish would need to be caught'.[21] Feed was the only one of Seafood Watch's criteria for which the cobia scored red on its traffic-light ratings. In their defence, fish farmers argue that catching small fish and feeding them to larger ones makes more efficient use of the feed, since there is less wastage than there would be in the wild: all the small fish caught are eaten in their entirety, and almost all the feeding fish make it to maturity. 'If you would leave those small pelagic fish in the sea it would be much less efficient than to take them out to make feeds,' argues Benetti. 'Tuna sometimes has to undertake a transoceanic migration to find food and then they need to eat, some say, sixty kilos of fish. The loss of energy that they incur is much higher than when they are in a cage.' Nor is it fair to compare the catching of fish for feed to the huge use of land to grow feed for livestock, land that could be used for human food.

Aquaculturists are also working to make feed production more efficient. For example, modern fish farms contain a rendering plant which takes all the by-products from the processing plant. 'They used to have to pay people to come and get it and throw it away,' says Benetti. 'Now they are making fishmeal or fish oil with it, mixing it with other ingredients to make pet food or even feeds for other species.' These efficiencies reduce the environmental footprint, but that need not be the motivation. 'Fishmeal and fish oil is the highest cost of aquaculture production, fifty, sixty per cent. So if you're a producer you want to be more efficient.' Self-interest is also driving other improvements. 'I can see a lot of progress towards circularity, but it's not because people are nice. They're there to make money. But sustainability and profitability come hand in hand.'

Advocates of aquaculture also claim that fish are much more efficient than land animals at converting feed, since being buoyant and cold-blooded they have lower energy needs. An established body of evidence supports this, based on a measure called the feed conversion ratio (FCR), which gauges the efficiency of converting feed to body mass. The lower the number, the more efficient the conversion of feed to flesh. Beef cattle has a typical FCR of around 6–10, pigs 2.7–5 and poultry 1.7–2, although it can be as low as 1.3 if it is a fast-growing caged variety.[22][23] The FCR for farmed fish and shrimp is typically 1–2.4, meaning that at its best it is more efficient than even the most intensively, quickly farmed chicken and much more efficient than pigs, sheep and cows.

Some researchers question the merits of FCR, arguing that nutrient conversion matters more than weight conversion and that 'despite lower FCRs in aquaculture, protein and calorie retention for aquaculture production is comparable to livestock production'.[24] But Benetti remains convinced that 'any way you look at it, aquaculture is the most efficient form of [animal] protein production hands down, because fish tend to be more efficient in terms of their physiological and energetic performance'. Even if farmed fish are no better than land livestock, they are more efficient than wild fish, which typically eat upwards of fifteen kilograms for every kilogram of weight added.

Seafood Watch scored Open Blue's cobia yellow on three other criteria, mainly due to unknowns: 'The risk of escapes is rated a moderate concern, and it's unknown if breeding between farmed and wild cobia could affect the genetic composition and fitness of wild populations.' It also found that data on antibiotic use were limited. The excessive use of antibiotics and other medications in aquaculture is as much of a concern as it is in agriculture, since it can lead to antimicrobial resistance, making bugs more dangerous for humans and other animals. Before entering the oceans, Open Blue's cobia are vaccinated against the various types of bacteria that could affect them in the waters off Panama. Brian O'Hanlon of Open Blue has said, 'Our practice is to only use medication when it's absolutely essential for the health of the fish.' However, Seafood Watch scored Open Blue 4/10 for its chemical use.

Open Blue shows how, for all aquaculture's potential, it still has many problems and challenges. Overall, Seafood Watch ranks its fish as a 'good alternative': not as good as its 'best choices' or as certified fish and seafood, but not on the 'avoid' list. This reflects the fact that aquaculture as a whole is still a problematic industry and even its best exemplars are far from perfect. In 2020, only 3 per cent of global aquaculture was covered by the two largest certification schemes, the Aquaculture Stewardship Council (ASC) and the Global Aquaculture Alliance–Best Aquaculture Practices (GAA–BAP).[25] By comparison, almost one in five of the world's wild fish catch are certified by the Marine Stewardship Council (MSC), with more than half of the global wild tuna catch now covered by it.[26]

Still, even many of aquaculture's biggest critics accept that it can be sustainable in its better forms. For example, the Dead Loss report rightly challenges the industry's narrative of 'a clean and healthy source of protein that is helping to revive coastal communities.' The most intensive industrialised farms, especially those inland and close to shore, are often deeply problematic. Despite these criticisms, it concludes 'aquaculture is a diverse farming practice, and we acknowledge that it can make a positive contribution to food security and livelihoods'.

Compassion in World Farming is also highly critical of the aquaculture industry, but it campaigns for higher standards, not for its abolition. It even acknowledges that 'fish can be farmed more humanely than conventional intensive farming'. The best practice of fish slaughter in farms like Open Blue's is better than that of most traditionally caught wild fish, and perhaps even better than some land animal slaughterhouses. The fish are effectively sucked out of the nets through a pipe and are individually stunned. Less stress results in better-quality flesh, so farmers have a commercial reason to kill quickly and painlessly, regardless of their welfare concerns.

The global environmental NGO WWF also warns that 'when farms are poorly managed, aquaculture can have substantial impacts on the environment, climate and society', but adds, 'when done responsibly, the impacts of aquaculture can be minimal' and that 'certain kinds of aquaculture can even be regenerative for the ocean'.[27] One such method is non-fed aquaculture, which, as the name indicates, does not require extracting feed from elsewhere in the seas or on land. It is used to grow molluscs, including clams; oysters and mussels; echinoderms, such as starfish, sea urchins and sea cucumbers; and seaweed.[28] Because the animals concerned have very basic central nervous systems, only the most absolutist vegans have welfare concerns about their use as food. Even Peter Singer, one of the world's most famous animal ethicists, said in the first edition of his landmark book *Animal Liberation* that molluscs (apart from octopus) could be eaten with impunity, and he would occasionally eat them himself, despite being a vegan. (He later decided to err on the side of caution, concluding that 'while one cannot with any confidence say that these creatures do feel pain, so one can equally have little confidence in saying that they do not feel pain'.)[29]

Non-fed aquaculture farms are not merely non-polluting, in many cases they are actively purifying. Because the animals feed on microscopic plants, detritus and nutrients, they act as water filters, often improving the water quality. Macroalgae (seaweeds) are 'nutrient strippers' that feed on inorganic nutrients, while molluscs and echinoderms are 'filter feeders' that eat dissolved organics and suspended solids. They can remove excess nutrients, such as nitrogen, that lead to eutrophication. They can also counter acidification by absorbing carbon. On top of all this, these foods are extremely nutritious.

Another system with similar advantages is integrated multi-trophic aquaculture (IMTA). This is defined as 'a balanced system that provides the by-products of one cultured species to another, which can achieve high income and environmental remediation'.[30] In other words, fish are farmed alongside molluscs, echinoderms and/or seaweed, and the latter feed on the waste the former produce. Chile has become the world's second largest producer of mussels largely as a result of adopting such systems, with salmon as the finfish. In Italy, sea bream and branzino (European seabass) are also being farmed with mussels. Such forms of aquaculture apply the same principles that made its very first forms sustainable: carp in the paddy fields were part of a symbiotic system in which the fish did not deplete or contaminate the waters but cleaned and enriched them. That too was a non-feed system.

It is unfortunate that modern aquaculture has taken its time to recognise the virtues of this ancient model. For example, mangroves are shrubs or trees that grow in coastal saline or brackish water. They are important biodiverse habitats. Not only do they sequester carbon, they act as buffers on coastlines, protecting them from storms and rising sea levels, and stopping salt water intruding into arable land. But 38 per cent of the world's mangrove habitats have been destroyed by prawn farming in South and Southeast Asia. Recently, however, some farmers have started to cultivate prawns among the intact mangroves. It is not yet clear whether this is as benign or even as helpful as the traditional rice–fish system, but it is at the very least less destructive than typical prawn farms.

It is hard to shake the intuition that the best fish must be wild, but Benetti points to several advantages of aquaculture: 'Fish farmed in Chile are harvested today, they are processed overnight and they are here in the market in Miami or New York in the next day or two, high quality, very fresh with very little waste. A wild salmon that is caught, for example, off Alaska can change hands seven times and take two weeks or longer before it reaches the final customer.' Some farmed fish may even be healthier than wild alternatives. People seek out salmon and tuna for their omega-3 fatty acids, but wild fish have to work harder, which means they have a larger muscle-to-fat ratio, so can have fewer omega-3s than farmed varieties.[31] In any case, the line between farmed and wild has been blurred. Alaskan wild salmon is world famous, but to help maintain wild stocks, around thirty hatcheries release nearly two billion reared juvenile salmon every year.[32] 'Wild' does not mean an absence of – sometimes quite extensive – human management.

In any case, the days when capture fishing was remotely natural are long gone. While most fishing boats are small and often unmotorised, the majority of seafood today is caught by huge trawlers which are like floating industrial units, spending months or even years at a time at sea, processing and freezing the catch on board. Around three quarters of the boats fishing in UK waters are small, but they catch less than 5 per cent of the total quota. The size of some of the larger vessels is incredible. In one year, just one boat caught half of all Northern Ireland's fish.[33] Some of their methods make aquaculture look gentle. Bottom trawlers and dredgers drag huge nets across the ocean floors, scooping up everything indiscriminately. One NGO compares it to bulldozing, with good reason: 'Seabed habitats from reefs to seagrass can be destroyed in minutes, often never to recover.'[34] One study estimated that the carbon dioxide released from the seabed from bottom trawling and dredging adds up to the same amount of emissions as are produced by the entire aviation industry.[35] This increases ocean acidification, decreases the sea's capacity to act as a carbon sink and results in more CO_2 getting into the atmosphere, fuelling global warming.[36]

All industrial capture fishing methods have problems with 'by-catch': sea life that is caught unintentionally and that is not used for food. WWF estimates that entanglement in fishing nets is the single largest cause of mortality for small cetaceans, killing over 300,000 small whales, dolphins and porpoises every year.[37] It published a study which estimated that 40.4 per cent of the global marine catch was bycatch.[38] Aquaculture may be ugly compared with a line and rod, but it is positively beauteous when compared with the large, rapacious capture fishing boats. And it is these, not aquaculture, which have caused the decline of the traditional small dayboat.

Benetti is convinced that aquaculture is the future. 'The bottom line is that, yes, in the past it has been developed at the expense of the environment, but it has improved dramatically and continues to improve its ecological efficiency and economic viability. As Winston Churchill said about democracy – except for all others, aquaculture is the worst form of animal production.'

The UN has also put its weight behind sustainable aquaculture with its Blue Transformation strategy, 'a vision for transforming aquatic food systems'. One of its three core objectives is 'sustainable aquaculture expansion' through improved governance and the development and transfer of technologies and best practices. When the history of the world's food system in the twenty-first century is told, it could be that the biggest changes occurred not on land, but in the world's waters.

12

ANIMALS AT THE
CROSSROADS

Falafel and fake meat in Utopia

'This is a totally amazing idea,' says Sam. 'It's going to come. For the moment people don't know what it is because they can't taste it. So we've been organising a few tastings, and once people put this in their mouth it changes everything.'

It's July 2022 and Sam is telling me about cultured meat, also known as cell-based, fake or lab-grown meat. This is a foodstuff that is chemically and – in theory, at least – nutritionally identical to animal protein, but created from cells in bioreactors. For Sam and other innovators, investors and enthusiasts, cultured meat is a food revolution. It promises meat without animals, a formula that hitherto has been a contradiction in terms. Advocates claim not that it will be as good as real meat, but that it will be better: for animals, for the environment, even for our health. Sam says their product will contain 'more nutritional elements like the proteins that you need and potentially less of the bad fats that you don't'.

Sam also argues that cultured meat is more environmentally sustainable, pointing to the vast amounts of water and crops required to raise livestock. 'The way we do it is a simplification of the system. We feed the cell directly rather than feeding the cereal that will feed the animal. We provide the cells with the optimised growth medium of water, sugars, amino acids, no more, no less, meaning that you don't have the wastage.' Until recently, this cell feed has been an obstacle to cultured meat being truly vegan as the cells have been fed on foetal bovine serum (FBS), drawn from the blood of a cow's foetus. However, now several biotech companies claim to have produced reliable and animal-free FBS substitutes. Vegan meat may not be an oxymoron for much longer.

What's more, Sam argues that cultured meat will help nations to become more self-sufficient in food supply. At the moment, many countries have to import huge quantities of meat because they don't have enough of the right kind of land to produce it. 'China is super interested in this kind of technology, because they would have sovereignty over the production of local meat. They won't have a question of intensive farming or extensive farming, they just won't have farming.'

It sounds wonderful. There's just one problem. 'For the moment it doesn't exist,' admits Sam. Cultured meat has been made and eaten, but not on anything like an industrial scale. The only such meat you could have bought commercially at the time of writing is some cultured chicken in Singapore, but even this has only been available for very limited periods. The bullish statements that regularly flow from cultured meat startups have not yet been matched by products on people's plates.

When I spoke to Sam, they were confident that their company would have a viable product soon. Lab and pilot-scale work were completed and Sam anticipated production of hundreds of kilos within six months. Sites for large factories with regulatory approval would be found by the end of the year and the first commercial products would be ready within twelve months. Sam believed that the price point would match that of natural meat five years from production and that when that point was reached, it would be 'transformational for the industry and for humanity'.

It turned out that Sam was a little optimistic. When I checked on progress eighteen months later, instead of producing hundreds of kilos, the company was still producing its 'first cut ... in limited quantities at its pilot production facility'. The regulatory submission was still being finalised, and no large-scale factory was yet in the pipeline. The only commercial products set to be available would be sold as 'part of exclusive tasting events curated in collaboration with select partners'.

Sam is not their real name. I interviewed twenty-eight people for this book and gave each one the opportunity to check and if necessary tweak the quotes I used from them. Sam was the only one to withdraw consent to be quoted. For all their missionary zeal, it took less than two years for them to withdraw their optimistic prophesies. Meat's second coming has been postponed, yet again.

The cultured-meat proto-industry is characterised by the kind of positive thinking Sam exuded. Its optimism is reflected in a techno-economic analysis (TEA) commissioned by the Good Food Institute (GFI), which describes itself as a 'nonprofit working internationally to accelerate alternative protein innovation'. The GFI's analysis of the TEA concluded that 'by 2030, cultivated meat could have lower overall environmental impacts, a smaller carbon footprint, and be cost-competitive with some forms of conventional meat'.[1] Numbers and deadlines vary, but this broad narrative has become received wisdom: within a few decades cultivated meat will deliver cheap, nutritious, sustainable alternatives to animal flesh. It's not a matter of *if*, only *when*.

Human geographer Alex Sexton and her colleagues have summarised five promises commonly made by cultured meat proponents. Sam has already given examples of three: it will be 'good for animals and the environment', it 'tastes like animal'; and it gives us 'healthier bodies'. A fourth is that it will 'feed the world', premised on the idea that in the future, as much meat will roll off production lines as we're willing to make. One company has talked about installing 'cellular agriculture life-cycle pods' in African refugee camps. Another announced a collaboration with local producers in Liberia. But grassroots cultured meat production to feed the poor is so far removed from the reality of where the technology is today that these can only be seen as wishful fantasies at best and as cynical PR at worst.

The fifth promise is 'control for sale'. This is the idea that 'the relocation of production into the spaces of technoscience is seen as safeguarding against the uncleanliness and risks associated with processes that are seemingly "closer" to nature'. An example of this is Sam's belief that cultured meat can provide a better, purer balance of fats and nutrients than nature can.

Sexton et al. argued that narratives have a central role in shaping how and what we eat. So it is not surprising that the people pushing cellular meat are finding persuasive stories to tell. However, on closer examination, many of these narratives feature shady characters and implausible plot twists.

Take the promise of 'healthier bodies'. The claims for the superior health-giving properties of plant-based burgers rest on comparisons of selected nutrients such as proteins and fats. The same boasts are made by makers of meat substitutes, who produce comparison tables to show how their products beat real meat. The makers of the plant-based Impossible Burger, for example, say that compared with ground beef, their burger has the same amount of protein, more fibre, eight times as much calcium, and less total fat and cholesterol.[2]

The idea that you can compare the healthiness of foods simply by listing these numbers is deeply questionable, as we shall see in chapter 16. Cultured meat is just muscle fibre which is then mixed with other ingredients like fat to make a kind of mince, shaped to produce burgers and faux steaks. It has to be fortified to add the micronutrients found in animal flesh. A traditional pasture-fed cow, in contrast, ingests a huge number of different microorganisms, fungi and nutrients from the grass and herbs it eats. So there is no way that cultured meat can ever be structurally the same as real meat. Even if you could identify every single micronutrient in beef and add it to the cell feed, the growing process is so different it cannot be assumed that the result will be the same. It is false to describe it as identical to animal meat, just made differently. Claims of nutritional equivalence or even superiority need to be taken with a pinch of salt.

Perhaps the most suspect story of all is the one about the technology's inexorable progress. When food writer Joe Fassler looked into the science behind the effusive claims made about the coming future of cultured meat, he didn't have to dig very deeply to discover that they stood on shallow, shaky foundations.[3]

Take the GFI report. It exudes optimism, but read it carefully and you will see that what is spun as the promise of cheap cultivated meat is in reality no more than a possibility. It noted that, at the time of its writing, 'current CM [cultured meat] production costs are an order of magnitude of 10,000 to 100 higher than benchmark values for comparable traditional meat products.'[4] Fassler calculated that for the report's claim about cost competitiveness by 2030 to be true, there would have to be a 4,000-fold reduction in costs in nine years. CE Delft, the research and consultancy company that prepared the report, calls the envisaged reduction in costs no more than 'feasible', while outlining the many and various challenges that would need to be overcome for it to be actual. The GFI carefully chose the word 'could' to describe the 2030 scenario.

Even taken on its own terms, the much-talked-up potential for cultured protein in the report is modest. The trade publication *Food Navigator* tried to calculate what would be required to replace

10 per cent of the world's animal meat with cultured protein by 2030, by analysing the report and quizzing Blake Byrne, former Business Innovation Specialist at GFI.[5] It found that each of the facilities sketched out in the analysis would require 130 bioreactor lines, with ten times the capacity of the largest mammalian cell culture facility constructed to date. Byrne said that to meet the 10 per cent target, we'd need '4,000 of these facilities to be operating at pretty much full capacity by 2030'. Each one is projected to cost $450 million, meaning the total cost of all of them would be $1.8 trillion. And, of course, the real costs of such cutting-edge projects almost always end up being far higher.

Then there is the projected retail price of the end product. Soon after the CE Delft report was published, it had to be corrected to raise the lowest-end modelled production cost of cultured protein from $5.66 per kg to $6.43. This is still more expensive than lean beef, while the cellular meat in question would be the less appetising 'slurry or paste made out of meat cells, comparable to very finely ground meat, suitable for further formulation into meat-consumer products'. Given that this is the most optimistic price from one of the most optimistic reports, it is not surprising that even its authors acknowledged that it would make no commercial sense. By comparison, another less partisan research paper concluded that 'the wholesale cost of cell-cultured meat is optimistically projected to be as low as $63/kg', which is almost ten times the price of prime steak.[6]

An even more gloomy prognosis was offered by another techno-economic analysis commissioned by Open Philanthropy, which funds research that it believes could have the maximum positive impact on humanity. Open Philanthropy sees the development of animal product alternatives as a key priority and is a major funder of the Good Food Institute. When it funded its own TEA into cultured meat it was as motivated as anyone to find a positive result. However, the author of the analysis, David Humbird, was unable to give one. His report is written in the suitably measured prose of an academic paper, but he could not have been more blunt when talking to Fassler. He said that when looking at how cultured-meat production could be scaled up, it was 'hard to find an angle that wasn't a ludicrous dead end'. He kept hitting up against a fractal 'Wall of No' in which 'every big no is made up of a hundred little nos'.

For example, existing bioreactors have to be kept 100 per cent sterile, which is a pharmaceutical rather than a food grade standard. But anything less than full sterility would not be feasible, since bacteria would multiply in the reactors faster than the cells. You also need a supply of amino acids, which Humbird calculated would add nearly $4 more to the cost per kilo of meat produced. CE Delft's much more optimistic 40 cents per kilo figure was based on the price of an amino acid on sale at the e-commerce marketplace Alibaba.com which turned out to be organic fertiliser, completely unsuitable for food. Humbird's conclusion was: 'Capital- and operating-cost analyses of conceptual cell-mass production facilities indicate economics that would likely preclude the affordability of their products as food.'[7]

This is not what the techno-optimists want to hear, and sometimes it seems that they are not even listening. Sam's response to the challenge of sterility was that 'I'm not a scientist but I understood that it's not that big a deal. It is feasible.' Many of the biologists working for his company were from the pharma industry, and Sam said, 'I trust that they will know how to scale it up.'

Like many in the field, Sam projected the wide-eyed optimism of an idealist. 'I'm just mesmerised by children. Whenever you explain to them how it works they say, "Why should we do it otherwise? Why should we get to kill an animal to eat if it's exactly the same amino acids that you need and potentially better?" I really put a lot of trust in children. Children have more wisdom. Maybe more clairvoyance, you could say.'

Sam was unmoved by the taunt that we've been promised commercial production is imminent ever since the world's first cultured-meat burger was cooked by Mark Post in 2013 and we're still waiting for the first full-scale commercial facility. In fact, Sam turned it on its head. 'If you compare it to any other technology, this is absolutely insane. Take Beyond Burger, which is just a formulation of some plants. It took them almost as much time to go to market and they still didn't reach price parity fifteen years later. So to me, what Mark Post and the rest have been doing is a miracle.'

Somehow, the message that cultivated meat is coming to a table near you soon has landed in a way in which more sober assessments have not. Hardly a day goes by without some new headline appearing about its relentless march. Mostly, however, these are reports of companies building pilot plants, developing pilot products, or making progress with regulatory approval, which sometimes means merely applying for it.

If it is true that the hype around cultivated meat is out of touch with reality, why are so many big players ploughing billions of dollars into its development? We can't rule out that this is a case of animal spirits running out of control. Markets move as herds, and if enough people start running in a certain direction, a stampede follows. Fassler describes one enthusiast on a private GFI video call saying that 'investor buy-in was the de facto proof that cultivated meat has legs'. In other words, he thought people wouldn't be investing if they didn't have good reason to do so. But this becomes a self-perpetuating justification. Someone invests, someone else thinks they must have their reasons and they too go looking for the next unicorn to buy into. Now there are two major investors, which increases the credibility of the investment, which makes others more likely to buy in, and so on.

If this seems too irrational to be true, consider the cautionary tale of Theranos, the tech startup that promised cheap and reliable blood tests. Not only was it unable to deliver, the company itself never had any good reason to believe that it could. In 2022, its CEO, Elizabeth Holmes, was convicted on four counts of criminal fraud. Silicon Valley has a culture of positive and blue-sky thinking, in which people take too literally the injunction to believe in the impossible.

Much as we have reason to be sceptical of the claims made for cultured meat, the counternarratives of the livestock industry are not above suspicion either. They claim that meat from animals is natural, traditional, 'real' as opposed to 'fake'. Yet modern industrial farming practices are light years away from the comforting images of grazing ruminants and rooting pigs. Fast-growing poultry and hormone-injected cattle are hardly natural. The debate over cultured meat should not be conducted as though it were a simple tale of technology versus nature, real versus fake, tradition versus progress.

Nor are there neat binaries of healthy versus unhealthy. Most of the foods that cultured meat hopes to replace would not be wholesome, grass-fed meats. That is why Henry Dimbleby, who is generally sceptical about ultra-processed food, isn't against invariably ultra-processed cell-based proteins. 'Because of the junk food cycle, I cannot see people voluntarily reducing their meat intake by enough. Given that a lot of that [meat] is in processed food, I would rather that it didn't destroy the environment at the same time. I think that is a pact worth making.'

Furthermore, the half-truths and selective facts bandied around in this debate come from parties on all sides. Tara Garnett points to pervasive 'straw manning' and 'bad faithism' involving 'the attribution of malign intentions to the person with whom you disagree'. One such bogeyman is 'big veganism', which the meat and livestock sector routinely says is trying to destroy it. 'I don't know who big veganism is,' says Garnett. 'Most people in this country are not even nearly vegan and many people who claim they are vegans are only vegans until it's time for dinner. A paper came out quite recently which showed the orders of magnitude difference between investment in alternative proteins and in the meat and livestock sector.' That study showed that in the United States and the European Union from 2014 to 2020, only 3 per cent of grants for research and innovation in animal and novel technologies were directed at new alternatives to animal products.[8]

Perhaps by the time you are reading this, affordable cultured meat will be in a supermarket near you. You might even be eating some right now. But the point of reasoned scepticism is not to dogmatically rule out possibilities. It is to be more realistic about probabilities. Commercially viable and widely available cultured meat is not an inevitability, and nor is it certain that if it does come, its impacts on the environment and our health will be as good as is claimed. We should be neither dismissive nor overzealous, but sceptically open-minded. And we should certainly not be planning for the future of the food system on the assumption that cellular meat will come good.

The rise of alternative proteins comes at a time when many are hoping for, even expecting, an end to all human use of animals for food. For much of history this wasn't a possibility. Human beings could not get their full nutritional needs from plants alone. Now, with the aid of supplements, we know that they can. It may be disputed whether such a fortified vegan diet is better for our health than an omnivorous one, but it is clear that people can live a healthy, long life either way. The production of animal proteins without animals could expand the range of a vegan diet to such an extent that the reasons for preferring actual meat, egg and dairy would be purely culinary. Many think that if this possibility were open to us, it would obviously be morally preferable to take it. Any minor reduction in gastronomic pleasure would be a small price to pay.[9]

We are approaching an unprecedented crossroads in human

history. Take one fork and humanity will look back in horror at how it ate so many other animals for so long. It will pity those who had no choice and damn most of our generation, who chose to continue eating animals long after we had to. To many, it seems inevitable that this is the road we will take.

But there are at least two other paths. On one we continue as we are, intensifying animal farming, using technology to increase yields and also, perhaps, to reduce suffering. Gene editing or modification might allow us to develop farm animals that feel no pain, or perhaps lack consciousness at all. Such zombie livestock may be disconcerting, but it is difficult to see what the moral objection would be. If we could make a chicken no more sentient than a vegetable, what would be wrong with eating it? No one has any qualms about chopping up a carrot for food.

The third road is commonly signposted as 'less and better' meat: shunning intensification and rearing only as many livestock as are compatible with ensuring the animals' well-being and respecting planetary boundaries. This has been the middle way to date for people horrified by industrial farming but unconvinced or unwilling to go vegan. But why would anyone take this route in the future if good synthetic animal proteins were available?

The arc of history and moral thought can seem to be bending towards the elimination of animal farming. Darwin blew away the idea that human beings were created differently from other beasts, which for millennia had been a main justification for their exploitation. We ultimately share a common ancestor with all animals, and in the case of primates, a close one. However, it wasn't difficult for vain humans to preserve their sense of superiority. As *Homo sapiens*, we judged ourselves to be the most evolved of all species, at least in terms of our moral and rational capacities. Our shared sentience mattered less than our supposedly unique intelligence.

Nonetheless, Darwin started us down a road that would inevitably lead us to some kind of moral reckoning and reassessment.

The more we have found out about the animal kingdom, the less any claims of a sharp divide between our capacities and those of other beasts have remained tenable. The gap has been squeezed by a philosophical pincer movement. From one side there is an increasing acceptance that supposedly unique human capacities are in fact also possessed by other animals. From the other, there is a realisation that little of what we do is down to our so-called higher capacities anyway. We are largely propelled by unconscious processes, cognitive shortcuts and instincts. David Hume was remarkably ahead of his time when, in the eighteenth century, he wrote 'Of the Reason of Animals'. Animals reasoned, he argued, not by deduction, but, like us, by generalising from past experience on the basis of inferences rooted more in instinct than in logic.[10]

Gradually, often reluctantly, humans have begun to accept that animals deserve to be treated as more than just biological automata. Once the line between humans and other animals was blurred, it became increasingly difficult to see where it should be drawn. More and more came to think that it shouldn't be drawn at all. This has led to calls for a step change in our treatment of animals. Ingrid Newkirk, the co-founder of PETA (People for the Ethical Treatment of Animals), has said, 'In the same way that racist and sexist views allowed us to discriminate against minorities and women, speciesism allowed us to inscribe an inferior status on animals and to regard them not as individuals, but as objects and means to fulfil our desires.' Similarly, the philosopher Peter Singer has argued, 'The taking into account of the interests of the being, whatever those interests may be [...] must, according to the principle of equality, be extended to all beings, black or white, masculine or feminine, human or nonhuman.'

The law in many countries has gradually been granting more and more protection to animals. In 2022, the UK passed the Animal Welfare (Sentience) Act, applying to vertebrates. It requires the government to establish and maintain an Animal

Sentience Committee, charged with monitoring whether and how government policy might have 'an adverse effect on the welfare of animals as sentient beings'.[11] UK law for the first time has legally acknowledged that non-humans are conscious too. Anything the government does that affects animals, in sectors from farming and food to construction and transport, will have to account for its impact on animal lives.

Supporters of this law expect more to follow. The Act was just one part of an Action Plan for Animal Welfare launched by the Secretary of State for Environment, Food and Rural Affairs, George Eustice, in May 2021. The plan proposed 'ending the export of live animals for slaughter and fattening', labelling food 'to make it easier for consumers to purchase food that aligns with their welfare values', 'ending the low-welfare practice of keeping primates as pets' and 'other reforms to improve farm welfare, including examining the use of cages for laying hens and farrowing crates for pigs'.[12] What makes this all the more remarkable is that this was being proposed not by a green, liberal or left-wing government, but by a Conservative one.

It is tempting to conclude that the tide of history is on the vegans' side. But so far, few have walked far down the road they have paved. Counting the number of vegans in the world is difficult, but on even the highest estimates, the country with the largest proportion in the world is India, with 9 per cent. Israel usually comes in the top three of global rankings, but is still only 5 per cent vegan. These statistics probably overestimate the numbers of vegans because behavioural studies have shown that many who say they are vegan do not eschew all animal products. One typical study showed that in 2012, 5 per cent of American adults identified as vegetarian but only 3 per cent always ate a vegetarian diet.[13] Meanwhile, few omnivores choose to purchase higher-welfare meat and dairy, with the majority still buying on price.

Our future direction is still undetermined. To decide which road to go down, we need to think about the fundamental ethical question of how we treat animals. Much of this thinking has already been done. Hardly anyone denies that animals are sentient – capable of perceiving and experiencing – and should not be caused to suffer without good reason. The essence of this argument is captured in the words of the nineteenth-century philosopher and reformer Jeremy Bentham. There is still no pithier formulation: 'The question is not, Can they *reason?*, nor, Can they *talk?* but, Can they *suffer?*' If the answer is yes, then we have reason 'why we should *not* be suffered to torment them'.[14]

Less quoted is what Bentham wrote before these famous lines:

There is very good reason why we should be suffered to eat such [non-human animals] as we like to eat: we are the better for it, and they are never the worse. They have none of those long-protracted anticipations of future misery which we have. The death they suffer in our hands commonly is, and always may be, a speedier, and by that means a less painful, one than that which would await them in the inevitable course of nature.

Bentham was no vegetarian, let alone a vegan. His reasons for not tormenting animals are incontestable. His reasons for eating them are less obviously compelling, but they remain robust. Bentham recognised that what makes human life worth preserving is not the mere fact that humans are sentient. Indeed, the ubiquity of sentience makes the idea of extending human-like rights to all animals absurd. Nature is overflowing with consciousness. Research suggests that even mosquitoes might be sentient.

Unlike other animals, however, we do not live just in the present, or within the narrow horizons of breeding seasons and other periods in the lifecycle. Our memories, plans and projects matter to us in ways that it is inconceivable they do for any other creature. When you kill any animal, you frustrate its natural desire to live.

But only when you kill a human being do you bring to a close a story that imbues both the past and the future with meaning.

Our human difference gives us reasons not to kill each other that go beyond simplistic injunctions to never kill or never shorten life at all. Human rationality and self-consciousness may not be entirely distinct from those of other animals, but they are far more developed. Even the most intelligent of other animals only ever lives instinctively. No dolphin has started an alternative cetacean community based on novel political values, for example. Whales do not choose to be childless because they have other projects or desires that matter more to them. Human culture is uniquely diverse and very distant from other species' primal evolutionary imperatives of survival and reproduction.

The line of thought Bentham started suggests that it is morally acceptable to kill and eat other animals, if we do it humanely. But still, if we don't have to, isn't it better not to? Many assume the answer is so obvious that the question is rhetorical. But it could be that we would lose something important were we to remove ourselves from the business of killing to eat. As we have seen, in traditional societies, there is an intimate relationship between people and the animals they keep or hunt. The Hadza eat baboons, the animal they believe they were created from. The Maasai use the same word, *inkishu*, for both cattle and their people. The Inuit believe that they are in a mutually beneficial pact with the seals they eat.

Time and again we find that the closer human beings have been to nature's natural cycles of life and death, the more they both respect other animals and are willing to eat them. This is not a flaw of 'primitive' people but a profound understanding of the true meaning of kinship with other creatures that is lost in more industrialised cultures. If you truly understand nature, you see that death and killing are inextricable parts of it. To refuse to be complicit in this harshness is, ironically, to repeat the mistake of human exceptionalism, by encouraging human beings to separate themselves from the hard realities of the food web. People who have a genuine feel for nature don't make this mistake. They have greater genuine reverence for animals than those whose alienation from true nature makes them repulsed by the idea of killing them.

In Ernest Hemingway's *The Old Man and the Sea*, we have a perhaps more relatable example of a person close to nature and reconciled with killing. The eponymous protagonist spends most of the book in pursuit of a marlin. And yet he empathises with the fish more than any vegetarian landlubber ever could. At one point he remembers catching a female marlin and the 'wild, panic-stricken, despairing fight that soon exhausted her'. All the while, her male mate had followed her, and at one point even 'jumped high into the air beside the boat to see where the female was'. The old man thought, 'That was the saddest thing I ever saw with them,' but still took the marlin he had caught that day, 'begged her pardon and butchered her promptly'.

Several lines of the novella combine almost religious reverence and a willingness to kill. At one point the old man addresses the fish he is pursuing and says, 'I love you and respect you very much. But I will kill you dead before this day ends.' And again, he says, 'I'll kill him though. In all his greatness and his glory.' For the old man, reverence does not stop the killing, but it does change the way it is done.

He even believes there is something wrong in what he is doing, that nothing can ultimately justify it. He resolves to complete his hunt, 'Although it is unjust.' 'His determination to kill him [the marlin] never relaxed in his sorrow for him,' writes Hemingway. 'There is no one worthy of eating him from the manner of his behaviour and his great dignity.' There are clear echoes here of how traditional hunters and pastoralists feel towards the animals they eat.

There seems to be something about acknowledging the cruelty

of nature that makes any refusal to partake in humane killing seem absurd. The sheer quantity of death and killing in nature is awe-inspiring. A single brown bear will eat up to thirty salmon in one day. Eagles bring a constant supply of small mammals and birds back to their nests to feed their young. Shoals of millions of sardines are fodder for larger predators like dolphins, who eat twenty-five to fifty pounds of fish every day. Worse, nature bestows sentience freely but has a total disregard for the welfare of those who possess it. When the sentient eagle carries away the sentient rabbit in its talons, who can imagine the terror of the poor little mammal? Salmon may feel pain, but the brown bears who intercept their return to their Alaskan spawning grounds and feast on them in their dozens don't make any effort to reduce it. The degree of death and suffering in the natural world would be gratuitous if it were the product of design. If God exists, he must be some kind of sadist.

That is not to say we should emulate his sadism. Despite the deeper connection traditional societies have with other animals, they too may often have been guilty of indifference to their welfare. For instance, common Maasai forms of ritual killing of cattle seem to be especially inhumane. The animals are either stabbed or suffocated to death. The method of suffocation, as described by Kaj Århem, is 'by smothering its mouth with a woman's skirt – a symbol of fertility and life – and by pouring milk and honey mead down its nostrils – the food of life and rebirth among men'. Århem is very articulate about the ritual significance of this: 'the very mixture of milk and mead, which is used to kill the sacrificial animal, is then drunk by the initiates, together with the blood of the sacrificed animal, to bring about their spiritual rebirth. By thus causing the sacrificial beast to die by the very substances which make people live, the sacrificial drama conveys the message that cattle die for people to live, which is another way of saying that, through its death, the sacrificial animal gives new life to men.'[15]

This seeming paradox of respect and a willingness to inflict a painful death would be a curio if it occurred once, but that it recurs time and again in traditional societies suggests it reveals something important and fundamental about humanity's relationship to other animals.

Of course, if we have the unique capacity to understand the pain of other creatures, we have a unique responsibility to use that understanding. But as Bentham pointed out, that may not require refraining from eating animals. Conscious life is the light that flickers all too briefly in what would otherwise be a dark universe. It is wonderful but it never lasts, and if we measured its value by its length, the whole of nature would seem worthless. To truly value sentience requires just two things. The first is never to cause more suffering to anything than is necessary. What should appal us is not that we eat the flesh of other animals but that we usually keep them in such dreadful conditions before putting them out of their misery. The second is to treat them with the same reverence that all traditional hunters, pastoralists, farmers and fisherfolk have done. We need to respect animals for the fleeting eruptions of consciousness that they are, not as though they had human-like life projects that we can cruelly cut short.

At the moment, the vast majority of humankind errs in one of two completely opposite directions. Most fail to respect animal sentience at all, treating livestock like meat machines. A growing minority, however, think of animals as though they were four-legged, feathered or finned versions of ourselves, creatures who deserve a long life and for whom death at anything other than an old age is a tragedy rather than an all-too-common fact of life. They are in denial, like the vegan cat-lover who refuses their companion animal meat. To love a cat and yet not accept the way it naturally lives is not to truly love it all, but simply to adore a sentimentalised, sanitised version of it.

Our choices about animal welfare reflect these two extremes. If humankind became vegan, we would be separating ourselves from the harsh realities of animal life. Death and suffering would still go on, it's just that we would have washed our hands of it. If we carry on as we are, we are making nature even crueller than it already is. The eagle's prey has a horrible death, but such torture is fleeting compared with that of too many farm animals.

If, on the other hand, we keep only as much livestock as we humanely can and treat it well, then we improve upon nature. We would need to keep no more of such livestock than the planet can sustain. This would result in much less animal husbandry than we have under mass industrial farming, but it would be significantly more than nothing. In such a future, the animals under our stewardship would have easier lives than those of their wild cousins, with medicines when they are sick and a compassionate, painless death when their time has come. The sentience we would then honour would be of an authentic kind: the in-the-present wonder of any conscious animal, whose life is incredible, but which never has any greater meaning and cannot be made more meaningful simply by virtue of it being made longer.

Humans may or may not be superior to other animals, but we are different. Only we are capable of full-blown morality. Only we can choose our actions on the basis of what we judge to be right or wrong, not merely acting on what instinct compels. So we could refrain, for example, from killing other animals – something a cat could never do. But the fact that we *can* do this doesn't mean that we *should*. The argument that we should avoid inflicting unnecessary suffering is irresistible, but, given the necessity of death and killing in nature, we need more reasons why we should always avoid ending life.

13

UNNATURAL BORNE KILLERS

Rats and bats in China

In early 2020, business was brisk in the Huanan Seafood Wholesale Market in Wuhan, China. The market's name is misleading, since many of its wares came from the land. A lot of exotic wild animals and game changed hands in this and the city's three other 'wet' markets, including Siberian weasels, masked palm civets, Chinese bamboo rats, Malayan porcupines, coypus, marmots and complex-toothed flying squirrels. According to one scientific study, thirty-one of the species sold for food or pets were – or, rather, were supposed to be – protected.

The market was about to gain an infamy it will never lose. On 9 January a sixty-one-year-old Wuhan resident died of a new coronavirus, soon to be identified as SARS-CoV-2. Coronaviruses range from the common cold to deadly MERS and SARS, causing diseases in mammals and birds, including respiratory infections in humans. The Huanan market was identified as the likely source of the first human case of Covid-19, as the virus came to be known. It was the beginning of a global pandemic that by the end of September had claimed one million lives. By the end of 2023, the official global death count was around seven million, although experts believe the true figure could be up to four times higher.[1]

In July 2022 a scientific paper was published that seemed to confirm the market as the epicentre of the outbreak. The researchers had analysed the distribution of positive samples taken by Chinese authorities in the market as well as of reported cases in the city. The distribution of cases clustered around the market. The further the distance from the market, the fewer victims per population there were. Evidence from the market itself seemed even more conclusive, with positive samples concentrated in the southwest corner of the market, where vendors had been selling live mammals, including raccoon dogs, hog badgers and red foxes. Researchers were even able to identify one specific stall as the likely source.[2] A second paper published the same month argued that the virus had two distinct lineages and that both could be traced to the Huanan market.[3]

Both papers were thorough pieces of detective work, but unfortunately they were not conclusive. Some argued that the pattern of positive samples was an artefact of the pattern of testing. Because the market was the early suspected source, more tests were done closer to it. If you look in one place more than in others, you are bound to find more positive cases there, even if they are no more concentrated than elsewhere. Further, the researchers did not have access to any live animal samples and so cannot confirm that any animals in the market actually had the virus. To add to suspicions, at the time of writing, China had still not released the gene sequences it holds from animals sold at the market. "These data could have – and should have – been shared three years ago,' said Tedros Adhanom Ghebreyesus, director-general of WHO.[4]

So the rival explanation cannot be ruled out: that the virus was actually a lab leak from the Wuhan Institute of Virology, which is known to have conducted research into coronaviruses. After all, diseases have escaped from labs before. The foot-and-mouth outbreak in the UK in 2007, which affected only cattle, is believed to have originated from a leak of infectious effluent from the Institute for Animal Health at Pirbright in Surrey, England. In 1971, a lab leak in Havana was responsible for an outbreak of African swine fever that left the disease endemic in Cuba. (Some blame the CIA.)

Or maybe, though it seems very unlikely, the Chinese government's insistence that imported frozen food was the culprit is true. Or perhaps there is some other cause we don't even suspect. But we don't need to wait until we have the final answer to take Covid-19 as a warning. Whether or not this particular virus originated from captured wildlife, we know that zoonotic diseases – those that pass from non-human animals to humans – exist and pose a major threat to public health. As well as viruses, non-human animals can transmit foodborne, waterborne, vector-borne and parasitic infections, as well as Rickettsia, prion diseases (when misfolded proteins affect normal proteins, causing cellular death), fungi, antimicrobial-resistant bacteria and other diseases caused by viruses. We have identified only a fraction of the zoonotic pathogens that pose a threat to human life.[5] An estimated 60 per cent of human infections originate in other animals, and this proportion is set to rise. Three out of every four new and emerging human infectious diseases 'jump species' to people. Such 'zoonotic spillover' events have happened on average twice a year over the last century.[6]

Even if Covid-19 is not such an event, this century has already seen at least two other major zoonotic spillovers: the SARS epidemic that started in China's Guangdong province in November 2002, and the MERS epidemic that began in Saudi Arabia in June 2012.[7] Both caused fewer than 900 deaths worldwide.[8] It is more than possible that both these and the Covid-19 outbreaks all originated in 'wet markets', open-air food markets where live animals are caged and slaughtered, often in cramped conditions, close to other foodstuffs. Nor is zoonotic infection a new threat. Both measles and smallpox are thought to have originated in animals. Measles passed from cattle to humans in the sixth century BCE, while smallpox is thought to have passed from rats to humans via camels in the third to second centuries BCE. More recently, non-human animals were the likely source of both HIV/AIDS and Ebola.

In fact, many zoonotic diseases are already in circulation, causing much disease and death. They don't receive much attention because they mainly circulate in poorer countries. These 'neglected zoonoses' include anthrax, brucellosis, rabies, pig tapeworm, echinococcosis (a parasitic disease caused by tapeworms), Japanese encephalitis, leptospirosis, Q fever, Lassa fever and sleeping sickness. They are responsible for 2.4 billion human infections and 2.2 million deaths every year.[9] Domestic animals, both livestock and pets, are largely responsible for their spread. Only one, the Lassa virus, is hosted exclusively in a wild animal, the multi-mammate rat. In addition to this, the health burden of foodborne diseases, mainly of animal origin, is estimated to be similar to that of the 'big three' infectious diseases, HIV/AIDS, malaria and tuberculosis.

And the situation is getting worse. Vector-borne diseases, spread by ticks and mosquitoes, have more than doubled in the USA in just two decades, with infected species increasing their geographical reach every year. Mammals alone host around 10,000 zoonotic viruses. Bird flu and swine fever are now regularly plaguing the world's livestock industry, interfering with food supply and animal health. In 2018, China had to slaughter half of its hogs to control an outbreak of African swine fever.[10]

A report by the Council for Agricultural Science and Technology (CAST) calls the globalised food chain a 'microbial perfect storm for emerging infectious diseases', warning that 'it only takes one incident or error in the value chain, anywhere in the world, to cause a global outbreak'. Its sobering conclusions are that a 'microbial threat anywhere is a threat everywhere', that 'zoonotic diseases will continue at an accelerated rate with significant consequences,' and that 'it is highly likely that the next pandemic will originate from animals'.[11] A 2019 study concluded that since 1940, 'agricultural drivers were associated with more than 25 per cent of all – and more than 50 per cent of zoonotic – infectious diseases that emerged in humans, proportions that will likely increase as agriculture expands and intensifies'.[12]

A landmark report by the United Nations Environment Programme (UNEP) and the International Livestock Research Institute (ILRI) authoritatively and clearly shows why the global food system presents particular risks. Of the seven major drivers of zoonotic diseases that it identifies, three are wholly to do with the food system: the increased human demand for animal protein; unsustainable agricultural intensification; and changes in food supply. And the other four significantly involve the food system: increased use and exploitation of wildlife; unsustainable utilisation of natural resources accelerated by urbanisation; land-use change and extractive industries; and increased travel and transportation. The risks are so clear that it is wrong to think of the Covid-19 pandemic as a rare and unforeseeable 'black swan' event. Zoonotic disease outbreaks are in fact 'a widely predicted consequence of how people source food, trade animals, and alter environments'.[13]

To understand why the food system presents a particular danger, you need to understand the three key risk factors for a zoonotic spillover: phylogenetic distance; abundance; and frequency of encounter. 'Phylogenetic distance' simply means how biologically similar animal species are to each other. The more similar the host, the easier it is for a virus to jump species. Transmission from a bonobo to a human is easier than from a cat. But because humans interact much more with cats than with bonobos, the felines may present a greater risk. The more hosts a virus has ('abundance') or the more frequent the encounters are between the host and a potentially infectible other species, the more opportunities it has to jump. If a virus is abundant enough and there is plenty of human contact, transmission can still happen where there is greater phylogenetic distance. It's a simple matter of probability: if the opportunity for something unlikely happening occurs often enough, it will eventually happen. That's why every week someone wins the lottery at odds of fourteen million to one. If more than fourteen million tickets are sold, then on average there will be a winner every week, even though from the point of view of that winner the odds were astronomically against them.

It is the combination of close contact and the abundance of livestock and game that makes the food system so vulnerable. The importance of phylogenetic closeness means that one of the biggest zoonotic threats comes from pigs. Both cattle and pigs are genetically closer to humans than poultry, sheep and goats, and pigs tend to be more intensively reared. Influenza A viruses regularly pass from pigs to humans, and vice versa. Add to that the fact that swine influenzas are also highly diverse, and many conclude that they present the greatest single zoonotic risk to human health. Indeed, the 2009 swine flu pandemic, caused by the H1N1pdm09 virus, led to anywhere between 150,000 and 575,000 deaths.[14]

Once a disease gets out, containing it becomes increasingly difficult. As the CAST report explains, 'the potential for establishment and movement of zoonoses has been accelerated and intensified both by our global interconnectedness and by the speed with which microbes, people, animals, and animal products can now travel and interact'. The report notes that 'microbes can now circumvent [sic] the globe faster than most of their incubation periods'.

Reading of all these risks, it might seem incredible that we're not being laid low by zoonotic pandemics more often. Our saving grace is that although zoonotic spillovers are a regular occurrence, they only cause a serious epidemic or pandemic if the pathogen then spreads fairly easily from human to human. If an animal infects a human but the human cannot infect another human, the spread of the disease is arrested at the first jump. Fortunately, this is usually what happens. So when making a comprehensive assessment of zoonotic risk, more attention needs to be paid to pathogens that are more likely to be passed from human to human.

While it is somewhat inevitable that the food supply presents the greatest risk of zoonotic infection, precisely how vulnerable it is depends on how it works. Unfortunately, several aspects of our contemporary food system increase the risks. One is our desire for more animal protein. While consumption of meat, fish, eggs and dairy in high-income countries has been fairly stable since the 1980s, in Southeast Asia the proportion of calories in the diet from both fish and animal products has doubled since the 1960s. South Asia and sub-Saharan Africa have also seen increases, though not as large. In all these regions, demand is expected to keep growing. As a result, over the last half century global meat production has gone up by 260 per cent, that of milk by 90 per cent, and that of eggs by 340 per cent, with no slowdown anticipated. The total weight of the world's farmed poultry is now nearly three times that of all wild birds, while the biomass of farmed mammals is around fifteen times that of all those in the wild.[15]

The planet's land mass, however, has not increased, with the inevitable result that there has been an intensification of animal agriculture, usually in the form of more industrialised production. This intensification has several consequences, all of which create a better environment for diseases to spread.

First, as the CAST report said, 'the movement towards intensive farming practices such as confined animal feeding operations (CAFO)' provides 'ample opportunity for rapid spread of infectious diseases'. Animals are kept closer together, often in conditions that are detrimental to their overall health. Hence they are both more susceptible to disease and more likely to be in contact with other diseased animals. The spread of swine flu, for example, was accelerated by the lack of physical distancing between the pigs. Intensive facilities are also more likely to be close to urban areas. Add to that the all-too-common low standards of sanitation and the poor management of animal waste, which is produced in huge amounts, and the risks of infection are clear.

As Jonathan Rushton, director of the Global Burden of Animal Diseases Programme and a professor of animal health and food systems economics, explained to me, factory farms are also dependent on off-farm services that act as potential routes of transmission. 'The most economically efficient systems tend to be large-scale intensive units that are feeding things into fairly narrow-based slaughter, dairy processing or manufacturing systems. These systems are efficient and produce relatively cheap food. But if something goes wrong in that system, then it has major consequences outside the individual farm unit.

'For example, the only slaughterhouse that can slaughter old sows, the females that are gone past their useful life in a herd, is in the south of England. That's a very efficient system in terms of utility of infrastructure. But it's a system that's very vulnerable to shocks. There are other examples. There's only one milk processing unit in Scotland, which means all the dairy farmers in Scotland put milk into one system. So there are vulnerabilities in our livestock systems in the UK that are now built in. If we're going to have systems that are about economic efficiency, we need to have some understanding about where the vulnerabilities lie and be prepared when things go wrong. And I'd say "when" rather than "if".'

Commodification is also a driver of potential infection. Gone are the days when most carcasses went to butchers to be sold as cuts. Most meat today is shipped to industrial facilities, where it is mixed with meat from other sources. Given that it only takes one infected beef carcass to contaminate around eight tons of ground beef, the risks of infection spread are obvious.[16] Modern industrial units might be assumed to be safer than traditional markets, but this is not always the case. In the early months of the Covid-19 pandemic, several meat-processing plants were centres of transmission because the cool, humid environments were ideal mediums in which the respiratory viruses could spread.

Such is the globalised nature of the food industry that the infrastructure issues are not contained within our borders. 'Half our meat in the UK comes from chickens,' says Rushton. 'The systems these chickens are in depend on feed grain and oil seed cake suppliers from around the globe. Some of those inputs can spread disease. We have had the experience of having different types of salmonella in chickens introduced through oil seed cakes into Europe. Those foodborne pathogens can be quite persistent and quite difficult to remove.'

It may seem obvious that since close contact and abundance increase the risks of zoonotic spillover, intensive animal farming is inherently riskier than the alternatives. But it is not that simple, says virologist Nick Johnson, who works for the Vector-Borne Diseases workgroup of the UK government's Animal and Plant Health Agency. 'We've been intensifying livestock relentlessly for years and occasionally it causes problems but on the whole, in itself, it doesn't,' he tells me. 'With intensification, the environment the animals are in is more controlled. So you can protect your animals from exposure to other things by increased biosecurity.' The CAST report supports this, while pointing out that although biosecurity practices have improved in large operations, smaller ones 'generally have minimal biosecurity in place'. In open-air, free-range farms, biosecurity cannot be assured. 'The challenge we have at the moment is avian flu, which is circulating in wild birds in this country,' says Johnson. 'It seems to be getting into the poultry supply and because it's intensely farmed, once this virus gets in, it's very destructive.'

Rushton explains that intensive and free-range systems pose different risks, which are hard to compare: 'The risks of getting a pathogen into a system, if it's spread by a wild animal, would probably be greater in a free range system compared to an intensive housing system. But the consequences of the introduction of a pathogen in those two systems are very different. In the extensive system it might spread quite slowly. But if you infect a group of animals housed in the intensive systems, then the transmission rates of the pathogens can be much faster. And because they're connected to other farms through the feed systems and the market systems, they could be spread beyond that point. So it's partly about the risk of introduction, but it's also important to recognise the consequences of what happens if you introduce a pathogen into those systems.'

One way in which intensive industrial livestock farming is evidently more problematic is in its routine use of antibiotics in animal feed as a prophylactic against infection, which is driving the evolution of antimicrobial-resistant (AMR) pathogens. The health toll of this is already so large that the CAST report called it 'the silent pandemic'. Some of the statistics it cites are shocking. Antibiotic-resistant bacteria and fungi already cause more than 2.8 million human infections and 35,000 deaths every year in the USA alone. Globally, in 2019 an estimated 1.27 million people died as a direct result of AMR pathogens, while they were a factor in nearly 5 million deaths. WHO warns that they could cause 10 million global deaths a year by 2050. Arable farming is also implicated, as many farmers spray their crops with antimicrobials to protect against fungal infections.

Increased demand for animal protein does not put pressure only on agriculture. Consumption of wild animals has also increased. For the poor, 'bushmeat' is a free source of animal protein. Game meat is generally considered to be traditional, nutritious and safe. Often it is, but some hunted species are potential vectors for zoonotic infection. Even if it is relatively rare for wild animals to be a source of a human disease outbreak, the more humans hunt them, the more frequent such infections will be. And the more rural and urban populations mix, the greater the risk that such outbreaks will spread. Johnson explains, 'Populations in Africa have hunted bushmeat for millennia, and occasionally we'd get a zoonotic transmission that may have caused a localised outbreak. But there wasn't then that secondary transfer into larger populations. Once it gets there, it really takes hold. Now that we have a very interconnected world, a single transfer from a primate into a human can lead to human to human transmission, and because of our increased population, it can spread rapidly. That is perhaps what we saw with Ebola in parts of West Africa.'

Both wild and farmed animals are increasingly transported, sometimes over very great distances. When transported live, the animals are often kept in cramped conditions, which means that infections are more likely to spread. Disease outbreaks are also more likely to be transmitted over greater distances than to be confined to small, local areas. Johnson says this is especially a problem in Africa. 'There's a virus called Rift Valley fever present in East Africa and because of the transfer of sheep and goats as part of the Hajj it was transported into Saudi Arabia and introduced into the Arabian Peninsula.'

Both Johnson and Rushton point to another driver of increased zoonotic risk: the conversion of virgin land to agricultural use, especially tropical forests. Every time we put livestock where they previously hadn't been, we expose them to novel pathogens and increase the chances of a new zoonotic transmission. 'Because of the diversity in the tropics, if we mow down a forest and turn it into an animal rearing facility there are viruses and bacteria that can then be exposed to livestock,' says Johnson. 'Potentially, these pathogens can jump to us. The classic example of that was Nipah virus, which could be put down to intensification of pig production in Malaysia. This increased exposure to fruit bats, and the virus jumped from the bats, to pigs, and then humans. It caused quite a large outbreak. They ended up slaughtering over one million pigs in Malaysia to try and get it under control, but it killed 105 people. That's the sort of unexpected thing that can happen when you destroy natural habitats and put intensive farming into uncharted territory.' And it is not just farm animals that are left more exposed to infection. 'Deforestation encourages people to go into areas where we have wild animals and we have contact with people with potential disease issues,' says Rushton.

One final problem is that genetic diversity provides a kind of natural protection against disease spreading too widely, since different animals will have different levels of immunity. But modern breeding creates more genetic uniformity, again exposing herds and flocks to more risk. In the wild, the loss of biodiversity also increases transmission risk, as does the reduction in habitat, forcing more species closer together.[17]

Add up all the vulnerabilities and weaknesses of the contemporary food system and it is easy to conclude that it is nothing but a failure. But Rushton reminds me that it is not without its successes. 'The animal health system has managed a range of infectious disease pathogens quite well over the last 100 years. We've removed very important zoonotic disease pathogens through surveillance and control systems, which has taken quite a lot of effort. If you look at something like bovine tuberculosis, which was a major cause of concern in Europe around the 1900s, it's no longer a big issue.' Another achievement is the almost complete removal of brucellosis from the cattle system in many countries. This bacterial disease is classed as a zoonosis, with human infection usually coming though ingestion of unpasteurised cheese or milk. It causes flu-like symptoms, such as fever, weakness and weight loss, and WHO describes it as having 'serious public health consequences'.[18]

On the other hand, because we rear many more chickens than

we used to do, in recent decades we have had more issues with Salmonella and Campylobacter, both bacteria that cause severe food poisoning. Rushton believes that Campylobacter, rather than an unknown zoonosis, is 'probably the biggest public health concern in terms of an infectious foodborne pathogen'. The bacteria can cause diarrhoea, fever, stomach cramps, nausea and vomiting for up to a week. Up to 10 per cent of victims suffer complications, which include potentially lethal septicemia, meningitis, inflammation of the gall bladder and appendicitis.[19] Although the *Guardian* newspaper has run a number of reports on the problem of Campylobacter in the poultry industry, public awareness of it remains low. 'It's like the word Campylobacter doesn't sound very threatening, but Salmonella does,' rues Rushton. There are around 60,000 reported cases of Campylobacter in the UK every year, and for every one there must be several that are not identified.[20]

Foodborne disease is a serious public health issue, even though it is one that could in theory be all but eliminated. Although the focus in recent years has understandably been on zoonoses, food can spread any number of other diseases and pathogens. Many of the drivers of zoonotic spillover are also risk factors for foodborne diseases, such as Salmonella and listeria. Incidences of these are rising in developed countries, and in the USA their economic burden is estimated to be between $50.1 and $77.7 billion per year.[21] There are also waterborne diseases, exacerbated by seas and rivers contaminated by agricultural pollution from fertilisers and manure.

We do need to keep the zoonotic and foodborne infection risk in perspective. Neither Johnson nor Rushton was particularly worried about the next zoonotic outbreak. Asked if he is kept awake at night by the prospect of the next nasty one, Johnson answers calmly in the negative. Rushton tells me, 'We're always keener to fight the sparks than deal with the fire we've got. I don't think we need to be sitting around worrying too hard about the next emerging pathogen, what it will be, how it enters society and how we react to it. We do need to have mechanisms where we try our best to avoid the release of these pathogens, because once they emerge and they start to spread between people, we can see it's very difficult to manage.'

The food system has always been both essential for supporting a healthy population and a potential source of sickness and disease. Before relatively modern inventions such as refrigeration, canning and pasteurisation, rotten food would often make people ill. While these innovations have made quotidian spoiling less of an issue, other changes have created new risks and raised the stakes. Food has always been able to make people ill, but today our food system could unleash a pandemic – and perhaps already has. As CAST sums it up, a combination of a more populous, mobile world and the modern food system has created 'a novel disease ecology where pathogen exposure and transmission across species is almost guaranteed. There is nowhere in the world from which we are remote and no one from whom we are disconnected. Numerous animal microbes are only a few mutations away from initiating new spillovers and outbreaks infecting humans.'

What can be done to reduce the risks? The UNEP/ILRI report came up with several recommendations.[22] All were framed by the 'One Health' approach adopted by the UN and its agencies. One Health 'recognizes that the health of humans, domestic and wild animals, plants, and the wider environment (including ecosystems) are closely linked and interdependent'. This holistic approach is key. In a world increasingly dominated by its human occupants, our fate is tied to the other living organisms we live with cheek by jowl.

Many of the steps needed to reduce the risk of zoonotic spillover and other animal-borne diseases are practical, technical ones: high safety standards, good hygiene practice, monitoring and testing, and so on. Better animal welfare is also critical: a more humane livestock industry is also a safer one. Reduced antibiotic use is essential and is already happening. After action by the FDA in 2015, antibiotic use in animal agriculture in the USA declined by 40 per cent.[23]

But one conclusion of the UNEP/ILRI report is more systemic: 'Increased support is necessary to build resilient agroecological food systems that rely on natural synergies and harness biological diversity for food production while protecting important wildlife habitats.' The endorsement of 'agroecology' in a UN report might seem surprising, but it's not a one-off. The FAO has formally adopted the '10 Elements of Agroecology' framework 'to support the design of differentiated paths for agriculture and food systems transformation'. These elements are named with big, aspirational abstract nouns that on closer examination turn out to be so open to interpretation that they prescribe little in detail: Responsible governance; Recycling; Efficiency; Diversity; Synergies; Human and social values; Co-creation and sharing of knowledge; Culture and food traditions; Resilience; Circular and solidarity economy. Everyone can be in favour of these, but disagree on how to achieve them.

The ten elements may be reduced to two general sets of principles. The first is that agriculture must be in harmony with the broader ecosystem, and this demands circular practices in which nothing is ultimately wasted. When farms work in this way, they are both resilient and efficient. Second, agriculture must be supportive of its human stakeholders, respecting workers, consumers and their cultures and traditions. This respect requires engagement and good governance. In short, agriculture must be in harmony with ecosystems and human societies.

Still, the term 'agroecology' is contested, claimed both by small, traditional mixed farms using no synthetic inputs, and by major international corporations that claim their industrial farms promote diversity, efficiency, circularity, resilience and every other agroecological virtue.[24] Indeed, such is the disagreement about what agroecology means that the FAO started to create a database of definitions.[25] This includes its own: 'Agroecology is a science that draws on social, biological and agricultural sciences and integrates these with traditional knowledge and farmer's knowledge.' It also includes more radical iterations, such as that contained in the Declaration of the International Forum for Agroecology, a lengthy document that says: 'Agroecology is a way of life and the language of Nature, that we learn as her children.'

The term 'agroecology' can be traced back to the 1920s, when scientists started to bring together the fields of ecology and agronomy to study the ways in which the complex interactions of plants, soil, animals and climate worked in agricultural systems. In this original sense it is an interdisciplinary field of study, drawing not only on the hard sciences but also on the social sciences such as sociology and anthropology. Increasingly it came to incorporate indigenous and practitioner knowledge too.

From the 1980s, however, agroecology has also become a name for a movement which brings a sharper political edge to the study of agriculture as an embedded ecosystem. Most notably, the term was taken up by the food sovereignty movement and became as much defined by what it stood against as by what it stood for. In this framing, agroecology can only be practised by peasant farmers using largely traditional methods, in opposition to industrialised, technological agriculture. It is also firmly anti-capitalist, seeing the ownership of land, seeds and the means of distribution by impersonal corporations as antithetical to agroecological values.

Now, however, the term 'agroecology' is even being used – critics say co-opted – by the same large food businesses that many older proponents of the idea decried. The French hypermarket chain Carrefour, for example, endorses the concept, saying that it uses methods that 'build on interactions between plants, animals, human beings and the environment ... in order to create healthier food'. With an apparent disinterest in and ignorance of agroecology's history, it calls it 'a new approach to agriculture which combines ecological, economic and social considerations'.[26]

As a result of this polyphony, many question whether the term has become too loose to serve any practical purpose. However, although the concept may be somewhat vague, it is not so thin as to be meaningless. Many aspects of the current food system are not among its desiderata. We have seen how most intensive livestock practices totally go against principles of circular agriculture, creating unmanageable amounts of manure and relying on feed grown thousands of miles away, often on land that was previously wooded. That such systems clearly contradict any conceivable conception of agroecology shows there are teeth in its apparently gentle bite.

It could even be argued that the vagueness of agroecology is its strength. The food system is inherently diverse, and so what we need is not an ideal which is highly prescriptive about details but rather a set of general principles farmers can follow in more than one way. If we take agroecology in its broader sense, without the ideological accretions of the food sovereignty movement, it could provide just such a broad, positive direction of travel for the food world. It leaves open exactly how farms work but says that however they do, they need to fulfil certain conditions. For many, this would be an unacceptable dilution of some of its core principles, but the more politicised versions of agroecology cannot claim historical precedence or ownership of the term. Further, as some commentators say, to insist on the most radical definition leaves it 'vulnerable to criticism from sceptics who perceive it as a dogmatic movement that restricts smallholder farmers, based on an ideological opposition to technology, modernisation and capitalism'.[27]

The UNEP/ILRI report makes some specific proposals. It ends with what it calls ten 'policy recommendations', but these are in fact areas needing attention, such as awareness, governance, finance, science, monitoring and regulation, incentives, biosecurity and control, capacity building, and operationalising the One Health approach. The eighth item on the list, however, concerns 'agriculture and wildlife habitats' and calls for the 'sustainable co-existence of agriculture and wildlife', 'investment in agro-ecological methods of food production', and the reduction of wildlife habitat destruction and fragmentation.

This is echoed in a white paper published by the One Health High-Level Expert Panel (OHHLEP), an august body created by, and giving guidance and inputs to, the 'Quadripartite' partner agencies, the FAO, UNEP, WHO and the World Organisation for Animal Health (WOAH). The panel concluded that 'prevention of pathogen spillover from animals to humans' requires 'addressing the drivers of disease emergence, namely ecological, meteorological and anthropogenic factors and activities that increase spillover risk, in order to reduce the risk of human infection'.[28]

The radical nature of these recommendations is easy to miss, but in effect both the high-level panel and the UNEP/ILRI report say that to reduce the risk of zoonotic disease spillover, we need to move away from the kinds of highly intensive, industrialised food production that currently dominate. This does not mean we have to revert to traditional small farms or organic systems. As we have seen, some farms can be extensive, industrial and green. But business as usual is not an option. For the prevention of foodborne illness as well as for broader environmental and social justice reasons, the mainstream needs to take a broadly agroecological turn towards more circular, holistic and humane forms of farming.

TAKING STOCK

Towards a Global Food Philosophy

It is hard to imagine that anyone who took an honest look at the place of fish and livestock in the modern industrialised food world would not conclude that something fundamental has to change. It is not just that the environmental impact of animal agriculture as it is currently practised is unsustainable. Our growing appreciation of the capacity of animals to feel pleasure and pain has made indifference to their well-being untenable. Yet at the same time, the growth of industrial agriculture has made the conditions in which they live much worse. Although it would be naive to believe that cruelty to animals is a modern invention, it has now been industrialised on an unprecedented scale. Our ethical awareness is increasingly pushing us in the opposite direction to which animal husbandry is going.

Our relationship with other animals requires a thoroughgoing rethink. Whether we continue to use animals for food or not, we should all be able to agree that we ought to treat them with much greater compassion. The historical precedents for this are limited.

In some cultures, notably in South Asia, many have refrained from eating animal flesh, taking only milk and eggs. Elsewhere, traditional societies have had an awe and reverence for nature that gave them deep respect for the animals whose flesh they ate. However, often this did not translate to treating those creatures with enough concern for their welfare. Perhaps knowing that nature was harsh, people felt no need to be softer themselves.

But it will not be enough to treat animals better. For both environmental and – in industrialised nations – health reasons we also have to address their oversized role in our food supply. For almost all the 300,000 years humans have walked the Earth, the use of other animals for food was necessary for our survival. Now, for the first time, we have the option of a vegan future. If we do not take it, our continued use of livestock and the methods we use to rear them will both stand in need of justification.

If we do continue to use animals for food, we need to think holistically about how we raise them, ensuring that livestock farming is as circular as possible. We have plenty of models to inspire us. The traditional rice–fish system provides a template for new forms of aquaculture such as non-fed and integrated multi-trophic systems. The cattle of the Pampas show how grazing animals can benefit habitats. New forms of circularity need to be developed, with waste from one farming sector becoming food or other inputs for another.

Although there is no doubt that we have to reduce our consumption of animal fats and proteins to meet our climate and sustainability goals, there can be a place for the right amount of properly circular animal farming. The cattle of the Pampas show that thanks to the biogenic cycle, ruminants grazing in the right areas can be carbon neutral and help maintain ecosystems. Animals fed on the parts of arable crops inedible to humans can also be highly efficient users of natural resources that would otherwise go to waste. One such unlikely virtuous synergy is that residue from oat milk production can be used to feed pigs and chickens, showing how increasing our consumption of plant-based products might sometimes make livestock farming more sustainable.[1]

Our survey of the ways in which we have used animals for food is also testament to the vital role of human resourcefulness. Those innovating today with the joint cultivation of sea bream and mussels are displaying the same ingenuity as the ancient Chinese who put carp in their paddy fields. We need to continue to be inventive because we cannot rely entirely on old farming systems. Climate change and the growing population mean that land such as the Pampas cannot provide all our meat, and the wild seas cannot provide all our fish. Whether cultured meat will earn its place as a positive innovation remains to be seen. But we have reason to be cautious about embracing a foodstuff that is as far removed as it could possibly be from the natural whole foods that have always been the basis of healthy diets.

With this resourceful ingenuity must come flexibility and diversity. We have to use every acre of the planet in the way that most suits it. Some parts of the world are ripe for grazing, while in others introducing ruminants would be disastrous. Some parts of the oceans are ideal sites for aquaculture, whereas some habitats must be left untouched. Different cultural preferences also mean that there is no one diet for all that promotes planetary and human health.

The need for the food world to be considered as a whole is also important to counter the spread of foodborne illnesses, including zoonotic diseases. The UN's One Health approach is exemplary in this regard, recognising that the well-being of humans is inextricably linked with that of animals and the environment. To promote this, agroecology in its broad, rather than its narrowly doctrinaire, sense could be a valuable guiding principle, encouraging circular, sustainable systems in which human beings are in harmony with each other and the rest of nature.

Our survey of how the world eats is not complete, but already we can see several elements of a global food philosophy recurring, in particular circularity, holism, plurality and resourcefulness. Two other values have been more notable by their absence – namely, equitability and compassion – while the case for including the idea of foodcentrism has been strong but not yet decisive. We now need to consider whether these seven values are sufficient and fit for the food future that awaits us.

PART FOUR

Technology

14

Editing nature

Corn and canola in Canada

You're eating a nice piece of organic Ruby Red grapefruit. Sure, it isn't as blemish-free as the non-organic alternative, but you're fine with that as the price of its naturalness. Of course, 'natural' does not necessarily mean that the fruit was just picked from a tree or bush. In this case, it was cultivated, and that means what you are eating is a specific cultivar that has been selected and grown, and isn't found in the wild. But what might surprise you is that the Ruby Red is not the result of a farmer simply choosing seeds from the most productive trees or grafting a scion from one tree to the rootstock of another. Rather, a plant was exposed to ionising radiation, creating more mutations in its seeds than would have occurred naturally. This process of 'mutagenesis' shuffles the genetic pack more violently than nature's more sedate mixing. The resulting plants are then compared to see which develops in the most desirable way. The Ruby Red had a darker flesh than the original pink, so the plant was put into commercial production.

In many parts of the world, the resulting cultivar can be grown and sold as organic.

Whether mutagenised crops should be certifiable as organic has become a matter of some dispute. The organic movement has long stood against genetically modified organisms (GMOs). But as IFOAM–Organics International acknowledges, 'there are genetic varieties in wide circulation and use (even by some organic producers) that have been developed through cell fusion, or through irradiation-induced or chemically-induced mutagenesis, or through in vitro mutagenic techniques'. While they 'call for identification of all such varieties' and their 'eventual replacement by varieties developed through breeding techniques that are compatible with fundamental tenets of organic breeding', for the moment, they are permitted.[1] The standards of neither the National Organic Program in the USA nor the Soil Association in the UK prohibit new mutation breeding.[2]

'Mutation' sounds repulsive until you remember that everything you eat is a mutant. Without mutation, there is no evolution. Every time a living thing reproduces, be it flora, fauna or fungi, there is a possibility that the genetic code will not be copied perfectly. If that results in a change to the organism that decreases its reproductive potential, the mutation will soon die out. If it enhances the organism's chances of reproducing, more specimens with the mutation will survive and over time they will increase their share of the overall population. This is natural selection.

Not all selection, however, is left entirely to nature. For millennia, human beings have been lending a hand. Farmers would select seeds from their plants for traits such as greater yield, flavour, or resistance to pests and drought. All of this improvement was done without anyone having any idea about why or how such selective breeding worked. No one knew about the theory of evolution, let alone about the role of genes in it. Indeed, when Darwin coined the term 'natural selection' he was drawing an analogy between what breeders were known to do and how nature works. Human beings were known to be selectors before Mother Nature was discovered to be one.

Natural selection and breeding by humans both rely on the same underlying mechanisms, but their purposes are quite different. More accurately, natural selection has no purpose. Survival of the fittest is not the *aim* of nature, it is rather the only thing that can happen when there is nothing or no one imposing any other goal. Humans, however, can give selection whatever purpose they want. Instead of letting nature select for 'fitness to survive', farmers select for fitness to be cultivated and to eat. They can breed for traits that are not intended to improve reproductive fitness, such as longer shelf life, firmer flesh or increased micronutrients. As a result, domesticated crops have become higher yielding, more nutritious and contain fewer toxins than their wild ancestors.

Sometimes humans can even choose to breed for traits that *reduce* reproductive fitness. Take pedigree (or purebred) dogs. These have been bred to accentuate certain features that human owners find desirable. This requires intentional inbreeding, a narrowing of the gene pool that is in any normal circumstances judged undesirable because it increases the risks of poor health. What's more, the 'desirable' traits themselves often cause health problems. Breeding for large dogs, such as Great Danes, increases the risk of bone and joint problems as well as heart disease. Breeding for very small dogs, such as chihuahuas, creates fragile bones. Flat-faced breeds such as pugs commonly have breathing difficulties. For all these reasons, pedigree dogs typically have worse health and lower life expectancy than mongrels.

We have been changing the genes of our crops and livestock from the dawn of agriculture. But one subset of modern methods differs significantly, in that it allows us to alter the genes directly. The most recently developed means of doing this is gene-editing (GE). This technique, perhaps unhelpfully, follows in the footsteps of the older technology of genetic modification. Genetically Modified Organisms have been controversial since the first GM produce, a tomato, was created in 1994. They polarise opinion and can provoke deep, emotional responses. It takes some effort to think about them anew, dispassionately. But if we are to understand the promises and risks of gene editing, we need to understand that in the complicated history of GMOs, the good and the bad are not always what we think they are.

The 'modification' in GMOs is the insertion of the DNA from one organism into a different one. Some 'transgenic' experiments sound eerie, such as inserting genes from jellyfish into mice to make them glow in the dark, or engineering goats to produce a spider silk protein in their milk. So it is little surprise that GMOs have provoked headlines about 'Frankenfoods'. However, most gene transfers are of bacteria or are from different members of the same species. Nor are such transfers the result of fiendish scientists' Promethean whims. Indeed, one of the first major attempts to develop a GM crop was a benign, philanthropic venture.

At the start of the twenty-first century, Golden Rice became the poster child for this emerging technology. It had been developed at the Swiss Federal Institute of Technology in Zürich in order to solve a huge malnutrition problem in Asia, where vitamin A deficiency resulted in a million deaths a year and half a million cases of blindness, with children the main victims. Golden Rice had been engineered to contain beta carotene, which the human body converts to vitamin A. This made it the world's first synthetically biofortified crop. The project was not-for-profit and the rice was to be made freely available to poor farmers in low- and middle-income countries, who would be able to save seeds to harvest the following year and so not be dependent on commercial seed sellers. More than twenty years after it was ready, however, it is still not available.

Over that time, many other GM crops have been planted and harvested. These are very much for profit and their key characteristics do not involve enhanced nutrition. The most popular GM crops are designed to work in conjunction with broad-spectrum herbicides that kill pretty much any plant they come into contact with except the GM crops, which have been bred to resist them. The best-known of these herbicides is glyphosate, better known under the brand names Roundup and Ranger Pro. If a farmer plants fields with a 'Roundup-ready' GM crop and then sprays the fields with glyphosate, everything dies except the crop. Weeds no longer compete with the crop for space, nutrients and water, and the farmer gets a better yield.

That may sound good, but concerns have been raised about the use of GM crops on health, environmental and social grounds. Regarding health, questions have been raised about both the crops themselves and the glyphosate used on the farms to help grow them.

For the general public, health concerns have always been paramount. When GMOs were new, these worries were entirely reasonable. Bill Tracy, a professor of agronomy at the University of Wisconsin–Madison, tells me that 'early on, and still to a large degree, GM was essentially controlled by [the argribusiness] Monsanto, and of course Monsanto was then and now a deeply mistrusted entity. They were saying it was perfectly safe, yet at the time, the USDA wouldn't give me anything. I asked Monsanto and they didn't respond. I did more digging and it was kind of weak. The media would call me up and say "Hey is this safe?" and all I could say is "Probably." No one would give me the information to say "yes" as a scientist.'

But, Tracy says, 'we now have the studies'. Or rather, 'it wasn't really a study, it was feeding it to millions of people, hogs and cattle'. Today, it is difficult to find an informed, non-partisan source with concerns about the effects of GM foods on human health.

National agencies such as the FDA in America and scientific organisations like the Royal Society say plainly that GM crops are safe to eat.[3] Nicola Patron, Synthetic Biology Group Leader at the Earlham Institute, sums up the expert consensus when she says that 'all crop breeding techniques involve rearrangements and changes to genes. The risks of using these new breeding technologies are no greater than for older breeding technologies, the products of which are subject to far fewer checks.' One such control is that food safety regulations do not allow toxins in synthetic food additives unless they are at less than 100th of the lowest level at which tests show they have no observable effects. According to zoologist John Krebs, if potatoes had to pass the same tests, they would probably be banned, as they contain high levels of poisons called glycoalkaloids.[4]

GM foods are perfectly safe, but the same cannot be said of the glyphosate used to help grow them. Many claim glyphosate causes cancer, and there is some truth in this. The WHO's International Agency for Research on Cancer (IARC) concluded in 2015 that the herbicide was 'probably carcinogenic to humans'.[5] Both Monsanto and Bayer, which bought Monsanto in 2018, have paid out millions of dollars to farmers who claim to have been made ill by it. In 2018 Monsanto lost a court case and was ordered to pay $289 million to a groundskeeper who contracted non-Hodgkin lymphoma, while in 2020 Bayer set aside more than $10 billion to settle tens of thousands of claims out of court.[6]

But if glyphosate is so dangerously toxic, why is it still licensed to use as safe in most of the world's countries? The reason is that of course glyphosate is toxic, as it is a herbicide, which makes it toxic by definition: it kills weeds. The question is not *if* it is toxic, but *how* toxic it is, and at what level of exposure. Glyphosate falls into category 2A ('probably carcinogenic to humans') of the IARC taxonomy, which includes substances that are found in a number of widely eaten foods, such as processed meats, alcoholic drinks, any charred or burned food, red meat and any hot beverage above 65°C.[7] That it is 'probably carcinogenic' to humans doesn't mean it is automatically unsafe to use. You would have to eat huge quantities of these foods to get cancer as a result. Likewise, you'd need a lot of exposure to glyphosate to get cancer from it. The exact amount is still not known, but the court cases and settlements so far have all involved agricultural workers exposed to vast amounts. There is no suggestion that the very small glyphosate residues sometimes found in food present any risk to human health. You ingest as many carcinogens from one cup of coffee as you do in a year from pesticide residues on food.[8] If you are regularly working with glyphosate, concerns about the health risks of your exposure are legitimate, but as someone who eats food made from glyphosate-treated GM crops, there is no good evidence that your health is at risk.

A second area of concern is the environment. Take contamination. Once planted, GM crops cannot be contained. Seeds from GM crops may blow into adjacent fields, leading to interbreeding. 'I can remember being in conferences where people who had never been in a corn field would stand up and say "We know how to control corn pollen,"' says Tracy. 'Nobody knows how to control corn pollen. It goes where it wants.' However, the language of 'contamination' is loaded. The more neutral term is 'cross-pollination', and this occurs in nature all the time. It would only be a problem if the GM crops were harmful in some way. In other words, unless there are good arguments that GM crops are in themselves dangerous, cross-pollination is not a problem.

Another environmental worry is that GM crops tend to be grown as large monocultures where there is massively reduced biodiversity. Fields where only the desired crop can grow sound great from the farmer's perspective, but they are much less hospitable to birds, insects and small mammals. This kind of farming is also more dependent on external inputs such as synthetic fertilisers. However, this is not an unavoidable consequence of using gene modification but a problem caused by how agribusinesses have chosen to deploy the technology. Furthermore, there are millions of hectares of environmentally unfriendly monocultures in the world which are not GMOs.

However, environmentalists have tended to be opposed to genetic modification in itself, not just as it has been most commonly used. This is especially true of some 'deep greens' who see all 'artificial' human creations as an impediment to a life lived more directly in touch with nature. They allow that there must be room for human-made buildings, tools and so on, but they prefer 'natural' materials such as wood and pottery to industrially made steel and concrete; green and animal manures to synthetic fertilisers; silk and cotton to polyester and Gore-Tex.

However, environmentalism comes in many shapes and forms, not all of them hostile to technology. An increasing number of greens reject the idea that we have to choose between environmentalism and technology. Ecomodernism is one such way of thinking. The Ecomodernist Manifesto states that 'we affirm one long-standing environmental ideal, that humanity must shrink its impacts on the environment to make more room for nature, while we reject another, that human societies must harmonise with nature to avoid economic and ecological collapse.'[9] Their argument is that we will do more damage to nature if we depend solely on natural resources: 'Natural systems will not, as a general rule, be protected or enhanced by the expansion of humankind's dependence upon them for sustenance and well-being.'

Ecomodernists claim to be more realistic than 'back to nature' environmentalists, and so also go by the name 'ecopragmatists'. They argue that to protect nature and create a sustainable future we need not less technology but smarter forms of it. This is sometimes caricatured as the idea that we don't need to fundamentally change how we live because 'technology will save us'. However, ecomodernists explicitly reject 'business as usual'. In their view, we need to decouple economic growth and environmental degradation, which to date have always gone together. We need environmental impacts to decline, even as the economy continues to grow. This won't happen by itself. 'Technological progress is not inevitable,' says the manifesto. 'Decoupling environmental impacts from economic outputs is not simply a function of market-driven innovation and efficient response to scarcity.'

Such ideas of 'green growth' are often ridiculed on the common-sense basis that an expanding economy requires expanding resources and you cannot have infinite growth on a finite planet. The latter statement is true, but it knocks down a straw man. No one is thinking about whether we will still need or want growth in a hundred years, let alone for eternity. Take infinity out of the equation and green growth is evidently possible, and we've already seen localised examples of it. Replace greenhouse gases with renewable energy, for example, and raw materials with recycled ones, and you can increase productive capacity while having less impact on the environment. Efficiency has always been a driver of growth, and the green economic revolution is all about more efficient use of resources, to the extent that we no longer need to extract new, non-renewable ones.

Ecomodernists point to various ways in which improved efficiency has led to, or can lead to, less impact on the environment. Since the mid-1960s, the amount of land required to feed the average person has halved, the amount of water used has been cut by nearly 25 per cent, and in developed nations there has even been a decrease in the amount of nitrogen pollution per unit of production. All this has been due to better use of technology, not to its abandonment. In contrast, pre-modern societies had a much bigger environmental footprint per person. As the Ecomodernist Manifesto says, 'a population of no more than one or two million

North Americans hunted most of the continent's large mammals into extinction in the late Pleistocene, while burning and clearing forests across the continent in the process.' If their lifestyles were not in aggregate as bad for the planet as ours today it is only because there were so few of them.

The Ecomodernist Manifesto was written and signed by many leading environmentalists, several of whom had themselves been on a journey from techno-scepticism, if not outright technophobia, to technophilia. Stewart Brand went from anti- to pro-nuclear power, Mark Lynas from opposition to transgenic crops to supporting them, Rachel Pritzker went from an advocate to a sceptic of the idea that eco-conscious activities like recycling, growing vegetables and using renewable energy are enough to save the planet, if we all did them. Whether you agree with them or not, ecomodernists show that a commitment to a set of values should not lead to an ossified set of beliefs about how to realise them. A conscientious environmentalist needs to challenge what true environmentalism requires, and that may change as the world, the facts and our understanding change.

As well as health and environmental objections, the third and perhaps greatest concern about GM is how it has given big 'agritech' companies even more power in the food system. Four companies – Bayer–Monsanto, DowDuPont/Corteva, ChemChina–Syngenta and BASF – dominate global agricultural seed sales, although how dominant they are depends on the crop and the location. Almost all cotton seed in Mexico is sold by Bayer–Monsanto, while in Central and Eastern Europe there is a lot of diversity of providers of wheat and barley.[10] Although this domination by a handful of multi-national companies may seem worrying, an OECD statistical analysis 'did not find any clear evidence that increases in market concentration raised seed prices or reduced innovation'.[11]

Whereas traditionally farmers saved seeds from harvests to plant the following year, modern hybrid seeds are subject to intellectual copyright and so are owned by the usually large companies that make them. Farmers can therefore legally be required to buy new seeds every year rather than use saved ones. Most of the time this is also good business for the farmer, since saved seed is less productive than new seed. Moreover, without the ability to keep earning from seeds, companies would not be able to justify the high research and development costs required to breed them.

Many argue that it is wrong for any private company to own a living organism, but the practice long predates GMOs. It should not therefore be surprising that GM crop manufacturers require farmers to buy new seeds every year, as well as the corresponding herbicides and pesticides. What changed was simply that at least one company, Monsanto, started to enforce its intellectual property rights more aggressively.

The most famous alleged instance was the Monsanto Canada Inc v Schmeiser case, the subject of both a documentary movie, *David versus Monsanto*, and a feature film, *Percy* (aka *Percy vs Goliath*), starring Christopher Walken and Christina Ricci.[12] The story is usually told in line with the documentary's synopsis: 'Imagine a storm blows across your property – and that now, without your knowledge or consent, genetically manipulated seeds are in the garden you have tended for years. A few days later, representatives of a multi-national corporation pay you a visit, demand that you surrender your produce – and simultaneously file a criminal complaint against you, with a fine of $200,000, for the illegal use of patented, genetically-manipulated seeds.'[13] The tale is presented as though Monsanto was suing farmers for growing their GM seeds without payment when the crops were the result of inadvertent contamination from neighbouring farms using the Monsanto seed. The reality, however, is more complex.

The case centres on the Saskatchewan farmer Percy Schmeiser, who in 1997 found Roundup-ready canola growing on an area of his field adjacent to the road used by trucks to deliver Monsanto canola seeds to neighbouring farms. He sprayed a three-to-four-acre area of the field with Roundup to see what would happen and around 60 per cent of the crop thrived, especially nearer the road. Crucially, he then used the seeds from that field to plant the following year's crop. This was the breach of patent Monsanto sued him over. Such lawsuits are not confined to GM seeds. Many crops and plants are patented and can only be grown under licence and are subject to the conventions of the International Union for the Protection of New Varieties of Plants (UPOV). Even organic growers use plenty of such patented seeds.

The Supreme Court ruled in favour of Monsanto, a verdict upheld after an appeal which also ruled that Schmeiser did not have to pay the company damages. Whatever the merits of the verdicts and the rightness or wrongness of Monsanto pursuing the case, it is plainly not an example of a farmer being sued for inadvertent contamination. There is no question that Schmeiser deliberately sowed the seeds. The same was true in the case of Bowman v Monsanto Co. Indiana farmer Vernon Bowman had saved seeds from Monsanto crops eight seasons running, which his contract with the company did not allow him to do. Again, the Supreme Court ruled in Monsanto's favour. Yet myths about farmers being sued for unintentional GMO contamination refuse to die.[14]

The history of GMOs is one of justified worries and unfounded scare stories. Most importantly it tells of the monopolisation of the technology by large companies that have used it to serve their own interests, not those of wider society. Assessing GMOs fairly is difficult because Roundup and the company that sold it, Monsanto, have become so demonised that all GM has become evil by association. But when agribusiness has applied GM in ways that are bad for the environment or small farmers, this should damn the companies, not the technology itself.

Any sober analysis would conclude that GM is neither an un-qualified success story nor a disaster. Some of its achievements are impressive. For example, the papaya ringspot virus almost wiped out Hawaii's papaya plantations in the 1990s as no varieties of the fruit had resistance to it. Resistant stains were bred by adding a gene from the virus to a papaya. Many credit this with saving the Hawaiian papaya, and now more than three quarters of farmers on the islands farm GM varieties.[15]

Still, the global public has not been won over by the idea of GMOs. Bans on their cultivation are in place in many European countries, including France, Germany, the Netherlands, Poland, Denmark, Italy and Croatia. Around a dozen countries elsewhere in the world also have bans, including Algeria, Turkey, Bhutan, Saudi Arabia, Ecuador, Peru and Venezuela. In many other countries, however, including the USA, not only are they permitted, they do not have to be labelled.[16] The ubiquity of GMOs in the global food chain means that bans on their consumption are im-practical, and so the most countries can do is insist on GM products being labelled, as the EU does. But there is no doubt that GMOs end up in countless foodstuffs, even in countries that tightly regu-late them, not least in the form of animal feeds such as soy. In 2017 the majority of animal feed in the EU was soy, mostly imported. Ninety per cent of it was GM, meaning that at least 40 per cent of animal feed in the EU is genetically modified. So, as the Royal Society explains, 'meat, milk and eggs from animals fed with GM crops is eaten in many countries including the UK'. But as the Finnish Ministry of Agriculture and Forestry says, 'an animal fed on feed of this type does not produce genetically modified foods'.[17] That is true: when you eat something you do not eat what it fed on. You do not eat manure when you eat potatoes grown in it, and you do not eat grass when you drink milk from a pasture-reared cow. Still, GMOs are in our food chain and sometimes we even eat them directly without realising. More than three quarters of hard cheese in the world is made with genetically engineered chymosin, a microbial rennet used in place of traditional animal rennet, in part because it is considered suitable for vegetarians.[18]

The story of GMOs is incomplete without the tale of what did *not* happen. Commercial GM crops have been widely resisted and vilified, yet they have become commonplace. At the same time, not-for-profit Golden Rice sits in university storage facilities uncultivated. Why?

Ed Regis tells the full story of the miracle crop that never got planted in his book *Golden Rice: The Imperiled Birth of a GMO Superfood*.[19] Regis says that the project was 'weighed down with all the political, ideological, and emotional baggage that has come to be associated with GMOs – stultifying government overregulation, fear and hostility, and criticism (much of it unfounded) from environmentalist and other activist organisations and individuals'.[20]

Leading the resistance was Greenpeace, a global environmental charity which enjoys a lot of support. In 2001 Greenpeace 'pointed out', as they happily continued to report twelve years later, that, 'people would need to consume vast quantities of [Golden] rice (over twelve times the normal daily intake) to obtain the recommended dietary allowance of vitamin A'.[21] This claim was made without evidence and later shown to be false. Bizarrely, other anti-GM groups used the opposite argument, with the Institute of Science in Society claiming that 'increasing the level of beta-carotene may cause vitamin A overdose to those [whose] diets provide adequate amounts of the vitamin', and Friends of the Earth saying that beta carotene in Golden Rice might 'produce derivatives that cause direct toxicity or abnormal embryonic development in those exposed to them'.[22]

George Church, a professor of genetics at Harvard Medical School, slammed Greenpeace for its role in hindering Golden Rice's development, saying in an interview, 'A million lives are at stake every year due to vitamin A deficiency, and Golden Rice was basically ready for use in 2002. . . . Every year that you delay it, that's another million people dead. That's mass murder on a high scale.' According to Church, in this story, the academics are David and Greenpeace is Goliath, with 'many, many times more funding than the groups that are developing the Golden Rice'.[23]

Regis attributes Golden Rice's failure mostly to a 'Byzantine web of rules, guidelines, requirements, restrictions, and prohibitions'. These are rooted in an international treaty called the Cartagena Protocol on Biosafety, which came into force in September 2003. By 2023, 173 countries had signed up.[24] The Protocol endorses the precautionary principle, as set out in the Rio Declaration issued by the United Nations Conference on Environment and Development in 1992. This stated that 'where there are threats of serious or irreversible damage, lack of full scientific certainty shall not be used as a reason for postponing cost-effective measures to prevent environmental degradation.'[25] This has been interpreted to mean that if a new biotechnology presents any serious risk, even if the probability of harm is extremely low, it should not be used until proven safe. Hence article 12 of the Cartagena Protocol states: 'Lack of scientific certainty [. . .] shall not prevent that Party from taking a decision [. . .] in order to avoid or minimise such potential adverse effects.'

The principle may sound sensible, but it demands a very high burden of proof, since absolute certainty is impossible in science. A mere shadow of doubt is enough to stop a technology from being used or even tested. Regis concludes, 'Had Golden Rice not faced overly restrictive regulatory conditions, it could have been cultivated by rice farmers and distributed throughout some of the poorest regions of South and Southeast Asia.'

If the regulatory burden is so onerous, how can commercial companies have overcome them? The answer is simple: money. Commercial crops overcome statutory resistance because in business the bottom line talks. Throw enough money at a problem and it will often go away. Golden Rice, in contrast, relied on goodwill, which was in short supply. This shows that if we erect obstacles to slow the development of technology, those seeking to develop it for altruistic purposes will be hampered more than those who are developing it for commercial gain. The fear that GMOs would become a tool of big business became a self-fulfilling prophecy because non-profits were hindered from using them.

Technology has been deeply embedded in our food system at least since the invention of the plough. Today, however, its role has massively increased. It is a truism that technology is rarely good or bad in itself and that it all depends on how it is used. On one side there are those who think that technology is overwhelmingly helpful and necessary for overcoming our challenges, and on the other are those who see the constant reaching for 'techno-fixes' not only as a distraction from deeper problems, but as the cause of many of them. Technology is too often seen as a get-out-of-jail-free card that enables us to carry on with an unsustainable system, when in reality it is no more than a sticking plaster. The danger of being too seduced by the opportunities of technology is that other options are left unexplored, in the belief that progress alone can save us.

GM crops have been used as such a sticking plaster. They have improved yields, but at the price of fields stripped of all biodiversity by the chemicals the GM crops have been engineered to resist. They have also consolidated corporate power in the food world. But it did not have to be this way. None of the downsides of GMOs have been due to the underlying technology itself. Rather, they have all arisen from the uses to which it was put. Many kinds of GM crops could and have been bred, including ones that are more drought- and pest-resistant, better yielding, or more nutritious. That the most successful crops have been designed to resist broad-spectrum herbicides is the result of the private sector taking the lead and pursuing its own priorities.

Today there is a new kind of gene modification technology, and there is a risk that the lessons of GM have not been learned and that history will repeat itself. Gene editing (GE) has been greeted as a potential saviour by some and as the second coming of the GMO Antichrist by others. GE leapt into public awareness with the development of CRISPR/Cas9 genetic scissors, commonly referred to simply as CRISPR technology. It was such a significant breakthrough that it won its developers, Emmanuelle Charpentier and Jennifer Doudna, the Nobel Prize in Chemistry 2020. CRISPR has many applications, including in medicine, but it has already been put to work in plant breeding. The Nobel Prize citation noted that its use has led to the development of rice varieties that absorb fewer heavy metals from the soil, reducing levels of cadmium and arsenic, as well as to crops that are more drought-, insect- and pest-resistant.[26]

Gene editing is, on paper, a less controversial technology than GM. Whereas GMOs incorporate genetic material from other organisms, gene editing can simply remove genes already in the organism without importing anything foreign.[27] This 'can' is important. In theory, GE could also add novel genetic material, as GM does. But for the purposes of this discussion, gene editing will be assumed to involve only altering the organism's own DNA. This follows the approach of the Swedish Board of Agriculture, which ruled that plants with foreign DNA introduced using CRISPR/Cas9 technology fall within the definition of GMOs, while edited plants lacking foreign DNA do not.[28] In other words, if CRISPR is used to introduce foreign genes, it is no longer doing gene editing, but is instead doing genetic modification.

GE foods face a great deal of opposition. GMOs established themselves in the food system without ever gaining widespread public acceptance and so have not 'softened up' the public, making it ready to embrace GE. Wariness about genetic modification remains high, meaning that many want to stop GE food coming through the door even when the room is already full of GMOs.

If public acceptance requires public understanding, CRISPR faces a big challenge. Even the name is baffling: it is an acronym for 'clustered regularly interspaced short palindromic repeats'. If you're not a chemist, any explanation of how it works is almost sure to leave you less than fully enlightened. In brief, it co-opts a bacterial antiviral defence system, using a synthetic guide RNA to deliver a protein called Cas9 to the precise point in a gene sequence that is to be cut, allowing target genes to be removed, with the option to replace them with others.

Still, gene editing has the potential to help improve the food supply in numerous ways. It could be used to breed plants and animals that are more resistant to heat, cold, drought, flooding, pests or disease as well as those that produce better yields. It could improve their nutritional content or remove so-called anti-nutrients, which inhibit the absorption of nutrients in digestion. Food allergens could be snipped out, allowing people with nut allergies, for example, to eat such foods again.

Supporters of such techniques argue that humankind has been genetically modifying food for millennia without knowing it, and has done so more recently in full knowledge and with explicit intent. As the FAO put it, scientific breeding has simply brought more 'speed and precision' to the process, and the new technique of gene editing is 'the latest advance in this continuum'.[29]

Patron argues that gene editing and traditional breeding are both techniques for rearranging genes to achieve desired ends. The difference is that 'applying genetic technologies to crop breeding makes the process of bringing combinations of beneficial sequences and genes together into the same plant easier. Because scientists know what changes are being made, the consequences of these changes are closely observed and extensively analysed even before the plants enter large-scale breeding programmes. The outcomes of gene editing are therefore more likely to be predictable.'[30]

Crucially, proponents of GE claim that the kind of modifications it delivers are indistinguishable from those that could have occurred from natural mutations. Whereas with a GMO you could tell that it had been modified because certain genes could not have got into the organism by natural processes, in a gene-edited organism, there is no such smoking gun. This, it is argued, means the resulting organisms present no special risks.

You don't need to buy into all the overexcited puff about gene editing to see its value. Bill Tracy is a supporter even though he thinks that 'technologists tend to overhype their invention' and that CRISPR is no exception. 'When they first came out with CRISPR it was like: it's incredibly accurate, nothing ever goes wrong. We very quickly learned that that was not true. The reason is that in many crops there's gene duplication.' A plant may contain slightly different versions of the same gene, each doing a different job, and trying to knock out one could knock out the other, with unintended consequences.

As with GMOs, most concerns about the risks to human health are misguided and disproportionate. It is bizarre to worry about the effects of a well-tested GE carrot when people in many countries are eating foods that are demonstrably bad for their health and causes of non-communicable diseases. To object to the slice of gene-edited tomato in your burger while happily eating all the other junk in it is a clear case of misplaced priorities.

Also as with GMOs, it is more important to think about how the technology is used and who benefits. Guy Poppy, Professor in Biological Sciences at the University of Southampton, is less worried about safety issues than he is about structural problems in the food system. Take concerns about crop diversity. 'Civilisation already relies on obtaining much of its calories from a few staple crops, which represent a fraction of one per cent of the total biodiversity which exists. [. . .] A diverse genome is more resilient to pests, diseases and climate change. Repeatedly breeding just a handful of cultivars can lead to wide-scale crop failure, as occurred with sugar cane in the 1970s.' These risks are higher if a handful of large firms dominate GE cultivars. But they are reduced if gene editing results in 'farmers using more species and cultivars'.[31] As with GMOs, much depends on whether those exploiting GE are doing so mainly for their own profit or for the general good.

Patron also makes a persuasive case that corporate bad practice is not a good enough reason to oppose the use of GE crops. She accepts that 'bad behaviour and poor corporate responsibility by companies should unquestionably be called out, curtailed and, where necessary, regulated', but argues that 'seeking to counter the behaviour of a few companies by suppressing the use of technologies with enormous potential that are being used in public development programmes to improve lives does not seem reasonable to me'.

Jennifer Doudna sums up what is perhaps the key issue: 'One risk that is often overlooked is the real possibility that some of the advances we make in genome editing will benefit a small fraction of society. With new technologies this is often the case at first, so we have to consciously work from the start to make new cures and agricultural tools that are accessible and affordable.'

Gene editing has the potential to level the playing field and give more power to non-profits. As plant molecular biologist Rebecca Mackelprang argues, the expense of licensing, research and development is so high with GMOs that it 'shuts small companies, academic researchers and NGOs out of the equation'. The more precise and predictable nature of CRISPR editing could allow genetically altered food to 'escape the dominant financial grasp of large seed companies'. But that is only if regulation becomes less onerous and costly.

However, most environmental NGOs have campaigned

vociferously against the spread of GM crops, and so far most have viewed GE crops as more of the same. The organic sector has also prided itself on remaining GMO free. For example, the US National Organic Standards Board (NOSB) excludes all genome-edited crops from organic certification.[32] The UK's Soil Association also refuses to countenance gene editing, saying in a statement that '"precision breeding" and "gene editing" have become shiny and attractive sounding terms used to rebrand newer forms of genetic modification.'[33] In 2020, the International Federation of Organic Agriculture Movements (IFOAM) issued a position statement which 'reaffirms its position that GMOs and their derivatives have no place in organic food and farming systems', classifying genome editing as a form of prohibited genetic engineering.[34]

Tracy sees opposition to any kind of gene modification to be so deeply entrenched in the organic movement that ending it would be virtually impossible. But he is not without all hope. 'Tomatoes get a lot of fungal diseases and the organic rule allows the use of copper as a fungicide. Copper fungicides have been used for hundreds, thousands of years, but everybody knows copper is toxic. If somebody came along today and said, "This is a brand new technology, let's use it," people would be scandalised and it probably wouldn't even be approved by the Environmental Protection Agency [EPA]. CRISPR and other GM technologies should be able to come up with a gene edited variety that enables us to get rid of that. I think that could be a game changer. I really don't see how the NOSB could say no, but due the intense politics they probably would.'

Raoul Adamchak, an organic farmer, also sees the potential benefits of CRISPR for organic farmers, again for tomatoes, by knocking out the genes that cause softening in heirloom varieties. Adamchak doesn't see any consistency in the ban on gene editing when it is clearly a better, more precise technology than mutagenesis. 'As long as mutational breeding is accepted by the National

Organic Program, then this type of CRISPR function should be accepted as well.' He also points out that organic growers can already use conventionally grown seed, as long as it is cultivated organically.

Patron also sees resistance to GE crops and acceptance of mutagenic ones as inconsistent. Following a European Court of Justice ruling in 2018, genome-edited plants were classified as genetically modified. But you could in theory end up with an identical plant that had been mutated using radiation or mutagenic chemicals, but that would not be classified as GM. Patron thinks this is illogical. 'When there are no new genes inserted, I struggle to understand how and why plants mutated with these technologies should be regulated in a different way.'

The FAO seems to have sized up the potential of gene editing just right. A 2022 report on gene editing and agrifood systems came to a rounded and measured conclusion of the risks and benefits, correctly judging that success or failure will depend on who ultimately benefits. It recognises the different objectives and incentives of the private and public sectors, but it is hopeful that 'collaboration between the two sectors is possible and can be beneficial'. It also resists the overenthusiasm that often accompanies technological breakthroughs, heralded as cure-alls, saying, 'Gene editing is not a stand-alone technology and is not the only solution for the problems currently faced by agrifood systems.'[35]

Sceptics will say that the history of agricultural technology suggests that big business will win and the small producers will be the losers, yet again. The experience of GMOs lends some weight to that concern. But small farmers have benefited from many other technologies, from better seeds to better irrigation systems to better mechanical equipment. There is no inevitability that the benefits of gene editing will all pile up on big business's plate. However, that risk is greater if gene editing and other novel technologies are rejected outright by those on the side of agroecological farming, peasant rights and human health. Environmentalism and technology can be allies, not enemies. If we made that mental shift, CRISPR could be seen as a potential tool for a more ecologically sustainable food system.

15

THE WASTE LANDS

Rullepølse and kyllingebrystfilet in Denmark

In traditional societies, little to no food goes to waste. Every edible part of an animal or plant is utilised. Western researchers found that the members of a Maasai community in northern Tanzania were outraged at the thought of intentionally wasting food, calling those who would do so 'lunatics'. Some even said it was worse than killing a person, because murder leads to one death whereas wasting food could result in several. The Yali, an indigenous tribe from West Papua, Indonesia that has very little contact with the modern world, had a similar reaction. They said it is better to give leftovers to other people or to feed pigs.

Attitudes towards waste are very different in industrialised nations. The researchers also spoke to urban Poles from Poznań, one of the biggest and richest cities in Poland. The Poznanians rarely judged wasting food to be immoral. Those who did cited global hunger and the environment as reasons.[1]

The authors of the study hypothesised that cultural differences in moral judgements could be adaptations to differing ecological conditions. (We considered why this should be so in chapter 2.) In the case of food waste, the key difference was thought to be in food security. This was very high in Poznań, with Poland, at the time of the study, ranking twenty-ninth in the Economist Intelligence Unit's Global Food Security Index, and with food shortages last seen in 1956. Food security was much weaker in Indonesia and Tanzania, which ranked seventy-first and ninety-fourth on the index, respectively.[2] Where food security is weaker, wasting food has bigger consequences so is condemned more. Societies with a cultural memory of scarcity may also continue to abhor waste, even if it no longer presents a risk. Such a memory may explain why many older Europeans who lived through or shortly after the Second World War still stick rigidly to the 'waste not, want not' principle.

Strictly speaking, the researchers should have said that moral norms are cultural adaptations to the *perceived* ecological challenges. If moral norms varied according to the *actual* ecological conditions, then everyone would be morally outraged at the amount of food and drink that goes uneaten, either as food waste or food loss. *Food loss* is defined as crop and livestock commodities destined for human consumption which are discarded before entering the retail sector. This could be because of failure to harvest, poor storage, deterioration in transport, or simply being left to rot because there is no buyer. *Food waste* is food removed from the human food supply chain in food manufacturing, retail, restaurants, food service and households. This includes unsold items as well as what people put into their rubbish bins.

Statistics on the amount of food lost or wasted are staggering. The United Nations Environment Programme (UNEP) estimates that 17 per cent of total global food production is wasted and around the same amount lost, meaning that around a third of food produced is not consumed. A total of 61 per cent of food waste comes from households, 26 per cent from food service and 13 per cent from retail. The global average for household waste is seventy-four kilograms per person annually, and this figure is broadly similar for lower-, middle- and high-income countries.[3]

Over recent decades, food waste and loss has become more of a salient moral issue across the world. One of the UN's Sustainable Development Goals is to 'halve per capita global food waste at the retail and consumer levels', along with the less specific aim of 'reducing food losses along production and supply chains'. The EAT–Lancet Commission, a global report into healthy, sustainable diets, thought that this goal was needed at the very minimum.[4] The World Resources Institute (WRI) says that meeting the goal would avoid the need to convert natural ecosystems equivalent in size to Argentina to agricultural land and would lower greenhouse gas emissions by more than those currently put out by Japan.[5]

However, food loss and waste statistics are not quite what they seem. First, they generally include the inedible parts of foods, such as shells, bones or stones. In low-income countries more people cook from raw ingredients that contain these parts, which might explain why their overall household food waste is similar to that in high-income ones. Second, everything is counted as lost or wasted irrespective of where it ends up. But clearly food that is put on compost heaps or in anaerobic digestion plants (which both produce energy and compost) is not as wasted as that which ends up in landfill. Third, we actually don't know how much food is wasted. In its most recent report, the UN said that it had high confidence in only seven countries' food waste records: Australia, Austria, Denmark, Germany, Sweden, the United Kingdom and the USA. The UN says that global estimates of food waste have relied on extrapolation from a small number of countries, often using old records.

So total food waste and loss figures could be overestimates, since they do not disaggregate edible and inedible parts. But given the fact that many countries do not have reliable data and that historically food waste has been underestimated, the figures could equally be as bad as or worse than they look. By any measure, a huge amount of food that could be eaten isn't, and whenever better measures are made, they tend to result in estimates of waste and loss going up, not down. In 2021, for example, the UN reported that 'global consumer food waste could be approximately twice the size of previous estimates'.[6]

Many believe reducing waste is essential for feeding the world. For example, the WRI opens its report into food waste and loss by asking 'How is the world going to feed nearly 10 billion people?' and argues that halving food waste 'would close the gap between food needed in 2050 and food available in 2010 by more than 20 per cent'.[7] However, this framing is questionable. Back in 1961, the world produced fewer than 2,200 calories per person per day, barely enough to cover the needs of its men and women, who on average need around 2,500 and 2,000 calories per day, respectively. By 2020, the world was producing much more food than its inhabitants eat: nearly 3,000 calories per person per day.[8] Even with the quantities that we waste, there is enough food in the world to feed everyone. Distribution and affordability are greater obstacles to good nutrition. But although hunger is not the problem now, it soon could be. With the global population still rising, and climate change and geopolitical instability already disrupting agriculture worldwide, in order to avert starvation, it could soon become imperative that we make as much use of what we produce as possible.

At the moment, the greatest impact of food waste is on climate change. UNEP estimates that 8 to 10 per cent of global greenhouse gas emissions are associated with food that is not consumed. As it says, 'If food loss and waste were a country, it would be the third biggest source of greenhouse gas emissions.' In poorer countries it increases food insecurity and everywhere it adds to biodiversity loss, because a lot of land is turned over to cultivation without it ultimately feeding anyone.

Every informed observer agrees that food waste and loss must be reduced. But can we do it?

Waste and loss are often portrayed as egregious, easily avoided if only people would take a bit more care about how much they buy and how they use it. But as with everything in the food world, it is highly complicated. The WRI identifies fifteen separate drivers of loss and waste, which we can illustrate by tracing the life cycle of a humble portion of rice.[9]

The first point of loss with any crop is when it is gathered. One study showed that the proportion of a rice crop lost at harvest ranged from as low as 1.1 per cent to as high as 28.2 per cent.[10] Some of this loss is inevitable. Walk around an olive or almond grove shortly after harvest and you'll find some fruits still on the tree or lying on the ground. Harvesting takes place when the bulk of the crop is ready, but there are always some parts of it that ripen early or late. It isn't possible to get everything. The traditional solution was gleaning, in which local people would take produce left behind after the harvests, or crops which were not harvested at all because it was not profitable to do so. In the Hebrew Bible, gleaning is enshrined in the law. In Deuteronomy 24:19 it says, 'When thou cuttest down thine harvest in thy field, and hast forgot a sheaf in the field, thou shalt not go again to fetch it: it shall be for the stranger, for the fatherless, and for the widow.' Gleaning is also endorsed in Leviticus. Due to this biblical mandate, in several Christian countries gleaning was a legal right of the poor. But in modern industrialised countries, gleaning is a pursuit of a few hardened environmentalists, not least because most people don't live near farms.

Efficient harvesting can keep this waste to a minimum, but this is often hampered by one or more of the other drivers of waste and loss. For instance, the bulk of the rice harvest losses occur during the stages of reaping, threshing and winnowing. These will be higher if there is inadequate equipment. Poor food-management practices, skills and knowledge can also contribute, with equipment being used incorrectly or the timings of the harvest being suboptimal.

Demographics can also hit harvesting. In many parts of the world, there is a shortage of agricultural labourers, as the work tends to be poorly paid and hard work. In low- and middle-income countries, many young people go to the cities to seek a better future, while in industrialised countries most people would rather do any job other than farm work. Climatic conditions also have an impact. For example, in Vietnam in 2022, heavy rains during the harvest damaged a lot of the grain, meaning that a large proportion of the harvest could not be used.

Once harvested, poor infrastructure and packaging can fail to keep the rice fresh, leading to spoilage. This could be due to a lack of access to financing for farmers, who are unable to invest in better storage. Another driver here can be economics. For instance, in years when the commodity price of rice is low, the costs of better storage may not be compensated for by the increased income from a larger crop. Indeed, when global production is very high the result is oversupply, so some farmers can't find buyers and the rice is stuck on the farm.

Policies and regulations such as trade tariffs and export controls may also result in rice going unsold. Farmers are at the mercy of often capricious governments. For instance, in early 2021 rice farmers around Ahero, a town in Kisumu, Kenya's third largest city, complained that they were left with 10,000 bags of unsold rice when the Kenya National Trading Corporation, which had agreed to buy their produce to sell to government institutions, suspended its purchasing.[11]

Poor supply-and-demand forecasting and planning is another

reason why some rice can't be sold. There are so many variables affecting demand that it is very difficult to plan the right sized crop. Grow too little and you could miss out on a bumper payday; grow too much and you could be looking at a loss.

Farmers are also at the mercy of inflexible procurement requirements. It is common for buyers – whether intermediaries, wholesalers or retailers – to require a farmer to have a certain quantity of a commodity like rice ready to sell without accepting any obligation to buy all of it. This is a major problem with fresh seasonal fruit and vegetables. A large supermarket may require its supplier to have a certain number of heads of lettuce ready, but if it is a cool, damp summer week, the buyer may only take half, leaving the farmer with the useless surplus. This isn't the only way in which retailers are very good at pushing waste upstream and downstream, which results in flattering statistics suggesting that they are responsible for only a small proportion of food loss and waste. Not only are suppliers often left with excess production, consumers are encouraged to buy more than they can eat by bulk deals and pricing that makes larger sizes more economic. Food waste campaigner Selina Juul says that this is more accurately described as 'buy three, pay for two, waste one'. Getting customers to buy more than they need is not a new strategy. It became the implicit business model of many Indian restaurants in the UK, where over-ordering became a kind of tradition for a large part of the clientele. Long before McDonald's started asking customers if they wanted to 'supersize' their meals, waiters were prompting theirs to order popadoms, side dishes, breads and sundries, resulting in huge quantities of food being cleared from overladen tables at the end of the evening.

Such waste as the retailers directly produce is partly due to failures of supply-and-demand forecasting and planning. But the big players have got so good at this that it is not a major problem. A bigger issue is norms and attitudes. Supermarkets like to have full shelves, as they know that half-empty ones look unappealing.

So they have historically tended to oversupply, preferring to throw out unsold loaves at the end of the day to running out of bread hours before closing. Products like uncooked rice, with their long shelf lives, are rarely wasted at the retail stage, except when the packaging is damaged. The bulk of retail food waste comes from fresh foods, including ready meals containing cooked rice.

Once the rice reaches homes, waste is often the result of a problem already encountered at the farm level: inadequate food management practices, skills and knowledge. Many households find themselves disposing of the contents of a bag or box found in the back of a cupboard after the best-before date has expired. Dates on packs are very conservative, and if the rice is stored properly – dry and in airtight containers – it can last long after the pack date. But if you are not confident in knowing the signs of mould (discolouration, visible growth, a rancid or otherwise bad smell), it can feel risky to cook it.

Many people routinely cook more than is needed for a meal and end up throwing a lot out. Rice is also a common side dish when eating Asian food in restaurants or as takeaways, and almost invariably more is served than is eaten. Many of us are aware that reheated rice carries the risk of food poisoning, thanks to the bacterium *Bacillus cereus*. Without understanding the full reasons why, some even avoid cold rice to be on the safe side. But the long histories of East Asian refried rice and Italian arancini (filled and fried rice balls) show that this is too cautious. The bacterium will not grow unless the cooked rice is left warm for at least a couple of hours and then reheated. Cold cooked rice is very low risk, and if it is cooled, put in a container and refrigerated within a few hours, it is perfectly safe to reheat.

Much household food waste is the result of bad meal planning. But a lot can be attributed to a basic lack of awareness. Too many of us have become used to abundance and have lost the thrifty mentality of previous generations. We don't think of food waste as an issue. Once we shift our mindset and see every item of food thrown away as a failure, we naturally adopt the habits that make food wastage more of a rarity.

Most of these drivers of waste can appear at different stages in the life cycle of a food. For example, we considered climatic conditions in relation to harvesting, but they can also lead to waste during transport, storage and retail stages, or even in people's homes. Inadequate food management practices, skills and knowledge can also be a problem at any stage.

Given that the drivers of waste identified by the WRI already simplify a very complex web of processes, tackling food waste is clearly far from straightforward. It requires a systemic, multi-pronged approach. But as we have seen before, sometimes complexities can blind us to relatively straightforward general truths. And we have good evidence that the drivers of change for complex problems can sometimes be quite simple.

If food waste and loss is such a complex problem, how come Denmark reduced its food waste by 25 per cent in just five years, between 2010 and 2015? This was the cumulative result of many small changes, but the main reason it happened was because of one woman and social media. Selina Juul was a graphic designer, 'not even a food person,' she told me. But, appalled to discover how much food was going to waste in her country, in 2008 she started a Facebook group *Stop Spild Af Mad* ('Stop wasting food'). Within a fortnight it had gone viral, and just three months later she was approached by REMA 1000, the biggest discount chain in Denmark, who asked her to help them reduce their waste. Among the steps they took was to end bulk discounts like 'Buy two, get one free'. They also started selling bananas individually, putting up signs saying, 'Take me, I'm single'. One retailer reported that after the change, instead of eighty to a hundred bananas being wasted every day, only around ten were.[12]

Before long, Juul was being called upon by the Danish Minister for the Environment, the United Nations, the European Union, the Vatican and Princess Mary of Denmark. She found herself featured by the BBC, CNN and the *New York Times*. She is widely credited with being the catalyst for Denmark's dramatic cut in food waste, winning multiple awards such as Dane of the Year in 2014 and the Nordic Council Nature and Environment Prize 2013.

It's a good-news story but a highly qualified one, because the great leap forward was a one-off. No other country has done as well as Denmark, where, it seems, the ducks uniquely lined up. 'Denmark is a small country,' says Juul. 'We are like a tribe, and it's very easy to get in the news if you have a good story, very easy to affect the population if there's a good cause.' The Danes were already very environmentally aware, and Juul was a charismatic frontwoman in an age where personality counts for a lot. In Britain, in contrast, the estimable Tristram Stuart has been at least as tireless at campaigning against food waste, but he lacks Juul's magnetism and is up against a citizenry that seems to resent even having to sort its recycling for collection. Whereas the Danish government embraced the cause with gusto and is developing a food waste strategy, in Britain the Environment Secretary appointed as the government's 'Food Surplus and Waste Champion' a man who ran a concierge firm for ultra-high net worth individuals, which had fifty staff in its Moscow office.[13]

Juul may also have been helped by avoiding the anti-capitalist and anti-corporate radicalism of many environmental movements. As she told CNN, 'Lots of environmental NGOs go out to rally against industrial actors, and it is the wrong approach. If you do that, they won't work with you. We don't scold anyone. We say: we are all part of the problem, and also the solution.'[14]

Despite the factors that went Juul's way, Denmark does not seem to have built much on its early success. It's hard to tell because of a lack of proper measurements. The original 25 per cent cut figure was an estimate made by the Danish Agriculture and Food Council, which did not collect its own statistics. Since then, there have been no consistent data. 'Food waste is not an exact science,' says Juul. 'Today we have the Danish Environmental Protection Agency and also the Danish Veterinary and Food Administration doing the food waste numbers. Unfortunately – and this is quite sad – their latest measurements and their previous measurements cannot be compared. We need to be able to compare, otherwise you cannot see if it's going backwards or whether it's going forwards. Right now, we simply do not know.'

The old maxim 'What gets measured gets managed' is crucial for food wastage. Around the world, advocates of food waste reduction advocate a 'Target-Measure-Act' approach. This isn't a three-step sequence but a trio of necessities. In order to act on waste and loss you need to have a clear target for the reductions you want to achieve and tools to measure their progress, so that actions are appropriate and effective.[15] Yet in most countries this basic requirement isn't being met. In the UK, for example, the government abandoned planned legislation to make food-waste reporting mandatory for large and medium-sized businesses in England.[16]

Reversals like this make Juul worried that a lot of countries are actually going backwards, as their priorities shift to the cost-of-living crisis and the effects of the war in Ukraine and other geopolitical upheavals. 'In Denmark at the moment there is less and less media exposure about food waste,' she says. 'Politicians are not as involved in the food waste agenda as they were. Sometimes I feel that everybody's waiting for everybody else to take action.'

Juul also warns that 'the fight against the food-waste agenda is on the verge of greenwashing'. Well-intentioned efforts risk getting caught up in this. She points to the food-waste app Too Good To Go, which she advised when it was set up. The idea is simple: shops, restaurants and cafés make any excess food left at the end of the day available for people to buy at a knock-down rate. The most common way to do this is to offer a 'magic bag' containing food worth much more than the total purchase price of its contents. It sounds great, and it has almost certainly reduced waste. But Juul claims that the app is 'no longer about saving food. In Denmark you can reserve the food two or three or four days in advance. How on earth do shops know that they will have five surplus breads three days in advance? That's crazy. I've spoken to a lot of supermarkets and bakeries and they said "We are using it as a sales channel." They also have quotas of how many magic bags they have to sell per day.'

There is also a big question mark over how much of that food waste is not avoided but, rather, passed on to the consumer. Magic bags will contain a mixture of items people want and those they don't; those they can't eat right now but can freeze and those they can't. 'The food waste just moves from the supermarket bin to your bin – and you have paid for it,' says Juul.

Juul argues that no scheme to distribute surplus food can be a solution because 'we need to talk about the *prevention* of overproduction of food. If you go to a store even five minutes before closing time, it has every product on the shelf. If you go to a restaurant, especially canteens, they continually overproduce 30 per cent more food. The biggest nightmare for a chef is that there's not enough food for the guests. This is overproduction and that is where it hurts. There are a lot of interests, economic interests, political interests, and it's not that easy.'

As we have seen, when the food system contains flaws, a common response is to demand more regulation. A few countries have started down that road with food waste and loss. Between 2016 and 2020 France passed a series of three laws making it illegal for supermarkets and other large food businesses to destroy edible leftover food. They are now obliged to donate it to charities, and actually receive tax breaks for all the food given away.

This is the kind of interventionist approach that many campaigners want to see more of. It always gets pushback from some advocates of free-market economics who see it as excessive government interference in the food economy. However, it is not a simple story of quasi-socialist state meddling versus capitalist free markets. Mainstream, market economics has in its toolkit a concept that can be used to make a strong economic case against any practice that has a negative environmental impact: externalities.

An 'externality' is an effect of an economic activity, the costs or benefits of which do not come back to the agent of that activity. These can be positive or negative. For example, if a farm pollutes a river but the farmer does not have to pay to clean it up or to stop the pollution getting there in the first place, people living downriver suffer from the negative externality. If, on the other hand, the farmer renovates an eyesore, everyone benefits from the improved view without any cost to them or any income to the farmer. This is a positive externality.

Economists agree that you can't force beneficiaries to pay for positive externalities, but economic actors should be accountable for any negative externalities they create. This can be achieved by a variety of regulations to prevent serious negative externalities occurring in the first place, with fines or other punishments if they are breached, and taxes to cover the costs of mitigating the harms caused.

In reality, many externalities have been conveniently ignored. This convenience is all too understandable. Were we to take all the externalities of our economy seriously, we would swiftly realise that so much of what we are able to buy at affordable prices depends upon bad things happening elsewhere, unseen. Cheap electronics depend on people working in poorly paid, polluting, often dangerous mines extracting rare earth minerals. Covering the costs of getting these metals ethically and sustainably would increase the prices of our phones, fridges, cars – pretty much everything modern life depends on. We've already seen how much cheap food depends on exploitation of people, the planet and farm animals.

However, before we conclude that orthodox economics can be used to justify taxing or banning any activity we don't like, we have to remember that not all negative *effects* are negative *externalities*. An example given by agricultural economist Jayson Lusk is that work in a meatpacking factory is riskier than in other industries, and more workers get injured. Many assume this means that such injuries are externalities of the meat industry. But Lusk argues, 'If you actually look at wages in meatpacking, they are higher than in other industries that aren't as risky. So yeah, we don't like to buy things where workers get hurt, but those workers are being compensated for their risk. It's just not a nice way to make a living. But if the wages are higher than they are for comparably physically demanding jobs, as they usually are, the negative effect is already being compensated for.'[17] In other words, the employer has already paid the cost of the externality.

Lusk may have picked the wrong example. The meat industry is notorious for poor practice. For instance, an exposé in 2021 revealed the 'open secret' that staff in many German slaughterhouses were low-paid Eastern Europeans often working in unsafe conditions.[18] But even with the caveat that not all bad consequences are technically externalities, it is obvious that the industrialised food system creates numerous negative externalities. Some, like poor animal welfare, cannot be mitigated by taxes and should simply not be allowed. The same is arguably true of much environmental degradation and pollution. No level of taxes could restore the habitats destroyed by the clearance of the Cerrado and the Amazon. In theory the climate-warming carbon released into the atmosphere could be offset, but in practice no tree-planting scheme could ever be as effective as not cutting down the established habitats already in place. And all this destruction is going to create huge costs in the near future. Rising sea levels and desertification are already starting to drive millions from their homes, while changing weather patterns are ruining harvests.

The food system is littered with externalities, from pollution, environmental degradation, greenhouse gas emissions and animal suffering, to virtual or actual slave labour. The FAO reported in 2023 that, globally, agrifood systems impose costs of at least $10 trillion every year.[19] Not only are these costs not paid for, some government policies actually help to create them, by subsidising synthetic inputs that pollute or contribute to global warming; by imposing import tariffs that prevent farmers in poorer countries from being able to profit from their produce; by incentivising farmers to plough up biodiverse habitats to grow feed for livestock. The illusion of cheap food – especially meat – is created by disguising its hidden costs.

Food waste arguably also creates negative externalities, so making its creators pay for these costs would not be authoritarian socialism, but good free-market economics. One report concluded that 'each year, food loss and waste leads to an estimated eight per cent of greenhouse gas emissions, consumes one-quarter of all water used by agriculture, and uses an area of land the size of China'. While not all of these are technically externalities, almost all the greenhouse gas emissions are costs not borne by the producers, the full value of water used is often not paid for, and the waste of land creates other economic penalties for society, such as raising land prices. The report also noted that 'the direct economic penalties of food loss and waste equate to around $1.25 trillion a year before these external factors are taken into account'.[20]

Juul, however, is cautious about legislation. 'I just delivered my input to the Minister for Food, Agriculture and Fisheries' Danish national food waste strategy, and what I suggest is not making a law. In France, they do have a food waste law, and I hear from my French colleagues that it's not working.' Many have praised the law, but Juul says 'charities then drown in food because many of them don't have the infrastructure, money or resources to get that food out to needy people. That's not a solution, it's just pushing the problem down the chain.' Indeed, when a team from the Pulitzer Center reported on the law, they also found that some of the supposedly 'edible' food donated did not pass muster, like yellowed broccoli. On the day of their visit, they saw three bins of food being thrown away.[21]

What Juul wants is 'a food waste prevention and reduction foundation funded by the government, for the fight against food waste. There are hundreds of organisations fighting against food waste and most of them are volunteer organisations. They have no money, they have no resources. They're paying expenses out of their own pockets, and this is not sustainable. In fifteen years, there will be only Selina because everybody else will be bankrupt. And maybe me too.'

One simple way to reduce food waste is to improve packaging. For example, as part of its waste-reduction push, REMA 1000 started to use two layers of packaging to extend the shelf life of its cold-cut meats like *rullepølse* (a kind of rolled pork) and *kyllingebrystfilet* (chicken breast), resulting in less being thrown away. The only downside, of course, is that this means more packaging, with all the waste and greenhouse gas emissions that come with it. And the modern food system produces a lot of packaging. In the UK, the packaging industry is worth more in financial terms than all the food that comes off farms.[22]

REMA 1000's cold cuts encapsulate the dilemmas and trade-offs involved with food packaging and waste. Loose fruit bruises more easily, leading to more being uneaten; leaves stay fresh and crisp for longer when packed in airtight, nitrogen-filled plastic bags; vacuum-packed sliced hams can be kept for months when they would otherwise dry up in days. Ideally, we want less waste and less packaging, but in practice, less of one often means more of the other. As a Swedish study put it, 'packaging is often considered an environmental villain, which can lead to missed opportunities for reducing food waste'.[23]

The right thing to do will vary from product to product, and there is some packaging that is purely cosmetic and egregious. Juul points to boxes of crackers that contain a plastic pack, and within that, several little plastic packs containing three or four crackers. But generally speaking, there is little doubt that food waste is a bigger problem than packaging. As another, earlier Swedish study concluded, 'Packaging that is altered in order to reduce food losses can lessen the total environmental impact and lead to large environmental gains, even if it is necessary to increase the environmental impact from the packaging itself.'

Much depends on the specifics of the food and the packaging. In that earlier Swedish study, they found that cheese had fifty-eight times more environmental impact than its packaging, whereas ketchup had less than twice. Still, these and the other three foods studied – bread, milk and beef – all had a bigger environmental footprint than their wrapping.[24] So while all packaging places a burden on planetary resources, when it is used well it helps to conserve them.

One obvious way to reduce the impact of packaging is through recycling. But once again, this isn't easy, as Louise Nicholls discovered when she was Corporate Head of Human Rights, Food Sustainability and Food Packaging at the British retailer M&S. The company tried to minimise the packaging it felt necessary to use, and made as much as possible 100 per cent recyclable. But 'recyclable' doesn't always mean 'recycled'. Too much of what could be recycled isn't, and recycling is an energy-intensive process with environmental impacts of its own. Another problem is the sheer variety of types of wrapping used in the food industry. M&S decided to reduce the eleven or so materials that it used for packaging to three in order to make it easier to be able to recycle them. But even then, problems remained. 'If we're talking about packaging, you have to talk about the fact that we have a failing infrastructure in the UK,' says Nicholls. Recycling should not be seen as a solution, but as damage limitation.

Legislation could, in theory, help to improve recycling and reduce the use of plastic, but so far it has been very limited. The UK government brought in a plastics packaging tax in 2022, the proceeds of which were meant to be invested in the infrastructure for recycling. But, as Nicholls reports, 'at the last moment the government decided that they wouldn't ring fence it for recycling and instead it's gone straight back into the Treasury. There's just so much stuff that could be done but it requires joined-up longer term thinking and it feels like lots of things are just tactical and short term.'

What can change this? Juul believes that for the fight against food waste to be won, pressure has to keep coming from the bottom up. 'The biggest impact is keeping people aware of food loss and food waste. When people act, other people act, the governments acts, the companies act.' However, well-intentioned activists, diligent shoppers and careful cookers cannot solve the waste and loss problem alone. The complexity of the issue requires action on many fronts, as illustrated by the WRI's detailed ten-point plan. Among its required actions, two of the most significant are the development of national strategies and the creation of national public–private partnerships. The former has become a familiar demand in many areas of food policy. Food is simply too big to be left to ad hoc, piecemeal initiatives and legislation. Similarly, solutions cannot be left to business, but nor can business be left out of them.

The Maasai and the Yali have a lot to teach us about the immorality of food waste. So do the Chinese, Japanese and Koreans encountered by the American agricultural scientist Franklin Hiram King in the first decade of the twentieth century:

Everything which can be made edible serves as food for man or domestic animals. Whatever cannot be eaten or worn is used for fuel. The wastes of the body, of fuel and of fabric worn beyond other use are taken back to the field; before doing so they are housed against waste from weather, compounded with intelligence and forethought and patiently laboured with through one, three or even six months, to bring them into the most efficient form to serve as manure for the soil or as feed for the crop.[25]

There is, however, one important difference between modern industrialised societies and traditional ones which could be an obstacle to adopting something closer to the moral norms of the latter around thrift. In small-scale societies, the consequences of waste are more evident, as are the identities of the wasters. In a modern city, all this is invisible. It is not public knowledge who throws everything into the garbage and who dutifully puts their food in waste containers for collection or on compost heaps. Nor is the amount of food wasted by different households evident. As for the consequences, there is no direct link between waste in Walthamstow and hunger in Harare. Furthermore, the contribution of any discarded part of a meal to increases in greenhouse gases is tiny, which makes it hard for many to care.

What traditional societies show us is that for moral norms to have social traction, they have to be rooted in values everyone shares and their breach has to be evident to all. These conditions are not met for food waste in most parts of the world. Fortunately, as the growing awareness and activism over waste shows, social values can change, sometimes quite quickly. Drink-driving went from being a bit of a laugh to *verboten* in a few decades; racism from a casual fact of life to a prosecutable offence. As people become more aware of the problems of food waste, we can expect social attitudes to change quickly. Juul points me to a survey that suggests that 94 per cent of the Danish population think there's much more focus on food waste today than fifteen years ago.[26]

And there are things authorities and civil society can do to make waste more visible. Regulation needs to be designed with care, or else it can be ineffectual at best or have unintended consequences at worst. We should rightly fear unwarranted state intrusion into our private lives, but no one should ever object to the state regulating behaviours that result in serious harms. Like drink-driving, littering and causing nuisance noise, excessive waste production carries a social cost that we should be obliged to pay. If we value our freedom to create waste more than we do the good of society and the planet, then something has gone very wrong indeed.

16

DIETARY ENGINEERING

Cans and candy on the International Space Station

In the popular imagination, space has represented the future, and by extension space food has been synonymous with the future of all food. Whatever people will eat in space will be eaten on the future Earth. The manufacturers of a British instant mashed potato played on these assumptions in a series of iconic 1970s television commercials. Aliens in their spaceship were shown laughing hysterically at how primitive humans still washed, peeled, boiled and mashed potatoes to eat them, instead of just opening a packet and adding hot water.

Space agencies such as NASA would like us to think that where they lead, Earth follows. In part to justify its huge funding, supporters of the space programme have often suggested that research for space travel results in major advances for terrestrial technology. For example, it is widely believed that NASA developed Teflon, the non-stick coating used on millions of frying pans around the world. In reality, NASA simply applied the technology and so helped raise its profile. The same is true of Velcro.[1]

When it comes to food, space exploration has contributed very little to eating on Earth. Vickie Kloeris, who worked at NASA in space food systems for thirty-four years, managing the food systems of the Shuttle and then of the International Space Station, tells me, 'When you look at the technology that NASA's been using since pretty much the beginning of the space programme, it's all old. Freeze drying has been around forever. Thermostabilisation of food, canning of food has been around forever. The most progressive thing that NASA has used in their food system is irradiated meat.'

One of the few genuine contributions to nutrition to have come out of the space programme is the use of algae (*Crypthecodinium cohnii*) that produces high levels of two essential fatty acids found in human breast milk that were absent from formula milks. This research allowed that nutritional deficiency to be corrected. But even this was not strictly a NASA innovation. Its scientists were looking at the uses of microalgae for food on long-duration interplanetary missions in the 1980s but never used any. When that programme finished, a number of them continued to work independently, going on to found Martek Biosciences. It was Martek, not NASA, that created the algae-based supplement Formulaid that is now added to most baby formula milks and given to some pregnant mothers.[2]

The reason space food is not a pioneer of Earth food is simple. On Earth, healthy, fresh, nutritious and tasty food is plentiful. In space, storage is limited, fresh deliveries impossible and cooking facilities minimal. So in space, you cannot have an optimal diet. The job of space nutritionists is to close the gap between what can be eaten on Earth and what can be eaten in space, not to open one up between special space food and ordinary Earth food.

Even a simple matter like storage creates problems. When the International Space Station was being planned, the idea was to have fridges and freezers for food but, says Kloeris, 'when the engineers started looking at the amount of power they were going to get from the solar arrays, they basically told the space station programme "You can either have freezers and refrigerators for food or you can have them for science. Your choice."' Chilled food was out, shelf-stable – food that stays fresh at room temperature – was in.

What's more, low or zero gravity and the vital importance of keeping any pieces of food from finding their way into vital machinery mean that there are many kinds of crumbly or powdery foods you just can't have. Most space meals come in pouches that allow a direct transfer of the food from packaging to mouth, to avoid even micro-spillages. You eat space food only because you have to. If Earth food were available, you'd always choose that.

What the space programme has taught us is that food really matters, not just as fuel. In the early days of space exploration, food was treated as a simple nutrition issue, a matter of human body engineering. That suited the early astronauts on short missions, who, says Kloeris, treated it like a camping trip, happy to survive on whatever they were given.

However, once astronauts were staying up for longer on the International Space Station, what they ate became much more important. Realising this, planners initially tried to maximise choice. So on Shuttle flights, astronauts had a 100 per cent preference menu, meaning that they selected what they would take with them from the range of available foods. However, when they tried to do this on longer missions, where food was sent up in cargo vehicles, the logistical complexities meant that astronauts often didn't get exactly what they asked for. This might not sound like a big problem, but creating an expectation that was not fulfilled led to real dissatisfaction. It turns out that the emotional and hedonic dimensions of what you eat on long space missions matter a great deal. NASA discovered that they had to nourish the astronauts emotionally as well as biologically. From then on, the astronauts would all eat a standard menu with a small proportion of preference items, striking a balance between operational efficiency and culinary satisfaction.

Many astronauts were surprised to find that food mattered so much to them. Kloeris remembers asking one who was due to go up to the Mir space station, where they would mainly be eating the Russian food, what NASA menu items he wanted sent up. 'He was like, "I don't have time for this. I'm too busy learning Russian and learning about Mir. Go back and look at my Shuttle menu and just pick something off there." When some of those crew members came back, they said "I should have put more thought into it." When you're there for four and a half months or something like that, the psychological importance of the food went way up.'

So what does satisfy the psychological needs of astronauts? 'I would say a lot of what goes in the preference containers is comfort food of some kind,' says Kloeris. 'It could be a commercial cookie that's not part of the NASA regular menu.'

It's not just *what* they eat that matters, it's also *how* they eat. Mealtimes together are highlights of the day. 'Joint meals were important during the Shuttle program and have continued to be important during the International Space Station program. This is especially true at holiday times or other special events like birthdays. There was always a lot of preparation and thought on the part of the crew regarding holiday meals such as Thanksgiving. They would decide as a crew what they wanted for the meal and then include that as part of their preference food.'

It has become evident that you can't separate the psychological and nutritional aspects of food. In the history of the US space programme, Skylab was the only mission where no crew members lost weight. The reason weight loss is so common on space missions is 'menu fatigue': when food becomes boring, the astronauts just don't eat enough of it. Kloeris explains that Skylab was different because 'they had had nutritional experiments on board and so they reported what they ate every day. That was analysed, and if they found that they weren't eating enough calories or enough of certain nutrients they were told what additional stuff they had to eat and so they made up for it. That's why they didn't lose weight.'

Menu fatigue has also been observed in army units subsisting on a limited range of MREs (meals ready to eat). Nor are humans the only animals to find variety in food pleasing: even creatures that are not culinarily discerning like it. Lab rats fed the same pellets day in, day out maintain weight, but when given variety they fatten up.[3] The desire for diversity is a useful evolutionary adaptation as it encourages us to get a wider variety of nutrients. What makes humans unique is that we will actually undereat if we don't get enough gastronomic stimulation.

The need to make space food as appealing as possible has become more urgent in the light of plans to send human beings to Mars. In the bipartisan NASA Authorization Act of 2010, the Americans set the goal of a crewed mission to Mars in the 2030s, while Elon Musk said in 2017 that his private company, SpaceX, would launch such a voyage in 2024.[4] Musk backtracked in 2023, tweeting, 'I must admit to being congenitally optimistic (SpaceX & Tesla wouldn't exist otherwise), but I think 5 years is possible and 10 years is highly likely.'[5]

This would be an extraordinary undertaking. There is only a small window every twenty-six months to launch such a mission because of the trajectories of the planets' orbits. In order to make the huge journey manageable you have to go when the distance between Earth at the time of launch and Mars at the time of arrival is shortest. Even then, it would take six to seven months to get there and the same to get back. Add time spent on the planet and you're looking at a two-year mission at minimum. This is a much longer trip than any have attempted before. The longest time to date anyone has been in space is 437 days (more than fourteen months), which Valeri Polyakov spent on the Russian Mir space station in 1994–95. Astronauts typically spend only six months on the International Space Station.

The major logistical problem is that whereas space stations in orbit around the world can be regularly restocked with supplies, no such delivery service is available in deep space. The mission would have to take all its supplies with it, which would require massive storage, or supplies would have to be sent ahead.

Either way, the food would have to last up to three years and still be palatable and nutritious. This might not seem too challenging because we have very long-life canned and dried products already. But although these products stay safe, they degrade nutritionally, presenting a problem if your entire diet depends on them.

There have been experiments in growing food in space, but this could never become a viable food source unless and until local supplies of water and nutrients were found. It's simple physics: it will always take more energy to take what is required to produce food than there is energy in the food produced. So although seed + water + growth medium = food, the left-hand side of the equation always adds up to more than the resulting right-hand side. The only way to balance the books would be to find a way of recycling human excrement and urine as growth media. Kloeris believes that 'in transit to Mars they will probably grow items but it's going to be more of a psychological benefit than anything else'. For now, a few salad leaves could enliven the travellers' diet and be part of a useful experiment, but they cannot feed a crew.

For all the ingenuity of NASA's scientists, creating space food that is truly delicious remains a challenge too far. In 2015, the European Space Agency tried to beat them to it by employing the services of the Michelin-starred chef Heston Blumenthal, whose famous 'molecular gastronomy' draws on the science of culinary experience. He created a number of dishes that the British astronaut Tim Peake took up to the International Space Station. Blumenthal's creations included beef and black truffle stew, Alaskan salmon, and bacon sandwiches. In the documentary about the project, Peake is shown appreciatively eating one of the meals in space, judging it to be a marked improvement. But that is quite a low bar. A taster on Earth reporting for *WIRED* confirmed that this was still a long way off gourmet cuisine. The bacon sandwich was 'peculiarly damp', a necessary consequence of the need to ensure no crumbs. Similarly, the apple crumble 'hit the spot with its sweet and tangy flavour, but did ooze out of the can rather than crumble'.[6] In space, where the senses of smell and taste work less well, the reviews would have been even worse. Crucially, these foods couldn't go to Mars anyway: they were canned, and for long missions the food has to go in lighter, more easily disposable pouches. No matter how good space food gets, it will never match even the simplest Earth food made from fresh ingredients at 9.8 m/s^2 gravity.

There is, however, one way in which space food has become a model for Earth food. In designing meals for astronauts, one of NASA's priorities is to produce meals which contain all the nutrients a human body needs, in the right proportions. In doing this, it thinks of the meals as nutritional aggregates: collections of macro- and micronutrients. Much of what we eat today is produced according to the same basic principle that the healthiness of food is determined by its itemised nutritional content. Processed foods have nutritional information labels that quantify certain key nutrients they contain, and many also list their vitamins and minerals, often added by fortification. Consumers are led to believe that this information allows them to compare the healthiness of different products. If one frozen pizza has less saturated fat than another, then, all other things being equal, it's healthier. If one cereal has added vitamins and iron and another doesn't, again, the former is healthier.

The idea that we can know how healthy a food is by analysing its nutritional content has become so widespread it might seem to be self-evidently true. However, Gyorgy Scrinis, an associate professor of food politics and policy, has pejoratively christened this 'nutritionism'. Nutritionism is the belief that the optimal diet can be defined purely in terms of its macro- and micronutrient composition: the different fats, proteins and carbohydrates as well as vitamins and minerals it contains. Scrinis tells me that 'nutritionism in its simplest definition is just the reductive understanding of food in terms of nutrients, particularly in terms of their health impacts. Nutritionism involves both a reductive focus on nutrients, rather than on foods and dietary patterns, and a reductive interpretation of the role of nutrients, which are taken out of any kind of context.'

Scrinis writes that 'single-nutrient reductionism often ignores or simplifies the interactions among nutrients within foods and within the body. It has also involved the premature translation of an observed statistical association between single nutrients and diseases into a deterministic or causal relationship, according to which single nutrients are claimed to directly cause, or at least increase the risk of, particular diseases. Nutrition scientists have also tended to exaggerate any beneficial or detrimental health effects of single nutrients.'[7]

Nutritionism leads on the one hand to the vilification of bogey foods. For example, saturated fats have long been demonised. But Scrinis argues that 'scientists now recognise that there are different types of saturated fats and they seem to behave differently depending on which type of food they're consumed in'. On the other hand, simplistic nutritionist thinking lies behind claims about miracle nutrients, celebrated for their quasi-magical properties, such as omega-3 fatty acids (accompanied by a damnation of omega-6s). Scrinis argues that even though there may be associations between some nutrients and health outcomes, suggesting a simple one-to-one causal relationship is too neat and reductive. The reality is much more complicated.

For example, Scrinis says that early, enthusiastic claims made for omega-3s haven't stood up to further study. Furthermore, there is evidence that the oils are prone to oxidisation, and, as one study put it, 'oxidised oils may have altered biological activity making them ineffective or harmful'. Many uncertainties remain, but it is clear that omega-3 oils found in, say, fresh fish are not identical to those found in processed supplements and so it cannot be assumed that any benefits of the former are also found in the latter.[8] This might explain why claims made in the 2000s that omega-3 supplements boosted schoolchildren's performance and helped with behavioural problems turned out to be unfounded.[9]

Scrinis traces some of the origins of the nutritionism paradigm to the discovery of the link between vitamin deficiencies and certain diseases and conditions, such as rickets and vitamin D and calcium; goitre and iodine; anaemia and iron; pellagra and niacin (vitamin B3); and scurvy and vitamin C. In all these cases, it was found that correcting the deficiency cured the disease. So a very tight and deterministic link was made between micronutrient intake and illness. However, these illnesses are the exceptions rather than the rule. Some health conditions may be a consequence of a specific nutritional deficiency, but if most illnesses could be fixed by tweaking nutrient contents, sickness would have been all but abolished by now. You can eat your way out of scurvy, but you can't eat your way out of cancer, or make yourself immune to it by following the right diet. Yet claims that you can have become widespread, fuelled by deep-rooted nutritionist assumptions.

Over time, researchers also started to link specific nutrient excesses or deficiencies with chronic illnesses, such as saturated fat and cardiovascular disease. But as Scrinis says, this is no small jump. 'Chronic diseases develop over many years, with people eating all sorts of foods and nutrients. So the idea that we can talk very definitively about the role of one nutrient in a chronic disease is quite problematic.' The idea that each and every chronic illness can be linked to over- or under-consumption of specific nutrients is a strong assumption not warranted by the evidence.

The anti-nutritionist case has recently been strengthened by the network scientist Albert-László Barabási. Trained as a physicist, Barabási went on to work on complex systems in nature, technology and society, including medicine and nutrition. Barabási makes two key related claims. The first is that for every nutrient that has been studied and well understood, there are countless others that we know little or nothing about. 'Our current understanding of the way food affects health is anchored in the 150 nutritional components that the United States Department of Agriculture (USDA) and other national databases track,' he writes. 'These nutritional components represent only a small fraction of the more than 26,000 distinct, definable biochemicals present in our food – many of which have documented effects on health but remain unquantified in any systematic fashion across different individual foods.'[10]

This seems incredible, but it is true. One of Barabási's favourite examples is garlic. We know that it is rich in manganese, vitamin B6 and selenium, just three of its sixty-seven nutritional components that are identified in the USDA's database. However, there are more than 2,306 distinct chemical components of a clove of garlic. Among those not listed by the USDA are allicin, which gives garlic its distinctive aroma, and luteolin, a type of flavonoid which some studies have suggested helps protect against cardiovascular disease. We know very little about the health effects of most of the other 2,237. Eighty-five per cent of the chemicals in plants remain unquantified, meaning that 'while their presence has been detected or inferred, their concentration in specific food ingredients remains unknown'. Many could have an important role in health.

Barabási's second point is that it is not simply that we know next to nothing about lots of chemical components in food. It's that the effects they have on our health depend on the extremely complicated ways in which they interact. Garlic, for example, is a major ingredient in the Mediterranean diet, so any red meat in it is usually accompanied by garlic. It turns out that the allicin blocks the production of trimethylamine N-oxide (TMAO) in the gut. Recent studies showed that 'patients with stable coronary heart disease had a fourfold greater risk of dying from any cause over the subsequent five years if they had high blood levels of TMAO'. This suggests that red meat is not good or bad for your health in and of itself. It depends on what is eaten with it. Barabási's complex systems approach can deal with this, whereas nutritionism's reductionism can't.

There are also good philosophical grounds for believing nutritionism is a mistake. The comparative philosopher Thomas Kasulis argues that there are two different, complementary ways of looking at the world. One is to see it as a mere collection of parts. Organisms are made of cells, cells are made of atoms, atoms of subatomic particles and so on. This is the reductive mode, which has been popular and successful in natural science. The other way is to understand what everything is in terms of its place in webs of interconnections. For example, from a reductive point of view, each individual human being can be described entirely without reference to anything else. But from a relational point of view, if we do that, we cannot see that a person is a parent, a child, a sibling, a member of a community, an employee, and so on. To fully understand what a person is, you have to understand their relation to other things.

Kasulis's point is not that one of the reductive or relational ways of seeing is right and one wrong. Both have their place. But we have to be aware of what we miss when we use one rather than the other, and of what each foregrounds. In nutrition, we have been led almost entirely by the reductive paradigm. But increasingly we have good reason to think that, from a nutritional point of view, the effects fats, proteins, carbohydrates, vitamins and minerals have on our bodies depend on their relation to the other elements in the foods in which they are consumed, and to the bodies that consume them. Iron is absorbed differently depending on whether it comes in liver, spinach or a pill. If you drink coffee, its absorption is also inhibited. There are endless such interactions, which means that it is never possible to say that two foods are nutritionally equivalent just because they contain identical amounts of a certain nutrient.

With nutrients, it is not just the *what*, it is also the *how*. Calcium in a tablet is absorbed by the body differently to the calcium in whole milk, which is in turn absorbed more efficiently than calcium in skimmed milk. Dietary fibre is not digested, but whether a food is high or low in it affects how that food is digested, and so how satiated a person feels, what their blood sugar response is, and so on. Like many bona fide mainstream nutrition experts, Vickie Kloeris agrees with all of this. 'Studies have shown that obtaining your nutrients in a food versus a supplement is superior,' she says. 'The problem is that there are so many interactions in a food that we don't know about. Those potentially beneficial interactions are lost with a pill. Plus your system actually works better when you have bulk food flowing through your system versus just drinking a drink or taking a pill.'

The apogee, or perhaps the nadir, of nutritionism is a product beloved of many Silicon Valley health hackers: Soylent. This brand has a mission: 'to make complete, sustainable nutrition accessible, appealing and affordable to all', which it aims to deliver through its range of bars, drinks and powders. It was developed by software engineers who thought that food too could be precision engineered. Its powders are sold as complete meals: you are supposed to be able to subsist entirely on them and get optimal nutrition.[11] It's as close as we get to space food for the mainstream market, and its appeal depends on customers buying into the nutritionist premise.

The fact that most people find products like Soylent repugnant suggests that nutritionism isn't accepted lock, stock and barrel. Nutritionist beliefs inform our thinking about food, but few consciously and completely sign up to it, at least not for human food. In the animal feed market, however, nutritionism has been out and proud for decades. Most pet foods and industrial animal feeds are sold as 'complete', meaning that there is nothing else the animal has to eat to be healthy. People seem to accept this message for their animals and think that pet food is a better option than whole food, but they are not so keen to feed themselves on the same principles.

Yet precisely these principles lie behind the idea that we can create highly processed foods that are engineered to contain the right amounts of everything we need and that this kind of food would actually be better than ordinary food, which we have to skilfully combine to get the same 'perfect' nutritional mix. Hence many processed foods, from breakfast cereals to energy bars, are fortified with vitamins and minerals so that they can be sold as healthier than unprocessed alternatives. Many also display their salt, sugar and fat contents, proudly showing that they fall within officially sanctioned levels.

The hijacking of nutritional claims for nefarious purposes has a very long history. In the 1950s, advertisements regularly made the claim that sugar could help you to lose weight. A 1953 advert asked, 'Which is less fattening?' with a picture of an apple and three teaspoons of 'pure' Domino Sugar. The answer was given in the fact that the sugar contained fewer calories. A 1959 advert by Sugar Information, Inc., an industry-funded body, claimed that sugar could help with weight loss because 'No other food satisfies your appetite so fast with so few calories.' As late as 1971 the same organisation was still promoting sugar as a 'diet dodge', again on the basis that because it is pure energy, it satisfies hunger quickly, giving you the willpower to resist eating more.[12]

The Quaker Oats company also provides a striking example of a food company taking full advantage of the nutritionist paradigm. It funded research into whether eating oats reduced cholesterol, which identified the soluble fibre beta glucan in oats as a key active component. Armed with the research, in 1997 the company managed to get the FDA to grant the first food-specific health claim – namely, that consumption of soluble fibre from oats lowered the risk of heart disease.[13]

It's not that such claims are entirely without substance. 'I'll take it for granted that if you eat enough oats they may help reduce your cholesterol, and maybe the beta glucan is one of the key components which facilitates that,' says Scrinis. 'What that proves, I think, is that if you have enough research money to throw at a particular food or a nutrient and look for some benefits, you'll find them. Why is that? Because all minimally processed foods are nutritious in one way or another. All foods – at least those that aren't ultra-processed – will have some healthful components. If you studied an apple, of course you're going to eventually find some potential health benefit. It's not that such claims are false. The problem is funding the studies and allowing companies to exaggerate the role of oats and beta glucan over everything else you might be eating in your diet.' This echoes a remark Marion Nestle makes in *Food Politics*: 'Because all foods and drinks include ingredients that are essential for life (calories, nutrients, or water), any one of them has the potential to be marketed for its health benefits.'[14] 'The nutritionism paradigm plays into the hands of big food companies,' says Scrinis. 'They love it because they can sell you a product by focusing on a particular nutrient, even if it's in an ultra-processed food.' What's more, 'nutritionism encourages the consumption of nutritionally engineered or nutritionally "improved" products – such as low-fat, low-calorie, or trans-fat-free varieties – rather than simply eating less of these foods.'[15]

Nutritionism helps industrial food manufacturers in other ways too. 'Nutrition scientists break down foods into their nutrient parts and then talk about those nutrients. Ultra-processed food companies break foods down into their component parts and then build them back up again, because it's very cheap to do that. And when they do that, they can also manipulate the nutrient profile to match what the current dietary advice is and find a way of marketing their products.'

Scrinis argues that the food industry not only used nutritionism to its own advantage, it played an important role in cultivating it. 'If we think back to the 70s and 80s, all these ultra-processed foods were emerging, but nutrition scientists were being very critical of them because they were high in sugar and salt and so on. They were also being critical of meat and dairy products because of their high saturated fat content. So they were using this reductive nutrient focus to criticise a whole lot of foods. But at that point the industry worked out how they could work with this, by focusing on particular nutrients in their products or manipulating their nutrient profile and then running with it to market them. So the meat industry focused on lean meat. The dairy industry focused on reduced fat, high protein or calcium content. With the rest of the processed foods, they took some of the fat out and they put sugar and a few vitamins in. They were also funding studies into these nutrients which they could use to market their products, and of course when they plaster nutrient claims all over their products, that sensitises everyone to the idea that nutrients are important.'

Nutritionist thinking by big business continues apace. The multinational company Unilever is making nutritional enhancement a key part of its drive to be a producer of healthier food, proudly saying 'We are fortifying our foods with vitamins and minerals to increase positive nutrition.' It has a target to 'double the number of products sold that deliver positive nutrition by 2025'.[16]

Nutritionist thinking leads to the labelling of foods according to their nutrient contents in the name of public health information. But Scrinis argues that nutritional labelling schemes play into the hands of the ultra-processors. 'They are actually designed to reward ultra-processed food. They're not for scoring whole foods.' By tweaking formulations, manufacturers can get their products seals of approval because of the nutrients measured on the label, even if as a whole the food is of poor nutritional quality. The dominance of the nutrient-led strategy leads to absurdities such as highly refined breakfast cereals with a high sugar content advertised as a 'good source of vitamin D'.[17] This has directly led to more consumption of unhealthy foods. For example, SnackWell's was a popular line of fat-free, high-sugar cookies introduced in America in 1992. It gave its name to the 'SnackWell effect' which, as Scrinis explains, referred to 'people eating more low-fat foods because they considered them healthier than regular, full-fat foods. They might have been tempted to eat two low-fat chocolate cookies instead of eating just one regular chocolate cookie.'[18]

To get some idea of just how nutritionally poor such foods are, consider Entenmann's fat-free fudge brownies, which contained 40 per cent of the recommended daily intake of sugar in one serving, no fibre and virtually no protein, vitamins or minerals.[19] There should be a special prize for any reader who can bear to read through the entire list of their ingredients:

Sugar, Nonfat Milk, Enriched Bleached Wheat Flour [Flour, Malted Barley Flour, Reduced Iron, Niacin, Thiamin Mononitrate (B1), Riboflavin (B2), Folic Acid], Egg Whites, Water, Corn Syrup, Dextrose, Defatted Cocoa (processed with Alkali), Chocolate Powder (Sugar, chocolate Liquor, Dextrose), Invert Sugar, Modified Food Starch (Tapioca, Corn, Rice), Salt, Soy Lecithin, Mono- and Diglycerides, Natural & Artificial Flavors, Leavening (Sodium Acid Pyrophosphate, Baking Soda, Monocalcium Phosphate, Sodium Aluminum Phosphate), Wheat Fiber, Potassium Sorbate (preservative), Sorbitan Monostearate, Wheat Gluten, Xanthan Gum, Guar Gum, Polysorbate 60, Agar, Sodium Stearoyl Lactylate, Propylene Glycol Monoesters, Oat Fiber, Artificial Color.

One complicating factor in nutritional science that has been getting more attention recently is the uniqueness of each individual eater. Healthy eating advice is based on population studies and averages. But no individual is an average and although all humans have the same basic physiology, every body is different. So there are high hopes for 'personalised nutrition': dietary advice that is tailored to our personal needs. This opens up opportunities not just for health. The business of personalised nutrition is growing rapidly, with the global market size set to reach $37.3 billion by 2030, increasing by 11 per cent each year.[20]

If we truly had such a thing, personalised nutrition would be transformative. When it comes to diet, one prescription does not fit all. Almost everyone has their dietary quirks, foods that most people find innocuous but that badly affect them personally. We also know that people have different blood sugar and fat responses, and absorb certain micronutrients differently. It would be wonderful to take this to the next level and use science to identify exactly which foods work or don't work for each of us, and in which combinations.

However, at the moment such genuinely personalised nutrition remains far off. Personalisation today remains extremely limited and arguably is often not truly personalised at all. Consider ZOE, a hugely successful health science company that believes 'there is no one right way to eat – the key lies in understanding your own biology'. People who sign up to ZOE send off stool and blood samples to have their gut microbiome content and blood fat levels measured, and fill in demographic and food frequency questionnaires. They also wear a blood sugar monitor for two weeks to assess their glucose responses to different foods. On the basis of the information collected, individual foods are scored, distinguishing between those you can enjoy 'freely', 'regularly' and 'in moderation'. A fourth category, 'once in a while', is not prefixed by the verb 'enjoy', which is a shame, because those tend to be the most enjoyable foods.

Whatever the merits of the programme, its personalisation is very limited. Blood sugar responses are incredibly variable and can be affected by all sorts of things other than your underlying long-term biological condition. Dietary advice based on your responses over just two weeks cannot be fully accurate. What's more, key data are taken from the responses to two meals of specially formulated muffins. But if the same person were to repeat these experiments weeks later, their results would rarely be identical and could be significantly different. The monitor used is not directly measuring blood sugar levels but, rather, correlates, so is prone to error. Similarly, blood fat results come from just one test on one day. As Kloeris says of this kind of approach (not referring to ZOE specifically), 'What they're doing is basically taking a snapshot and saying this is where you are right now. I can see that there's some value in that. But at the same time, even as it varies from person to person, it also varies within a person over time. So what your particular status is today may not be your typical status.'

All this information is used to rate thousands of specific foods. The scores it gives are predictions, extrapolations from a limited set of personalised data, drawing mostly on how people with similar test results responded. Finally, although the programme draws on lots of population-level data, only three personal biomarkers are used: blood fat, blood sugar response and gut microbiome. These are clearly important, but they give us far from a holistic view of how our body processes food.

Given that fully personalised nutrition doesn't yet exist, we have many reasons to be sceptical of anything that passes as such. ZOE claims fantastic results, saying that 70 per cent of participants have more energy and 85 per cent improve their gut health, but these figures are based on a survey of 450 people who followed the programme closely.[21] This is not even close to being a proper randomised control trial. Respondents are to some extent self-selecting and motivated to be enthusiastic, given the hundreds of pounds they have invested in the programme in the hope of improved health. At the time of writing, ZOE was promising the publication of a randomised control trial, but had only released the abstract, not the full paper, which was still undergoing peer review. This abstract did not contain enough information for the efficacy of the programme to be assessed.[22]

More importantly, most people eat erratically and not always very well, but while on the programme participants are highly aware of what they are eating, having to log every meal in an app, and they are guided towards options that any dietician would recognise as healthy. Under these conditions, we should expect most people on the programme to be eating significantly better than usual and so feeling better than usual. This doesn't show that the limited personalisation of the advice is the decisive factor. As Kloeris says, 'Some people are paying so little attention to their diet that just the fact that you get them to focus on it is probably going to improve it.' A ZOE spokesperson as good as acknowledged that it didn't matter if the claimed benefits of the programme were not mostly due to the personalisation, telling me that 'the vast majority (more than 99%) of the population don't follow dietary guidelines and advice so if our approach helps in both ways (personalised and public health guidelines) we think it's a good thing.'

Kloeris also thinks that there aren't enough data yet to be confident that customising diets reliably delivers significant benefits. 'It seems to me as a scientist you would have to spend about two years figuring me out from a metabolic perspective before you could even have the data to propose a customised diet.' She acknowledges that the figure of two years was plucked out of the air to make her point, but says she is sure that whatever the correct length of observation is, two weeks is not enough.

We should be sceptical of personalised nutrition until it is fully proven, and not just because its advocates oversell what it can currently deliver. Emphasising personalised nutrition shifts responsibility for healthy eating squarely on to the individual, taking pressure off both governments and businesses to tackle the dominance of unhealthy foods in the marketplace. As Marion Nestle tells me, 'Personalised nutrition is nice for rich people. But it's not a public health solution to public health problems.' Tim Lang is also against all forms of advice that 'individualise our food problems' and 'see salvation in private choices'.[23] He tells me, 'Modern food dilemmas are at the population and mass planetary level, so unless the 'choice' has that mass scale, the food crises are likely to intensify rather than subside.'

Personalised nutrition also creates opportunities for food manufacturers to sell premium products that can be used to improve your scores. Take the gut microbiome. Most people are told that they need to increase the diversity of their gut biota. There is a simple way to do this: eat a wide variety of fibrous plants. But the gut microbiome fad has led to the launch of any number of processed products that promise to help your gut. Some, like kimchi and kefir, are minimally processed and healthy, albeit generally quite expensive and not necessary for good gut health. Others are highly processed products with ingredients like 'prebiotics', which can be less healthy than simpler whole foods that are at least as effective in helping nurture your gut microbiota.

Gyorgy Scrinis is a sceptic of personalised nutrition, for reasons rooted in two important concepts he uses as part of his critique of nutritionism. One is 'biomarker reductionism', defined as a 'reductive focus on, and interpretation of, bodily health in terms of particular biomarkers (biological markers).' For example, poor cholesterol test results or a high or low body mass index are widely taken to be indicative of a medical problem, irrespective of other facts about your general health. A worse than average blood sugar response could categorise you as 'pre-diabetic' even if it is stable over time and therefore not 'pre' any medical condition at all. Scrinis sums up the medical historian Robert Aronowitz's view as follows: 'there has been a continual slippage and blurring of risk factors and disease determinants, such that risk factors have been treated by medical experts as if they were causal factors. These risk factors have even been interpreted as diseases or health conditions in their own right and therefore in need of treatment. Risk factors for coronary heart disease, such as hypertension (high blood pressure) and hyperlipidemia (high blood cholesterol) are now directly treated with blood pressure drugs and cholesterol-lowering statins.'[24]

A second concept is the 'myth of nutritional precision'. Many scientists exaggerate the extent to which we know that particular nutrients have specific health effects, good or bad. This leads to advice like 'avoid saturated fat', irrespective of whether it comes in a processed pork sausage or cashew nuts.

Although it might look like personalised nutrition moves away from the reductionism of nutritionism, Scrinis says, 'I actually think quite the opposite. I think personalised nutrition is a manifestation of the idea of precision nutrition which is actually super reductive. It's not just reducing food to nutrients, but also reducing bodily health to a few biomarkers. When you reduce your body to a few biomarkers and then make definitive claims that these markers indicate that you need to eat this or that food, that's more reductionism than personalisation. It's actually de-personalising nutrition in many ways.'

Human beings are in a real sense biological machines and we have learned a great deal about how we work. However, the paradox of learning is that the more you understand, the more you find out how much you don't understand. Nutrition is so complicated that we ought to have more humility about our capacity to finetune it. Ironically, the more we find out about the details, the more we realise that our best bet is to focus instead on the bigger picture. Rather than hubristically trying to micro-manage our diets to optimise health and longevity, based on a few biomarkers, we should simply focus on eating a diet based on real, whole foods. Of course, you can't sell that advice, and nor can you sell anything off the back of it. A problem for the health and wellness industry, however, can be a solution for the rest of us.

Nutritionism remains a powerful paradigm. Some, like the late Mike Gibney, a professor emeritus of food and health at University College Dublin, sign up to its central tenets explicitly, even if they do not use the term. I asked him if there was any nutritional reason to prefer a butcher-made free-range pork sausage over a meat substitute made with all sorts of highly processed vegetable proteins and thickeners, if they had the same salt, sugar, fat and micronutrient content, and so were identical in terms of nutritional composition. He replied, 'There's no nutritional reason. No food enters my body as anything other than nutrients or phytochemicals and that's what does the damage to my body. If I have too much salt, it may raise my blood pressure. If I have too much sugar, it may destroy my teeth. If I eat too much saturated fat, it would raise my blood cholesterol.'

However, most mainstream nutritionists are beginning to accept at least parts of the critique against the nutritionist paradigm. In particular, a consensus is emerging that the form in which we ingest food makes an important difference to how we digest and process it. For example, if you eat a whole fruit the sugars will be released into your bloodstream more slowly than if you were to blitz it into a smoothie, even though atom for atom it would add up to the same thing. The nutritional profile of both the whole fruit and the smoothie would be identical, but the former is better for us than the latter. This is a clear and uncontroversial demonstration that you can have identical nutritional composition without nutritional equivalence.

Scrinis is clear that 'the critique of nutritionism is not that we shouldn't be studying nutrients, or that studying individual nutrients isn't useful. It is how we study them and how we interpret them. In particular, we need to put that nutrient knowledge in the context of foods and dietary patterns.' It is entirely sensible that the nutrient profile of foods is a major factor in planning the meals of astronauts and that we think about the balance of nutrients in our diets. We only go wrong when we try to meet our nutritional needs by running through a checklist of its components, rather than thinking about the habits and patterns that shape our eating.

17

THE GOOD, THE BAD
AND THE PROCESSED

Milk and margarine in France

What do you get if you mix one egg, 150ml of milk, 60g of plain flour and a pinch of salt? Unless you are a total stranger to the kitchen, you'll probably easily identify this as a batter mix. Nor do you need to be Antonio Carluccio to know that a little oil, fairly small quantities of onion, celery and garlic, a few pounds of minced beef or pork, a pinch of mixed herbs, a squeeze of tomato purée and some canned chopped tomatoes are the ingredients for a pasta sauce. But what on earth is this?

Water, Plant Protein (13 per cent) (Soy), Sunflower Oil, Coconut Oil, Thickener (Methylcellulose), Spices, Yeast Extract, Cultured Dextrose, Salt, Modified Starch, Citric Acid, Flavours, Apple Extract, Cacao Extract, Antioxidant (Mixed Tocopherols), Zinc Gluconate, Niacin (Vitamin B3), Pyridoxine Hydrochloride (Vitamin B6), Riboflavin (Vitamin B2), Vitamin B12.

This is not a list of ingredients for any recipe that you would cook in your home. The inclusion of ingredients like methylcellulose, mixed tocopherols and zinc gluconate and the fortification with vitamins tell you straight away that this is an industrially produced food. The fact that a plant protein is the biggest ingredient after water is a clue that this is some kind of meat substitute. How you would know which one, however, is a mystery. It is in fact a faux pork sausage.[1]

Such concoctions are relative newcomers to our food world, but the processing of raw food to make it more palatable, safer, or easier to store or eat is almost as old as humanity itself. Ralph Early, who has spent his whole career working in industry and academe with or on processed food, suggests that the first food processing was cooking over fire. 'The heat treatment of the meat changed the texture and made it easier to chew. Although they didn't realise it at the time, it also enabled the release of nutrients more effectively in digestion.' He conjectures that serendipity was probably responsible for the discovery of this and many other early forms of processing. The first cooked meat was the result of raw meat being dropped into the flames; meat that was hung near the fire to keep flies away became smoked, which helped preserve it; bread dough was accidentally dropped in water and the resulting fermented brew had a strange but pleasant effect on those who drank it.

In modern usage, we reserve the term 'processing' for what we do to food between taking it in its raw state and cooking or eating it. It is only fairly recently that we began to systematically apply science and technology to this. One of the most significant innovations was spurred by Napoleon Bonaparte offering a prize of 12,000 francs in 1795 to whoever could come up with a better way of preserving food, in order to feed his conquering armies. It took fourteen years for the confectioner Nicolas Appert to win the prize for his method of heating and sealing food in airtight glass jars. In 1804, Appert opened the world's first food bottling factory, in Massy, near Paris. Six years later, a London broker called Peter Durand obtained a patent for a method of preservation based on Appert's principles but using metal tins. In 1813, the men he'd sold his patent to the year before, Bryan Donkin and John Hall, opened the first canning factory in the world, in Bermondsey, South London. Today, cans and jars are still widely used for both cheap staples and prized speciality products, such as Portuguese sardines and Italian tomatoes. The global canned food market today is worth around $118 billion.[2]

A second important leap in food processing was Louis Pasteur's development of the heat treatment of milk, patented in 1865. The eponymous process of pasteurisation keeps milk fresh for days, when it would otherwise become potentially unsafe in hours.

Both these applications of food technology address three inter-related core desiderata of food products: safety, stability and long shelf life. We take food safety for granted today, but historically bad food was a constant source of illness, mostly as a result of decay or adulteration. Some foods, like fish, meat and salad leaves, quickly go off or become unpalatable if they are not kept in exactly the right conditions, hence the need for stability. Finally, the longer food can be kept both safe and palatable, the less we waste, which is why increased shelf life is, all other things being equal, a boon.

But not all early modern developments in food processing have stood the test of time as well as canning and pasteurisation. Take margarine, another invention developed in response to a prize, this time offered by Napoleon III to find an alternative to increasingly expensive and scarce butter. Like many food technologists, the chemist Hippolyte Mège-Mouriès was trying to produce more, cheaper and healthier food, a noble goal at a time when so many struggled to get enough nutrition. He had already developed a method for making bread that resulted in a 14 per cent increase in production with the same quantity of ingredients. His cumbersome method required fermenting the groats (the hulled wheat kernels) in water and tartaric acid, which were then strained and added to the flour.[3] For this, Napoleon III awarded him the Légion d'Honneur in 1861. He also fortified chocolate with calcium phosphate and protein in an attempt to make it more nutritious. Mège-Mouriès's work was studied across Europe.

Creating a cheap spread for the masses was another benevolent ambition. Mège-Mouriès started experimenting with a saturated fatty acid recently discovered by Michel Eugène Chevreul, *acide margarique* (margaric acid or heptadecanoic acid). He created a substance called oleomargarine from processed beef tallow and skimmed milk, which he patented in 1869. Its name derived from the Ancient Greek word for pearl, *márgar* (μάργαρος), on account of the pearly appearance of the fat produced.

A British patent application details just how complex and lengthy Mège-Mouriès's process of production was:

A fatty body identical in chemical composition with butter is obtained from fresh suet by crushing it between rollers under a stream of water, further washing it and then digesting it with agricultural gastric juice. The fat is extracted, melted, passed through a sieve and poured into boxes to set, after which it is cut into pieces, which are wrapped in cloths and pressed between hot plates. A fatty body is expressed and may be agitated in a closed vessel, cooled, cut up, bleached with acid and washed with water. This purified fat is mixed at animal heat (104°F) with water containing small quantities of bicarbonate of soda, casein of cold milk and mammary tissues along with yellow coloring matter. This is digested, allowed to settle, decanted and cooled and yields a preserved butter. Fresh butter is obtained by agitating the above mixture until a cream is formed, which is then treated as usual to obtain the butter.[4]

Reading some recipes is mouth-watering. This is more stomach-churning. In order for the margarine to be appealing, colourings were added to make it look more like butter, since in its unadulterated state most margarine is white. Indeed, to prevent it being passed off as butter, for many years several territories banned the use of yellow colouring, and in some US states it had to be dyed pink.[5]

In this we see a clear forerunner of the kind of industrial processing that was to become ubiquitous in the twentieth century. Margarine ushered in an era when we would do things to foods that transformed them to a degree unprecedented in human history.

But the tale of margarine is a cautionary one. Mège-Mouriès's oleomargarine didn't initially take off as a mass-market product. That required the invention of a process called hydrogenation, patented by Wilhelm Normann in 1902. As the name suggests, the process binds additional hydrogen atoms to the fats, converting unsaturated fatty acids into saturated ones.

Hydrogenation creates trans fatty acids (also known as trans fats). These are unsaturated fats that are solid at room temperature. Trans fats also occur naturally, but in very much smaller quantities than other fats.

Hydrogenation allowed the animal fats in margarine to be replaced with cheaper vegetable oils. As a result, margarine became increasingly popular, and by 1970, five million metric tons were being produced worldwide per year.[6] It was marketed as a health food, high in polyunsaturated fats, better for us than butter laden with saturated fat. It was not just spread on bread, but was also used as an ingredient in industrial baked products.

But it started to become clear that trans fats were very bad for our health. Trans fat increases 'bad' LDL cholesterol while lowering 'good' HDL cholesterol. According to the WHO, 'Approximately 540,000 deaths each year can be attributed to intake of industrially produced trans-fatty acids.' It adds, 'Trans fat has no known health benefits.'[7]

Gyorgy Scrinis argues that the embrace of margarine as a health food is rooted in the nutritionist way of thinking. 'We rejected butter just because margarine has a little bit less saturated fat in it. Taking that one nutrient out of context and exaggerating our knowledge of saturated fats led in this case to the promotion of margarine, which has gone through many stages of technological processing and has many additives. It's not surprising that years later nutrition scientists changed their minds about the benefits of margarine versus butter.'

Many governments legislated to limit the amounts of trans fat in our diets. In the USA, the FDA ordered its elimination from food processing by June 2018. So food technologists set to work fixing the problem they had created, and today most margarine contains much lower levels of trans fats or none at all. Hydrogenation was 'improved' by adjusting the temperature, pressure, and length of time involved in the process, by adding new catalysts, and by applying yet more complex techniques. One of the most important of these is chemical or enzymatic transesterification. It is virtually impossible to describe this process in terms that a non-chemist could understand. One of the (relatively) clearest definitions is: 'a process in which triacylglycerides from a variety of feedstock such as nonedible oil seeds, vegetable oils, animal fats or tallow, waste cooking oil, and microbial lipids or single cell oil (from algae, oleaginous yeast, filamentous fungi and bacteria) are converted into fatty acid methyl esters (biodiesel) in the presence of alcohol (methanol or ethanol)'.[8]

'Transesterification' is a process that few understand and none reproduce in their own kitchens. That makes it a prime example of 'ultra-processing': the industrial transformation of food that goes beyond what humans have been doing for the vast majority of our existence. In many high-income countries, including the USA, the UK and Canada, more than half of the population's calorie intake comes from ultra-processed foods (UPFs), with sales still growing by around 1 per cent per year. In middle-income countries such as Brazil, Mexico and Chile, between one fifth and one third of calories come from UPFs, but growth is even stronger, averaging around 10 per cent per year. A study of the growth of UPFs concluded that 'a transition towards a more highly-processed global diet is not only underway, but also continuing apace'.[9]

There is now strong evidence that increased consumption of UPFs is associated with significantly worse health outcomes. One major meta-analysis found a 'possible association between high UPF consumption, worse cardiometabolic risk profile [...], and greater risk of all-cause mortality, CVD, cerebrovascular disease and depression'.[10] Another reached very similar conclusions, also noting that 'no study reported an association between UPF and beneficial health outcomes' and that 'beneficial outcomes were associated with diets higher in unprocessed and minimally processed foods'.[11]

Correlation is not causation, so these associations are not by themselves proof that UPFs are unhealthy. UPFs tend to be higher in fat, sugar and salt than less processed foods, as well as having fewer micronutrients. This raises the possibility that the problem with UPFs is their typical ingredients, not the ultra-processing itself. UPFs also tend to be eaten more by the less well-off, who tend to have worse health for myriad other reasons. However, many studies have tried to account for these confounding variables and have still found a strong association with worse health, suggesting that causation is at work. One widely cited study led by Kevin Hall fed two groups of people with either minimally processed or ultra-processed meals that were identical in terms of their energy density and their carbohydrate, fat, protein, sugar, sodium and fibre content. Participants were allowed to eat as little or as much as they wanted. In just two weeks, those following the ultra-processed diet gained on average 0.9 kg, while those following the minimally processed diet lost the same amount.[12]

Despite the tide turning against UPFs, not everyone is convinced that they deserve to be demonised. After all, processing is ubiquitous and often benign. Even the nutritionist Carlos Monteiro, who has done more than anyone else to define the category of UPF, has written, 'Most foods as purchased and consumed are processed to some extent. For this reason, accounts that are critical of "processed food" are not useful.'[13] So are UPFs fundamentally different to other processed foods, or is the distinction between the two arbitrary? And if there is a meaningful difference, are all UPFs bad for us or do we need to distinguish between better and worse varieties?

Think of an ultra-processed food and you'll probably think of the kind of product that contains a list of ingredients like the vegan sausage at the beginning of this chapter. Another paradigmatic example is the ubiquitous puffed, savoury, crispy snack. Ralph Early provides an unappetising summary of the process used to make these. 'You take your raw potatoes, smash them up and end up with a cold slurry of potato starch. You then process that in some way, perhaps enzymically to change the nature of the starch. You then dehydrate it to make a powder. Somebody takes that modified potato starch powder, adds water, flavourings, colourings, etc. to make a paste and then they put it into an extruder which pops shaped pieces into hot oil for frying.' This is clearly much more transformative than traditional processing and it is hard to see how it can result in nutritious food. As Early says, 'All the structure and the nutrients that we would find in a potato cooked from raw have been completely transformed into an entirely different food material.'

But many seemingly innocuous, even healthy, products also fall into the UPF category. One is Marmite, a yeast extract popular in Britain that has been eaten since the late nineteenth century. Another is a venerable brand of no added sugar muesli, which is classified as a UPF because it contains milk powders.[14] Examples

336

like these raise the question of whether the term 'ultra-processed' catches too many foods in its net, and whether it is useful for distinguishing between healthy and non-healthy options.

To answer these questions, we need to have a more precise idea of what a UPF is. It is obvious enough that a fake sausage or a savoury puff is ultra-processed. But what about sliced bread, frozen pizza or a bar of dark chocolate?

The best-known and most-used definition of a UPF is the one used in the NOVA classification system, developed by Carlos Monteiro. NOVA places foods into four groups. Group 1 is unprocessed or minimally processed foods, like eggs, pasteurised milk, grains, fruits and vegetables. Group 2 is processed culinary ingredients, such as oils, butter, sugar and salt, which are produced by methods such as pressing, refining, grinding, milling and drying. Group 3 comprises processed foods such as bread, cheese, jam, dry biscuits. These are modified foods, made by combining ingredients from groups 1 and 2. Group 4, ultra-processed foods, are defined as 'not modified foods but formulations made mostly or entirely from substances derived from foods and additives, with little if any intact Group 1 food and drink products'. They include soft drinks, sweet or savoury packaged snacks, reconstituted meat products and pre-prepared frozen dishes.[15]

Ultra-processed foods have several distinctive characteristics. First, the processes used to make them are industrial ones that cannot be reproduced easily or sometimes at all in a domestic kitchen. Second, they involve ingredients that are exclusively used in industry and again would not or could not be found in any home, such as emulsifiers, sweeteners, thickeners, gelling and glazing agents. These ingredients are often themselves produced by the kinds of industrial processes characteristic of UPFs. Typically these are ingredients such as potato starch, high-fructose corn syrup and skimmed milk powder that are fractioned – that is to say, extracted and refined – from whole foods.

You would expect such a classification system to have grey areas and borderline cases. But because NOVA's function is to determine whether a particular food is a UPF or not, it is forced to turn the fuzzy borders of the categories into hard ones. To be able to do this, it needs to specify its criteria in detail, and that is where the devil dwells. For example, Group 4 foods contain 'substances not commonly used in culinary preparations', but whereas American kitchens often contain corn starch, French ones rarely do. Hence a French assessor may categorise a food differently from an American one. Cultural factors also explain why some forms of processing are seen as acceptable merely because they are traditional. Coffee torrefaction, for example, is a method of roasting that adds sugar in order to increase shelf life and impart a more palatable flavour to robusta beans, which are cheaper than better quality arabica beans. Torrefaction today is often done on an industrial scale and at high temperatures, which increases levels of acrylamide, a carcinogenic compound. While there is no evidence that the levels are high enough to pose a health risk, the same could be said of many of the compounds in UPFs. Still, coffee is placed in Group 1, seemingly just because it is seen as a traditional, minimally processed drink, irrespective of how high-impact the roasting process is.

Critics often latch on to these ambiguities and inconsistencies to question the very coherence of the idea of UPFs, arguing that unless it can be clearly defined how the concept is applied, it cannot be meaningful. Further evidence for the imprecision of the term 'UPF' comes from a French study that asked food and nutrition specialists to assign a variety of foods to their correct NOVA groups. Despite all the evaluators being experts, the study concluded that the overall consistency of their classifications was low, even when ingredient information was available. The authors concluded that the NOVA groups were 'not clearly defined' and that their results 'suggest current NOVA criteria do not allow for robust and functional food assignments'.[16] Scrinis dismisses this as a study that has been 'designed by people who wanted to debunk NOVA'. But even if it exaggerated the ambiguities and inconsistencies in NOVA, it seems undeniable that there are some.

Another contentious aspect of NOVA is that it incorporates some political as well as nutritional criteria. It distinguishes between good and bad processing not only in terms of its nature and extent but also according to its purpose. Canning and pasteurisation were done in the service of safety, stability and shelf life. Now, palatability and cost are the main drivers.

Take palatability. Industrial food is often designed to get as close as possible to the so-called bliss point discovered by the American Howard Moskowitz. Moskowitz is a psychophysicist who studied the relationships between physical stimuli and sensations and perceptions. He applied this science to market research and product development, realising that when foods contain the right balance of fat, sugar and salt, people love to eat them, and eat more of them. Moskowitz was personally involved in the development of Cherry Vanilla Dr Pepper and Prego spaghetti sauce, but his insights have been used extensively in the food industry to create what critics call 'hyper-palatable' foods.

Monteiro also points out that 'ultra-processed food products are usually packaged attractively and marketed intensively' and are 'designed to displace all other food groups'. He says 'marketing strategies used worldwide include vivid packaging, health claims, special deals with retailers to secure prime shelf space, establishment of franchised catering outlets, and campaigns using social, electronic, broadcast and print media, including to children and in schools, often with vast budgets'.[17]

One typical study showed that in the UK, for every pound spent by the government on promoting healthy eating, more than thirty were spent on advertising junk food, the worst subset of UPFs.[18] In the early 2000s, Coca-Cola and PepsiCo combined spent more on marketing than the entire budget of the World Health

Organization.[19] 'When was the last time you saw adverts on TV for fruits and vegetables?' asks Early.

But the purposes, palatability and marketing of foods do not in themselves tell us anything about their nutritional value. If ultra-processing is bad for us it must be because of its nature, not because of the motives of those who use it. As two commentators put it, 'whether a manufacturer's primary intention for producing a UPF is to generate high profits is difficult to measure'. Nor is it clear why a producer of less processed food should not be just as motivated by profit or the desire to appeal.[20]

The argument that 'ultra-processed' is a somewhat vague and ambiguous category seems incontrovertible. Rather than dispute it, a better response is to argue that we should not be surprised or concerned that UPF is less than perfectly defined. Very few concepts have clear and unequivocal applications. We can define 'gold' precisely as the metal that has seventy-nine protons and seventy-nine electrons in the nuclei of its atoms. We can also say with absolute clarity that a fat is unsaturated if it has at least one double bond within the fatty acid chain, otherwise it is saturated. But many other concepts have vaguer or more arbitrary boundaries. For example, 'snacks' are whatever foods we decide to eat between meals, and what we call a 'meal' is itself a social convention. There is nothing a nut, a pot of yogurt and a slice of cake have in common that makes them all inherently snacks. It is simply that we choose to eat them as snack foods. Even the term 'healthy' is imprecise, as it depends on the quantity and regularity of consumption.

Other food categories are also somewhat unscientific. Take the difference between fruits and nuts. From a botanical perspective, fruits develop from the flowering parts of plants, and nuts are fruits that have a kernel protected by a hard shell. From a culinary perspective, however, the terms fruit and nut refer to edible parts of plants, divided up somewhat arbitrarily on the basis of their similarities as foods. In culinary terms, tomatoes are vegetables, even though they are botanically fruits, and we do not usually think of non-edible fruits and nuts such as holly berries and acorns as fruits or nuts at all. Strawberries and apples are also both not 'true fruits' in the botanical sense.

The concept 'ultra-processed food' is more like that of 'snack' or 'culinary fruit' than it is like that of 'gold' or 'saturated fat'. UPFs do not have an unequivocal, objective 'essence'. It is a category we have invented for our own purposes and so there will inevitably be some element of arbitrariness in how we use it. Processing is a matter of degree, and so it is up to us where we choose to draw a line and say, 'Beyond this point, processing becomes ultra-processing.' So rather than thinking of UPF and non-UPF as binary categories, we should think of a spectrum of processing, with the most highly processed foods at one end and things like apples and berries, which we can eat straight from the plant, at the other. We should also expect there to be a lot of variety within the UPF part of the spectrum, from foods that just cross the threshold on the basis of a single added ingredient or process, to foodstuffs that could never be made in a domestic kitchen, even if you have access to industrial ingredients.

However, this reply does not address the criticism that the inclusion of motivation and purpose in the definition of UPF is an unnecessary muddying of already opaque waters. But Scrinis defends UPF's political dimension, arguing that it is 'actually key to the definition, because the only way we can really understand what is in these foods and why they might be harmful is if we understand that they're being produced by bad actors who are so hell bent on making a profit they will put anything on the shelves'. To appreciate the force of this point, you need to understand that people like Monteiro and Scrinis are trying to change the whole framework in which we think about food. Instead of seeing it as composed of individual items we put into our stomachs, they want to see it as embedded in a rich network of cultural and political practices. To fix our health problems we cannot just think about what to eat or not. We have to think about the whole food system. If UPFs are a problem, it is not going to be solved unless we address the source of the problem: the food industry.

It seems indisputable that any attempt to draw a line between processed and ultra-processed is going to result in some anomalies, grey areas and contested cases. There is also a question mark over the inclusion of political and motivational criteria, even if there are some good reasons for doing this. But there is still sufficient coherence to the concept for it to be meaningful. Aristotle famously advised us to only expect as much precision as the subject matter allows. UPFs cannot be defined with mathematical precision, but the term is precise enough for our purposes.

UPF may be a meaningful, albeit not a precise, category. But is it really the case that UPFs are inherently bad for us? After all, the fact that most venomous reptiles are snakes does not mean all snakes are venomous reptiles. So even if it is true, as it seems it is, that the most unhealthy foods are ultra-processed, that does not necessarily mean all ultra-processed foods are unhealthy.

Some industrial processes and ingredients may be perfectly good alternatives to domestic ones. Some foods may contain a small enough proportion of ultra-processed components that it doesn't really matter.

Sceptics argue that no one has yet shown why being ultra-processed in itself makes a food less healthy. To show that, you would need to establish the causal pathways by which UPFs cause harm to health, and this has not yet been done. Even the researchers who found weight gain among those following a UPF diet acknowledged that their study 'was not designed to identify the cause of the observed differences in energy intake'. Although NOVA advocates talk darkly about the harms done by food additives, critics say that with the exception of trans fats, which have now been removed or reduced from most processed foods, there isn't a single other widely used additive that has been established to be bad for our health.

But it is common in nutrition to discover a strong association before identifying the precise causal mechanisms. These are the final pieces of the jigsaw, slotted into place once the bigger picture has already become clear. As a commentary in the leading medical journal *The Lancet* put it, 'Although evidence still needs to be strengthened to establish a causal link, it is rapidly accumulating.' It is probably the case that UPFs are unhealthy for a variety of reasons, not because they contain one killer compound. Ultra-processing creates substances such as furans, which we have only recently found can cause liver damage in excessive quantities. Other evidence is emerging. Many UPFs make use of emulsifiers which have been found in mice to induce 'metabolic perturbations, alterations to the gut microbiota, inflammation, and colon carcinogenesis'.[21] Just as this book was going to press, another study came out that tracked 95,442 adults and found positive associations between the risk of cardiovascular disease and the intake of several emulsifiers.[22]

Highly processed food also tends to be less satiating: because it is so processed and tends to be low in fibre, it doesn't stimulate the digestive system as much as whole foods, and so the stomach doesn't send the brain the signals that it has eaten enough. That could explain why UPFs are associated with obesity. Again, that would not necessarily mean ultra-processing is itself the problem. As Mike Gibney explained to me, 'If you take an apple, it would take me five minutes to eat it. If I pureed it, I'd have it down in ten seconds. Processing changes the texture of a food and texture plays a huge role in the rate of eating. The texture matters, not whether it is ultra-processed or not.' In support, Gibney cited a study by a team including Ciarán Forde, who has worked a lot on texture. The study concludes that 'texture-based differences in

ER [eating rate] and meal energy density contribute to observed differences in energy intake between minimally processed and ultra-processed meals' and that food texture – not degree of processing – 'accounted for observed differences in the amount (g) of food consumed across minimally processed and ultra-processed diets'.[23]

Interestingly, the authors also found that energy intake was lowest when harder texture was combined with lower-energy-density minimally processed foods within a meal, evidence that there may be something about UPFs that makes them worse. It is also striking that one of Gibney's papers sceptical of the supposed harms of UPF cited as evidence several papers that, overall, came down clearly against ultra-processed food.[24] One of these concluded that 'higher intakes of MPF [minimally processed food] and lower intakes of UPF were associated with the most healthful dietary profiles'[25] and another that 'decreasing the dietary share of ultra-processed foods is a rational and effective way to improve the nutritional quality of US diets'.[26]

Scrinis accepts that there haven't been many studies on the causal pathways of UPFs. But we have enough evidence about what goes into them and how they are made to see that 'it's no great surprise or accident that these foods are not satiating and that people might over-consume them. They have been designed over many decades by food companies to do just that. That's not a conspiracy theory, it's food corporation strategy 101.'

The ideas of the network scientist Albert-László Barabási, whom we met in the last chapter, could also explain why we know so little about the causal pathways linking UPFs to poor health. Barabási argues that many of the molecules in food are not nutrients, but that does not mean they have no impact on health. For example, polyphenols are known to be good for us, probably in the main because of their antioxidant properties. However, as Barabási explains, 'your metabolism does not process polyphenols'. Rather, 'they're broken up by bacteria, get into your bloodstream and bind to different human proteins and they affect health by blocking certain activities of those proteins and activating others'.[27] Many compounds that are not nutrients similarly modify or control activities in the body. But 'while the impact of food processing on basic nutritional components is well studied,' he writes, 'little is known about the impact of processing on the thousands of chemicals found in the nutritional dark matter.'

Barabási is treading on new ground, and it may turn out that this 'nutritional dark matter' doesn't do very much after all. Even so, once you start to think of nutrition as a complex system in which each compound or chemical behaves differently depending on how it relates to innumerable others, the idea that ultra-processing won't have any effect on how foods are metabolised becomes implausible. Perhaps the reason we have so little evidence about how UPFs cause ill health is that hardly any evidence has been collected, so absence of evidence is not evidence of absence.

Still, it is undeniable that, as one study put it, 'foods most commonly assigned to NOVA4 [. . .] could vary substantially in their nutrient profiles'. NOVA4 groups together foods as disparate as turkey twizzlers, Snickers ice cream bars, mass-produced wholemeal bread, Quorn and fortified unsweetened soymilk.[28] We cannot judge the relative healthiness of a food solely by asking if it is ultra-processed or not. A home-made chocolate nemesis should be eaten in more moderation than an industrially produced wholemeal loaf or a natural yogurt with a little added stabiliser. A recent study showed that although, overall, 'higher consumption of UPF was associated with a higher risk of multimorbidity of cancer and cardiometabolic diseases', this was not true of several UPF sub-categories. In particular, 'ultra-processed breads and cereals showed an inverse association with the risk of multimorbidity', while even 'sweets and desserts, savory snacks, plant-based alternatives, ready-to-eat/heat and mixed dishes were not associated with risk of multimorbidity'.[29] There is other published evidence that several foods classified as UPFs currently make a positive difference to at least some people's diets. One study concluded that 'breakfast cereals make a significant contribution to the micronutrient intake of the low-income UK population'.[30] Another review said that bread – the vast majority of which is made using the industrial Chorleywood process and so is classified as ultra-processed – 'continues to play an important role in the current UK diet, contributing to intakes of carbohydrate (as starch), fibre, protein and numerous vitamins and minerals including calcium, iron and thiamin', noting that 'bread is also low in saturates and free sugars'.[31] Yet another meta-analysis, surveying multiple studies, found that although consumption of UPFs in general is associated with an increased risk of all-cause mortality, higher consumption of breakfast cereals was associated with decreased risk. They concluded that 'the health consequences of UPF must be carefully assessed, given that this broad term includes various food components that can cause different health outcomes'.[32]

In summary, most nutritionists would agree with the assessment of Bridget Benelam of the British Nutrition Foundation, who said that 'UPF classification is broad and also includes foods such as sliced wholemeal bread, wholegrain cereals, low fat fruit yogurts and baked beans, all of which could be included in a healthy diet according to current UK healthy eating advice'.[33]

However, to use this as a reason to reject the UPF category as unhelpful arguably misses the point. No one is claiming that all UPFs are equally bad for us. 'It really is important to understand that all foods within that category are not the same,' says Scrinis. 'Different UPF products will vary greatly in terms of the quantities and proportions of ultra-processed ingredients and additives. Of course each product will therefore vary in terms of their dietary impact and potential long-term health impact. But what matters more is some of their common characteristics and collective impact.

This includes not only what these products contain, but what they don't contain, and also what they displace from our diets.'

Every time we complain that the NOVA classification doesn't rank specific foods fairly, we're falling back into the old way of thinking about nutrition in terms of individual components of a diet rather than its overall structure and pattern. 'The epidemiological studies reveal that it's the proportion of UPFs in the diet that is a source of poor diets and health outcomes. That's a very different sort of argument from saying that each individual product is harmful,' says Scrinis. 'It's the ultra-processed dietary pattern that is problematic, not just the individual products.'

Adopting the 'dietary pattern approach' would require a fundamental shift in our thinking. Scrinis gives the example of sugar, which comes under NOVA category 2, processed culinary ingredients, along with other things like vegetable oils, butter and salt. As Scrinis says, standard nutritional guidelines say 'these are bad ingredients: minimise them; moderate your consumption; reduce, reduce, reduce. The NOVA classification does something very different. It says if you are using these ingredients in your kitchen that's a good thing, because it means you're cooking and if you're cooking, you're probably creating quite nutritious meals. Go for it. We're not going to tell you how much butter to slather on that bread or how much oil to use.'

Many recent headlines suggest that the case against ultra-processed food is closed. However, a statement by the UK government's Scientific Advisory Committee on Nutrition (SACN) in 2023 sums up the current state of play more accurately. It says: 'The SRs [systematic reviews] identified have consistently reported that increased consumption of (ultra-) processed foods was associated with increased risks of adverse health outcomes. However, there are uncertainties around the quality of evidence available.' A particular worry is that 'consumption of (ultra-) processed foods may be an indicator of other unhealthy dietary patterns and lifestyle behaviours. Diets high in (ultra-) processed foods are often energy dense, high in saturated fat, salt or free sugars, high in processed meat, and/or low in fruit and vegetables and fibre.'[34]

The Nordic Council of Ministers was even more circumspect when it issued its updated nutrition recommendations for its member states, Denmark, Finland, Iceland, Norway and Sweden. It reported that 'despite the observed association between ultra-processed food and health outcomes ... the categorisation of foods as ultra-processed foods does not add to the already existing food classifications and recommendations'. It found that 'no qualified SRs [systematic reviews] are available on the health effect of UPF'. Still, it noted that 'diets high in ultra-processed foods tend to be nutritiously unbalanced and are less likely to adhere to the overall [Nordic Nutrition Recommendations 2023] than minimally processed foods'. In other words, avoid nutritionally unbalanced diets and you will automatically avoid bad UPFs. You do not need to avoid UPFs per se.[35]

Some Latin American countries, in contrast, have included references to UPFs in their dietary advice, including Brazil, Uruguay, Ecuador and Peru. Brazil, for example, urges its citizens to 'avoid ultra-processed foods', citing problems with ingredients (they are 'nutritionally unbalanced'), formulation and presentation (they 'tend to be consumed in excess, and displace natural or minimally processed foods'), and their 'means of production, distribution, marketing, and consumption', which 'damage culture, social life, and the environment'.[36] France, meanwhile, advises reduced consumption of 'ultra-transformed' foods.

'Ultra-processed food' is in many ways too broad and unscientific a concept, and we need to be careful not to assume everything that falls under the description is equally bad, or bad at all. Like cakes and candies, these products are not going to hurt anyone in moderation. Some may actually be positively good for us, at least in certain circumstances. Think of the shakes packed with energy and nutrients given to sick patients who have trouble eating. You wouldn't want to live on them permanently, but you might well be kept alive by them in the short run. We don't yet have a full understanding of the risks of UPFs, and several aspects of their definition are questionable. In the future, a finer-grained tool than NOVA may be needed to distinguish the most harmful highly processed foods. But despite its limitations, the Scientific Advisory Committee on Nutrition concluded that NOVA was 'the only processed food classification that met SACN's initial screening criteria as being potentially suitable for use in the UK'.

The case against ultra-processed foods is not that the category is clear-cut and everything in it is bad for our health. The fact that it is technically possible to eat badly by consuming nothing but artisan cake made with minimally processed ingredients, or to eat well by carefully picking out the small minority of good UPFs, is a quibble. It would be naive to expect all UPFs to be equally unhealthy. Indeed, we should not assume that all will necessarily be unhealthy. Still, all other things being equal, the proportion of UPFs in our diet should be much lower than it is in many countries. If you're mostly eating food that is homemade or cooked from scratch, your diet is very likely to be good. If you're mostly eating industrially produced food, your diet is almost certainly bad. As we've seen before, the food world is extremely complicated, but sometimes the best general direction of travel is crystal clear.

TAKING STOCK

Towards a Global Food Philosophy

The history of human technology is one of millennia of small advances followed by just a few centuries of accelerating development. There have surely been more technological advances in the last two hundred years than there had been in the previous two hundred thousand. The main reason for this is the ever-increasing pace at which our understanding of nature has grown since the beginning of the scientific revolution in the sixteenth century. Modern science has created innumerable opportunities for us to apply our knowledge of how the world works to develop techniques to make it work for us.

However, science never stands still, and we have to challenge some of the fixed ideas we have about it if it is to remain the servant of progress. Most scientific achievements have been the result of breaking the world down into manageable parts, and discovering the laws that govern how they work. However, science is also the study of systems, and increasingly this is where its cutting edge lies. The properties of any part of the world cannot be fully revealed by isolating it. Its nature can only be fully understood once we understand how it interacts with other parts. For example, as a chemical, nitrogen is nitrogen, but it behaves differently in the atmosphere to how it does when fixed in the soil. Similarly, a vitamin in a whole fruit is absorbed differently to a pure vitamin in a pill; manure is pollution if disposed of in one way, a fertiliser if used in another; methane emissions increase Earth's temperature in some situations but not in others. In the vast and complex food world, these interactions are of vital importance. When looking at the use of technology for food, the need is always to take a holistic, systems-level approach.

Consider genetic modification. It is easy to assume that the key question is 'are GMOs safe?' and that the answer is found by looking at what happens if you eat or plant one. However, the most important issues and problems with GMOs can only be seen if you look at the systems in which they are used. GM maize may be safe and healthy, but it is damaging if it is sown in vast monocultures in which biodiversity is all but eliminated by broad-spectrum herbicides. GM crops could help peasant farmers, but not if their manufacture and distribution is controlled by a handful of multi-national companies, helping to consolidate their power in the food system.

Similarly, we cannot understand the problems and challenges of waste if we focus on the individual items that are lost along the supply chain. We have to think about why waste is created at every stage and the often structural reasons for this, such as buyers' terms of trade, growers' lack of resources, governments' ill-conceived policies. Waste is minimised in a food system that is as circular as possible, and circularity can only be achieved at a systems level. Actions by individuals, companies and civil society groups are not enough.

The need for a holistic perspective is also evident in nutrition. The space programme showed the limitations of reducing food to nutrients and treating it simply as fuel. Eating needs to be pleasurable not only for psychological and social reasons, but for the sake of our bodies. Nor can the healthiness of individual foods be separated from their place in our dietary patterns. Nonetheless, it is clear that, in general, the healthiest foods are real foods, less processed and made from whole ingredients. Other types of food can feature in our diets, but they should not be the core of them.

How technology has been used and misused also tells us about the value of human resourcefulness. During the green revolution our inventiveness saved millions from starvation. However, we need to have some humility, recognising that there is always more that we don't know and that we often cannot foresee the effects on the whole of our manipulation of a part. The precautionary principle is perhaps too ambiguous and crude a tool to keep hubris in check. We might be better to adopt the Scottish Enlightenment philosopher David Hume's maxim, 'a weaker evidence can never destroy a stronger'.[1] History has given us strong evidence that the only sustainable food systems are circular ones; that the healthiest foods are whole foods; that there is no one right way to eat, cook or farm; that if power is granted to vested interests they will abuse it. Whenever our ingenuity suggests something that goes against these and other well-established principles, the evidence is always going to be stacked up against it, the burden of proof on those who claim that the old rules don't apply.

We also need a whole systems approach to address issues of inequity in the food world. GMOs could be used to make the food system fairer, but in practice they have been taken advantage of by those who already have most power. Truly personalised nutrition could help everyone, or it could further the health gap between those with the money to afford it and those without, while also encouraging the belief that good nutrition is a purely personal responsibility which governments need do nothing about. Waste has to be understood as an equity issue because it imposes externalities on society: costs in terms of habitat loss and pollution that the manufacturers of surplus food don't have to pay for.

Technology is often presented as something that offers highly targeted solutions, transformative interventions at specific points in a system. Sometimes it can do that. But every technology ends up as part of a wider system, and if that is dysfunctional, the technology only ends up helping to entrench its flaws. To use technology better, we need to use it as part of a broader strategy to reshape systems to make them more circular, equitable and sustainable.

CONCLUSION

A Global Food Philosophy

The food world is a remarkably complex and diverse ecosystem, a hybrid of nature and artifice. It has expanded to use more land and more resources to feed more people than ever before. Yet every informed observer of it, from whatever specialism, agrees that it is not looking healthy – for people, for the planet or for other animals. It is riddled with systemic injustices, with some getting fat while others starve, both literally and metaphorically. It has become a living hell for much, if not most, of the livestock within it. And it is environmentally unsustainable, requiring too many inputs while producing too many harmful outputs.

Yet the principles that should govern our management of the food world are neither controversial nor hard to identify. They have been evident throughout our historical and global survey, as have the many vices that have blighted the food system. They can be brought together and boiled down into seven pillars of food wisdom.

Arguably, the keystone principle is *holism*. Time and again we have seen that every part of the food world is connected to every other. But too often we fail to join the dots, finding apparent solutions somewhere that either shift the problems elsewhere or create new ones. Forests are felled in South America to feed livestock in Europe; fertilisers increase yields on fields and create run-off that destroys life in the rivers; ultra-processing enables the manufacture of cheap, tasty foods which years later turn out to diminish the health of people who eat too many of them; waste is reduced in the retail sector at the cost of increasing it for producers and consumers. In a globalised world where we are more interconnected than ever, the need for holistic thinking has never been greater.

We need to get away from the atomistic mode of thought that has dominated in the West, in which we think of the aspects of the food world as discrete elements, building blocks that can be fiddled with individually. Instead we need to recapture a sense of the relationality of all being. The nature of each individual thing, person or animal is determined by how it stands in relation to other things. Maize can be a nutritious food or a highly processed ingredient for junk. Fish excrement can be toxic waste or food for molluscs. Burning forests can lead to catastrophic habitat and carbon sink loss or it can be part of a sustainable shifting cultivation system.

Terms like 'holism' and 'relationality' might sound abstract and nebulous. However, together they mean more or less the same as the more scientific phrase 'systems thinking', which is increasingly popular in the physical and social sciences. As Roberta Sonnino explains it, 'Systems thinking suggests that, in complex systems such as food, causality is not necessarily evident, known, stable and linear; there are "causal loops" between multiple variables'.[1] The systems approach is more rigorous, thorough and complicated than alternatives that only focus on the elements in a system and don't consider how their interactions change them.

Systems thinking is linked to probably the most uncontroversial principle for a healthy food world: *circularity*. Any sustainable food system requires a balance of inputs and outputs, and historically the best way to achieve this has been through regenerative cycles. On the Pampas, the cattle needed only to graze, and with traditional herd intensities the grasses were not only able to recover, the urine and manure of the livestock helped them to flourish. Hunter-gatherers moved around their territories, only taking as much from each part as would allow for regrowth and repopulation the next year. Efficient mixed farms waste nothing and require little extra to be brought in. Plants inedible to humans feed livestock, while manure from the animals feeds the ground.

The advent of truly renewable energy means that for the first time the circle need not be entirely closed. For example, if we could start to produce nitrogen fertilisers efficiently using renewable energy, we could have an infinite source of agricultural inputs. (Without any further innovations, we would have enough of the other two main fertilisers for some time. Phosphorus would run out near the end of the century and potassium by the end of the twenty-third.)[2] It may even be vital that farming is *not* a hermetically sealed loop. Ken Giller argues that in many low- and middle-income countries, 'the lack of nitrogen has actually driven land use change and caused biodiversity loss. Poorly productive agriculture leads to soil degradation and delivers only ecosystem disservices.'[3]

The circularity we need in the twenty-first century will not all be of the kind practised by mixed farms. We may see more of it at regional, national or even international levels. Specialised farms can be part of a circular food world if they are linked with farms with different specialisations, so that waste from each one becomes a resource for the others.

Another principle that should be uncontentious is *plurality*. The environments and peoples of the globe are vastly different, so the idea that one mode of farming, manufacture, or even eating should be practised by all people at all times in all places is absurd. Given that human ingenuity and adaptability have fed us for millennia, it would be perverse to demand that everyone follows the exact same path, and to stop people laying down new ones.

Yet many advocate 'one-size-fits-all' solutions, such as the Mediterranean diet, organic farming, intensification, direct trade, eating locally. People also talk about finding things that work and then 'scaling them up' so that they become more widely adopted. Sophia Murphy, Executive Director of the Institute for Agriculture and Trade Policy (IATP), says, 'This fascination with scaling up seems to me very misguided, because often what works locally will not globally, and the good rule globally won't apply in every situation.'[4]

Pluralism does not mean 'anything goes'. Acceptable ways of growing, processing and eating food have to conform to the other principles of our global food philosophy. But it should be obvious that many different ways of working and being pass this test, as may some new ways that are yet to come.

In his absorbing book *An Edible History of Humanity*, Tom Standage succinctly sums up the case for pluralism. 'To ensure an adequate supply of food as the world population heads towards its peak and climate change shifts long-established patterns of agriculture, it will be necessary to assemble the largest possible toolbox of agricultural techniques. . . . It is far too simplistic to suggest that the world faces a choice between organic fundamentalism on the one hand and blind faith in biotechnology on the other. The future of food production, and of mankind, surely lies in the wide and fertile middle ground in between.'[5]

Together, the principles of circularity, plurality and holism meet in the Confucian value of harmony, which requires difference in order to achieve balance. Murphy echoed this when she compared the food system to music. 'You don't all need to have the same piece of music in front of you to make a symphony, you can play different things, and it can harmonise.' Diversity is not the enemy of harmony; it is a precondition of it, in the food world as in music.

A fourth principle is that the food world should be *foodcentric*, by which I mean it should have food at its heart. This might sound puzzling: how could food not be at the centre of the food world? But there are at least three ways in which foodcentrism has been undermined. First of all, much of the world's agricultural land has been given over to the production of plants as commodities to be used as ingredients in industrial production, not as whole foods to be eaten as they are or cooked in homes. Of course, there has to be a role for commodity crops in a modern food system. But commodification has gone too far and has distorted the ways we grow, process and eat food. Much of what we now eat is arguably not food at all but what Michael Pollan colourfully called 'edible food-like substances'.[6] In industrialised nations too many people eat too much food that has been processed too much. We know from the hunter-gatherers, the Inuit, the Maasai and the people who eat the best diets today that we are healthier when our diets are based on whole foods.

Second, food is not just a collection of nutrients, consumed as fuel. This goes beyond the increasing realisation that nutrition cannot be reduced to check boxes of fats, carbohydrates, proteins, vitamins and minerals. As the pioneering French Enlightenment food writer Jean Anthelme Brillat-Savarin wrote, 'Animals feed themselves; human beings eat.'[7] We need food for our psychological and social nourishment, not just for the fitness of our bodies. And because, as the holistic principle implies, we are psychosomatic wholes, these elements cannot be disentangled. We've seen from astronauts and soldiers that when food is just fuel, physical as well as mental health suffers.

Third, too much of the food system is driven by corporates whose main goal is to make profit, not to provide food. That is hardly their fault and making profit is no crime. But the market needs to be regulated so that the best way to make money is to sell wholesome, fair and humane food.

A fifth principle of a global food philosophy is *resourcefulness*. The incredible diversity of ways of managing the food world testifies to the adaptability and inventiveness of human beings. Yet it seems that some would seek to stop this, or at least limit it. Too impressed by what we have done so far, they believe we already know all that we need to know, and fear future innovations rather than seek them. But there should be no going back to old ways, and wise admirers of traditional practices recognise this. The best organic farmers, for example, are not trying to return to some Arcadian past but are using technology to help them maximise their use of manures, water and feed, or manage their herds and flocks.

While technophobia is a mistake, some agents in the food system suffer from the opposite vice of excessive technophilia. They fail to spot the difference between helpful technological solutions and hasty 'techno-fixes' which ignore systemic problems and seek to resolve difficulties by the application of a silicon-based sticking plaster. Rather than being too enamoured of the past, they are too dismissive of it. Between these two extremes lies what I have called *technophronesis*.[8] *Phronesis* is an Ancient Greek term meaning 'practical wisdom', implying an ability to make case-by-case judgements on the basis of learned experience. Hence *technophronesis* enables us to judge whether any given technology is unnecessary, extravagant, wasteful, or useful, on its own merits and without preconceptions.

One reason why resourcefulness is an apt name for this principle is that the idea of being 'resource-full' contrasts with the recent tendency for the food system to be 'resource-emptying'. Think of how rainforests have been cleared to grow livestock feed, oceans left depleted by over-fishing, aquifers emptied to irrigate huge arable farms. It is undeniable that we have been hollowing out the food world by extracting resources from it at a faster rate than we can replace them. A resourceful approach is about carefully making the most of our resources as possible, not carelessly making use of the most resources as possible.

In being pluralistic, circular, holistic, foodcentric and resourceful, the food world of the near future would be emulating the best of the past. But there are two principles that ought also to guide us which no food system to date has entirely followed, and which most have contradicted. The first is that our management of the food world should be *compassionate*. Even traditional societies that have revered other animals have not tended to treat them with as much care as we all could and should. Post-Darwin, with all we know about animal nervous systems and behaviour, ignorance about their capacity to suffer can no longer be an excuse for cruel practices. All should agree that our food world should be a humane one, even though exactly what that requires is still a matter of much dispute, with some advocating an animal-free food future and others a high-welfare one.

We could also use the word 'humane'. Although this might seem too anthropomorphic, as Sky Carrithers said, in a sense 'humane' is precisely the right adjective, because only humans have the capacity to adjust their behaviour towards other animals. Our care for other animals only becomes anthropomorphism when we forget our human difference and think that compassion requires us to treat them as though they had minds just like ours, with projects, plans and rich autobiographical memories.

A second almost unprecedented principle is that our food world should be *equitable*. Some traditional societies, such as hunter-gatherers, Maasai and Inuit, have been largely internally equitable, without wealth or food being concentrated in the hands of a few while others go without. However, from a twenty-first-century perspective most traditional societies have been extremely inequitable with regard to sex, with men tending to have more power and status. Also, while small societies and communities have been internally egalitarian, little if any thought was given to fairness beyond the community.

Equitability today requires a degree of democratic accountability. As the Food Ethics Council's Food and Fairness Inquiry concluded, fairness in the food system requires fair shares, fair play (the ability to participate on equal terms) and fair say.[9] The food world has no single leader, but power within it is highly concentrated, with large businesses having too much and many citizens having far too little. In addition to having the ability to feed ourselves well as consumers, we also need the right and capacity to act as 'food citizens', whether we take up that opportunity or not. The denial of that right to peasant farmers led to resistance in the form of the birth of the global food sovereignty movement. Citizens of industrialised nations need to recognise that they too have that right but that they have not exercised it, allowing themselves to become largely passive consumers.

If we were to adopt the principles of Holism, Circularity, Pluralism, Foodcentrism, Resourcefulness, Compassion and Equitability, many of the desiderata we have for the food world would come along for the ride. Everyone is in favour of sustainability, and that is what we would get if we followed these seven principles. Similarly, a circular, plural and resourceful food system is also an efficient one. When the main things people want flow naturally from a set of principles, that is a good sign that those principles are the right ones.

The fact that it is so hard to disagree with these principles might be taken as a sign that they are too woolly, too thin. If you advocate something that no one is against, how can you be advocating something worth fighting for? In this case, however, the almost self-evident virtues of the principles are a strength, because we can see that they are not being followed. Everyone agrees with them but hardly any one is acting in accordance with them. Our food world is more full of holes than it is a harmonious holistic unity. Pollution leaks from it, externalities flow from it. Circularity is a virtue more honoured in the breach than it is in the observance. Pluralism is under constant pressure from the march of homogeneous, intensive industrialised farming, and from governments imposing or incentivising a small number of systems for cultivation, manufacture and distribution. Large companies dominate every sector of the food economy, their hegemony pushing out the plurality of small and local actors. Instead of being resourceful, we are depleting resources. Technology is too often rejected out of hand, as in the case of gene editing, or adopted too hastily and too much, as has been the case with synthetic fertilisers, broad-spectrum herbicides, insecticides and antibiotics. No honest observer could call the dominant systems of animal farming humane. It is too often pure doublespeak to talk of animal 'husbandry', given that word's association with care. Equitability is just as elusive, with farmers the world over receiving a pittance for crops and animal products that make retailers and manufacturers rich and provide cheap food for consumers living much more comfortable lifestyles. And no one could say that the food world is foodcentric when all the while it is built around trade in commodities, healthy eating advice is based on nutrients, and in many countries only a minority of meals are prepared with fresh, whole ingredients.

If the seven principles were followed, we would see major changes. We would have much higher standards of animal welfare. The power of large businesses to shape the food world in their own interests rather than in those of humankind would be curbed. The externalities of the food system would be properly measured and either paid for or not allowed to occur in the first place. Every country would have a proper land use framework to achieve the right balance between agricultural productivity, conservation and regeneration. Our diets would shift away from highly processed foods made from commodities towards ones based on whole foods. Farmers and farm labourers would receive a much fairer share of the price paid by consumers. And every citizen would have not only a voice in how the food world was shaped, but real power to use it.

Reshaping the food world will not be easy. Tara Garnett talks of 'a kind of unholy cycle between governments, corporates, and us – citizens and consumers in our different incarnations. There are politicians saying "we're not going to do anything because no one's going to vote for them"; corporates saying "we need a level playing field and if we do X then everyone's going to go to our competitors instead and we will lose out"; and then consumers saying *"they*, the government, have to do something." How do you break that cycle? The only answer I have is the answer that everyone will give you, which is that you need people with a certain courage and vision. It's giving people something to believe in and a reason for doing something.'

Henry Dimbleby also sees the scale of the challenge, saying, 'If there was an obvious win–win solution, it would have happened by now. There are economic forces, there are cultural forces which are shaped by but also shape the economics, and then there's just inertia in the system, which is a really powerful force. To change our way of thinking about food involves broad scale things like breaking down corporate power, changing the incentives, getting government to have a vision, changing our entire work–life balance, changing our whole attitude to food, changing our educational system, changing trading relations, and so on and so on.'

But we should not fall into fatalism. As Dimbleby says, history shows that 'our food culture changes wildly all the time and it's a mistake to think that somehow just because you're in a certain system you need to be stuck there'.

Too many calls for change are utopian, requiring a wholesale shift of values that is not going to happen. If healing the food world depends on the downfall of global capitalism, near-universal adoption of organic farming, everyone going vegan, all animal proteins coming from bioreactors, people losing their taste for 'bliss point' foods or the dismantling of large food corporations, then we are already lost. Fortunately, we do not need to tear the whole system down and start again. Positive change depends only on people recognising that the values we already hold are discordant with the food system that we have and that values and practices can be brought into harmony by a series of adjustments, some radical, but all ad hoc and doable. The will for change and the possibility for change can converge, join forces and transform how the world eats for the better.

Notes

Introduction

1 FAO (2018), p. 1
2 Dimbleby (2023), p. 19
3 Sellars (1962), p. 35
4 FAO, IFAD, UNICEF, WFP and WHO (2023), p. 27
5 WHO (2021)
6 www.worldpopulationreview.com/country-rankings/obesity-rates-by-country (accessed 30 November 2023)
7 Pickett et al. (2005)
8 United Nations Department of Economic and Social Affairs, Population Division (2022)
9 FAO (2016), p. 10
10 Crippa et al. (2021)
11 Benton et al. (2021)
12 Whiting (2022); Council for Agricultural Science and Technology (2022), p. 34
13 Kraamwinkel et al. (2021)
14 FAO (2020) p. 110
15 www.gov.uk/government/publications/water-stressed-areas-2021-classification (accessed 30 November 2023)
16 Krebs (2013), p. 96
17 Lang et al. (2009), p. 298

1 The hunter-gatherers

1 Brundtland (1987)
2 Crittenden et al. (2017a)
3 www.hsph.harvard.edu/nutritionsource/healthy-weight/diet-reviews/paleo-diet (accessed 30 November 2023)
4 Warinner (2019)
5 Lederberg and McCray (2001)
6 Ungar et al. (2008)
7 Smits et al. (2017)
8 DiGiulio (2023)
9 Marlowe et al. (2014)
10 Berbesque & Marlowe (2009); Berbesque et al. (2011)
11 Hawkes et al. (2001)
12 Marshall (1961)
13 Paley (2014)
14 Benenson (2014)
15 Borgerhoff Mulder (2017)
16 Margulis & Sagan (1987)
17 GfK (2015)

2 The outliers

1 Oiye et al. (2009)
2 Ho et al. (1972)
3 Oiye et al. (2009)
4 Gadsby & Steele (2004)
5 Jenkinson (2020)
6 Fediuk (2000)
7 Kuhnlein et al. (2009)
8 Popkin (2002)
9 Oiye et al. (2009)
10 Bjerregaard et al. (2003)
11 Munch-Andersen et al. (2012)
12 Galvin et al. (2015)
13 Bjerregaard et al. (2003)
14 Borré (1991)
15 Bowman (2016)
16 King (1911) p. 16
17 Ohta (1987)
18 www.maasai-association.org/maasai.html (accessed 30 November 2023)
19 Quammen (2021)

20 Århem (1989)

21 Baggini (2012)

22 Tybur et al. (2016)

23 Talhelm et al. (2014)

3 Humanity's greatest mistake?

1 Rapsomanikis (2015)

2 https://data.worldbank.org/indicator/SP.RUR.TOTL.ZS?locations=BT (accessed 30 November 2023)

3 www.nationalcouncil.bt/en/content/constitution_of_bhutan (accessed 30 November 2023)

4 https://worldhappiness.report/about (accessed 30 November 2023)

5 https://ourworldindata.org/grapher/share-people-vaccinated-covid?country=CUB~USA~OWID_WRL~BTN~CAN~GBR (accessed 30 November 2023)

6 Helliwell et al. (2019)

7 Diamond (1999)

8 Cohen (1989)

9 O'Connell (2009)

10 Crittenden et al. (2017b)

11 O'Connell (2009)

12 Shrestha et al. (2021)

13 World Bank Group (2017)

14 World Bank (2023)

15 Wangda & Wangdi (2021)

16 Kinga (2008)

17 Ritchie (2021b)

18 Food Corporation of Bhutan (2022)

19 Tshering (2023)

20 von Bernstorff & Sangay (2017)

21 Lorenzen (2019)

22 Lorenzen & von Bernstorff (2019)

23 World Food Programme (2022a)

24 World Food Programme (2022b)

4 The intensive turn

1 www.atlasbig.com/en-us/countries-tomato-production (accessed 30 November 2023)

2 van der Heide et al. (2011)

3 Statistics Netherlands (2017)

4 World Bank (2022)
5 Krebs (2013), p. 92; Brassley & Soffe (2016), p. 92
6 Krebs (2013), p. 92
7 Standage (2009), p. 216, p. 232
8 https://themansholtletter.hetnieuweinstituut.nl/sites/default/files/brief_
   mansholt_malfatti_en1.pdf (accessed 30 November 2023)
9 Quist (2023)
10 VPRO World Stories (2017)
11 Viviano (2017)
12 IPPC Secretariat (2021)
13 Brassley & Soffe (2016), p. 25, Mesnage et al. (2021)
14 The Royal Society (2009)
15 BBC Television (2023)
16 https://leaf.eco/farming/ifm (accessed 30 November 2023)
17 Westerman (1999)
18 Compson (2022)
19 Nordhaus, T. & Shah, S. (2022)
20 Cusworth & Garnett (2022)
21 www.fao.org/conservation-agriculture (accessed 30 November 2023)
22 Viviano (2017)

5 From food to commodity

1 www.researchandmarkets.com/report/cocoa-processing (accessed 30
   November 2023)
2 ICCO (2023)
3 Bhutada (2020)
4 Bentley (2023)
5 Hotel Chocolat (2020)
6 Higonnet et al. (2017)
7 FAO & US Department of Agriculture (2023)
8 Page (2022)
9 WHO & FAO (2002) pp. 1–2
10 USDA Consultative Group (2010), p. 9
11 Whoriskey & Siegel (2019), Whoriskey (2019), Mufson (2019)
12 *The Economist* (2022a)

6 Hard labour

1 Laing (2017), p. 26
2 Slave Voyages (2020)
3 BBC Bitesize (2023), Standage (2009), p. 115

4 Lodhi (2015)
5 Brode (1907), Ali (2022)
6 Standage (2009), p. 94
7 Sheriff (1987) pp. 2, 35, 48
8 Brode (1907), p. 109
9 Brode (1907), p. 12
10 Stanley (1961) 7 November 1876
11 Brode (1907), p. 12
12 Gates (2017)
13 Lodhi (2015)
14 Glover (2014)
15 New American Economy Research Fund (2021)
16 Jones & Awokoya (2023)
17 Dumpis (2001)
18 McAndrew (2022)
19 International Labour Organization et al. (2022)
20 Jones & Awokoya (2023)
21 https://makechocolatefair.org/en/probleme/child-labour-cocoa-farming (accessed 30 November 2023)
22 Eurostat (2020)
23 Bentham (1843)
24 Pendergrast (2011), www.macrotrends.net/2535/coffee-prices-historical-chart-data (accessed 30 November 2023)
25 Fairtrade Foundation, personal correspondence
26 Scott et al. (2008)
27 Fairtrade Foundation, personal correspondence

7 The big business of food

1 Speed & Murray (2023)
2 Friedmann & McMichael (1989)
3 Table Debates (2023)
4 Nestle (2013), ch. 8 & 9
5 Guerrera (2009)
6 *Ford Times* (1916), p. 106
7 Friedman (1962), p. 110
8 Guerrera (2009)
9 https://ourworldindata.org/grapher/daily-per-capita-caloric-supply (accessed 30 November 2023)
10 Lang et al. (2009), p. 114
11 Lang et al. (2009), p. 3
12 Nestle (2013), p. 4

13 *The Economist* (2014)
14 Macpherson et al. (1999)
15 *The Economist* (2019)
16 *The Economist* (2022d)
17 Morrison (2022)
18 *The Economist* (2022c)
19 Bris (2021)
20 www.nestle.com/about/how-we-do-business/purpose-values (accessed 30 November 2023)
21 Evans (2021)
22 https://betterchicken.org.uk/better-chicken-commitment (accessed 30 November 2023)
23 BBC News (2019)
24 https://bostonteaparty.co.uk/blog/post.php?s=another-plea-for-conscious-sipping (accessed 30 November 2023)
25 Talman (2023)
26 *The Economist* (2022c)
27 Harford (2005)
28 Baggini (2014) p. 124
29 Bauer (2019)
30 Canning (2022)
31 Nestle (2013), p. 111
32 Dimbleby & Lewis (2023), p. 47
33 WHO (2023)
34 Biscourp et al. (2013)
35 Edge by Ascential (2021)

8 Who governs?

1 Gaidar (2007)
2 *The Economist* (2022b)
3 Jones et al. (2023)
4 United Nations (1945)
5 General Agreement on Tariffs and Trade (1986)
6 General Agreement on Tariffs and Trade (1986) Article XI
7 Pearce & Sharma (2000)
8 Brundtland (1987)
9 WTO (1995)
10 Vidal (2017)
11 Euractiv (2006)
12 Hoekman et al. (2008)
13 Bartholomeusz (2019)

14 Larch (2022)
15 Economist Impact (2021), Economist Impact (2022)
16 FAO (2008)
17 FAO (2012a), p. 36
18 Bailey & Wellesley (2017)
19 Dimbleby & Lewis (2023), p. 17
20 Ministry of Agriculture and Forestry of Finland (2017), p. 5
21 Forbes (accessed 21 November 2023)
22 World Bank (2020)
23 GEM (2022)
24 Pro Luomu (2023)
25 Statista (2023)
26 Finnish National Agency for Education (accessed 21 November 2023)
27 Finnish National Agency for Education (2019)
28 City of Helsinki, Education Division (2019)
29 Laitinen et al. (2021)
30 Siegel (2016)
31 McClure (2021)
32 Finnish National Agency for Education (2019)
33 Väärikkälä et al. (2019)
34 FAO (2019)
35 MUFPP (2015)
36 Calancie et al. (2018)
37 OECD (2021), pp. 162–64
38 Arisoy et all (2023)
39 Coulson & Sonnino (2019)
40 Schiff et al. (2022)
41 Brons et al. (2022)

9 Culture and identity

1 https://terroni.co.uk (accessed 30 November 2023)
2 Vigna (2023)
3 Wilson (2015)
4 Loreti (2023)
5 Århem (1989)
6 Borré (1991)
7 Kuhnlein et al. (2009)
8 Lopez-Ridaura et al. (2021)
9 Bender (2014), p. 80
10 Carlile et al. (2021)
11 La Via Campesina (2021)

12 www.wfp.org/wfp-food-basket (accessed 30 November 2023)
13 www.unrefugees.org/news/refugee-camps-explained (accessed 30 November 2023)
14 Mehelin (2022)
15 Snowdon (2019b), Snowdon (2019c)
16 Thapa (2021)
17 Sarma (2021)
18 UNHCR (2022)
19 Thakral (2018)
20 duBois (2020)
21 Snowdon (2019a)
22 Brillat-Savarin (1825) Prolegemona
23 Ringquist et al. (2016)
24 Curtis et al. (2021)
25 Euromonitor International (2021)

Taking Stock: Towards a Global Food Philosophy

1 Sen (2009)

10 From extensive grazing to exploded chickens

1 OECD (2023a)
2 Cook (2023)
3 Watts et al. (2016)
4 Gutman (2018), Misculin (2008)
5 FAO (2017)
6 Missouri Coalition for the Environment (2019)
7 Colley & Wasley (2022)
8 Wakabayashi & Fu (2023)
9 Farm Animal Welfare Council (2009)
10 www.ciwf.org.uk/your-food/meat-poultry/veal (accessed 30 November 2023)
11 www.ufaw.org.uk/why-ufaws-work-is-important/lameness (accessed 30 November 2023), https://ahdb.org.uk/knowledge-library/lameness-in-dairy-cows (accessed 30 November 2023)
12 www.ciwf.org.uk/factory-farming/animal-cruelty (accessed 30 November 2023)
13 FoodIndustry.com (2022)
14 McKay (2021)
15 Gerber et al. (2013)
16 Rossi (2015)
17 Valdes (2022)

18 Rossi (2015)

19 www.worldwildlife.org/industries/soy (accessed 30 November 2023)

20 Rossi (2015)

21 FAO (2012b)

22 www.worldwildlife.org/places/cerrado (accessed 30 November 2023)

23 Castaño-Sánchez et al. (2021)

24 OECD (2023b)

25 Garcia et al. (2021)

26 WWF (2021)

27 WWF (2020)

28 *The Economist* (2010)

29 https://en.unesco.org/biosphere/lac/cerrado (accessed 30 November 2023)

30 FAO (2022a)

31 Ritchie (2017)

32 Chemnitz & Becheva (2014)

33 Ritchie (2021a)

34 Chang et al. (2021)

35 Krebs (2013), p. 109

36 CLEAR Center (2021)

37 Authority for Consumers and Markets (2015)

38 Gibson (2020)

39 https://corporate.marksandspencer.com/media/press-releases/ms-becomes-first-national-retailer-offer-new-entry-tier-offer-higher-welfare-0 (accessed 30 November 2023)

40 Reuters (2021), Deutsche Welle (2021)

41 Animal Equality (2022)

42 Heyden (2015)

43 Chicken Welfare Hub (2022)

44 Accurity (2022)

45 Britton (2022)

46 Siddique (2023)

47 VPRO World Stories (2017)

48 Willett et al. (2019)

49 U.S. Department of Agriculture & U.S. Department of Health and Human Services (2020)

50 McManus (2023)

11 Out of the blue

1 FAO (2022b), p. 43

2 Rabanal (1988) ch. 2

3 FAO (2005)

4 Ritchie (2019); FAO (2022b), p. 26
5 Mood et al. (2023)
6 FAO (2022b)
7 Oceana in the UK (2023)
8 Minderoo Foundation (2021)
9 FAO (2022b)
10 South Florida PBS (2017)
11 Naylor et al. (2021a)
12 https://ourworldindata.org/grapher/fish-and-seafood-consumption-per-capita?tab=table (accessed 30 November 2023)
13 FAO (2022b)
14 Blaxter & Garnett (2022)
15 Mood et al. (2023)
16 www.ciwf.org.uk/farm-animals/fish/fish-welfare/ (accessed 30 November 2023)
17 Just Economics (2021), p. 9
18 Thorstad & Finstad (2018)
19 Just Economics (2021)
20 South Florida PBS (2017)
21 https://prod.seafoodwatch.org/recommendation/cobia/cobia-39613?species=295 (accessed 30 November 2023)
22 Fry et al. (2018)
23 Pradeep (2020)
24 Fry et al. (2018)
25 Naylor et al. (2021b)
26 Marine Stewardship Council (2023)
27 www.wwf.org.uk/what-we-do/aquaculture (accessed 1 December 2023)
28 DeWeerdt (2017)
29 Singer (2015)
30 Mohsen & Yang (2021)
31 Harvard Health (2015)
32 Wilson (2023)
33 Lang (2020), p. 211
34 https://uk.oceana.org/our-campaigns/habitat-protection (accessed 4 December 2023)
35 McVeigh (2021)
36 Sala et al. (2021)
37 www.worldwildlife.org/threats/bycatch (accessed 4 December 2023)
38 Davies et al. (2009)

12 Animals at the crossroads

1 Vergeer et al. (2021)
2 Impossible Foods (2021)
3 Fassler (2021)
4 Vergeer et al. (2021)
5 Southey (2021)
6 Garrison et al. (2022)
7 Humbird (2021)
8 Vallone & Lambin (2023)
9 Parts of this section are adapted from Baggini (2021)
10 Hume (1748) §9
11 Animal Welfare (Sentience) Act (2022)
12 Department for Environment, Food and Rural Affairs (2021)
13 Rosenfeld & Burrow (2017)
14 Bentham (1789) Chapter 17
15 Arhem (1989)

13 Unnatural borne killers

1 Adam (2022), https://covid19.who.int (accessed 4 December 2023)
2 Worobey et al. (2022)
3 Pekar et al. (2022)
4 Tedros (2023)
5 Council for Agricultural Science and Technology (2022)
6 Kappelle et al. (2020)
7 Hewings-Martin (2020)
8 https://covid19.who.int (accessed 4 December 2023)
9 Council for Agricultural Science and Technology (2022)
10 Ibid
11 Ibid
12 Rohr et al. (2019)
13 Kappelle et al. (2020)
14 Dawood et al. (2012)
15 Bar-On et al. (2018)
16 Council for Agricultural Science and Technology (2022)
17 Ibid
18 www.who.int/news-room/fact-sheets/detail/brucellosis (accessed 4 December 2023)
19 https://marlerclark.com/news_events/the-long-term-physical-effects-of-campylobacter (accessed 4 December 2023)
20 UK Health Security Agency (2023)

21 Council for Agricultural Science and Technology (2022)
22 Kappelle et al. (2020)
23 Council for Agricultural Science and Technology (2022)
24 Carlile & Garnett (2021)
25 www.fao.org/agroecology/knowledge/definitions/en (accessed 4 December 2023)
26 Carrefour (2018)
27 Carlile & Garnett (2021)
28 One Health High Level Expert Panel (2023)

Taking Stock: Towards a Global Food Philosophy

1 Boztas & Penna (2022)

14 Editing nature

1   IFOAM (2017)
2   Soil Association (2023)
3   The Royal Society (2016), FDA (2022)
4   Krebs (2013), p. 53
5   Guyton et al. (2015)
6   BBC News (2018), Cohen (2020)
7   Steen, Juliette (2019)
8   Krebs (2013), p. 52
9   Asafu-Adjaye et al. (2015)
10 Deconinck (2019)
11 OECD (2018)
12 Johnson (2020)
13 Verhaag (2009)
14 Katiraee (2021a, 2021b)
15 The Royal Society (2016)
16 https://worldpopulationreview.com/country-rankings/countries-that-ban-gmos. (accessed 4 December 2023)
17 Ministry of Agriculture and Forestry of Finland (2017)
18 Johnson & Lucey (2006)
19 Regis (2019a)
20 Regis (2019b)
21 Cotter (2013)
22 Lobbywatch (2004), Science in Society (2006)
23 Church (2016)
24 Secretariat of the Convention on Biological Diversity (2000)
25 United Nations Department of Economic and Social Affairs (1992)
    Principle 15

26 www.nobelprize.org/prizes/chemistry/2020/prize-announcement (accessed 4 December 2023)
27 Massel (2023), Poppy (2021)
28 Garnett et al. (2017)
29 FAO (2022c)
30 Patron & Price (2021)
31 Poppy (2021)
32 Monaco (2019)
33 Payton (2022)
34 IFOAM (2017)
35 FAO (2022c)

15 The waste lands

1 Misiak et al. (2018)
2 Economist Intelligence Unit (2012)
3 United Nations Environment Programme (2012)
4 Willett et al. (2019)
5 Flanagan et al. (2019)
6 United Nations Environment Programme (2012)
7 Flanagan et al. (2019)
8 Roser et al. (2013)
9 Flanagan et al. (2019)
10 Qu et al. (2021)
11 Ojina (2021)
12 Rodionova (2017)
13 Department for Environment, Food & Rural Affairs (2018), Mason (2022)
14 CNN (2017)
15 WRAP (2023), Flanagan et al. (2019)
16 Uba, Estelle (2023)
17 Kessler & Brock (2022)
18 Solomon et al. (2021)
19 FAO (2023), p. 21
20 Food and Land Use Coalition (2019)
21 Saltzman et al. (2019)
22 Lang (2020), p. 244
23 Williams et al. (2020)
24 Williams & Wikström (2011)
25 King (1911), p. 34
26 Effersøe (2023)

16 Dietary engineering

1 Nunley (2019)
2 www.spacefoundation.org/space_technology_hal/micro-algae-nutritional-supplements-and-products-from-space-research (accessed 4 December 2023)
3 Krebs (2013), p. 28
4 Wall (2020)
5 Musk (2023)
6 Reynolds (2016)
7 Scrinis (2013), p. 6
8 Albert et al. (2013)
9 University of Birmingham (2018), Goldacre (2008)
10 Barabási et al. (2019)
11 https://soylent.com (accessed 5 December 2023)
12 Oatman (2012)
13 Fitzsimmons (2011)
14 Nestle (2013), p. 315
15 Scrinis (2013), p. 36
16 www.unilever.com/planet-and-society/positive-nutrition/strategy-and-goals (accessed 5 December 2023)
17 Scrinis (2013), p. 8
18 Ibid. p.107
19 www.innit.com/nutrition/entenmanns-fudge-brownie/p/00072030009858 (accessed 5 December 2023)
20 SkyQuest Technology (2023)
21 https://joinzoe.com/results-reviews (accessed 5 December 2023)
22 Bermingham et al. (2023)
23 Lang (2020), p. 13
24 Scrinis (2013), p. 78

17 The good, the bad and the processed

1 https://impossiblefoods.com/gb-en/products/sausage (accessed 5 December 2023)
2 Mordor Intelligence (2018)
3 Horsford (1861)
4 List (2006)
5 Scrinis (2013), p. 135
6 Parmentier (2007)
7 WHO (2018)
8 Bardhan et at (2021)
9 Baker et al. (2020)
10 Pagliai et al. (2020)

11 Elizabeth et al. (2020)
12 Hall et al. (2019)
13 Monteiro et al. (2019)
14 Loth (2020)
15 https://world.openfoodfacts.org/nova (accessed 6 December 2023)
16 Braesco et al. (2022)
17 Monteiro et al. (2017)
18 O'Dowd (2017)
19 Lang et al. (2009), p. 157
20 Fraanje & Garnett (2019)
21 Srour & Touvier (2021)
22 Sellem et al. (2023)
23 Teo et al. (2022)
24 Gibney et al. (2017)
25 Adams & White (2015)
26 Martínez Steele et al. (2017)
27 Khosla Ventures (2022)
28 Fraanje & Garnett (2019)
29 Cordova et al. (2023)
30 Holmes et al. (2012)
31 Lockyer & Spiro (2020)
32 Taneri et al. (2022)
33 Science Media Centre (2023)
34 Scientific Advisory Committee on Nutrition (2023)
35 Blomhoff et al. (2023)
36 Ministry of Health of Brazil (2015)

Taking Stock: Towards a Global Food Philosophy

1 Hume (1748) §10.1

Conclusion: A Global Food Philosophy

1 Sonnino et al. (2018)
2 Brassley & Soffe (2016), p. 13
3 Giller (2023)
4 Kessler & Brock (2021)
5 Standage (2009), p. 237
6 Pollan (2008)
7 Brillat-Savarin (1825) Prolegomena
8 Baggini (2014) ch. 10
9 Food Ethics Council (2010)

References

Accurity (2022) 'Swiss referendum results on key issues', 26 September. www.accurity.ch/2022/09/26/swiss-referendum-voters-support-ahv-reforms-reject-farming-and-withholding-tax-reforms/

Adam, David (2022) 'The pandemic's true death toll: Millions more than official counts', *Nature*, 601, pp. 312–15. doi.org/10.1038/d41586-022-00104-8.

Adams, Jean and White, Martin (2015) 'Characterisation of UK diets according to degree of food processing and associations with socio-demographics and obesity: Cross-sectional analysis of UK National Diet and Nutrition Survey (2008–12)', *International Journal of Behavioral Nutrition and Physical Activity*, 12, p. 160. doi.org/10.1186/s12966-015-0317-y.

Albert, B., Cameron-Smith, D., Hofman, P. and Cutfield, W. (2013) 'Oxidation of marine omega-3 supplements and human health', *BioMed Research International*, 2013, 464921. doi.org/10.1155/2013/464921.

Ali, Adam (2022) *Zanj revolt in the Abbasid Caliphate*. Oxford: Oxford University Press.

Animal Equality (2022) 'Italy bans the killing of male chicks in an effort led by animal equality', *Animal*

Equality, 4 August. https://animalequality.org/news/
italy-bans-the-killing-of-male-chicks/

Animal Welfare (Sentience) Act 2022. c.20. www.legislation.gov.uk/
ukpga/2022/22/enacted

Arhem, Kaj (1989) 'Maasai food symbolism: The cultural
connotations of milk, meat, and blood in the pastoral maasai
diet', *Anthropos: International Review of Anthropology and
Linguistics*, 84, pp. 1–23. jstor.org/stable/40461671

Arisoy, Elmas, Leipoldkouami, Knut J. and Messam, Koumi
Hounsinou (2023) 'The expanding role of public procurement
in Africa's economic development', *World Bank*, 17 January.
https://blogs.worldbank.org/governance/expanding-role-public-
procurement-africas-economic-development

Asafu-Adjaye, J., Blomqvist, L., Brand, S., Brook, B., DeFries, R., Ellis,
E., Foreman, C., Keith, D., Lewis, M., Lynas, M., Nordhaus, T.,
Pielke, R., Pritzker, R., Roy, J., Sagoff, M., Shellenberger, M.,
Stone, R. and Teague, P. (2015) 'An Ecomodernist Manifesto',
Ecomodernism.org. doi.org/10.13140/RG.2.1.1974.0646

Authority for Consumers and Markets (2015) 'Industry-wide
arrangements for the so-called Chicken of Tomorrow
restrict competition', *Netherlands Authority for Consumers and
Markets (ACM)*, 26 January. www.acm.nl/en/publications/
publication/13761/Industry-wide-arrangements-for-the-so-
called-Chicken-of-Tomorrow-restrict-competition

Baggini, Julian (2012) 'Patricia Churchland, the really nice guy
materialist, interview', *Philosophers' Magazine*, 57, 2nd quarter,
pp. 60–70.

Baggini, Julian (2014) *The virtues of the table*. London: Granta.

Baggini, Julian (2021) 'Of beasts and men', *New Humanist*, winter.
https://newhumanist.org.uk/articles/5891/of-beasts-and-men

Bailey, Rob and Wellesley, Laura (2017) 'Chokepoints
and vulnerabilities in global food trade',
Chatham House. www.chathamhouse.org/2017/06/
chokepoints-and-vulnerabilities-global-food-trade-0/
executive-summary

Baker, P., Machado, P., Santos, T., Sievert, K., Backholer, K.,

Hadjikakou, M., Russell, C., Huse, O., Bell, A., Scrinis, G., Worsley, A., Friel, S. and Lawrence, M. (2020) 'Ultra-processed foods and the nutrition transition: Global, regional and national trends, food systems transformations and political economy drivers', *Obesity Reviews*, 21. doi.org/10.1111/obr.13126

Barabási, A., Menichetti, G. and Loscalzo, J. (2019) 'The unmapped chemical complexity of our diet', *Nature Food*, 1. doi.org/10.1038/s43016-019-0005-1.

Bardhan, P., Deka, A., Bhattacharya, S. S., Mandal, M. and Kataki, R. (2022) 'Economical aspect in biomass to biofuel production'. doi.org/10.1016/B978-0-12-824388-6.00003-8, in Suzana Yusup and Nor Adilla Rashidi (eds) (2021) *Value-chain of biofuels*. San Diego: Elsevier.

Bar-On, Y., Phillips, R. and Milo, R. (2018) 'The biomass distribution on Earth', *Proceedings of the National Academy of Sciences*, 115, 201711842. doi.org/10.1073/pnas.1711842115.

Bartholomeusz, Stephen (2019) 'Trump is threatening to blow up the WTO – and potentially cause anarchy', *Sydney Morning Herald*, 19 November. www.smh.com.au/business/markets/trump-is-threatening-to-blow-up-the-wto-and-potentially-cause-anarchy-20191119-p53bxw.html

Bauer, Joanne (2019) 'Can benefit corporations fix what's wrong with business and human rights?' *Rights CoLab*, 5 January. https://rightscolab.org/do-benefit-corporations-respect-human-rights

BBC Bitesize (2023) 'The transatlantic slave trade overview'. www.bbc.co.uk/bitesize/topics/z2qj6sg/articles/zfkfn9q

BBC News (2018) 'Monsanto ordered to pay $289m damages in Roundup cancer trial', *BBC News*, 11 August. www.bbc.co.uk/news/world-us-canada-45152546

BBC News (2019) 'Coffee cup ban: Boston Tea Party's sales fall by £250k', *BBC News*, 2 April. www.bbc.co.uk/news/uk-england-bristol-47629820

BBC Television (2023) *Saving our Wild Isles*.

Bender, David A. (2014) *Nutrition: A very short introduction*. Oxford: Oxford University Press.

Benenson, B. (dir.) (2014) *The Hadza: Last of the First* (Film). Benenson Productions.

Bentham, Jeremy (1789) *An introduction to the principles of morals and legislation*. London: T. Payne.

Bentham, Jeremy (1843) 'Anarchical fallacies', in *The works of Jeremy Bentham*, vol. 2. Edinburgh: William Tait.

Bentley, Scott (2023) 'The forgotten origin', *Caffeine*, 51.

Benton, T., Bieg, C., Harwatt, H., Wellesley, L. and Pudasaini, R. (2021) 'Food system impacts on biodiversity loss: Three levers for food system transformation in support of nature', *Chatham House*. doi.org/10.13140/RG.2.2.34045.28640.

Berbesque, J. C. and Marlowe, F. W. (2009) 'Sex differences in food preferences of Hadza hunter-gatherers', *Evolutionary Psychology*, 7(4), pp. 601–16. doi. org/10.1177/147470490900700409

Berbesque. J. C., Marlowe, F.W. and Crittenden, A. N. (2011) 'Sex differences in Hadza eating frequency by food type', *American Journal of Human Biology*, May–June 23(3), pp. 339–45. doi. org/10.1002/ajhb.21139

Bermingham, K. M., Linenberg, I., Polidori, L., Wolf, J., Bulsiewicz, W. J., Spector, T. D. and Berry, S. E. (2023) 'Improved cardiometabolic health using a personalised nutrition approach: The ZOE Method Study', *Proceedings*, 91(1), p. 55. doi.org/10.3390/proceedings2023091055

Bhutada, Govind (2020) 'Cocoa's bittersweet supply chain in one visualization', *World Economic Forum*, 4 November. www.weforum.org/agenda/2020/11/cocoa-chocolate-supply-chain-business-bar-africa-exports/

Biscourp, Pierre, Boutin, Xavier and Vergé, Thibaud (2013) 'The effects of retail regulations on prices: Evidence from the Loi Galland', *Economic Journal*, 123(573), pp. 1279–1312. doi. org/10.1111/ecoj.12045

Bjerregaard, Peter, Young, Kue and Hegele, Robert (2003) 'Low incidence of cardiovascular disease among the Inuit: What is the evidence?' *Atherosclerosis*, 166, pp. 351–7. doi.org/10.1016/S0021-9150(02)00364-7

Blaxter, Tamsin and Garnett, Tara (2022) 'Primed for power: A short cultural history of protein', *TABLE* (University of Oxford, Swedish University of Agricultural Sciences and Wageningen University and Research). doi.org/10.56661/ba271ef5

Blomhoff, R., Andersen, R., Arnesen, E., Christensen, J., Eneroth, H., Erkkola, M., Gudanaviciene, I., Halldorsson, T., Høyer-Lund, A., Lemming, E., Meltzer, H., Pitsi, T., Schwab, U., Siksna, I., Thorsdottir, I. and Trolle, E. (2023) *Nordic nutrition recommendations 2023.* doi.org/10.6027/nord2023-003

Borgerhoff Mulder, M. (2017) 'Review of *Demography and evolutionary ecology of hadza hunter-gatherers* by Nicholas Blurton Jones', *Human Nature*, 28, 117–127. doi.org/10.1007/s12110-016-9280-9

Borré, Kristen (1991) 'Seal blood, Inuit blood, and diet: A biocultural model of physiology and cultural identity', *Medical Anthropology Quarterly*, 5, pp. 48–62. doi.org/10.1525/maq.1991.5.1.02a00080

Bowman, David (2016) 'Aboriginal fire management: Part of the solution to destructive bushfires', *The Conversation*, 22 February. https://theconversation.com/aboriginal-fire-management-part-of-the-solution-to-destructive-bushfires-55032

Boztas, Senay and Penna, Dominic (2022) 'Oat milk producers accused of hypocrisy over selling byproducts as animal feed', *Daily Telegraph*, 5 December. www.telegraph.co.uk/world-news/2022/12/05/oat-milk-producers-accused-hypocrisy-selling-byproducts-animal/

Braesco, V., Souchon, I., Sauvant, P., Haurogné, T., Maillot, M., Féart, C. and Darmon, N. (2022) 'Ultra-processed foods: How functional is the NOVA system?' *European Journal of Clinical Nutrition*, 76, pp. 1–9. doi.org/10.1038/s41430-022-01099-1

Brassley, Paul and Soffe, Richard (2016) *Agriculture: A very short introduction.* Oxford: Oxford University Press.

Brillat-Savarin, Jean Anthelme (1825/1990) *The physiology of taste*, trans. Anne Drayton. London: Penguin.

Bris, Arturo (2021) 'Danone's CEO has been ousted for being progressive: Blame society not activist shareholders', *The Conversation*, 19 March. https://theconversation.com/danones-ceo-has-been-ousted-for-being-progressive-blame-society-not-activist-shareholders-157383

Britton, Cordelia (2022) 'Judicial review challenging using frankenchickens granted', *The Humane League UK*, 23 September. https://thehumaneleague.org.uk/article/judicial-review-challenging-the-use-of-frankenchickens-granted

Brode, Heinrich (1907) *Tippoo Tib: The story of his career in Central Africa*. London: Edward Arnold.

Brons, Anke, Oosterveer, Peter and Wertheim-Heck, Sigrid (2022) 'In- and exclusion in urban food governance: Exploring networks and power in the city of Almere', *Journal of Environmental Policy & Planning*, 24, pp. 1–17. doi.org/10.1080/1523908X.2022.2057936

Brundtland, G. H. (1987) *Our common future: Report of the World Commission on Environment and Development*. United Nations. https://sustainabledevelopment.un.org/content/documents/5987our-common-future.pdf

Calancie, Larissa, Cooksey-Stowers, Kristen, Palmer, Anne, Frost, Natasha, Calhoun, Holly, Piner, Abbey and Webb, Karen (2018) 'Toward a community impact assessment for Food Policy Councils: Identifying potential impact domains', *Journal of Agriculture, Food Systems, and Community Development*, 8, pp. 1–14. doi.org/10.5304/jafscd.2018.083.001

Canning, Anna (2022) 'Nespresso: Known for human rights violations, now B Corp certified', *Fair World Project*, 4 May. https://fairworldproject.org/b-corp-nespresso-human-rights/

Carlile, Rachel and Garnett, Tara (2021) 'What is agroecology?' TABLE Explainer Series. *TABLE* (University of Oxford, Swedish University of Agricultural Sciences and Wageningen University & Research). doi.org/10.56661/96cf1b98

Carlile, R., Kessler, M. and Garnett, T. (2021) 'What is food sovereignty?' TABLE Explainer Series. *TABLE* (University of Oxford, Swedish University of Agricultural Sciences and

Wageningen University & Research). www.tabledebates.org/building-blocks/food-sovereignty

Carrefour (2018) 'What is agroecology?' *Carrefour*, 22 February. www.carrefour.com/en/news/what-agroecology

Castaño-Sánchez, J. P., Izaurralde, C. and Haynes, K. (2021) 'Conversion of grassland to cropland is increasing carbon emissions', *NASA Harvest*, 23 August. www.nasaharvest.org/news/conversion-grassland-cropland-increasing-carbon-emissions

Chang, J., Ciais, P., Gasser, T., Smith, P., Herrero, M., Havlík, P., Obersteiner, M., Guenet, B., Goll, D., Li, W., Naipal, V., Peng, S., Qiu, C., Tian, H., Viovy, N., Yue, C. and Zhu, D. (2021) 'Climate warming from managed grasslands cancels the cooling effect of carbon sinks in sparsely grazed and natural grasslands', *Nature Communications*, 12. doi.org/10.1038/s41467-020-20406-7

Chemnitz, C. and Becheva, S. (eds) (2014) *The meat atlas*. Heinrich Böll Foundation/Friends of the Earth Europe. https://cz.boell.org/sites/default/files/meat_atlas2014.pdf

Chicken Welfare Hub (2022) 'Chicken welfare hub focuses on longevity of hens', *VIV Europe*. www.viveurope.nl/about/viv-europe-22-theme/huborange-chickenwelfarehub/

Church, George (2016) 'The augmented human being', *Edge*, 30 March. www.edge.org/conversation/george_church-the-augmented-human-being

City of Helsinki, Education Division (2019) 'Helsinki's curriculum for early childhood education and care', City of Helsinki, Education Division. www.hel.fi/static/liitteet-2019/KasKo/vare/Helsinki_Vasu_EN_Sivut.pdf

CLEAR Center (2021) 'Why methane from cattle warms the climate differently than CO2 from fossil fuels', *CLEAR Center*, 16 November. https://clear.ucdavis.edu/explainers/why-methane-cattle-warms-climate-differently-co2-fossil-fuels

CNN (2017) 'The Danish recipe to cut food waste' [Video], *CNN*, 21 July. https://edition.cnn.com/videos/world/2017/07/21/going-green-selina-juul-food-waste.cnn

Cohen, Mark Nathan (1989) *Health and the rise of civilization*, New Haven, CT: Yale University Press.

Cohen, Patricia (2020) 'Roundup maker to pay $10 billion to settle cancer suits', *New York Times*, 24 June. www.nytimes.com/2020/06/24/business/roundup-settlement-lawsuits.html

Colley, Claire and Wasley, Andrew (2022) 'UK has more than 1,000 livestock mega-farms, investigation reveals', *Guardian*, 18 August. www.theguardian.com/environment/2022/aug/18/uk-has-more-than-1000-livestock-mega-farms-investigation-reveals

Compson, Sarah (2022) 'Bringing down organic by focussing on yields alone, sets us all up to fail', Soil Association, 14 October. www.soilassociation.org/blogs/2022/october/14/bringing-down-organic-by-focussing-on-yields-alone-sets-us-all-up-to-fail/

Cook, Rob (2023) 'World beef consumption: Ranking of countries (USDA)', *Beef2Live*, 28 November. www.beef2live.com/story-world-beef-consumption-ranking-countries-243-106879

Cordova, R., Viallon, V., Fontvieille, E., Peruchet-Noray, L., Jansana, A., Wagner, K., Kyrø, C., Tjønneland, A., Katzke, V., Bajracharya, R., Schulze, M., Masala, G., Sieri, S., Panico, S., Ricceri, F., Tumino, R., Boer, J., Verschuren, W., Schouw, Y. and Freisling, H. (2023) 'Consumption of ultra-processed foods and risk of multimorbidity of cancer and cardiometabolic diseases: A multinational cohort study', *The Lancet Regional Health – Europe*. doi.org/10.1016/j.lanepe.2023.100771

Cotter, Janet (2013) 'Golden illusion: The broken promises of "Golden" Rice', *Greenpeace International*. www.greenpeace.org/static/planet4-international-stateless/2013/10/08786be5-458-golden-illusion-ge-goldenrice.pdf

Coulson, Helen and Sonnino, Roberta (2019) 'Re-scaling the politics of food: Place-based urban food governance in the UK', *Geoforum*, 98. doi.org/10.1016/j.geoforum.2018.11.010

Council for Agricultural Science and Technology (CAST) (2022) *Zoonotic diseases in animal agriculture and beyond: A One Health perspective*. Ames, Iowa: Council for Agricultural Science and Technology.

Crippa, M., Solazzo, E., Guizzardi, D. et al. (2021) 'Food systems are responsible for a third of global anthropogenic GHG emissions', *Nature Food*, 2, pp. 198–209. doi.org/10.1038/s43016-021-00225-9

Crittenden, Alyssa and Schnorr, Stephanie (2017a) 'Current views on hunter-gatherer nutrition and the evolution of the human diet', *American Journal of Physical Anthropology*, 162, e23148. doi.org/10.1002/ajpa.23148

Crittenden, A. N., Sorrentino, J., Moonie, S. A., Peterson, M., Mabulla, A. and Ungar, P. S. (2017b) 'Oral health in transition: The Hadza foragers of Tanzania,' *PloS one*, 12(3), e0172197. doe.org/10.1371/journal.pone.0172197

Curtis, M., Quiring, K., Theofilou, B. and Björnsjö, A. (2021) *Life reimagined: Mapping the motivations that matter for today's consumers.* Accenture. www.accenture.com/content/dam/accenture/final/a-com-migration/custom/_acnmedia/thought-leadership-assets/pdf-4/Accenture-Life-Reimagined-Full-Report.pdf

Cusworth, G. and Garnett, T. (2023) 'What is regenerative agriculture?' *TABLE Debates*, 20 June. www.tabledebates.org/building-blocks/what-is-regenerative-agriculture

Davies, R. W. D., Cripps, S. J., Nickson, A. and Porter, G. (2009) 'Defining and estimating global marine fisheries bycatch', *Marine Policy*, 33(4). doi.org/10.1016/j.marpol.2009.01.003.

Dawood, F., Iuliano, A., Reed, C., Meltzer, M., Shay, D., Cheng, P., Bandaranayake, D., Breiman, R., Brooks, W. A., Buchy, P., Feikin, D., Fowler, K., Gordon, A., Hien, N., Horby, P., Huang, S., Katz, M., Krishnan, A., Xmf, D. and Widdowson, M. (2012) 'Estimated global mortality associated with the first 12 months of 2009 pandemic influenza A H1N1 virus circulation: A modelling study', *Lancet Infectious Diseases*, 12(9), pp. 687–95. doi.org/10.1016/S1473-3099(12)70121-4.

Deconinck, Koen. (2019) 'From Big Six to Big Four: New OECD study sheds light on concentration and competition in seed markets', *Seed World Europe*, 27 February. https://european-seed.com/2019/02/from-big-six-to-big-four-new-oecd-study-

sheds-light-on-concentration-and-competition-in-seed-
markets

Department for Environment, Food & Rural Affairs (2018) 'Gove
appoints Food Waste Champion', 31 December. www.gov.uk/
government/news/gove-appoints-food-waste-champion

Department for Environment, Food and Rural Affairs (2021)
Action Plan for Animal Welfare, 12 May. www.gov.uk/
government/publications/action-plan-for-animal-welfare/
action-plan-for-animal-welfare

Deutsche Welle (2021) 'Germany bans male chick culling
from 2022', *Deutsche Welle*, 21 May. www.dw.com/en/
germany-bans-male-chick-culling-from-2022/a-57603148

DeWeerdt, Sarah (2017) 'Sea change', *Nature*, 550, S54–S58. doi.
org/10.1038/550S54a

Diamond, Jared (1999) 'The worst mistake in the history of the
human race', *Discover Magazine*, 1 May.

DiGiulio, S. (2023) 'What is the paleo diet and can it help you lose
weight?' *TODAY.com*, 31 January. www.today.com/health/diet-
fitness/paleo-diet-rcna68193#anchor-Whataboutallthatredmeat

Dimbleby, Henry (2022) *National Food Strategy: The Plan (Part Two:
Final Report)*, National Food Strategy.

Dimbleby, Henry, with Lewis, Jemima (2023) *Ravenous: How to get
ourselves and our planet into shape*. London: Profile.

duBois, Brook (2020) 'A masala recipe spells home for
Rohingya refugees in Bangladesh', *World Food Programme
Insight/Medium*, 21 January. https://medium.com/
world-food-programme-insight/a-family-recipe-a-sense-of-
home-115ed5731bae

Dukpa, Wangda and Wangdi, Jamyang Tashi (2021) 'The situation
of family farming in Bhutan', in Shrestha et al., *United Nations
Decade of Family Farming 2019–2028: Regional Action Plan to
implement the UNDFF for achieving the SDGs in South Asia.*
SAARC Agriculture Center, FAO, Asian Farmers' Association
and International Cooperative Alliance Asia and Pacific.

Dumpis, Tom (2001) 'UK's growing reliance on Moroccan fruit
and vegetables', *Morocco World News*, 23 March. www.

moroccoworldnews.com/2021/03/338013/uks-growing-reliance-on-moroccan-fruit-and-vegetables

Economist, The (2010) 'The miracle of the Cerrado', The Economist, 26 August. www.economist.com/briefing/2010/08/26/the-miracle-of-the-cerrado

Economist, The (2014) 'In search of the good business', The Economist, 9 August. www.economist.com/business/2014/08/09/in-search-of-the-good-business

Economist, The (2019) 'How to rev up Unilever', The Economist, 2 May. www.economist.com/business/2019/05/04/how-to-rev-up-unilever

Economist, The (2022a) 'Bean counters', The Economist, 1 January. www.economist.com/middle-east-and-africa/2022/01/01/middlemen-are-the-invisible-links-in-african-agriculture

Economist, The (2022b) 'Costly food and energy are fostering global unrest', The Economist, 19 July. www.economist.com/international/2022/06/23/costly-food-and-energy-are-fostering-global-unrest

Economist, The (2022c) 'The fundamental contradiction of ESG is being laid bare', The Economist, 21 October. www.economist.com/leaders/2022/09/29/the-fundamental-contradiction-of-esg-is-being-laid-bare

Economist, The (2022d) 'Unilever's problems will not go away with its boss', The Economist, 21 October. www.economist.com/business/2022/09/29/unilevers-problems-will-not-go-away-with-its-boss

Economist Impact (2021) 'Food Sustainability Index 2021', Economist Impact. https://impact.economist.com/projects/foodsustainability/

Economist Impact (2022) 'Global Food Security Index 2022', Economist Impact. https://impact.economist.com/sustainability/project/food-security-index/

Economist Intelligence Unit (2012) 'Global Food Security Index 2012', Economist Intelligence Unit. https://impact.economist.com/sustainability/project/food-security-index/resources/EIU_Global_Food_Security_Index_-_2012_Findings_Methodology.pdf

Edge by Ascential (2021) 'Leading hyper-stores and supermarket retailers in Europe based on estimated sales in 2021 and 2026 (in billion U.S. dollars)', *Statista*, 17 August. www.statista.com/statistics/1261153/leading-hyper-stores-supermarkets-europe/

Effersøe, Flemming (2023) 'Undersøgelse: Danskerne har i dag et meget stærkere fokus på madspild', *Dagligvarehandlen*, 31 July. https://dagligvarehandlen.dk/madspild/undersoegelse-danskerne-har-i-dag-et-meget-staerkere-fokus-pa-madspild

Elizabeth, L., Machado, P., Kolby, M., Baker, P. and Lawrence, M. (2020) 'Ultra-processed foods and health outcomes: A narrative review', *Nutrients*, 12(7). doi.org/10.3390/nu12071955

Euractiv (2006) 'EU GMO ban was illegal, WTO rules', *Euractiv. com*, 12 May. www.euractiv.com. www.euractiv.com/section/trade-society/news/eu-gmo-ban-was-illegal-wto-rules/

Euromonitor International (2021) 'Top 10 global consumer trends 2021', *Euromonitor International*. www.euromonitor.com/top-10-global-consumer-trends-2021/report

Eurostat (2020) 'How much are households spending on food?' *Eurostat*, 28 December. https://ec.europa.eu/eurostat/web/products-eurostat-news/-/ddn-20201228-1

Evans, Judith (2021) 'Nestlé document says majority of its food portfolio is unhealthy', *Financial Times*, 31 May. www.ft.com/content/4c98d410-38b1-4be8-95b2-d029e054f492

Food and Agriculture Organization of the United Nations (FAO) (2005) 'Rice fish culture, China'. www.fao.org/giahs/giahsaroundtheworld/designated-sites/asia-and-the-pacific/rice-fish-culture/en/

Food and Agriculture Organization of the United Nations (FAO) (2008) 'An introduction to the basic concepts of food security'. www.fao.org/3/al936e/al936e00.pdf

Food and Agriculture Organization of the United Nations (FAO) (2012a) *Statistical pocketbook 2012: World food and agriculture*.

Food and Agriculture Organization of the United Nations (FAO) (2012b) 'Livestock and landscapes'. www.fao.org/3/ar591e/ar591e.pdf

Food and Agriculture Organization of the United Nations (FAO)

(2016) 'Food and agriculture key to achieving the 2030 Agenda for Sustainable Development'.

Food and Agriculture Organization of the United Nations (FAO) (2017) 'The future of food and agriculture: Trends and challenges'. www.fao.org/agrifood-economics/publications/detail/en/c/1475516/

Food and Agriculture Organization of the United Nations (FAO) (2018) 'Sustainable food systems: Concept and framework'. www.fao.org/3/ca2079en/CA2079EN.pdf

Food and Agriculture Organization of the United Nations (FAO) (2019) 'FAO framework for the Urban Food Agenda'. doi.org/10.4060/ca3151en

Food and Agriculture Organization of the United Nations (FAO) (2020) 'The state of food and agriculture 2020: Overcoming water challenges in agriculture'. doi.org/10.4060/cb1447en

Food and Agriculture Organization of the United Nations (FAO) (2022a) 'More fuel for the food/feed debate'. www.fao.org/3/cc3134en/cc3134en.pdf

Food and Agriculture Organization of the United Nations (FAO) (2022b) 'The state of world fisheries and aquaculture 2022: Towards blue transformation'. doi.org/10.4060/cc0461en

Food and Agriculture Organization of the United Nations (FAO) (2022c) 'Gene editing and agrifood systems'. doi.org/10.4060/cc3579en

Food and Agriculture Organization of the United Nations (FAO) (2023) 'The state of food and agriculture 2023: Revealing the true cost of food to transform agrifood systems'. doi.org/10.4060/cc7724en

FAO, IFAD, UNICEF, WFP and WHO (2023) 'The state of food security and nutrition in the world 2023: Urbanization, agrifood systems transformation and healthy diets across the rural–urban continuum'. doi.org/10.4060/cc3017en

FAO and US Department of Agriculture (2023) 'Worldwide production of grain in 2022/23, by type', *Statista*, 8 February. www.statista.com/statistics/263977/world-grain-production-by-type/

Farm Animal Welfare Council (2009) 'Five freedoms', *The National Archives*, 16 April. https://webarchive.nationalarchives.gov.uk/ ukgwa/20121010012427/http://www.fawc.org.uk/freedoms.htm

Fassler, Joe (2021) 'Lab-grown meat is supposed to be inevitable: The science tells a different story', *The Counter*, 22 September. https://thecounter.org/lab-grown-cultivated-meat-cost-at-scale/

FDA (US Food and Drug Administration) (2022) 'GMOs and your health', *FDA*, July. www.fda.gov/media/135280/download

Fediuk, Karen (2000) 'Vitamin C in the Inuit diet: Past and present': A thesis submitted to the Faculty of Graduate Studies and Research in partial fulfilment of the requirements for the degree of Master of Science, School of Dietetics and Human Nutrition, McGill University, Montreal.

Finnish National Agency for Education (2019) 'Student meals benefiting health and communities', Finnish National Agency for Education, *Guides and Handbooks 2019: 5c.* www.oph.fi/en/statistics-and-publications/publications/ student-meals-benefiting-health-and-communities

Finnish National Agency for Education (2023) 'School meals in Finland', *Finnish National Agency for Education.* www.oph.fi/en/ education-and-qualifications/school-meals-finland (accessed 21 November 2023).

Fitzsimmons, Robert (2011) 'Oh, what those oats can do: Quaker Oats, the Food and Drug Administration, and the market value of scientific evidence 1984 to 2010', *Comprehensive Reviews in Food Science and Food Safety*, 11, pp. 56–99. doi. org/10.1111/j.1541-4337.2011.00170.x

Flanagan, K., Robertson, K. and Hanson, C. (2019) 'Reducing food loss and waste: Setting a global action agenda', *World Resources Institute.* doi.org/10.46830/wrirpt.18.00130

Food and Land Use Coalition (2019) 'Growing better: Ten critical transitions to transform food and land use', *Food and Land Use Coalition.* www.foodandlandusecoalition.org/wp-content/ uploads/2019/09/FOLU-GrowingBetter-GlobalReport.pdf

Food Corporation of Bhutan (2022) *Annual Report, 2022.* https://fcbl. bt/drukfood/hr/report/Annual Report 2022.pdf

Food Ethics Council (2010) 'Food justice: The report of the Food and Fairness Inquiry'. www.foodethicscouncil.org/wp-content/uploads/2010 FoodJustice.pdf

FoodIndustry.com (2022) 'What is a CAFO?' www.foodindustry.com/articles/what-is-a-cafo/

Forbes (2023) 'Best countries for business'. www.forbes.com/best-countries-for-business/list/#tab:overall (accessed 21 November 2023).

Ford Motor Company (1916) 'An outside vision', *Ford Times*, October, p. 106.

Fraanje, Walter and Garnett, Tara (2019) 'What is ultra-processed food? And why do people disagree about its utility as a concept?' (Foodsource: building blocks.) Food Climate Research Network, University of Oxford. https://tabledebates.org/sites/default/files/2021-12/FCRN Building Block – What is ultra-processed food.pdf

Friedman, Milton (1962) *Capitalism and freedom*. Chicago: University of Chicago Press.

Friedmann, Harriet and McMichael, Philip (1989) 'Agriculture and the state system: The rise and fall of national agricultures, 1870 to the present', *Sociologia Ruralis*, 29(2), pp. 93–117. doi.org/10.1111/j.1467-9523.1989.tb00360.x

Fry, J., Mailloux, N., Love, D., Milli, M. and Cao, L. (2018) 'Feed conversion efficiency in aquaculture: Do we measure it correctly?' *Environmental Research Letters*, 13, 024017. doi.org/10.1088/1748-9326/aaa273

Gadsby, P. and Steele, L. (2004) 'The Inuit paradox', *Discover Magazine*, 20 January. https://www.discovermagazine.com/health/the-inuit-paradox

Gaidar, Yegor (2007) 'The Soviet collapse: Grain and oil', American Enterprise Institute for Public Policy Research. www.aei.org/wp-content/uploads/2011/10/20070419_Gaidar.pdf

Galvin, Kathleen, Beeton, Tyler, Boone, Randall and BurnSilver, Shauna (2015) 'Nutritional status of Maasai pastoralists under change', *Human Ecology*, 43. doi.org/10.1007/s10745-015-9749-x

Garcia, M., Rijk, G. and Piotrowski, M. (2021) 'Key Cerrado

deforesters in 2020 linked to the clearing of more than 110,000 hectares', *Chain Reaction Research*. https://chain reactionresearch.com/report/cerrado-deforestation-2020-soy-beef/

Garnett, T., Adamchak. R. and Eldridge, H. (2017) 'Perspectives on organic agriculture and new plant breeding techniques', *Table Debates*, 8 November. https://tabledebates.org/blog/perspectives-organic-agriculture-and-new-plant-breeding-techniques

Garrison, G., Biermacher, J. and Brorsen, W. (2022) 'How much will large-scale production of cell-cultured meat cost?' *Journal of Agriculture and Food Research*, 10. 100358. doi.org/10.1016/j.jafr.2022.100358

Gates, Jr, Henry Louis (2017) *Africa's great civilizations*. PBS TV, episode 6.

General Agreement on Tariffs and Trade (1986). Text of the General Agreement on Tariffs and Trade. World Trade Organization. www.wto.org/english/docs_e/legal_e/gatt47_e.pdf

Gerber, P. J., Steinfeld, H., Henderson, B., Mottet, A., Opio, C., Dijkman, J., Falcucci, A. and Tempio, G. (2013) 'Tackling climate change through livestock: A global assessment of emissions and mitigation opportunities', FAO. www.fao.org/3/i3437e/i3437e00.htm

GfK. (2015) 'Number of hours spent cooking per week among consumers worldwide as of June 2014, by country', *Statista*, 30 March. www.statista.com/statistics/420719/time-spent-cooking-per-week-among-consumers-by-country/

Ghebreyesus, Tedros Adhanom (2023) 'WHO Director-General's opening remarks at the media briefing', WHO, 17 March. www.who.int/director-general/speeches/detail/who-director-general-s-opening-remarks-at-the-media-briefing-on-covid-19---11-march-2020

Gibney, M., Forde, C., Mullally, D. and Gibney, E. (2017) 'Ultra-processed foods in human health: A critical appraisal', *American Journal of Clinical Nutrition*, 106. ajcn160440. doi.org/10.3945/ajcn.117.160440

Gibson, Rachel (2020) 'Dutch slower growing chickens require less antibiotics than fast growing chickens', Compassion in World Farming. www.ciwf.org.uk/media/7441136/dutch-slower-growing-broilers-require-less-antibiotics-than-fast-growing-chickens-updated-2020.pdf

Giller, Ken (2023) 'Opening academic year 2023–2024: Land sharing and land sparing?' [Video], YouTube/Wageningen University & Research, 6 September. www.youtube.com/watch?v=f2V9SwOiuKY

Global Entrepreneurship Monitor (GEM) (2022) Global Entrepreneurship Monitor 2021/2022 Global Report: Opportunity Amid Disruption. GEM.

Glover, Andrew (2014) 'Slavery "worse" 10 years after Morecambe Bay tragedy', *BBC News*, 5 February. www.bbc.co.uk/news/uk-england-25914594

Goldacre, Ben (2008) 'Fish oil pills, exam results and a belated retreat', *Guardian*, 29 March. www.theguardian.com/commentisfree/2008/mar/29/5

Guerrera, Francesco (2009) 'Welch condemns share price focus', *Financial Times*, 12 March. www.ft.com/content/294ff1f2-0f27-11de-ba10-0000779fd2ac

Gutman, Daniel (2018) 'As it recovers, Argentina's beef production faces environmental impact questions', Inter Press Service, 6 August. www.ipsnews.net/2018/08/argentinas-beef-production-recovers-faces-questions-environmental-impacts/

Guyton, K., Loomis, D., Grosse, Y., Ghissassi, F., Tallaa, L., Guha, N., Scoccianti, C., Mattock, H. and Straif, K. (2015) 'Carcinogenicity of tetrachlorvinphos, parathion, malathion, diazinon, and glyphosate', *The Lancet: Oncology*, 16(5), pp. 490–1. doi.org/10.1016/S1470-2045(15)70134-8

Hall, K., Ayuketah, A., Brychta, R., Cai, H., Cassimatis, T., Chen, K., Chung, S., Costa, E., Courville, A., Darcey, V., Fletcher, L., Forde, C., Gharib, A., Guo, J., Howard, R., Joseph, P., McGehee, S., Ouwerkerk, R., Raisinger, K. and Zhou, M. (2019) 'Ultra-processed diets cause excess calorie intake and weight gain: An inpatient randomized controlled trial of ad libitum food intake', *Cell Metabolism*, 30(1), pp. 67–77.E3. doi. org/10.1016/j.cmet.2019.05.008

Harford, Tim (2005) *The Undercover Economist*. London: Penguin.

Harvard Health (2015) 'Finding omega-3 fats in fish: Farmed versus wild', *Harvard Health*, 23 December. www.health.harvard.edu/ blog/finding-omega-3-fats-in-fish-farmed-versus-wild-2015122 38909

Hawkes, K., O'Connell, James and Blurton-Jones, Nicholas (2001) 'Hadza meat sharing', *Evolution and Human Behavior*, 22, pp. 113–42. doi.org/10.1016/s1090-5138(00)00066-0

Helliwell, J., Layard, R. and Sachs, J. (2019) *World Happiness Report 2019*. New York: Sustainable Development Solutions Network.

Hewings-Martin, Yella (2020) 'How do SARS and MERS compare with COVID-19?' *Medical News Today*, 10 April. www.medical newstoday.com/articles/how-do-sars-and-mers-compare-with-covid-19#MERS

Heyden, Tom (2015) 'The cows that queue up to milk themselves', *BBC News*, 7 May. www.bbc.co.uk/news/magazine-32610257

Higonnet, Etelle, Bellantonio, Marisa and Hurowitz, Glenn (2017) *Chocolate's dark secret: How the coca industry destroys national parks*. Washington, DC: Mighty Earth. www.mightyearth.org/ wp-content/uploads/2017/09/chocolates_dark_secret_english_ web.pdf

Ho, Kang-Jey, Mikkelson, Belma, Lewis, Lena, Feldman, Sheldon and Taylor, C. (1972) 'Alaskan Arctic Eskimo: Responses to a customary high fat diet', *American Journal of Clinical Nutrition*, 25, pp. 737–45. doi.org/10.1093/ajcn/25.8.737

Hoekman, Bernard, Horn, Henrik and Mavroidis, Petros (2008) 'Winners and losers in the panel stage of the WTO Dispute Settlement System', *Research Institute of Industrial Economics*, Working Paper Series no. 769. doi.org/10.1093/acprof: oso/9780195383614.003.0008

Holmes, B., Kaffa, N., Campbell, K. and Sanders, T. (2012) 'The contribution of breakfast cereals to the nutritional intake of materially deprived UK population', *European Journal of Clinical Nutrition*, 66, pp. 10–17. doi.org/10.1038/ejcn.2011.143

Horsford, Eben Norton (1861) *The theory and art of bread-making: A new process without the use of ferment*. Cambridge, MA: Welch, Bigelow, and Company.

Hotel Chocolat (2020) 'How much cocoa is in milk chocolate?' *Hotel Chocolat*, 9 March. www.hotelchocolat.com/uk/blog/food%2Bdrink/how-much-cocoa-is-in-milk-chocolate.html

Humbird, David (2021) 'Scale-up economics for cultured meat', *Biotechnology and Bioengineering*, 118. doi.org/10.1002/bit.27848

Hume, David (1748) *An enquiry concerning human understanding*. London: A. Millar.

ICCO (2023), 28 February. Global leading countries of cocoa bean processing from 2021/2022–2022/2023 (in 1,000 metric tons). *Statista*. www.statista.com/statistics/238242/leading-countries-of-global-cocoa-bean-processing/

IFOAM – Organics International (2017) 'Genetic engineering and genetically modified organisms', *IFOAM*, position paper. www.ifoam.bio/sites/default/files/2020-03/position_genetic_engineering_and_gmos.pdf

Impossible Foods (2021) 'Are Impossible™ products healthy?' *Impossible Foods*, 13 December. https://impossiblefoods.com/blog/are-impossible-products-healthy

International Agency for Research on Cancer (IARC) (2015) Some organophosphate insecticides and herbicides: Tetrachlorvinphos, parathion, malathion, diazinon and glyphosate, *IARC IARC Monographs programme on the evaluation of the carcinogenic risk of chemicals to humans*, 112. IARC Working Group, Lyon; 3–10 March.

International Labour Organization (ILO), Walk Free and International Organization for Migration (IOM) (2022) 'Global estimates of modern slavery: Forced labour and forced marriage', ILO. doi.org/10.54394/CHUI5986

International Plant Protection Convention (IPPC) Secretariat (2021) 'Scientific review of the impact of climate change on plant pests: A global challenge to prevent and mitigate plant pest risks in agriculture, forestry and ecosystems', FAO. doi.org/10.4060/cb4769en

Jenkinson, Andrew (2020) *Why we eat (too much): The new science of appetite*. London: Penguin.

Johnson, Clark (dir.) (2020) *Percy* (Film). Scythia Films, May Street Productions, Inferno Pictures Inc.

Johnson, Mark and Lucey, J. A. (2006) 'Major technological advances and trends in cheese', *Journal of Dairy Science*, 89, pp. 1174–8. doi.org/10.3168/jds.S0022-0302(06)72186-5

Jones A. et al. (2023) 'Scoping potential routes to UK civil unrest via the food system: Results of a structured expert elicitation', *Sustainability*,15(20), 14783. doi.org/10.3390/su152014783

Jones, T. and Awokoya, A. (2023) 'Are your tinned tomatoes picked by slave labour?' *Guardian*, 2 March. www.theguardian.com/world/2019/jun/20/tomatoes-italy-mafia-migrant-labour-modern-slavery

Just Economics (2021) 'Dead loss: The high cost of poor salmon farming practices', Just Economics Research Ltd. https://www.justeconomics.co.uk/dead-loss

Kappelle, M., Grace, D., Refisch, J., Wright, C., Wernecke, B., Barbieri, M., Karesh, W., Machalaba, C., Fraenkel, A., Macmillan, S., Bett, B. and Lee, H. S. (2020) 'Preventing the next pandemic: Zoonotic diseases and how to break the chain of transmission', United Nations Environment Programme & International Livestock Research Institute. www.unep.org/resources/report/preventing-future-zoonotic-disease-outbreaks-protecting-environment-animals-and?_ga=2.4791667.1753871421.1701239488-2000171075.1701239488

Katiraee, Layla (2021a) 'GMO patent controversy 2: Supreme Court cases of farmers Bowman and Schmeiser', *Gene Literacy Project*, 16 December. https://geneticliteracyproject.org/2021/12/16/gmo-patent-controversy-2-supreme-court-cases-farmers-bowman-schmeiser

Katiraee, Layla (2021b) 'GMO patent controversy 3: Does Monsanto sue farmers for inadvertent GMO "contamination"?' *Gene Literacy Project*, 17 December. https://geneticliteracyproject.org/2021/12/17/gmo-patent-controversy-3-monsanto-sue-farmers-inadvertent-gmo-contamination

Kessler, Matthew and Brock, Samara (hosts) (2021) 'Sophia Murphy on "getting the global rules right"', Table Debates, 8 July, *Feed*, episode 12 [Podcast]. https://tabledebates.org/podcast/episode12

Kessler, Matthew and Brock, Samara (hosts) (2022) 'Jayson Lusk on markets and consumer power,' Table Debates, 7 July, *Feed*, episode 27 [Podcast]. https://tabledebates.org/podcast/episode27

Khosla Ventures (2022) 'The dark matter of nutrition: From the foodome to network medicine' [Video], 2 August. www.youtube.com/watch?v=FNfrp4giFll

King, F. H. (1911) *Farmers of forty centuries, or Permanent agriculture in China, Korea and Japan*. Madison, WI: Mrs. F. H. King.

Kinga, Sonam (2008) 'Reciprocal exchange and community vitality: The case of Gortshom Village in eastern Bhutan', *Towards Global Transformation: Proceedings of the Third International Conference on Gross National Happiness*. Thimphu, Bhutan: Centre for Bhutan Studies.

Kraamwinkel, C. T., Beaulieu, A., Dias, T. et al. (2021) 'Planetary limits to soil degradation', *Nature: Communications Earth & Environment*, 2, article 249 (2021). doi.org/10.1038/s43247-021-00323-3

Krebs, John (2013) *Food: A very short introduction*. Oxford: Oxford University Press.

Kuhnlein, Harriet, Erasmus, Bill and Spigelski, Dina (2009) *Indigenous peoples' food systems: The many dimensions of culture, diversity and environment for nutrition and health*. Rome: FAO and Centre for Indigenous Peoples' Nutrition and Environment (CINE).

Laing, Stuart (2017) *Tippu Tip: Ivory, slavery and discovery in the scramble for Africa*. Surbiton, UK: Medina Publishing.

Laitinen, Aija, Tilles-Tirkkonen, Tanja, Karhunen, Leila and Talvia, Sanna (2021) 'Food education in Finnish primary education: Defining themes and learning objectives using the Delphi technique', *British Food Journal*, 123, pp. 404–27. doi.org/10.1108/BFJ-02-2021-0174.

Lang, Tim (2020) *Feeding Britain: Our food problems and how to fix them*. London: Penguin.

Lang, T., Barling, D. and Caraher, M. (2009) *Food policy: Integrating health, environment and society*. Oxford: Oxford University Press.

Larch, M., Yalcin, E., and Yotov, Y. V. (2022) 'Valuing the impact of the World Trade Organization', Department for International Trade. www.gov.uk/government/publications/the-value-of-the-world-trade-organization-impacts

Lederberg, J. and McCray, A. T. (2001) ''Ome sweet 'omics: A genealogical treasury of words', the *Scientist*, 15(7), pp. 8-9.

List, Gary R. (2006) 'Giants of the past: Hippolyte Mège (1817–1880)', *Inform*, 17(4) (April), p. 264. https://web.archive.org/web/20181215053212/http://lipidlibrary.aocs.org/History/content.cfm?ItemNumber=39276

Lobbywatch (2004) 'The green revolution and genetic engineering', 26 November. www.lobbywatch.org/archive2.asp?arcid=4662.

Lockyer, Stacey and Spiro, A. (2020) 'The role of bread in the UK diet: An update', *Nutrition Bulletin*, 45, pp. 133–64. doi.org/10.1111/nbu.12435.

Lodhi, Abdulaziz (2015) 'Slavery and the slave trade in eastern Africa'. doi.org/10.13140/RG.2.1.3949.8969.

Lopez-Ridaura, Santiago, Barba-Escoto, Luis, Reyna-Ramirez, Cristian, Sum, Carlos, Palacios Rojas, Natalia and Gerard, Bruno (2021) 'Maize intercropping in the milpa system: Diversity, extent and importance for nutritional security in the western highlands of Guatemala', *Scientific Reports*, 11. doi.org/10.1038/s41598-021-82784-2.

Lorenzen, Hannes (2019) 'Bhutan: Spearheading a transition to organics?' *ARC2020*, 17 January. www.arc2020.eu/bhutan-spearheading-a-transition-to-organics/

Lorenzen, Hannes and von Bernstorff, Adrian (2019) 'Bhutan: An economy for food sovereignty and organic farming', *ARC2020*, 18 February. www.arc2020.eu/bhutan-food-sovereignty-and-organic-farming/

Loreti, Lara (2023) 'Il professor Grandi e la cucina italiana', *La*

Repubblica, 27 March. www.repubblica.it/il-gusto/2023/03/27/
news/il_professor_grandi_e_la_cucina_italiana_ricostruisco_la_
storia_non_metto_in_dubbio_la_qualita_dei_piatti-393844169/

Loth, Shefalee (2020) 'Five ultra-processed foods you shouldn't
dismiss', *Which?*, 6 February. www.which.co.uk/news/
article/five-ultra-processed-foods-you-shouldnt-dismiss-
aXlGr9Z5Dn18

Macpherson, W., with Cook, T., Sentamu, J. and Stone. R. 1999.
*The Stephen Lawrence Inquiry: Report of an Inquiry by Sir
William Macpherson of Cluny*, CM 4262-I. (Stationery Office)

Margulis, Lynn, and Sagan, Dorion (1987) *Microcosmos: Four Billion
Years of Evolution from Our Microbial Ancestors* (HarperCollins)

Marine Stewardship Council (2023) Celebrating Sustainable
Seafood: The Marine Stewardship Council Annual Report
2022–23. *Marine Stewardship Council.* www.msc.org/docs/
default-source/default-document-library/about-the-msc/msc-
annual-report-2022-2023.pdf

Marlowe, Frank, Berbesque, J. Colette, Wood, Brian, Crittenden,
Alyssa, Porter, Claire and Mabulla, Audax (2014) 'Honey,
Hadza, hunter-gatherers, and human evolution', *Journal
of Human Evolution*, 71, pp. 119–28. doi.org/10.1016/j.
jhevol.2014.03.006.

Marshall, L. (1961) 'Sharing, talking, and giving: Relief of
social tensions among !Kung bushmen', *Africa: Journal
of the International African Institute*, 31(3), pp. 231–49. doi.
org/10.2307/1157263.

Martínez Steele, E., Popkin, B. M., Swinburn, B. and Monteiro,
C. A. (2017) 'The share of ultra-processed foods and the
overall nutritional quality of diets in the US: Evidence
from a nationally representative cross-sectional study',
Population Health Metrics, 15, article 6 (2017). doi.org/10.1186/
s12963-017-0119-3.

Mason, Rowena (2022) 'Starmer calls on Tories to sack co-
chair Ben Elliot over party links to Russia', *Guardian*,
5 March. www.theguardian.com/politics/2022/mar/04/
starmer-calls-on-tories-to-sack-co-chair-ben-elliot

Massel, Karen (2023) 'What's the latest on GMOs and gene-edited foods – and what are the concerns? An expert explains', *The Conversation*, 7 May. https://theconversation.com/whats-the-latest-on-gmos-and-gene-edited-foods-and-what-are-the-concerns-an-expert-explains-204275

McAndrew, Catherine (2022) 'Solidarity with migrant landworkers in Europe', *Landworkers Alliance*, 16 May. https://landworkers alliance.org.uk/solidarity-with-migrant-workers-in-europe/

McClure, Tess (2021) 'Emissions from cows on New Zealand dairy farms reach record levels', *Guardian*, 5 August. www.theguardian.com/world/2021/aug/05/emissions-from-cows-on-new-zealand-dairy-farms-reach-record-levels

McKay, Hannah (2021) 'CAFOs (concentrated animal feeding operations): Why are they bad?' *Sentient Media*, 29 September. https://sentientmedia.org/cafo/

McManus, K. D. (2023) 'A practical guide to the Mediterranean diet', *Harvard Health*, 22 March. www.health.harvard.edu/blog/a-practical-guide-to-the-mediterranean-diet-2019032116194

McVeigh, Karen (2021) 'Bottom trawling releases as much carbon as air travel, landmark study finds', *Guardian*, 17 March. www.theguardian.com/environment/2021/mar/17/trawling-for-fish-releases-as-much-carbon-as-air-travel-report-finds-climate-crisis

Mehelin, Nalifa (2022) 'Night in the Rohingya camps: WFP storyteller reminisces his life, now and then', *World Food Programme Insight/Medium*, 6 January. https://medium.com/world-food-programme-insight/night-in-the-rohingya-camps-wfp-storyteller-reminisces-his-life-now-and-then-ebfee16b6cc5

Mesnage, R., Szekacs, A. and Zaller, J. (2021) 'Herbicides: Brief history, agricultural use, and potential alternatives for weed control', doi.org/10.1016/B978-0-12-823674-1.00002-X. In: Robin Mesnage and Johann G. Zaller (eds) (2021) *Herbicides: Chemistry, efficacy, toxicology, and environmental impacts* (Amsterdam: Elsevier).

Minderoo Foundation (2021) 'The Global Fishing Index 2021:

Assessing the sustainability of the world's marine fisheries.'
www.minderoo.org/global-fishing-index

Ministry of Agriculture and Forestry of Finland (2017) 'Food2030:
Finland feeds us and the world.' Government report on
food policy. https://mmm.fi/en/food-and-agriculture/policy/
food-policy

Ministry of Health of Brazil (2015) 'Dietary guidelines for the
Brazilian population.' https://bvsms.saude.gov.br/bvs/
publicacoes/dietary_guidelines_brazilian_population.pdf

Misculin, Nicolas (2008) 'Argentine cattle move from Pampas to
feedlots', *Reuters*, 18 December. www.reuters.com/article/
us-argentina-feedlots-idUSTRE4BH02B2008121

Misiak, M., Butovskaya, M. and Sorokowski, P. (2018) 'Ecology
shapes moral judgments towards food-wasting behavior:
Evidence from the Yali of West Papua, the Ngorongoro
Maasai, and Poles', *Appetite*, 125. doi.org/10.1016/j.
appet.2017.12.031.

Missouri Coalition for the Environment (2019) 'What should
you know about CAFOs?' *Missouri Coalition for the
Environment*, 25 October. https://storymaps.arcgis.com/
stories/476f09dad5f941518b5c92b091acb91e

Mohsen, Mohamed and Yang, Hongsheng (2021) 'Sea cucumbers
mariculture'. doi/org/10.1016/B978-0-12-824377-0.00009-8.
In: Mohamed Mohsen and Hongsheng Yang (eds) (2021) *Sea
cucumbers: Aquaculture, biology and ecology* (Cambridge, MA:
Academic Press).

Monaco, Emily (2019) 'Synthetic biology and gene editing aren't
organic, says NOSB', *Organic Authority*, 7 May. www.organic
authority.com/buzz-news/synthetic-biology-and-gene-editing-
arent-organic-says-nosb

Monteiro, C., Cannon, G., Levy, R., Moubarac, J., Louzada, M.,
Rauber, F., Khandpur, N., Cediel, G., Neri, D., Martinez
Steele, E., Baraldi, L. and Jaime, P. (2019) 'Ultra-processed
foods: What they are and how to identify them', *Public Health
Nutrition*, 22, pp. 1–6. doi.org/10.1017/S1368980018003762.

Monteiro, C., Cannon, G., Moubarac, J., Levy, R., Louzada, M. L.

and Jaime, P. (2017) 'The UN Decade of Nutrition, the NOVA food classification and the trouble with ultra-processing', *Public Health Nutrition*, 21 (special issue 1), pp. 5–17. doi. org/10.1017/S1368980017000234.

Mood, A., Lara, E., Boyland, N. and Brooke, P. (2023) 'Estimating global numbers of farmed fishes killed for food annually from 1990 to 2019', *Animal Welfare*, 32, E12. doi.org/10.1017/awf.2023.4.

Mordor Intelligence (2018) 'Canned food market value worldwide from 2018 to 2023', *Statista*, 15 March. www.statista.com/ statistics/1007114/global-canned-food-market-value/

Morrison, Oliver (2022) 'Dispose with purpose? Unilever has "lost the plot" by fixating on sustainability, claims influential UK fund manager', *Food Navigator Europe*, 12 January. www.foodnavigator.com/Article/2022/01/12/ Dispose-with-purpose-Unilever-has-lost-the-plot-by-fixating-on-sustainability-claims-influential-UK-fund-manager#

MUFPP (2015) Milan urban food policy pact (MUFPP). www. milanurbanfoodpolicypact.org/wp-content/uploads/2020/12/ Milan-Urban-Food-Policy-Pact-EN.pdf

Mufson, S. (2019) 'Mars Inc. vowed to stop deforestation in West Africa. It failed', *Washington Post*, 29 October. www.washington post.com/graphics/2019/national/climate-environment/ mars-chocolate-deforestation-climate-change-west-africa/

Munch-Andersen, Thor, Olsen, David, Søndergaard, Hans, Daugaard, Jens, Bysted, Anette, Christensen, Dirk, Saltin, Bengt and Helge, Jørn (2012) 'Metabolic profile in two physically active Inuit groups consuming either a western or traditional Inuit diet', *International Journal of Circumpolar Health*, 71, 17342. doi.org/10.3402/ijch.v71i0.17342.

Musk, Elon (@elonmusk) (2023) 'I must admit to being congenitally optimistic ...' *Twitter*, 9 February. https://twitter.com/ elonmusk/status/1623824862673518592?s=20

Naylor, R., Kishore, A., Sumaila, R., Issifu, I., Hunter, B., Belton, B., Bush, S., Cao, L., Gelcich, S., Gephart, J., Golden, C., Jonell, M., Koehn, J., Little, D., Thilsted, S., Tigchelaar, M. and Crona, B. (2021a) 'Blue food demand across geographic

and temporal scales', *Nature Communications*, 12, 5413. doi.
org/10.1038/s41467-021-25516-4.

Naylor, R., Troell, M., Little, D., Hardy, R., Bush, S., Shumway,
S., Lubchenco, J., Cao, L., Klinger, D. and Buschmann, A.
(2021b) 'A 20-year retrospective review of global aquaculture',
Nature, 591, 551–63. doi.org/10.1038/s41586-021-03308-6.

Nestle, Marion (2013) *Food politics: How the food industry influences
nutrition and health* (Tenth anniversary edn.). Berkeley, CA:
University of California Press.

New American Economy Research Fund (2021) 'Immigration and
Agriculture', 16 August. https://research.newamericaneconomy.
org/report/immigration-and-agriculture/

Nordhaus, T. and Shah, S. (2022) 'Sri Lanka's organic farming
experiment went catastrophically wrong', *Foreign
Policy*, 20 May. https://foreignpolicy.com/2022/03/05/
sri-lanka-organic-farming-crisis

Nunley, Deana (host) (2019) 'Small steps, giant leaps', episode
25: NASA technology transfer [Podcast], 11 December.
www.nasa.gov/podcasts/small-steps-giant-leaps/
small-steps-giant-leaps-episode-25-nasa-technology-transfer/

Oatman, Maddie (2012) 'Enjoy an ice cream cone shortly before
lunch', *Mother Jones*, 31 October. www.motherjones.com/
media/2012/10/classic-ads-from-big-sugar/

Oceana in the UK (2023) 'Taking stock: The state of UK fish
populations 2023', Macalister Elliott and Partners Ltd. for
Oceana. https://uk.oceana.org/reports/taking-stock-2023/.

O'Connell, Sanjida (2009) 'Is farming the root of all evil?' the
Telegraph, 23 June. www.telegraph.co.uk/news/science/science-
news/5604296/Is-farming-the-root-of-all-evil.html

O'Dowd, Adrian (2017) 'Spending on junk food advertising is nearly
30 times what government spends on promoting healthy
eating', *BMJ*, 359, j4677. doi.org/10.1136/bmj.j4677.

Ohta, Itaru (1987) 'Livestock individual identification among the
Turkana: The animal classification and naming in the pastoral
livestock management', *African Study Monographs*, 8(1), pp.
1–69. doi.org/10.14989/68024.

Oiye, S. H., Simel, J. O., Oniang'o, R. U. and Johns, T. I. (2009) 'The Maasai food system and food and nutrition security' in: H. Kuhnlein, B. Erasmus and D. Spigelski (eds), *Indigenous peoples' food systems: The many dimensions of culture, diversity and environment for nutrition and health*, Rome: FAO and Centre for Indigenous Peoples' Nutrition and Environment (CINE), pp. 231–49.

Ojina, Elizabeth (2021) 'Ahero farmers stuck with more than 10,000 bags of rice', *Nation*, 11 January. https://nation.africa/kenya/counties/kisumu/ahero-farmers-unable-sell-rice-3253714

One Health High Level Expert Panel (2023) 'Prevention of zoonotic spillover', *World Health Organization*. www.who.int/publications/m/item/prevention-of-zoonotic-spillover

Organisation for Economic Co-operation and Development (OECD) (2018) 'Concentration in seed markets: Potential effects and policy responses.' doi.org/10.1787/9789264308367-en.

Organisation for Economic Co-operation and Development (OECD) (2021) 'Government at a glance 2021.' doi.org/10.1787/1c258f55-en.

Organisation for Economic Co-operation and Development (OECD) (2023a) 'Meat consumption (indicator).' doi.org/10.1787/fa290fd0-en.

Organisation for Economic Co-operation and Development (OECD) (2023b) 'Agricultural support (indicator).' doi.org/10.1787/6ea85c58-en.

Page, M. L. (2022) 'Bananas threatened by devastating fungus given temporary resistance', *New Scientist*, 28 September. www.newscientist.com/article/2338753-bananas-threatened-by-devastating-fungus-given-temporary-resistance/

Pagliai, G., Dinu, M., Madarena, M., Bonaccio, M., Iacoviello, L. and Sofi, F. (2020) 'Consumption of ultra-processed foods and health status: A systematic review and meta-analysis', *British Journal of Nutrition*, 125, pp. 308–18. doi.org/10.1017/S0007114520002688.

Paley, Matthieu (2014) 'We are what we eat: Hunting the Hadza way with bows, arrows, and ingenuity', *National Geographic*, 10 December. www.nationalgeographic.com/photography/article/we-are-what-we-eat-hunting-the-hadza-way-with-bows-arrows-and-ingenuity

Parmentier, Michel (2007) 'Formulation of margarines: Up to the third generation and what beyond', *European Journal of Lipid Science and Technology*, 109, pp. 1051–2. doi.org/10.1002/ejlt.200700222.

Patron, Nicola and Price, Catherine (2021) 'Should we genetically edit the food we eat? We asked two experts', *The Conversation*, 11 August. https://theconversation.com/should-we-genetically-edit-the-food-we-eat-we-asked-two-experts-162959

Payton, Louise (2022) 'UK government proposed gene editing/modification deregulation for plants, crops and animals', *Soil Association*, 12 May. www.soilassociation.org/blogs/2022/may/12/despite-major-opposition-government-are-progressing-plans-to-allow-unregulated-genetic-modification-of-plants-and-food-crops/

Pearce, R. and Sharma, R. (2000) Agreement on Agriculture, Module 3: Export Subsidies. FAO. www.fao.org/3/x7353e/X7353e03.html

Pekar, J., Magee, A., Parker, E., Moshiri, N., Izhikevich, K., Havens, J., Gangavarapu, K., Serrano, L., Crits-Christoph, A., Matteson, N., Zeller, M., Levy, J., Wang, J., Hughes, S., Jungmin, L., Park, H., Park, M., Ching, K., Lin, R. and Wertheim, J. (2022) The molecular epidemiology of multiple zoonotic origins of SARS-CoV-2. *Science*, 377(6609), pp. 960–6. doi.org/10.1126/science.abp8337.

Pendergrast, Mark (2011) 'A boom and bust culture', *New York Times*, 9 March. www.nytimes.com/roomfordebate/2011/03/09/coffee-the-new-shaky-commodity/a-boom-and-bust-culture

Pickett, K., Kelly, S., Brunner, E., Lobstein, T. and Wilkinson, R. (2005) 'Wider income gaps, wider waistbands? An ecological study of obesity and income inequality', *Journal of Epidemiology and Community Health*, 59, pp. 670–4. doi.org/10.1136/jech.2004.028795.

Pollan, Michael (2008) *In defence of food*. London: Penguin.

Popkin, Barry (2002) 'Part II. What is unique about the experience in lower- and middle-income less-industrialised countries compared with the very-high income industrialised countries?' *Public Health Nutrition*, 5(1a), pp. 205–14. doi.org/10.1079/PHN2001295.

Poppy, Guy (2021) 'Gene-edited crops: Expert Q+A on what field trials could mean for the future of food', *The Conversation*, 30 September. https://theconversation.com/gene-edited-crops-expert-q-a-on-what-field-trials-could-mean-for-the-future-of-food-168983

Pradeep (2020) 'The ultimate guide to FCR (feed conversion ratio)', *NavFarm*, 22 September. www.navfarm.com/blog/fcr-guide/

Pro Luomu (Finnish Organic Food Association) (2023) 'Organics in Finland 2022.' https://proluomu.fi/wp-content/uploads/2023/09/organics-in-finland-2022.pdf

Qu, Xue, Kojima, Daizo, Wu, Laping and Ando, Mitsuyoshi (2021) 'The losses in the rice harvest process: A review', *Sustainability*, 13(17), 9627. doi.org/10.3390/su13179627.

Quammen, David (2021) 'Can good come from Maasai lion killings in the Serengeti?' *National Geographic*, 3 May. www.nationalgeographic.com/animals/article/140428-serengeti-ngorongoro-conservation-area-tanzania-lions-maasai-craig-packer-lion-guardians-world

Quist, Zazala (2023) 'Is the Dutch farming system as sustainable as David Attenborough thinks?' *Ecochain*, 10 August. https://ecochain.com/knowledge/david-attenborough-dutch-agriculture/

Rabanal, Herminio R. (1988) *History of aquaculture*. ASEAN/UNDP/FAO Regional Small-Scale Coastal Fisheries Development Project. www.fao.org/3/ag158e/AG158E00.htm

Rapsomanikis, George (2015) 'The economic lives of smallholder farmers.' Rome: FAO. doi.org/10.13140/RG.2.1.3223.9440.

Regis, Ed (2019a) *Golden Rice: The imperiled birth of a GMO superfood*. Baltimore, MD: Johns Hopkins University Press.

Regis, Ed (2019b) 'The true story of the genetically modified superfood that almost saved millions', *Foreign Policy*, 17

October. https://foreignpolicy.com/2019/10/17/golden-rice-genetically-modified-superfood-almost-saved-millions

Reuters (2021) 'France bans crushing and gassing of male chicks from 2022', *Reuters*, 18 July. www.reuters.com/world/europe/france-bans-crushing-gassing-male-chicks-2022-2021-07-18/

Reynolds, Matt (2016) 'Heston Blumenthal's ISS menu: Bacon sarnies and Alaskan salmon', *Wired*, 12 March. www.wired.co.uk/article/heston-blumenthal-documentary-dinner-in-space-tim-peake

Ringquist, J., Phillips, T., Renner, B., Sides. R., Stuart, K., Baum, M. and Flannery J. (2016) 'Capitalizing on the shifting consumer food value equation.' Deloitte. www2.deloitte.com/content/dam/Deloitte/us/Documents/consumer-business/us-fmi-gma-report.pdf

Ritchie, Hannah (2017) 'How much of the world's land would we need in order to feed the global population with the average diet of a given country?' *Our World in Data*, 3 October. https://ourworldindata.org/agricultural-land-by-global-diets

Ritchie, Hannah (2019) 'The world now produces more seafood from fish farms than wild catch', *Our World in Data*, 13 September. https://ourworldindata.org/rise-of-aquaculture

Ritchie, Hannah (2021a) 'If the world adopted a plant-based diet we would reduce global agricultural land use from 4 to 1 billion hectares', *Our World in Data*, 4 March. https://ourworldindata.org/land-use-diets

Ritchie, Hannah (2021b) 'Smallholders produce one-third of the world's food, less than half of what many headlines claim', *Our World in Data*, 9 August. https://ourworldindata.org/smallholder-food-production

Rodionova, Zlata (2017) 'Denmark reduces food waste by 25% in five years with the help of one woman – Selina Juul', the *Independent*, 28 February. www.independent.co.uk/news/business/news/denmark-reduce-food-waste-25-per-cent-five-years-help-selina-juul-scandanavia-a7604061.html

Rohr, J., Barrett, C., Civitello, D., Craft, M., Delius, B., DeLeo, G., Hudson, P., Jouanard, N., Nguyen, K. H, Ostfeld, R., Remais,

J., Riveau, G., Sokolow, S. and Tilman, D. (2019) 'Emerging human infectious diseases and the links to global food production', *Nature Sustainability*, 2, 445–56. doi.org/10.1038/s41893-019-0293-3.

Rosenfeld, Daniel L. and Burrow, Anthony L. (2017) 'The unified model of vegetarian identity: A conceptual framework for understanding plant-based food choices', *Appetite*, 112, pp. 78–95. doi.org/10.1016/j.appet.2017.01.017.

Roser, M., Ritchie, H. and Rosado, P. (2013) 'Food supply', *Our World in Data*, 5 March. https://ourworldindata.org/food-supply

Rossi, Leonardo (2015) 'From dream to nightmare', *D+C (Development and Cooperation)*, 10 September. www.dandc.eu/en/article/cattle-industry-argentina-changing-rapidly-not-better

Royal Society, The (2009) 'Reaping the benefits: Science and the sustainable intensification of global agriculture.' https://royalsociety.org/topics-policy/publications/2009/reaping-benefits/

Royal Society, The (2016) 'GM plants: Questions and answers', May. https://royalsociety.org/topics-policy/projects/gm-plants

Sala, E., Mayorga, J., Bradley, D., Cabral, R., Atwood, T., Auber, A., Cheung, W., Costello, C., Ferretti, F., Friedlander, A., Gaines, S., Garilao, C., Goodell, W., Halpern, B., Hinson, A., Kaschner, K., Kesner-Reyes, K., Leprieur, F., Mcgowan, J. and Lubchenco, J. (2021) 'Protecting the global ocean for biodiversity, food and climate', *Nature*, 592, pp. 1–6. doi.org/10.1038/s41586-021-03371-z.

Saltzman, M., Livesay, C., Bittman, M., Martelli, J. and Gouffran, D. (2019) 'Is France's groundbreaking food-waste law working?' *PBS Newshour*, 31 August. https://pulitzercenter.org/stories/frances-groundbreaking-food-waste-law-working

Sarma, Atanu (2021) 'Social cohesion: When food offers an occasion for bonding', *World Food Programme Insight/Medium*, 16 December. https://medium.com/world-food-programme-insight/social-cohesion-when-food-gives-the-taste-of-bonding-e1c748e13296

Schiff, Rebecca, Levkoe, Charles and Wilkinson, Ashley (2022)

'Food policy councils: A 20-year scoping review (1999–2019)', *Frontiers in Sustainable Food Systems*, 6, 868995. doi. org/10.3389/fsufs.2022.868995.

Science in Society (2006) 'GM crops and microbes for health or public health hazards?' *Science in Society*, 16 November. www.i-sis.org.uk/GMCMHPHH.php

Science Media Centre (2023) 'Expert reaction to SACN (Scientific Advisory Committee on Nutrition) statement on processed foods and health', *Science Media Centre*, 11 July. www. sciencemediacentre.org/expert-reaction-to-sacn-scientific-advisory-committee-on-nutrition-statement-on-processed-foods-and-health

Scientific Advisory Committee on Nutrition (SACN) (2023) 'SACN statement on processed foods and health: Summary report', Office for Health Improvement and Disparities, 11 July. www.gov.uk/government/publications/ sacn-statement-on-processed-foods-and-health/sacn-statement-on-processed-foods-and-health-summary-report

Scott, C., Sutherland, J. and Taylor, A. (2008) 'Affordability of the UK's Eatwell guide', *Food Foundation*, 5 September. https://foodfoundation.org.uk/publication/ affordability-uks-eatwell-guide

Scrinis, Gyorgy (2013) *Nutritionism: The science and politics of dietary advice*. New York: Columbia University Press.

Secretariat of the Convention on Biological Diversity (2000) Cartagena Protocol on Biosafety to the Convention on Biological Diversity. https://bch.cbd.int/protocol/text/

Sellars, Wilfrid (1962) 'Philosophy and the scientific image of man,' in Robert Colodny (ed.), *Frontiers of science and philosophy* (Pittsburgh: University of Pittsburgh Press), pp. 35–78.

Sellem, L.& Srour, B., Javaux, G., Chazelas, E., Chassaing, B., Viennois, E., Debras, C., Salamé, C., Druesne-Pecollo, N., Esseddik, Y., Szabo de Edelenyi, F., Agaësse, C., Sa, A., Lutchia, R., Louveau, E., Huybrechts, I., Pierre, F., Coumoul, X., Fezeu, L. and Touvier, M. (2023) 'Food additive emulsifiers and risk of cardiovascular disease in the

NutriNet-Santé cohort: Prospective cohort study', *BMJ*, 382, e076058. doi.org/10.1136/bmj-2023-076058.

Sen, Amartya (2009) *The Idea of Justice*. London: Allen Lane/ Cambridge, MA: Belknap Press of Harvard University Press.

Sheriff, Abdul (1987) *Slaves, spices and ivory in Zanzibar: Integration of an East African Commerical Empire into the World Economy, 1770–1873*. London: James Currey.

Shrestha, R. B., Ferrand, P., Penunia, M. E., Dave, M. and Ali, Y. (eds) (2021) *United Nations Decade of Family Farming 2019– 2028: Regional action plan to implement the UNDFF for achieving the SDGs in South Asia*. SAARC Agriculture Center, FAO, Asian Farmers' Association and International Cooperative Alliance Asia and Pacific. doi.org/10.4060/cb5030en.

Siddique, Haroon (2023) 'Animal welfare groups lose court challenge over "Frankenchickens"', *Guardian*, 24 May. www. theguardian.com/world/2023/may/24/animal-welfare-groups-lose-court-challenge-over-frankenchickens

Siegel, Josh (2016) 'What happened when New Zealand got rid of government subsidies for farmers', *Daily Signal*, 22 September. www.dailysignal.com/2016/09/22/what-happened-when-new-zealand-got-rid-of-government-subsidies-for-farmers/

Singer, Peter (2015) *Animal liberation: A new ethics for our treatment of animals* (40th anniversary edn.). New York: HarperCollins.

SkyQuest Technology (2023) 'Customize food in your plate: Personalized nutrition market set to soar past USD 37.3 billion by 2030', *GlobeNewswire News Room*, 4 July. www. globenewswire.com/en/news-release/2023/07/04/2698844/0/ en/Customize-Food-In-Your-Plate-Personalized-Nutrition-Market-Set-to-Soar-Past-USD-37-3-Billion-by-2030.html

Slave Voyages (2020) 'Estimated share of African slaves who did not survive the Middle Passage journey to the Americas each year from 1501 to 1866', *Statista*, 1 January. www.statista.com/ statistics/1143458/annual-share-slaves-deaths-during-middle-passage/

Smits, S. A., Leach, J., Sonnenburg, E. D., Gonzalez, C. G., Lichtman, J. S., Reid, G., Knight, R., Manjurano, A.,

Changalucha, J., Elias, J. E., Dominguez-Bello, M. G. and Sonnenburg, J. L. (2017) 'Seasonal cycling in the gut microbiome of the Hadza hunter-gatherers of Tanzania', *Science*, 25 August, 357(6353), pp. 802–06. doi.org/10.1126/science.aan4834.

Snowdon, Gemma (2019a) 'I'm very excited to cook this new dish', *World Food Programme Insight/Medium*, 11 March. https://medium.com/world-food-programme-insight/im-very-excited-to-cook-this-new-dish-ea70b23b64c7

Snowdon, Gemma (2019b) 'Rohingya families rediscover the joy of mealtimes', *World Food Programme Insight/Medium*, 8 May. https://medium.com/world-food-programme-insight/in-pictures-rediscovering-the-joy-of-family-mealtime-20ecc2f3fb4

Snowdon, Gemma (2019c) 'Fathers at the forefront of fighting malnutrition', *World Food Programme Insight/Medium*, 13 July. https://medium.com/world-food-programme-insight/in-pictures-fathers-at-the-forefront-of-nutrition-2d4d1c365f90

Soil Association (2023) 'Organic standards for Great Britain: Farming and growing', Version 1.3, 25 May. www.soilassociation.org/media/25986/sa-gb-farming-growing.pdf

Solomon, E., Hopkins, V. and Vladkov, A. (2021) 'Inside Germany's abattoirs: The human cost of cheap meat', *Financial Times*, 9/10 January. www.ft.com/content/7b77ec15-7384-42d0-9da0-76c4b7f0872b

Sonnino, R., Tegoni, C. and Cunto, A. (2018) 'The challenge of systemic food change: Insights from cities', *Cities*, 85. doi.org/10.1016/j.cities.2018.08.008.

South Florida PBS (2017) 'The future of seafood', YouTube/ChangingSeasTV. www.youtube.com/watch?v=eff-Z0NdwzY

Southey, Flora (2021) 'Cell-based disruption: How many factories, and at what capacity, are required to supply 10% of the meat market?' *FoodNavigator Europe*, 13 August. www.foodnavigator.com/Article/2021/08/13/Cell-based-disruption-How-many-factories-and-at-what-capacity-are-required-to-supply-10-of-the-meat-market

SpaceX (2017) 'Elon Musk: We can launch a manned mission to Mars by 2024' [Video], *Guardian*, 29 September.

Speed, Madeleine and Murray, Christine (2023) 'How a Mexican beer became the US best-seller', *Financial Times*, 25 August. www.ft.com/content/0f746f09-a082-422e-9845-0f2a6e4b860b

Srour, Bernard and Touvier, Mathilde (2021) 'Ultra-processed foods and human health: What do we already know and what will further research tell us?' *EClinicalMedicine*, 32, 100747. doi.org/10.1016/j.eclinm.2021.100747.

Standage, Tom (2009) *An edible history of humanity*. London: Atlantic Books.

Stanley, Henry Morton (1961) *The exploration diaries of H. M. Stanley*, New York: Vanguard Press.

Statista (2023) 'Organic food market in the United Kingdom (UK).' www.statista.com/study/21709/organic-food-market-in-the-uk-statista-dossier/

Statistics Netherlands (2017) 'Agricultural production in the period 1950–2015', 31 January. www.cbs.nl/en-gb/news/2017/05/agricultural-production-in-the-period-1950-2015

Steen, Juliette (2019) '17 Carcinogenic foods you probably eat every day', *HuffPost UK*, 2 October. www.huffingtonpost.co.uk/entry/17-carcinogenic-foods-you-probably-eat-every-day_n_6108760ee4b0999d2084f9db

Table Debates (2023) 'Philip McMichael on the "Corporate food regime"' (season 2, episode 14), *Feed podcast*, 2 February. https://tabledebates.org/podcast/episode37

Talhelm, Thomas, Zhang, Xuemin, Oishi, Shigehiro, Shimin, C, Duan, D, Lan, Xuezhao and Kitayama, Shinobu (2023) 'Large-scale psychological differences within china explained by rice versus wheat agriculture', *Science*, 344(6184), pp. 603–08. doi.org/10.1126/science.1246850

Talman, Kristen (2023) 'How "ESG" came to mean everything and nothing', *BBC*, 15 November. www.bbc.com/worklife/article/20231114-how-esg-came-to-mean-everything-and-nothing

Taneri, P., Wehrli, F., Diaz, Z. M., Itodo, O., Salvador, D., Raeisi-Dehkordi, H., Bally, L., Minder, B., Jong, J., Carmelli,

J., Bano, A., Glisic, M. and Muka, T. (2022) 'Association between ultra-processed food intake and all-cause mortality: A systematic review and meta-analysis', *American Journal of Epidemiology*, 191(7), pp. 1323–35. doi.org/10.1093/aje/kwac039.

Teo, P. S., Lim, A., Goh, A. T., Janani, R., Choy, J., McCrickerd, K. and Forde, C. (2022) 'Texture-based differences in eating rate influence energy intake for minimally processed and ultra-processed meals', *American Journal of Clinical Nutrition*, 116(1), pp. 244–54. doi.org/10.1093/ajcn/nqac068.

Thakral, Shelley (2018) 'Empowering refugee women for food security and nutrition', *World Food Programme Insight/Medium*, 16 January. https://medium.com/world-food-programme-insight/empowering-refugee-women-for-food-security-and-nutrition-53b1476b338c

Thapa, Seetashma (2021) 'I knew it would be a challenge, but I was determined to do my part', *World Food Programme Insight/Medium*, 11 December. https://medium.com/world-food-programme-insight/i-knew-it-would-be-a-challenge-but-i-was-determined-to-do-my-part-70ea594c4650

Thorstad, Eva B. and Finstad, Bengt (2018) 'Impacts of salmon lice emanating from salmon farms on wild Atlantic salmon and sea trout', NINA Report 1449. https://brage.nina.no/nina-xmlui/bitstream/handle/11250/2475746/1449.pdf

Tshering, Lotay (2023) 'State of the nation.' Royal Government of Bhutan. www.pmo.gov.bt/wp-content/uploads/2019/09/SoTNR-2023.pdf

Tybur, Joshua, Inbar, Yoel, Aarøe, Lene, Barclay, Pat, Barlow, Fiona, Barra, Mícheál, Becker, D., Borovoi, Leah, Choi, Incheol, Choi, Jongan, Consedine, Nathan, Conway, Alan, Conway, Jane, Conway, Paul, Cubela Adoric, Vera, Demirci, Ekin, Fernandez, Ana, Ferreira, Diogo, Ishii, Keiko and Žeželj, Iris (2016) 'Parasite stress and pathogen avoidance relate to distinct dimensions of political ideology across 30 nations', *Proceedings of the National Academy of Sciences*, 113. doi.org/10.1073/pnas.1607398113.

Uba, Estelle (2023) 'Ministers criticised for scrapping new

food waste laws for England', *Guardian*, 17 August. www.
theguardian.com/environment/2023/aug/17/ministers-
criticised-for-scrapping-new-food-waste-laws-for-england

UK Health Security Agency (2023) 'Campylobacter data
2010 to 2019', 4 May. www.gov.uk/government/
publications/campylobacter-infection-annual-data/
campylobacter-data-2010-to-2019

Ungar, Peter, Grine, Frederick and Teaford, Mark (2008) 'Diet in
early Homo: A review of the evidence and a new model of
adaptive versatility', *Annual Review of Anthropology*, 35. doi.
org/10.1146/annurev.anthro.35.081705.123153.

UNHCR (2022) 'Refugee data finder: Data insights.' www.unhcr.
org/refugee-statistics/insights/explainers/refugee-host-
countries-income-level.html

United Nations (1945) 'Charter of the United Nations,' 24 October.
www.un.org/en/about-us/un-charter/full-text

United Nations Department of Economic and Social Affairs (1992)
Report of the United Nations Conference on Environment
and Development (Rio de Janeiro, 3–14 June 1992). Annex
I: Rio Declaration on Environment and Development.
www.un.org/en/development/desa/population/migration/
generalassembly/docs/globalcompact/A_CONF.151_26_Vol.I_
Declaration.pdf

United Nations Department of Economic and Social Affairs,
Population Division (2022) 'World population prospects 2022:
Summary of results.' UN DESA/POP/2022/TR/NO. 3.
www.un.org/development/desa/pd/sites/www.un.org.
development.desa.pd/files/wpp2022_summary_of_results.pdf

United Nations Environment Programme (2021) Food Waste
Index Report 2021. www.unep.org/resources/report/
unep-food-waste-index-report-2021

University of Birmingham (2018) 'Omega fish oils don't improve
school children's reading skills or memory, study finds,'
16 March. www.birmingham.ac.uk/news-archive/2018/
omega-fish-oils-dont-improve-school-childrens-reading-skills-
or-memory-study-finds

US Department of Agriculture (USDA) Consultative Group (2010) 'Federal Register Notice published March 11, 2010, 75 Fed. Reg. 11512,' 30 April. www.dol.gov/sites/dolgov/files/ILAB/legacy/files/statement10.pdf

US Department of Agriculture and US Department of Health and Human Services (2020) *Dietary guidelines for Americans, 2020–2025*, 9th edn. www.dietaryguidelines.gov/sites/default/files/2021-03/Dietary_Guidelines_for_Americans-2020-2025.pdf

Väärikkälä, Sofia, Hänninen, Laura and Nevas, Mari (2019) 'Assessment of welfare problems in Finnish cattle and pig farms based on official inspection reports', *Animals*, 9(5), p. 263. doi.org/10.3390/ani9050263.

Valdes, Costanza (2022) 'Brazil's momentum as a global agricultural supplier faces headwinds', *USDA Economic Research Service*, 27 September. www.ers.usda.gov/amber-waves/2022/september/brazil-s-momentum-as-a-global-agricultural-supplier-faces-headwinds/

Vallone, Simona and Lambin, Eric (2023) 'Public policies and vested interests preserve the animal farming status quo at the expense of animal product analogs', *One Earth*, 6. doi.org/10.1016/j.oneear.2023.07.013.

van der Heide, C. M., Silvis, H. J. and Heijman, W. J. (2011) 'Agriculture in the Netherlands: Its recent past, current state and perspectives', *Applied Studies in Agribusiness and Commerce*, 5(1–2), pp. 23–28. doi.org/10.19041/APSTRACT/2011/1-2/3.

Vergeer, R., Sinke, P. and Odegard, I. (2021) 'TEA of cultivated meat', *CE Delft*. https://cedelft.eu/publications/tea-of-cultivated-meat/

Verhaag, Bertram (dir.) (2009) *David versus Monsanto* (Film). DENKmal-Film Verhaag GmbH.

Via Campesina, La (2021) 'Food sovereignty, a manifesto for the future of our planet', *La Via Campesina*, 13 February. https://viacampesina.org/en/food-sovereignty-a-manifesto-for-the-future-of-our-planet-la-via-campesina/

Vidal, J., Borger, J. and Watt, N. (2017) 'US wins WTO backing in

war with Europe over GM food', *Guardian*, 8 May.
www.theguardian.com/science/2006/feb/08/gm.wto

Vigna, Giovanni (2023) 'Financial Times contro la cucina italiana,
Coldiretti e Salvini replicano: "Un attacco surreale"',
Corriere Della Sera, 27 March. www.corriere.it/cook/
news/23_marzo_27/fake-news-cucina-italiana-coldiretti-
salvini-grandi-un-attacco-surreale-ca304560-cc12-11ed-a33d-
c3013907eff7.shtml

Viviano, Frank (2017) 'This tiny country feeds the world', *National
Geographic*, September. www.nationalgeographic.com/
magazine/article/holland-agriculture-sustainable-farming

von Bernstorff, Adrian and Farmer Sangay (2017) 'Agricultural
sustainability in Bhutan: A perspective', *The Druk Journal*.
http://drukjournal.bt/agricultural-sustainability-in-bhutan-a-
perspective/

VPRO World Stories (2017) 'Dutch free range farming: The
Netherlands from above' [Video], 14 September. www.
youtube.com/watch?v=WL_nNwbjlQA

Wakabayashi, Daisuke and Fu, Claire (2023) 'China's bid to
improve food production? Giant towers of pigs', *New York
Times*, 8 February. www.nytimes.com/2023/02/08/business/
china-pork-farms.html

Wall, Mike (2020) 'SpaceX's 1st crewed Mars mission could launch
as early as 2024, Elon Musk says', *Space.com*, 3 December.
www.space.com/spacex-launch-astronauts-mars-2024#

Warinner, C. (Physicians Committee) (2019) 'Anthropologist
debunks the Paleo Diet' [Video], 7 May. www.youtube.com/
watch?v=FNIoKmMq6cs

Watts, P., Davis, R., Keane, O., Luttrell, M. M., Tucker, R. W.,
Stafford, R. and Janke, S. (2016) 'Beef cattle feedlots: Design
and construction.' Meat & Livestock Australia. www.mla.
com.au/globalassets/mla-corporate/research-and-development/
program-areas/feeding-finishing-and-nutrition/feedlot-design-
manual/design-manual.pdf

Westerman, Frank (1999) *De graanrepubliek*, p. 229. Amsterdam:
Atlas.

Whiting, Kate (2022) '6 charts that show the state of biodiversity and nature loss – and how we can go nature positive', *World Economic Forum*, 17 October. www.weforum.org/agenda/2022/10/nature-loss-biodiversity-wwf/

WHO (2018) 'Nutrition: Trans fat,' 3 May. www.who.int/news-room/questions-and-answers/item/nutrition-trans-fat

WHO (2021) 'Obesity and overweight,' 9 June. www.who.int/news-room/fact-sheets/detail/obesity-and-overweight

WHO (2023) 'Use of non-sugar sweeteners: WHO guideline,' 15 May. www.who.int/news/item/15-05-2023-who-advises-not-to-use-non-sugar-sweeteners-for-weight-control-in-newly-released-guideline

WHO and FAO (2002) 'Diet, nutrition and the prevention of chronic diseases,' *WHO Technical Report Series*, 916. www.who.int/publications/i/item/924120916X

Whoriskey, P. (2019) 'Chocolate companies sell "certified cocoa". But some of those farms use child labor, harm forests', *Washington Post*, 28 October. www.washingtonpost.com/business/2019/10/23/chocolate-companies-say-their-cocoa-is-certified-some-farms-use-child-labor-thousands-are-protected-forests/

Whoriskey, P. and Siegel, R. (2019) 'Hershey, Nestlé and Mars broke their pledges to end child labor in chocolate production', *Washington Post*, 5 June. www.washingtonpost.com/graphics/2019/business/hershey-nestle-mars-chocolate-child-labor-west-africa/

Willett, Walter, Rockström, Johan, Loken, Brent, Springmann, Marco, Lang, Tim, Vermeulen, Sonja, Garnett, Tara, Tilman, David, Declerck, Fabrice, Wood, Amanda, Jonell, Malin, Clark, Michael, Gordon, Line, Fanzo, Jessica, Hawkes, Corinna, Zurayk, Rami, Rivera, Juan, Vries, Wim, Sibanda, Lindiwe and Murray, Christopher (2019) 'Food in the Anthropocene: The EAT–Lancet Commission on healthy diets from sustainable food systems', *Lancet*, 393. doi.org/10.1016/S0140-6736(18)31788-4.

Williams, H., Lindström, A., Trischler, J., Wikström, F. and Rowe,

Z. (2020) 'Avoiding food becoming waste in households: The role of packaging in consumers' practices across different food categories', *Journal of Cleaner Production*, 265, 121775. doi/org/10.1016/j.jclepro.2020.121775.

Williams, Helén and Wikström, Fredrik (2011) 'Environmental impact of packaging and food losses in a life cycle perspective: A comparative analysis of five food items', *Journal of Cleaner Production*, 19, pp. 43–8. doi.org/10.1016/j.jclepro.2010.08.008.

Wilson, Bee (2015) *First bite: How we learn to eat*. London: Fourth Estate.

Wilson, L. (2023) 'Alaska salmon fisheries enhancement annual report 2022.' Alaska Department of Fish and Game, Division of Commercial Fisheries, Regional Information Report No. 5J23-04. www.adfg.alaska.gov/FedAidPDFs/RIR.5J.2023.04.pdf

World Bank Group (2017) Bhutan Living Standards Survey Report. National Statistics Bureau of Bhutan. http://documents.worldbank.org/curated/en/628171596185674486/Bhutan-Living-Standards-Survey-Report-2017

World Bank (2020) 'Ease of doing business scores 2020.' https://archive.doingbusiness.org/en/scores

World Bank (2022) 'Food products exports by country US$000 2021: WITS data', *World Integrated Trade Solution*. https://wits.worldbank.org/CountryProfile/en/Country/WLD/Year/LTST/TradeFlow/Export/Partner/by-country/Product/16-24_FoodProd

World Bank (2023) 'Bhutan: Share of economic sectors in the gross domestic product (GDP) from 2011 to 2021', *Statista*, 19 September. www.statista.com/statistics/527319/share-of-economic-sectors-in-the-gdp-in-bhutan/

World Food Programme (2022a) 'Evaluation of WFP's support to smallholder farmers and its expanded portfolio across the agriculture value chain in Bhutan.' https://docs.wfp.org/api/documents/WFP-0000139663/download/

World Food Programme (2022b) 'Fill the nutrient gap – Bhutan.' www.wfp.org/publications/fill-nutrient-gap-bhutan

Worobey, M., Levy, J., Serrano, L., Crits-Christoph, A., Pekar, J., Goldstein, S., Rasmussen, A., Kraemer, M., Newman, C., Koopmans, M., Suchard, M., Wertheim, J., Lemey, P., Robertson, D., Garry, R., Holmes, E., Rambaut, A. and Andersen, K. (2022) 'The Huanan Seafood Wholesale Market in Wuhan was the early epicenter of the COVID-19 pandemic', *Science*, 377. doi.org/10.1126/science.abp8715.

WRAP (2023) 'The food waste reduction roadmap: Executive summary.' https://wrap.org.uk/resources/guide/introduction-food-waste-reduction-roadmap-and-how-get-involved#download-file

WTO (1995) 'Sanitary and phytosanitary measures: Text of the agreement.' World Trade Organization. www.wto.org/english/tratop_e/sps_e/spsagr_e.htm

WWF (2020) 'Cerrado destruction increases by 13%, and biome loses 7.3 thousand km^2 of native vegetation', 23 December. www.wwf.org.br/?77611/cerrado-prodes-destruction-deforestation-increase-123

WWF (2021) 'New study shows illegalities in 94% of converted ecosystems in the Amazon and the Cerrado', 17 May. https://wwf.panda.org/wwf_news/?2518441/New-study-shows-illegalities-in-94-of-converted-ecosystems-in-the-Amazon-and-the-Cerrado

CREDITS

EDITOR	Bella Lacey
COPY-EDITOR	Mandy Woods
PROOFREADER	Kate Shearman
COVER DESIGN	James Jones
MARKETING	Simon Heafield
SALES	Noel Murphy
PUBLICITY	Lamorna Elmer
INTERNATIONAL RIGHTS	Isabella Depiazzi
PRODUCTION DIRECTOR	Sarah Wasley
MANAGING EDITOR	Christine Lo
LITERARY AGENT	Lizzy Kremer
LITERARY AGENT'S ASSISTANTS	Maddalena Cavaciuti and Orli Vogt-Vincent
EXISTENTIAL SUPPORT	Antonia Macaro

INTERVIEWEES

Daniel D. Benetti, Professor of Marine Ecosystems & Society,
University of Miami
Simran Bindra, Co-founder, Kokoa Kamili
Sky Carrithers, Owner/manager, Estancia Ranquilco
Ulrike Čokl, Co-founder, The Bhutan Network
Alyssa Crittenden, Professor of Anthropology, University of
Nevada, Las Vegas
Henry Dimbleby, Co-founder of Leon and food campaigner
Ralph Early, Food scientist, food ethicist and food writer
Tara Garnett, Director of Table, Oxford Martin School, University
of Oxford
Mike Gibney, Emeritus Professor of Food & Health, University
College Dublin
Ken Giller, Emeritus Professor of Plant Production Systems,
Wageningen University
Albert Hoekerswever, Co-founder, HubOranje!
Spencer Hyman, Co-founder, Cocoa Runners
Noud Janssen, Co-founder, HubOranje!
Nicholas Johnson, Professor of Animal Health and Production,
University of Glasgow
Selina Juul, Chair and Founder, Stop Wasting Food Movement
(*Stop Spild Af Mad*)
Vickie Kloeris, Retired Former Manager of Space Food Systems,
NASA
Tim Lang, Emeritus Professor of Food Policy at City University
London
Marion Nestle, Professor Emerita of Nutrition, Food Studies &
Public Health, New York University
Steven Newman, Managing Director, BioDiversity International
Ltd
Louise Nicholls, Managing Director, Suseco.org
Barnaby Peacocke, Senior Consultant, International Development
Jonathan Rushton, Professor of Animal Health & Food Systems
Economics, University of Liverpool

Gyorgy Scrinis, Associate Professor of Food Politics & Policy, University of Melbourne

Roberta Sonnino, Professor of Sustainable Food Systems, University of Surrey

Jeff Steinberg, Founder and Managing Director, Latitude Craft Chocolate

Bill Tracy, Professor of Agronomy, University of Wisconsin–Madison

Martin van Ittersum, Professor, Plant Production Systems Group, Wageningen University

BOOKSHOP SALES

UK: Kellie Balseiro, Sam Brown, Luke Crabb, Sarah Davison-Aitkins, Richard Evans, Richard Fortey, Sue Jackson, Rosy Locke, John McColgan, Mel Tyrrell, Jeremy Wood.

Export: Amelie Brutal, Viki Cheung, Mallory Ladd, Bridget Lane.

SUPPORTERS

Corinna Algranti, John Boyd, Paul Breach, Eddie Bullock, Mark Cohen, Ruth Colvin, Jennifer Cornbleet, Susan Costello, Harry Davies, Paul Devine, Matt Evans, Timo Hannay, Carlien Hillebrink, Spencer Hyman, Rune Isene, Carol Jefferson-Davies, Duane Kelly, Dan Kettmann, Kris Krimel, Veronica Lawlor, Michael Lawton, Michael Leigh, Janet Lentzos, Robert Little, Rosmarie Maran, Marilyn Mason, James Nathan, Frank Newhofer, Brian Pagano, John Park, Keith Robinson, Magdalena Rogier, Jason Schock, Bill Singleton, David Sutherland, Windsor Viney, Anthea Windsor, Frederick Woodbridge.

INDEX

ABOUT THE AUTHOR

Julian Baggini's books include the *Sunday Times*-bestselling *How the World Thinks, How to Think Like a Philosopher, The Virtues of the Table* and the bestseller *The Pig That Wants to be Eaten*, all published by Granta Books. He has served as the Academic Director of the Royal Institute of Philosophy and is a member of the Food Ethics Council. He has written for the *Guardian*, the *TLS*, the *Financial Times* and *Prospect*, among other publications, and for academic journals and think tanks. His website is julianbaggini.com.